the arab world's legacy

The
Arab World's
Legacy

ESSAYS BY
CHARLES ISSAWI

The Darwin Press, Inc.
Princeton, New Jersey

Library of Congress Cataloging in Publication Data
Main entry under title:
Issawi, Charles Philip.
    The Arab world's legacy.

    1. Arab countries—History—Addresses, essays, lectures. 2. Civilization, Arab—Addresses, essays, lectures. 3. Near East—Addresses, essays, lectures. I. Title.
DS37.7.187   909'.04927   81-3279
ISBN 0-87850-039-1   AACR2

Printed in the United States of America

To Janina

Contents

PREFACE

The following essays were written over a span of more than thirty years. They cover a wide variety of topics—including cultural history, economic history, and politics—and differ considerably in method and style. They do, however, have one thing in common, which gives them an underlying unity: they each deal with that fascinating entity, the Middle East, and more particularly with its large Arab component, as seen by an observer who has spent a lifetime studying the subject. They are sketches of a vast, sprawling, ancient building, drawn by an amateur artist who has visited it again and again, looked at it from many angles, and dwelt within some of its courtyards and halls. Combined, these sketches may give an idea of some aspects of the size, complexity, and basic structure of the edifice.

Two of the essays are published here for the first time. The others have been reproduced exactly as they appeared, except for a short postscript to one of them and the addition of a paragraph in another. No attempt has been made to bring them up to date by taking into account either more recent developments or the large body of knowledge that has accumulated since their publication. Some of the earliest essays are, in certain respects, out of date, but I believe that their main conclusions still stand and that the insights they provide have not lost their value.

The time range covered in this book is a very long one—from the seventh to the twentieth century—but no apology is offered for this. The past is very much a part of the present in the Middle East. To change the metaphor, Middle Eastern society is a tree with very deep roots, and the fruits it bears are nourished by the soil of previous centuries. No one wishing to understand contemporary trends can afford not to ask himself certain questions about the formative period of classical Islamic civilization.

These essays represent some of the questions that pose themselves and some of the tentative answers that ensue. I hope they will stimulate the reader to pursue further some of the topics discussed and to raise additional questions. If they do, they will have served their purpose to the fullest extent.

Princeton, 1981

1

The Christian-Muslim Frontier in the Mediterranean:
A HISTORY OF TWO PENINSULAS

Much has been written about the unity of the Mediterranean, and rightly. For no one who has traveled in that region can fail to notice not only the great similarity of landscape and physical conditions of its various parts, but also the similarity of the temperament, physical appearance, outlook and way of life of its many peoples. And yet there is a profound cultural cleavage in the Mediterranean, splitting it into Christian and Muslim halves. This split coincides with the break in the shoreline of the Mediterranean formed by the Straits of Gibraltar at one end and the Dardanelles and the Bosphorus at the other, a break that marks the conventional borders of Europe with Africa on the one hand and Asia on the other.

Christian and Muslim Zones

It cannot be said that these straits constitute formidable natural obstacles—indeed it is possible to swim across all three. But they do mark the limits of two of the major religions of the world. South of them, the only Mediterranean country where Christians claim to be a majority is tiny Lebanon (the claim is disputed and the facts are obscure, but this does not affect the argument), and to the north the only country with a Muslim majority—a very small one—is the equally tiny Albania; in neither does the total population reach the 1.5 million mark. Muslim minorities, aggregating some 3.3 million, are to be found in Yugoslavia, Bulgaria, Greece, and Rumania, and there are a further 2.3 million Muslims in European Turkey. These are matched by Christian minorities, totaling nearly 3 million, in Egypt, Syria, Turkey, Iraq, and Jordan, plus 1.5 million European settlers in North Africa.[1] In both halves the previous religion has been extirpated

Reprinted with permission from the *Political Science Quarterly* 76, December 1961, 544-54.

from what was formerly one of its most brilliant centers: in North Africa, the home of Cyprian and Augustine, native Christianity seems to have died out in the twelfth century; in Spain, the home of Ibn Hazm and Averroes, Islam disappeared in the seventeenth century.

Moreover, in both halves, during the last hundred years or so, a process of polarization has been taking place, with Muslims moving southeast and native Christians northwest. In the decades immediately preceding the First World War tens of thousands of Turks and other Muslims left the European parts of the shrinking Ottoman Empire and settled in Anatolia and hundreds of thousands of Greeks, Armenians, and Christian Arabs emigrated westward to various parts of the world. The upheavals and tragedies of the First World War accelerated the process: almost all the Armenians left in Turkey emigrated, as did 1.2 million Greeks, who were replaced by over 600,000 Turkish- or Greek-speaking Muslims from Greece. The exodus of Turks from the Balkans continued in the interwar period, and rose once more in 1950-51, owing to mass expulsion from Bulgaria; altogether, between 1923 and 1954, Turkey received over one million immigrants. At the same time, emigration of Christians from the southern half was rising rapidly, though here the outflow was not so much of native Christians, albeit that continued, as of the descendants of European immigrants who had settled in Arab lands in the late nineteenth and early twentieth centuries. The most noteworthy movements were those of Italians from Libya after 1943, of various Europeans from Egypt following the Suez crisis of 1956, and of Frenchmen from Morocco, Tunisia, and, to a much smaller extent, Algeria; total Christian emigration from these countries since the Second World War has been about 500,000, and the process is by no means at an end.

Geographical Background

The purpose of this essay is to trace the steps by which Christianity and Islam reached their present boundaries. Before doing so, however, it is necessary to draw attention to two geographical features of the Mediterranean. First, the main islands—Sicily, Sardinia, Corsica, the Balearics, Crete, and also Malta—are closer to the Christian than to the Muslim half; the only significant exception is Cyprus, the others being Ruwad off the Syrian coast, Jerba and Kerkenna off the Tunisian, and the tiny Pantelleria and Lampedusa group. This enumeration of course excludes islands in the seas opening on the Mediterranean, namely the Adriatic and Aegean. Secondly, each end of the Mediterranean is dominated by a large peninsula— the Anatolian and the Iberian, which are very roughly equal in size, Anatolia being one-fifth larger than Iberia; each peninsula is cut off from its mainland by a very high mountain range—the Taurus and Armenian mountains, with the Caucasus in the rear, and the Pyrenees—and juts toward the strait marking it off from the opposite mainland. It will be seen that much of the history of the interaction of Christianity and Islam in the Mediterranean revolves around these two peninsulas.

Historical Phases

Pre-Islamic. Of the pre-Muslim history of the Mediterranean, only one characteristic need be noted. The coasts of Anatolia had been subjected to a very powerful Greek influence, and those of North Africa and Southeast Spain to a somewhat less powerful, but nonetheless real, Punic influence. In other words, each peninsula was tied by a strong bond to what was to become a powerful element in the religion which subsequently dominated the *other* half. This initial cultural influence probably retarded the absorption of Iberia into Christianity and Anatolia into Islam.

Early Onslaught. Islam had no sooner burst out from Arabia, in 633, than it headed for Constantinople. The first siege took place in 669, the second in 674-80, and the third and last in 716. All three were beaten off, and the Arabs withdrew to Syria. Henceforth, for over three centuries, Arabs and Byzantines exchanged border raids across a line that shifted back and forth along the base of the Anatolian peninsula. In the second half of the tenth century, under the vigorous "Macedonian" dynasty, the Byzantines pushed deep into Syria, occupying Aleppo, Baalbek, and several coastal cities, but they were later forced back toward their Anatolian base.

However, almost simultaneously with their last unsuccessful attack on Constantinople, the Muslims crossed the Straits of Gibraltar, in 711. By 732 they had passed the Pyrenees, reached the south of France, been defeated at the battle of Tours and pushed back. Here, too, for over three centuries, the battle lines swung back and forth in Northern Spain. Here, too, the vigorous Omayyad dynasty pushed deeper into Christian territory in the second half of the tenth century, its campaigns culminating in the sack of Santiago de Compostela in 997. At the same time, sea raids were taking place across the

Mediterranean. Muslim attacks on the Italian and French coasts were frequent in the ninth and tenth centuries, as were Christian attacks on the North African coasts in the eleventh and twelfth centuries.

The Conquest of the Peninsulas. Neither John Tzimisces nor Al Mansur found worthy successors, and the weakness of the Byzantine Empire on the one hand and the Spanish Muslim states on the other was soon dramatically demonstrated. In 1071 the Turks under Seljuk leadership won the decisive battle of Manzikert (Malazgerd), which opened before them the whole of Anatolia and allowed them to raid as far as the sea of Marmora. Simultaneously, a Christian offensive in Spain led to the no less important capture of Toledo, in 1085, which also opened the way to Andalusia and the Muslim south and allowed the Spaniards to raid as far as Cadiz.

But both of these disasters provoked strong reactions from the more vigorous and barbarous co-religionists of the victims, who rushed across the Straits to their help. In the East came the First Crusade of 1096 and the subsequent expeditions. These succeeded in pushing back the Seljuks some distance and thus postponed for several centuries the Muslim conquest of Byzantium, but in the process inflicted fatal damage on its cultural and social structure. Similarly in the West the Almoravids (Al Murabitun) crossed over from Africa in 1086 and by defeating the Spaniards at Al Zallaqa gave a new lease of life to Muslim Spain; they were followed in 1145 by the Almohades (Al Muwahhidun). But here, too, a high price was paid in cultural deterioration and religious intolerance.

In both peninsulas, however, the halted advance was resumed after a century or so. In Anatolia, by the end of the twelfth century, the Seljuks and Ghazis pushed back toward the Straits, and in the fourteenth century their place was taken by the more vigorous Ottomans, who obtained their first foothold in Europe in 1354. And in the West, the victories of Ferdinand III of Castile (1217-52), following the decisive battle of Las Navas de Tolosa in 1212, resulted in the conquest of practically the whole of southern Spain, a conquest that was confirmed by the victory of Rio Salado in 1340. Ferdinand actually occupied, by treaty, some African fortresses, and in 1415 the Portuguese started a systematic conquest of Africa with the capture of Ceuta.

At this stage, the fate of both remnants, Constantinople and its immediate neighborhood, and the Kingdom of Granada, was sealed, but their fall was delayed by misfortunes that befell their enemies. The victory of Timur Leng over Bayazid I at Ankara, in 1402, shook the Ottoman state and it took another half century to regain enough strength to attack and capture Constantinople in 1453. And the hostilities between Castile, Aragon, and Portugal, the feudal anarchy prevailing and the wars of succession, delayed the final conquest of Granada until 1492. The fall of both cities aroused deep emotions in Christianity and Islam, but neither led to positive action by the co-religionists of the defeated party to avenge its loss—not even when Granada sent a desperate appeal to the newly Muslim Istanbul, just as, fifty years earlier, Constantinople had in vain appealed to Christendom.

The Struggle Between the Peninsulas. Much of the sixteenth century was dominated by a bitter struggle between the two peninsulas, which formed the bases of the two major world powers of the day, the Spain of Charles V and Philip II, and the Turkey of Selim I and Suleiman. It may be added, parenthetically, that their population was roughly equal, Spain having some 8 million and Portugal 1 million, while Anatolia had over 5 million, with another 6 million in European Turkey.[2] The powers not only clashed directly in the Mediterranean but pursued their landward expansion. The Ottomans were pushed back from Vienna in 1529, with Imperial help, and in the same year the Spaniards were expelled from Algiers, with Ottoman help. Both powers renewed their assaults, and registered notable successes, such as the capture of Tunis in 1535 and Buda in 1541, but neither could concentrate all its forces on the other since each was distracted by another power and by a religious schism in its rear. For Spain the power was France and the schism Protestantism, while for the Ottomans it was Iran and Shiism. At the same time, it may be noted, the other Iberian power, Portugal, was making desperate efforts to conquer Morocco and was vigorously fighting the Turks in the Red Sea.[3]

The Spaniards remained in North Africa until the eighteenth century and returned, together with the French and Italians, in the nineteenth and twentieth centuries, and the Ottomans stayed in the Balkans until the twentieth, but all ultimately failed not only in that they lost their empires but, more important, in that the religion and basic culture of their subjects did not change.

The Islands. The history of the islands may be briefly told. The Muslim onslaught of the eighth-tenth centuries resulted in the total or partial occupation of Cyprus, Crete, Sicily, Malta, and the Balearics and in frequent raids on Corsica and Sardinia. But with the passing of sea power to the Christians in the tenth-eleventh centuries all these islands were recaptured. In the sixteenth and seventeenth centuries the Turks reconquered Cyprus and Crete, but they did not change their fundamentally Christian character and, except for the island of Ruwad off the Syrian shore and those of Jerba and Kerkenna of the Tunisian, Cyprus is the only island with Muslim inhabitants, Crete having lost its Muslims after the First World War.

Underlying Factors

Any attempt to explain the phenomena noted above must take up three separate, though interrelated, questions: What were the factors that influenced the general position of the Christian-Muslim frontier? What were the factors that brought about the ultimate inclusion of Anatolia in the Muslim zone and Iberia in the Christian? And what factors determined the sequence of events?

The Christian-Muslim Frontier. Various explanations have been given for the failure of Islam to spread further north than it did. Some of these are based on physical geography. The most obvious is the existence of the Mediterranean. For although Islam has spread across seas, notably into East Africa and Indonesia, most of its advance has been over land, and the presence of a large body of water, which was more often an arena of warfare than a channel of trade, must have constituted a serious obstacle. Again, nearly six centuries ago, Ibn Khaldun entitled one of the chapters in his *Prolegomena*, "Arabs Conquer only Plains";[4] it is a fact that Islam was carried into most of the mountainous regions lying on the periphery of the Arab World (Anatolia, Caucasus, Spain, and, to a certain extent, Morocco) chiefly by Turks and Berbers, and it may well be that the high mountain chains of Southern Europe acted as an effective barrier to Arab, and subsequent Muslim, invasion and expansion.

A second geographical explanation, which complements the first, is based on climate. Islam grew up in, and adapted itself to, a dry region. The main habitat of the Muslim peoples is the vast zone stretching from the Atlantic Ocean to China, where marked aridity is either a year-round or at least a seasonal phenomenon.[5] The tropical forests lying south of this zone have for centuries acted as a barrier against Islam and it is only recently that, helped by European pacification of these regions and by improved communications and by the spread of modern medicine, Islam has once more resumed its southern advance. But the forests of the north have proved insurmountable obstacles; a possible explanation of this resistance may be that "in the oak-forested Balkan mountains or in the area of Chinese civilization the ban on pork has slowed down conversions,"[6] and pig-raising is one of the main traditional forms of livelihood in the Balkans—though it should be added that pig-raising was also widespread in Anatolia.

This leads to a third explanation, of a sociological nature. Although it had its origin in sedentary Mecca and Madina, Islam spread rapidly among nomads, the group best adapted for life in an arid zone. As a French geographer put it so well:

The frontiers of Islam seem to coincide very generally with those of pastoral nomadism, or at least with regions that the nomads could influence politically. . . . The contrast between the Islamic and Christian shores of the Mediterranean shows perfectly this difference between a shore completely controlled by nomads, who find their natural home in the neighboring deserts, and a shore unified into a solid peasant civilization, against which invasions simply peter out.[7]

As the same author points out, this is also true of the southern frontier of Islam in Africa.[8]

A complementary sociological explanation, also given by Planhol, stresses the crucial role of cities and trade routes in the peaceful penetration of Islam:

The expansion of Islam seems therefore to be linked to means of communication; the religion spreads along trade routes and in coastal areas but is hindered by all natural obstacles to social life (mountain ranges and densely forested areas) as well as by the simple inertia of the rural population. . . . The Moslem religion may be thought of as a sort of gigantic octopus, the arms of which reach far down the main roads and project far in front of the animal's actual body.[9]

This explanation fits very well with the expansion of Islam in Eastern Africa and Southeast Asia since, until the irruption of the Portuguese at the beginning of the sixteenth century, the Muslims dominated the Indian Ocean and were its main traders. But although during most of the ninth and tenth centuries Muslims dominated the Mediterranean and captured most of its islands, they never obtained control over the trade between the Muslim and Christian worlds, which, important as it was to Europe, was of minor significance to the Muslims compared with the Eastern trade. This trade, which before the Muslim conquest had been largely conducted by Syrians and other eastern Mediterraneans, remained in the hands first of the Byzantines,[10] then of the southern Italians (Amalfites, Neapolitans, and others) and later of the northern Italians (Pisans, Genoese, Venetians, and Florentines), Provençals, and Catalans. And by the eleventh century sea power had definitely passed into Christian hands, where it was to stay with one brief interruption in the sixteenth century.[11]

Two other explanations, based on long-term relations between the major civilizations, may be briefly considered. E. F. Gautier has pointed out that the westernmost limits of Islam coincided with those of the Carthaginian domain, namely, Southeastern Spain and Sicily.[12] But a better fit can be shown between the limits of the Arab world and the area inhabited by various Semitic peoples before the Arab conquest.[13] Secondly, there is the question of the relation between the three major civilizations of the Western world in medieval times: the Islamic, the Orthodox Christian, and the Western Christian, to use the terms adopted by Toynbee; but this is better discussed under the next heading.

The Incorporation of Anatolia in Islam and the Reincorporation of Iberia in Christendom. Some of the factors noted in the previous paragraphs may help to explain why Islam finally incorporated Anatolia but failed to hold on to Iberia. In the first place, the Anatolian peninsula is distinctly more arid than the Iberian: it receives less precipitation over the year, its dry season is much longer, and it contains larger stretches of arid land.[14] Secondly, the interior of the Anatolian peninsula is somewhat less broken up than that of the Iberian, and fewer barriers impede the advance of the invader once he has succeeded in penetrating the mountain chains ringing Anatolia. Thirdly, and as a consequence of these two phenomena, there is the existence of the vast dry central plateau of Anatolia. This plateau has, from time immemorial, furnished the ideal conditions for the rise of the pastoral nomadic groups so closely associated with Islam, and made it possible for these nomads to grow in numbers and acquire sufficient strength to overwhelm the sedentary inhabitants of the periphery.

Another, more significant, difference between the two peninsulas is that Anatolia lies next to the heartland of Islam, the Arab-Persian area, whereas Iberia lies next to the heartland of Western Christendom, the French-Italian area. Islam conquered Anatolia through the Turks, who had been converted and civilized in the course of their passage through the Persian and Arab countries. It attempted to use for the same purpose the Berbers in Spain, but here it was operating very far from its base. North Africa was not comparable to Iran and the Levant as a cultural training ground, and the Berbers proved no match for the Galicians and Franks, drawing strength from the adjacent Christian heartland.

This leads to a still more important factor, the cultural. The Arabs seized Spain from the Arian Visigoths and the Turks conquered Anatolia from the Byzantines and took the Balkans from other Orthodox peoples. But neither Arabs nor Turks succeeded in penetrating deep into, or holding for a long time appreciable portions of, the continental domain of the much tougher Catholic Christian civilization.[15]

A comparison of the three civilizations in the medieval and modern periods leads to the following conclusions. The Orthodox civilization, although far more vigorous than the clichés "Byzantine decadence" and "Byzantinism" would suggest, and although for several centuries it showed both great fortitude against external attacks and considerable inner creativity, finally succumbed before the Islamic. The Islamic civilization also showed great strength in many fields of economic, scientific, and artistic activity and in addition to overwhelming Byzantium (which had been weakened by the Crusades) it made deep inroads into the domain of the Hindu civilization. But neither could compare with emerging Western Christian civilization, the most active and powerful the world has yet seen. Already by the eleventh century, Western Christianity had taken the offensive against Islam in Spain, Sicily, North Africa, and, even closer to the heart of Islam, in Palestine. And with every year that passed, Western Christendom gained over Islam in economic and cultural strength and could generally more than hold its own in war as well.

In these circumstances, what is puzzling is not that Islam did not spread farther north but that the counter-offensives of Western Christendom in the twelfth, sixteenth, and nineteenth centuries produced so little results in the religious field. In spite of quite long periods of European occupation, not one of the Muslim countries of Asia or Africa has witnessed any substantial conversion to Christianity, or become permanently incorporated in Christendom, and this is the greatest witness to the continued strength of Islam.

The Sequence of Events. The question of the factors determining the sequence of events outlined above must be raised, but the present writer must also confess his utter inability to answer it. The remarkable parallelism between the development of events at both ends of the Mediterranean, the synchronism of ebb and flow, is surely more than a coincidence or an optical illusion. It may point to some profound and as yet unsuspected rhythms in the history of the contact of civilizations. The question is a fascinating one, but it is still unanswered.

NOTES

1. These figures, which are approximate, have been compiled from various sources, notably Louis Massignon, ed., *Annuaire du Monde Musulman* (Paris 1955); *Statesman's Yearbook; Encyclopedia of Islam; Encyclopedia Britannica*; and national yearbooks; an attempt has been made to bring the available figures up to date.

2. The figures for Spain and Portugal are taken from Fernand Braudel, *La Méditerranée et le Monde méditerranéen à l'époque de Philippe II* (Paris 1949), p. 348, and those for the Ottoman Empire from O. L. Barkan, "Essai sur les données statistiques des registres de recensement dans l'Empire Ottoman aux XVe and XVIe siècles," *Journal of the Economic and Social History of the Orient*, vol. 1, Part I, 1957.

3. Other interesting points in the relations of the two peninsulas include the parallel attempts of each to form an alliance with the chief enemy of its rival, Turkey with France, and Spain with Iran; the emigration of the Jews from Iberia to the Ottoman Empire, where they were warmly welcomed; the regionalism that prevailed in both until their unification at the end of the fifteenth century; and the cultural symbiosis of Christians, Muslims and Jews in both until mounting intolerance in the Spanish and Ottoman religious establishments undid the effects of the tolerance formerly shown by the rulers. I am indebted for some of these, and other, points to Professor Bernard Lewis.

4. Ibn Khaldun, *Prolegomena*, edited by Quatremère (Paris 1858), vol. I, p. 269.

5. See Charles Issawi, "The Bases of Arab Unity," *International Affairs*, XXXI (January 1955), p. 36, and the maps in Peveril Meigs, *World Distribution of Arid and Semi-Arid Homoclimates*, Unesco mimeographed document NSI/A21/37/rev. (Paris, December 28, 1952).

6. Xavier de Planhol, *The World of Islam* (Ithaca 1959), p. 121.

7. *Ibid.*, p. 123.

8. See also the remarks on "desert power" in Bernard Lewis, *The Arabs in History* (London 1958), p. 55.

9. Planhol, *op. cit.*, p. 104.

10. A small amount of trade was carried on through Spain and France, by Rhadanite Jews.

11. This topic is discussed in a very interesting but not always reliable book by Archibald R. Lewis, *Naval Power and Trade in the Mediterranean* (Princeton 1951) and in the excellent contribution by Robert S. Lopez, "The Trade of Medieval Europe: The South" in M. Postan and E. E. Rich (eds.), *The Cambridge Economic History of Europe* (Cambridge 1952), vol. II, *Trade and Industry in the Middle Ages.*

12. E. F. Gautier, *Moeurs et coutumes des musulmans* (Paris 1949), p. 142.

13. Charles Issawi, *loc. cit.*

14. The greater aridity of Anatolia, and the greater length of its dry season, are brought out clearly both by maps showing total annual or quarterly rainfall [see Food and Agricultural Organization, *FAO Mediterranean Development Project* (Rome 1959), p. 8 and *The Oxford Atlas* (1958), pp. i-v.] and by maps showing climatic regions such as those in Meigs, *op. cit.*, and *Goode's World Atlas* (1960), pp. 8-9.

15. The Arabs were beaten off at Tours, and held parts of southern Italy only briefly; the Turks were pushed back at Vienna, Vicenza and Taranto and held Croatia and large parts of Hungary for a comparatively short period of time.

2

The Area and Population
of the Arab Empire:

AN ESSAY IN SPECULATION

As a distinguished classicist pointed out: "There is no subject of the first importance in ancient scholarship in which our thoughts are vaguer, in which we almost refuse to think (because the evidence is unsatisfactory) than that of population."[1] The reasons for this are not far to seek: demographic studies depend on statistics and, as an eminent social historian has reminded us, "There can be no statistics unless someone has first done the counting. In history often nobody has until relatively recently."[2] This is particularly true of the Islamic Middle East where, until the Ottoman period, there was very little counting of things and even less of persons. In such circumstances, to resume the quotation from Hobsbawm, "We have no statistics but only informed estimates, or more or less wild guesses. The best we can expect is orders of magnitude." Given this, almost the only tools available to the demographically-minded historian are extrapolation, collection of scattered data on cognate subjects, and comparison, and all have been used in this study. Backward extrapolation has been made from the figures available for the beginning of the nineteenth century and forward extrapolation from the various estimates for the Roman Empire, both being adjusted in the light of what we know of the course of the political, economic, and medical history of the countries concerned. Data on taxation, cultivated area, size of cities and size of armies have served as a check on some of the magnitudes thus obtained. Lastly, a further check has been provided by comparing the figures on total population and population density so derived with the corresponding ones for the Roman, Byzantine, and Ottoman empires, which, with the Arab, dominated the Mediterranean region for nearly 2,000 years.

Reprinted from *The Islamic Middle East, 700-1900*, edited by A. L. Udovitch, copyright © 1981, by The Darwin Press, Inc. (Princeton, New Jersey). I am indebted to my colleagues Nina Garsoian, D. M. Dunlop, and Hassanein Rabie for valuable criticism of an earlier draft and to Professors E. Ashtor, Andrew M. Watson, and Mohamed Talbi for comments and suggestions.

23

Needless to say this paper is very derivative: it contains no first-hand research and depends heavily on the work of other scholars, notably on that of Josiah C. Russell. It is also highly conjectural, and the results it presents are very tentative.

Demographic estimates are not only conjectural but are liable to be revised sharply upward or downward, according to both new archeological and historical evidence and, also, to prevailing moods. The tone was set by David Hume when, in an essay that is a model of reasoning on historical and social questions, he demolished Montesquieu's assertion that the world's population in his time was not one-fiftieth of what it had been in that of Julius Caesar and showed convincingly that, on the contrary, it had appreciably risen.[3] The estimate-cycles have continued since. Beloch's figures for the Roman Empire, referred to below, represent a sharp reduction from previous estimates; they were revised upward during the next fifty years, but in the last two or three decades these revisions have, in turn, been scaled down, especially the ones concerning the size of cities. Similar cycles are observable in estimates for other parts of the world; for example, the very large figures given for the population of Mexico by the early Spanish writers were utterly discredited but recently have been rehabilitated.[4] Estimates for the Middle East and North Africa also fluctuate up and down.

Roman Empire, Second Century A.D.

Estimates of the area and population of the Roman Empire begin with Beloch's excellent study[5] which, for nearly a century, has been the starting point for almost all subsequent work. His totals of 3,340,000 square kilometers and 54,000,000 inhabitants at the death of Augustus, in A.D. 14, however, understate both the extent and population at its zenith. For one thing, Beloch's table does not cover the areas conquered in the first and second centuries: Britain, Mauretania Tingitana, Arabia Petraea, and Dacia, for which estimates have been included in Table I.[6] More important, nearly all scholars agree that population grew for almost two centuries after Augustus. Table I summarizes the available information. The first column gives Beloch's figures for area, with rough estimates added (in brackets) by the present writer. The second column reproduces Beloch's figures on population. The third gives various estimates of population in the first or second centuries, which are discussed in detail below.

Divisions of the Empire. The constituent parts of the empire have been divided into three groups, according to their subsequent

TABLE I: AREA AND POPULATION OF ROMAN EMPIRE

	(1) Area (000 sq. kms.)	(2) Population A.D. 14 (millions)	(3) Population 2nd century (millions)
Group A			
Spain	590	6.0	6.0-7.0
Sicily	26	0.6	0.7-0.9
Africa	400	6.0	4.0-5.0
Cyrenaica	15	0.5	0.5
Egypt	28	5.0	6.0-7.0
Syria	109	6.0	5.0-6.0
Add			
Mauretania Tingitana	(100)	-	0.5
Arabia Petraea	(100)	-	-
	1,368	24.1	22.7-26.9
Group B			
Danubian provinces	430	2.0	2.0
Greek peninsula	267	3.0	3.0
Province of Asia	135	6.0 ⎫	10.0-13.0
Other Asia Minor	412	7.0 ⎭	
Cyprus	10	0.5	0.5
Add			
Dacia	(100)	-	0.5
	1,354	18.5	16.0-19.0
Group C			
Italy	250	6.0	8.0-15.0
Sardinia, Corsica	33	0.5	0.5
Narbonensis	100	1.5 ⎫	8.0-12.0
Three Gauls	535	3.4 ⎭	
Add			
Britain	(150)	-	0.5-1.5
	1,068	11.4	17.0-29.0
Grand Total	3,790	54.0	55.7-74.9

history. Group A covers those countries that were conquered by the Arabs. Group B includes those that remained under Byzantine rule after the initial Arab invasions. Group C consists of all the rest.

SPAIN. For some time, the prevalent view was that Beloch's figure of 6 million understated the population of the Iberian peninsula, and that the total grew appreciably until the end of the second century, but more recent estimates have again reduced the totals. Bouchier suggested that the population doubled between the death of Caesar and the principate of Hadrian, an estimate that was accepted by van Nostrand.[7] Menendez Pidal put the total at 9 or even 12 million, a figure regarded as much too high by contemporary scholars, including Russell, who reduced it back to 6 million.[8] In the table, a range of 6 to 7 million has been indicated.

SICILY. Beloch's figure of 600,000 is regarded as "far too conservative" by V. M. Scramuzza, who goes on to say: "Our estimate of 750,000 is probably nearer the actual figure, though still quite conservative. Beloch himself does not exclude 800,000 or even 900,000."[9] A range of 700,000 to 900,000 has been given in the table.

NORTH AFRICA. Evidence on this subject is contradictory. For Libya, Richard Goodchild, curator of the Department of Antiquities of Cyrenaica, suggested a total population of 1,000,000 to 1,500,000, about equally divided between Cyrenaica and Tripolitania.[10] This implies a somewhat larger figure for Cyrenaica than Beloch's of 500,000. On the other hand, Russell estimated the population of rural Tripolitania at only 100,000 and put the total for Roman Africa (which excluded Cyrenaica) at 4,300,000.[11] In the table, a range of 4 to 5 million has been given for Africa, and Beloch's figure of 500,000 has been kept for Cyrenaica. An arbitrary figure of 500,000 has been assigned to Mauretania Tingitana, which was not included by Beloch. Laroui, summing up the recent research of such French scholars as C. Courtois, C. Saumagne, and G. Picard, put the area, excluding deserts, at 350,000 square kilometers and the population at 3.5 million.[12]

EGYPT. Estimates for Egypt also vary, but somewhat less. Some writers are prepared to accept Josephus' figure of a population of 7,500,000 excluding Alexandria, which may have had a quarter of a million inhabitants, though the figure of 500,000 for Alexandria suggested by Beloch is now regarded as being too high.[13] Josephus was quoting a figure given by Herod Agrippa, who may have been trying to dissuade the Jews from revolting against Rome.[14] Diodorus, writing in 60-30 B.C., stated that Ptolemaic Egypt "as can be seen from the holy records" had a population of about 7 million, and in his day had at least 3 million. Walek-Czernicki put the population of Egypt at the end of the Ptolemaic era at 8 to 8.5 million, and in the first century A.D. at 8.5 to 9 milion, but subsequently reduced the latter figure to 7.5 million.[15] Based on certain assumptions regarding tax returns and the cultivated area, Russell estimated the population at 4,500,000, but his methods and results are questionable. In the table, a range of 6 to 7 million has been used.

SYRIA. Beloch's figures of 5 to 6 million for geographical Syria, including 2 million in Palestine, were regarded as somewhat conservative by Heichelheim, who stated that an estimate of 10 million for Syria, Lebanon, Palestine, and Transjordan is "by no means improbable,"[16] and Lammens suggested a figure of 7 million.[17] Russell, on the other hand, does not believe that the population exceeded 4 to 4.5 million.[18] A range of 5 to 6 million has been used in the table; this covers both Roman Syria and "Arabia." The subtotal for Group A ranges between 22.7 and 26.9 million.

ASIA MINOR. Very little work has been done on Group B, except for its largest single constituent, Asia Minor. Broughton's calculations confirmed those of Beloch, and showed a total of about 13,000,000.[19] Russell, however, believes that this figure is exaggerated and reduces it to 8.8 million.[20] But this in turn may be too low since his own estimate for the fifth century is 11.6 million. Russell does accept Beloch's figures for Greece and the Danubian lands.

In the table, a range of 10 to 13 million has been shown for Asia Minor, all Beloch's other figures have been kept unchanged, and an arbitrary addition of 500,000 has been made to cover Dacia. The subtotal for Group B is, therefore, 16 to 19 million.

ITALY. For Group C, on the other hand, several estimates are available, with widely varying figures. Tenney Frank put the population of Italy under Augustus at 14,000,000 and under Claudius, in A.D. 48, "doubtless over 15,000,000"; these figures seem to exclude the islands.[21] Russell, however, cuts the figure down to around 8 million, including the islands. The difference arises from conflicting interpretations as to whether the word citizen (*civis*), as used in the Roman censuses, covered only free males above the age of seventeen or both free males and females above that age.[22] A range of 8 to 15 million has therefore been given in the table.

GAUL. Beloch's figures are rejected as far too low by several French historians, whose own estimates are in turn suspiciously high. Grenier, discussing Camille Jullian's suggestion of 20 to 30 million, said: "Disons plutôt, pour le moment de la conquête, de 15 à 20 millions,"[23] and in a subsequent work raised his figure to 24 million,[24] while Lot quoted a total of 20 million.[25] Russell's figures are much lower, 6 to 8 million. In the table, a range of 8 to 12 million has been shown.

BRITAIN. For Roman Britain, which covered the "southern two-thirds of Great Britain, as far north as the Tyne-Solway isthmus," Collingwood discussed estimates ranging between half a million and a million and a half and opined that: "The truth is most likely somewhere between the two figures."[26] This range has been shown in the table.

The subtotal for Group C shows a very wide range, from 17 to 29 million.

Adding up the three subtotals gives a grand total ranging from 55.7 million to 74.9 million, or say 60 to 70 million. These figures are in line with various other estimates. Thus Cavaignac, adjusting Beloch's figures for some underestimates and for the omission of children, put the population under Augustus at 80 million, a figure that seems acceptable to many other students.[27] However, his estimate of a total population of 150 million by A.D. 180 is generally regarded as far too high, even granted that much evidence points to an increase between the time of Augustus and that of Marcus Aurelius. Conversely, M. I. Finley gives the same total for the reigns of both Augustus and Hadrian, about 60 million, which seems to imply no growth.[28]

Arab Empire, Eighth Century A.D.

Estimates of Roman population are tentative, but at least they are based on some statistical information. As Finley points out: "Whether anyone, in or out of government, actually knew the latter figure [i.e., of total population] is much to be doubted. Although censuses were taken, they were irregular, and they came at different times in different provinces. Their sole purpose was to bring the tax roles up to date."[29] But for pre-Ottoman Islam, although we have some figures on tax receipts—which presumably must have been partly based on some head counts—estimates of town populations by Muslim, Jewish, and European travelers, army lists and, for Egypt, cadastral surveys, we do not have a single official population figure. Nor do we have such records as the parish registers of Europe, from which so much can be learned regarding age distribution, family structure, and demographic trends. Any statement on the subject must, therefore, be inferential and extremely tentative. Indeed a leading authority, discussing the Muslim country about which most information is available, Egypt, says, "Poliak . . . suggested the figure of 3 million for the beginning of the fourteenth century. I would not, myself, feel able to speculate."[30]

Area and Population of the Arab Empire. Before discussing population, however, it is necessary to determine the approximate area of the Arab Empire at its widest extent, just before the fall of the Umayyads in 750. Table II is divided into two groups of countries: Group A, which had formed part of the Roman Empire and for which the figures on area given in Table I have been used to facilitate comparison;[31] and Group B, which includes the lands

TABLE II: AREA AND POPULATION OF ARAB EMPIRE

	(1) Gross Area (000 sq. km.)	(2) Inhabited Area (000 sq. km.)	(3) Population (millions)
Group A			
Spain	590	590	5.0-6.0
North Africa	1,584[1]	515	3.0-4.0
Egypt	1,001	28	4.0-5.0
Syria	222[2]	109	3.0-4.0
	3,397	1,242	15.0-19.0
Group B			
Arabia	3,173[3]	159	1.5-2.0
Iraq	435	131	5.0-6.0
Iran	1,648	412	3.0-4.0
Afghanistan	647	129	1.0-1.5
Central Asia	(200)	20	0.5-1.0
India	(300)	75	2.0-3.0
	6,403	926	13.0-17.5
Grand Total	9,800	2,168	28.0-36.5

1. One third of the total area of Algeria (2,382,000 square kilometers), Libya (1,760,000), Morocco (445,000), and Tunisia (164,000).

2. Two thirds of the combined areas of Israel, Jordan, Lebanon, and Syria.

3. Total of Saudi Arabia (2,150,000 square kilometers), Yemen (483,000), Oman (212,000), and Kuwait, Bahrain, Qatar, and United Arab Emirates (328,000).

Source: Gross Area, *United Nations Statistical Yearbook;* other figures, see text.

further east. But here a major difficulty arises. It will be noticed
that in his estimates of the area of Egypt, Syria, and North Africa
Beloch used figures of inhabited or cultivated land, not of total area—
thus Egypt is assigned 28,000 square kilometers, not the 1,000,000
lying within its geographical limits. Some such adjustment is required
for Group B, and hence Table II includes two columns, showing
gross and inhabited area respectively. It has been assumed that
the inhabited area constituted the following percentages of the countries in question: Iraq 30, Iran 25, northwest India 25, Afghanistan
20, central Asia 10, Yemen 10, and the rest of Arabia 5 percent.
If these assumptions are at all correct, four broad conclusions follow:

First, the total gross area of the Arab Empire was some 9 to 10
million square kilometers, or almost twice as large as that of the
Roman Empire, even if the latter be "grossed" by adding the desert
area of Egypt and that part of the North African deserts under its
control.

Secondly, the inhabited area of the Arab Empire was less than
two-thirds that of the Roman. If, however, the latter is adjusted
to take into account the vast tracts of forests, mountains, and wastes,
the difference between the two is considerably reduced, though
perhaps not eliminated.

Thirdly, the gross area of the part not previously included in the
Roman Empire (Group B) was nearly twice as large as that which
had been (Group A).

Lastly, the inhabited area of Group B was somewhat smaller than
that of Group A.

Since absolutely no figures are available for the Islamic period—
except for the unsatisfactory Ottoman ones for Syria discussed later
(in "Ottoman Empire, Sixteenth Century")—estimates, or rather more
or less informed guesses, regarding population must be based on
such data as the figures available for the beginning of the nineteenth
century, the conjectural Roman figures, and information on cultivated area, taxation, urban population, size of armies, and probable
demographic trends.

Before doing so, however, one further remark is in order: the
population of the Arab Empire was almost certainly not below 20
million and not above 60 million. The first statement rests on the
fact that, around 1800, the population of the countries in question—
excluding Spain and Sicily—may, with a high degree of confidence,

be estimated at well over 20 million, and the assumption is that in the High Middle Ages it was not lower. The second statement rests on the fact that in 1930—after several decades of unprecedentedly rapid growth, including substantial European and Jewish immigration—the population stood at about 70 million, and the assumption is that it must have been much smaller at every single previous point in its long history.

GROUP A. Three general observations may be made. First, it is agreed by all historians that the countries in this group, like other parts of the Roman Empire, suffered a sharp drop in population after the second century owing to the combined effects of insecurity, economic decline and, above all, successive plagues, especially the great plague of the early sixth century. Secondly, the end of the eighteenth century also represents a period of deep economic decline. Thirdly, one gets the strong impression that even at their most prosperous, the countries in this group, with the exception of Spain, were not as thickly populated as they had been under the Romans.[32] This gives us plausible upper and lower limits for a range of guesses.

Spain. Russell judges that, by the time of the Arab conquest, the population of Iberia had declined to some 3 to 4 million. Some improvement probably took place under Arab rule and, for the end of the eighth century, he puts the total at 4 million, a figure based on estimates of urban population. Growth seems to have continued till the end of the eleventh century. By the end of the thirteenth century, the population is more reliably (because of the availability of Christian records) put at 8.3 million,[33] and there is good reason to believe that, at its height, the population of Muslim Spain was somewhat larger than that of Roman Spain; a guess of 5 to 6 million for the eighth century may therefore not be too far out, with perhaps an additional one or two million at the height of Muslim rule.

North Africa. There seems little doubt regarding the drop in population following the revolts of the third and fourth centuries,[34] the Vandal invasion and the Byzantine reconquest, as well as the plagues. The cultivated area seems to have shrunk very considerably. Russell estimates that the population fell by more than half between the second century and the year A.D. 422, from 4.3 to 2.0 million, and even that does not take into account the Vandals and Byzantines! He puts the population under the caliphate at 1.9 million.[35] But this figure seems too low when compared to available estimates for the nineteenth century: Algeria 2.5 to 3 million in 1800-30, Tunisia one million in 1881 and apparently not much less at the beginning of the century, Libya 600,000 in 1911, and Morocco 3 to 3.5 million in 1914.[36] On the other hand, there is the fact that in 1800 North Africa had much larger cities than in the early Islamic period. Perhaps a range of 3 to 4 million seems appropriate, with the probability of appreciable growth, possibly to 5 to 6 million, until the middle of the eleventh century, when the Banū Hilāl and Banū Sulaym invasions, and other disturbances, caused a sharp setback.[37]

Egypt. Much more research has been done on Egypt than on any other Arab country, and there is wide agreement regarding trends if not magnitudes. Pestilence and other misfortunes drastically reduced both the cultivated area and the population in the third century. This was followed by a slow revival succeeded, in turn, by a sharp decline in the sixth century.[38] Russell puts the total population at the end of the seventh century at 2.5 to 2.6 million, and notes that this agrees with the estimate made by Napoleon's *savants* and the "census" of 1821. But, as Gabriel Baer[39] has demonstrated, extrapolating backward from the much more reliable censuses taken at the end of the nineteenth century shows that 2.5 million is too low for 1800, and at least 3 million seems more reasonable. Now it is unlikely that the population of Egypt after a century of Arab rule, when the initial disruption had subsided, should have been smaller than at the end of the very anarchic and depressed eighteenth century. Gibb, who also regarded the French estimate of 2.5 million as too low, thought that "in the fourteenth century it is not likely to have exceeded four millions,"[40] and Dols gives higher figures. It may be added that, basing himself mainly on tax and cadastral figures, Russell states that the population of Egypt fell to a low of 1.5 million in the tenth to eleventh centuries, rose to a peak of just over 4 million by the middle of the fourteenth, and was then reduced by the plague to some 3.15 to 3.36 million.

In a communication to the present writer, Professor E. Ashtor stated that the evidence on grain prices and wages leaves no doubt that the population of Egypt grew considerably in the eighth to tenth centuries. Equally surely, there was a sharp fall at the beginning of the thirteenth century. He believes that an estimate of 3 to 4 million for the eighth century is too low, and thinks that the eleventh-century peak was distinctly over 5 million. A range of 4 to 5 million has therefore been given in Table II, and the eleventh-century peak may well have been higher. As regards the Ottoman period, Russell's figures of 3.15 to 3.36 million for the period after the Black Death, taken in conjunction with the revised estimate of 3 million or over for 1800 suggest that, overall, there was no substantial change, though there were of course sharp fluctuations caused by plagues and famines, with subsequent recoveries, as well as by changed economic conditions. Thus André Raymond, in his monumental study of Cairo, estimates the city's population in both 1798 and the early sixteenth century at about 250,000, but believes that around 1660-70 it may have reached a peak of 350,000.[41]

Syria. Here, by contrast, information is extremely scanty. Even for the nineteenth century no reliable figures are available; various estimates by British consular agents in the 1830s, based on tax returns, range from 1,000,000 to 1,864,000, but most of them fall between 1,250,000 and 1,450,000. By the First World War, the figure had risen to around 3.5 million.[42] Russell's conclusion is that "an estimate of 3 million would be reasonable for Syrian population of about A.D. 720; about two-thirds of the estimated population for Roman Syria. By the end of the century Syria probably numbered 4 million."[43] Ashtor is inclined to believe that these estimates are somewhat too low. First, he believes that Syria's population under the Romans was higher than is suggested by Beloch. Secondly, he points out that, in the first century of Muslim rule, there was a large immigration of Bedouins and Persians, which more than offset the emigration of Greek town dwellers. Under the Umayyads, a series of plagues and earthquakes kept population down, at about 3.5 million, but there was an upsurge under the Abbasids. For the thirteenth to fourteenth centuries, Ziadeh puts the population of the 29 towns at 304,000 and, assuming that this represents one-seventh to one-eighth of the total, estimates the latter at 2 to 2.5 million.[44] A range of 3 to 4 million has been given in Table II, with the proviso that in the ninth to tenth centuries the total may have been nearer 5 million.[45]

The total for Group A around A.D. 750 is therefore between 15 and 19 million, compared to 25 million during the Roman period. But, as noted above, it is not unreasonable to assume that in the next two or three centuries population rose, along with economic development, and at its peak the area covered in Table II may well have been close to 20 million inhabitants.

GROUP B. Stepping out of the borders of the Roman Empire means entering an almost entirely uncharted—and perhaps unchartable—demographic terrain.

Arabia. Even today the population of the peninsula is not clearly determined, though a total of 10 to 12 million seems reasonable. Writing some ten years ago, the leading authority on Arabia, George Rentz, stated: "One may doubt whether the total approaches 10,000,000, and it may fall several millions short of this figure."[46] During the First World War an official British publication stated: "It is usually guessed to be from five to eight millions. The lower of these figures is probably nearest to the truth."[47] For the caliphate, Russell gives a figure of one million,[48] but I see no reason to believe that in 750 the population of Arabia was less than one-fifth of what it might have been in 1900, and a guess of 1.5 to 2.0 million has been put in Table II.

Iraq. For Iraq, the evidence is not much better. Beloch thought that in Parthian and Sasanian times the population of Babylonia was "scarcely less than 6 to 8 million." Russell puts the population of the Valley at 9.1 million. Robert Adams[49] indicates that the population of Lower Diyala reached a peak of 800,000 around A.D. 800, or slightly more than the figure for 1957; at the latter date, according to the census, the whole of Iraq had 6,538,000 inhabitants. These high figures receive some confirmation from two sources. On the one hand, the descriptions of the Arab geographers leave the impression of an intensively cultivated and thickly-settled country.[50] And on the other, figures on tax returns—which however are subject to widely varying interpretations—are generally higher than those for Egypt.[51] The range of 5 to 6 million shown in the table probably represents the peak of Iraq's population. Already by A.D. 1100, according to Adams, the population of Lower Diyala had halved and the Mongol invasion reduced it to less than a tenth, a figure which persisted until the nineteenth century, when the total for Iraq may have been around 1 to 1.5 million.[52] Not until the 1950s did Iraq's population pass the 6 million mark.

Iran, Afghanistan, Central Asia, and India. Russell puts the population of the "Plateau"—a term he uses to cover the area stretching from Mesopotamia to Marw—at 4.6 million, a figure that seems too low. At the beginning of the nineteenth century the population of present-day Iran was probably not below 5 million. This in turn almost certainly represents a reduction from the Safavid level.[53] Perhaps a range of 3 to 4 million for eighth-century Iran may be given, with the proviso that the population probably grew appreciably until the eleventh or twelfth century, was sharply reduced during the Mongol invasions, and then slowly grew again until the seventeenth century. Adding purely arbitrary guesses of 1 to 1.5 million for Afghanistan, 500,000 to 1,000,000 for central Asia, and 2 to 3 million for the Indian provinces gives a range of 13.0 to 17.5 million for Group B. Needless to say, these figures are based mainly on guesswork. If they are at all acceptable, they would suggest that, in the eighth century, the Arab Empire may have had a population of about 30 to 35 million, as against Russell's estimate of 23.3 million. In the course of the two following centuries, the total almost certainly grew,[54] perhaps to 35 to 40 million, including 1,000,000 for Sicily, Cyprus, and the other islands conquered during that period.

Of course, these figures rest heavily on the assumption that the population of the southern Mediterranean decreased during and after the decline of Rome. If a different, and rather improbable, assumption be made (viz., that it remained at its Roman peak), the population of Group A in Table II would rise to about 25 million and, retaining the figure of 15 million for Group B, the total to some 40 million. On a third, and also improbable, assumption (viz., that the population in the eighth century was no larger than at the beginning of the nineteenth, and assigning a figure of 5 million to Spain), the total for Group A would fall to some 13 million and the grand total to 28 million.

Byzantine Empire, Eleventh Century

This section will be very brief, since it is based entirely on three studies: by Russell, Vryonis, and especially Charanis, who exhaustively and critically reviewed the literature on Byzantine demography.[55]

First as regards area, Andreades put it at 1,010,000 square kilometers under Justinian and, following the great losses to the Arabs and a recovery under the Macedonian dynasty, at 545,000 in 1024.[56] But this figure seems much too small. Basil's rule extended over the whole of Anatolia and the southern Balkans, as well as parts of Syria, Transcaucasia, and Italy.[57] Ignoring the latter group, the total area may be put at about 1.2 million square kilometers; this represents the combined areas of present day Turkey (781,000),

Greece (132,000), Bulgaria (111,000), Albania (29,000), and one-half to two-thirds of Yugoslavia's area of 256,000 square kilometers.

As for population, perhaps the safest statement is that of Beck regarding the time of Justinian: "weit über 10 millionen und weit unter 40. Mehr zu sagen, ist illusorisch, aber schon eine solche Spanne ist mehr als nichts."[58] Stein ventured the following figures: 30 million under Justinian, 20 million during the first half of the eleventh century, 10 to 12 million under the Comneni and 5 million during the reign of Michael VIII Palaeologus.[59] Russell gives the following table, in millions (figures in brackets added):[60]

A.D.	Greece	Balkans	Asia Minor	Total
1	3.0	2.0	8.8	13.8
350	2.0	3.0	11.6	16.6
600	1.2	1.8	7.0	10.0
800	2.0	3.0	8.0	13.0
1000	5.0	2.5	8.0	(15.0-16.0)
1200	4.0	2.0	7.0	(13.0)
1340	2.0	2.0	8.0	(12.0)

More recently, Russell has suggested that the population of Anatolia remained around 8 million till the eleventh century, declining to 6 million by the thirteenth century.[61] Perhaps a guess of 15 to 20 million indicates the order of magnitude around the year 1000; this range derives some support from the figures for the Ottoman Empire given in the next section and also from the totals for Group B in Table I. Almost the only points on which there seems to be some agreement are summarized as follows by Charanis, a statement which Vryonis seems to accept:[62]

At the beginning of the sixth century the combined population of the regions which constituted the eastern empire was more than the combined population of the same regions at the beginning of the fourth century. A decline set in in 541 and this decline continued, or at the most there was no appreciable increase, down to about the middle of the ninth century. Meanwhile the empire suffered huge losses in population by the conquests of the Arabs and the occupation of virtually all the Balkan peninsula by the Slavs. A new era began towards the end of the ninth century and lasted till 1071. The huge territorial expansion of the empire during this period added, of course, greatly to its population, but there was also an increase in the old provinces. The loss of the eastern provinces following Manzikert decreased the population of the empire, but there was also a decline in the course of the twelfth century in that part of Asia Minor which had been recovered by Alexius Comnenus and his immediate successor. In the Balkan peninsula, beginning with the end of the ninth century, but especially after the Bulgarian wars, a definite increase set in and this increase continued almost down to the end of the twelfth century. No figures can be given for any one of these periods.

Ottoman Empire, Sixteenth Century

This section, too, is brief since the spade work has already been done by Ömer Barkan, whose population figures, based on the Ottoman *defter*, are more accurate than any pre-nineteenth-century ones used in this article.[63]

For the purposes of this study, the Ottoman Empire under Sulaymān may be divided into three parts. First, European Turkey has been taken to include the territories of present-day European Turkey (24,000 square kilometers), Greece, Bulgaria, Albania, and Yugoslavia (see previous section), Hungary (93,000), and Romania (238,000), a total of 883,000 square kilometers. The inclusion of Ottoman territories beyond the Dniester brings the total up to one million square kilometers or so. Secondly, there is Anatolia, with its present area of 757,000 square kilometers. Thirdly, there are the Arab lands: Syria, Iraq, Egypt, and North Africa;[64] for these Beloch's figures have been used, with a total of 683,000. Allowing for the Arabian coastlands held along the Red Sea and Persian Gulf, the figure is brought up to some 750,000. The grand total was therefore around 2.5 million square kilometers, or about twice as large as the Byzantine Empire.

Barkan's figures of population, based on the number of "hearths" in 1520-1535 multiplied by 5 is as follows:[65] European Turkey (including Istanbul) 5,959,000; Anatolia 5,162,000, Syria 571,000—a total of 11,692,000. This figure needs, however, considerable upward adjustment. First Barkan himself proposes an addition of 10 to 15 percent to take into account "les lacunes laissées par certaines classes militaires et les esclaves," raising the total to 12 to 12.5 million. Secondly, as he also points out, the figures for eastern Anatolia and Syria are certainly underestimates, due to instability caused by wars and invasions.[66]

Thirdly, the population figures for Europe do not cover the Trans-Danubian provinces, the inclusion of which would, presumably, raise the total by another 1 to 2 million. However, it should be noted that Barkan's figures are comparable with the ones given above for the Byzantine Empire. Fourthly, they also omit Iraq, which was not conquered until 1555, and which demands the addition of another 500,000 to 1,000,000, and a small number must also be added for the Arabian coastlands. Fifthly, an adjustment must be made for Egypt and North Africa, and here the figures offered by Braudel and adopted by Barkan (viz., 2 to 3 million for each area) may be accepted.[67] Lastly, Barkan draws attention to the fact that population grew appreciably until the end of the sixteenth century, a fact confirmed by Cook's very careful study. Cook gives good reason to believe that in the later sixteenth century the population of "a large part of Anatolia" was about half its 1940 level,[68] which would indicate some 8 million for the whole peninsula.

Braudel suggested for the end of the sixteenth century the following figures, in millions: European Turkey 8, Asiatic Turkey 8, Egypt 2 to 3, North Africa 2 to 3, giving a total of 20 to 22 million. On the basis of as yet unpublished research, Barkan is inclined to raise the total to 30 or even 35 million. It may be added that there seems to have been a sharp population decline in the next two centuries so that, according to the census of 1831, the population of Anatolia was only about 5.2 million and that of Rumelia and Istanbul 4.4 million.[69]

Conclusions

The findings may now be summarized. Once more it is necessary to point out that many of the figures are no better than guesses, but I believe some magnitudes may be established and some conclusions drawn.

First, as regards area, the Arab Empire, with some 9 to 10 million square kilometers, was by far the largest. However, if the empty desert regions are excluded, its inhabited area, a little over 2 million square kilometers, is well below that of the Roman Empire (perhaps 3 million inhabited square kilometers out of a gross area of some 3.5 to 4 million), and about equal to that of the Ottoman Empire (probably some 2 million out of a gross area of 2.5 million). The Byzantine Empire is far smaller, with a total area of about 1.2 million square kilometers, of which perhaps 1 million were inhabited.

These figures deserve attention since they cast some light on the political as well as the demographic history of these empires. Of the four, the Arab was easily the largest, followed by the Roman and Ottoman, with the Byzantine by far the smallest. Their geographical structure and texture was also very different. The Arab Empire was the most sprawling (its maximum length from Morocco to central Asia being over 4,000 miles) and the Byzantine the most compact; a vegetation or population map shows that the Arab Empire consisted of little islands of cultivated and settled areas surrounded by vast seas of desert, whereas in the others, especially the Roman, cultivation and settlement were more continuous. Lastly, they differed in respect to accessibility by sea, at a time when water transport was both vastly cheaper and (except for couriers) somewhat swifter than land transport. The Roman Empire was fortunate in that the bulk of its population lived within an ellipse centered on Rome and enveloping the shores of the Mediterranean; no point in this ellipse was more than a few days' journey by sea from Rome. The bulk of the Byzantine population was also concentrated in the areas along or near the shores of the Mediterranean and Black Sea to which Constantinople had easy access by sea; however, both the northern Balkan and eastern Anatolian provinces were remote from the sea, and correspondingly difficult to control.

The same is even truer of the Ottoman Empire, which spread further inland in both directions than did the Byzantine. However, the worst placed was undoubtedly the Arab, whose provinces stretched far into the heart of Asia and whose coastal areas bordered on two completely unconnected seas (after the silting of the Nile-Red Sea canal), the Mediterranean and the Arabian, with its Red Sea and Persian Gulf arms.

These factors help to explain the varying length of the period during which the empires retained their unity. The Arab split far more quickly than the others: by A.D. 800, or within 150 years of its foundation, it was already broken up into several independent states. Both Roman and Ottoman unity lasted longer: around 600 years. But, even if one were to put the break up of the Byzantine Empire as early as 1204 (the Fourth Crusade), it lasted about 800 years, and, by 1453, it had lasted a thousand years.

The question of the survival of the empires against external attack (as distinct from the preservation of internal unity) is another matter, since it has to take account of numerous additional factors, such as the state of technology, organization, and solidarity within each empire, compared to both its civilized and barbarian neighbors, and clearly lies outside the scope of this paper.

In population, the Roman Empire, with its 60 to 70 million inhabitants in the second century, towers above the rest. It has been suggested that at its highest point, in the ninth or tenth centuries, the population of the Arab Empire (by then no longer one political unit) may have been some 35 to 40 million. For Byzantium, a total of 15 to 20 million has been suggested for the post-Justinian peak, early in the eleventh century. For the Ottoman Empire, the highest point reached may have been 30 to 35 million, at the end of the sixteenth century.

These results are summarized in Table III. The table brings out an additional interesting fact: the density of population in the inhabited areas. The closeness of the figures for the Arab, Byzantine, and Ottoman empires is striking, the more so since the figures for the area were arrived at completely independently of those for population. Of course the closeness of the density figures may be fortuitous, but it is not unexpected given the essential similarity of the climatic, technological, and social conditions in the three empires, and it gives some additional confirmation of the population estimates. The somewhat higher density of the Roman Empire may perhaps be explained by the more favorable climate—particularly the more abundant rainfall of the northern Mediterranean region, compared to the southern—and greater internal security.

TABLE III: AREA AND POPULATION OF THE FOUR EMPIRES

	Roman (2nd century)	Arab (10th century)	Byzantine (11th century)	Ottoman (16th century)
Gross area (million sq. kms.)	3.5-4	9-10	1.2	2.5
Inhabited Area (million sq. kms.)	(3)	(2)	(1)	(2)
Population (millions)	60-70	35-40	15-20	30-35
Density per sq. km. of inhabited area	20-23	17.5-20	15-20	15-17.5

In conclusion, one may suggest a few lines of research that could throw some light on population size and trends. Much more can be done to estimate the population of the cities, using both literary and archaeological evidence and drawing on demographic and anthropological findings to determine the average size of households. The studies of Jean Sauvaget on Aleppo, Marcel Clerget, André Raymond and Janet Abu-Lughod on Cairo, Roger Le Tourneau on Fez, Jacob Lassner on Baghdad, and Richard Bulliet on Nishapur, to mention only a few, show what can be done in that direction. Data on the size and composition of armies and tax returns should also be collected systematically and compared. Perhaps most importantly, much work remains to be done on the spread of settlement at various periods, the extent of the cultivated area, and the kind of crops grown. When all this has been done, it should be possible to provide something more solid than the more or less informed guesses that have been given here. In the meantime, we can say, with the distinguished economist Simon Kuznets, that "speculation is an effective way of presenting a broad view of the field . . . . so long as it is recognized as a collection of hunches calling for further investigation, rather than a set of fully tested conclusions, little harm and much good may result."[70]

NOTES

1. A. W. Gomme, *The Population of Ancient Athens* (Chicago 1927), p. 1.

2. E. Hobsbawm, *Industry and Empire* (London 1968), p. 11.

3. David Hume, "Of The Populousness of Ancient Nations," *Essays Literary, Moral and Political*.

4. See J. H. Parry, *The Spanish Seaborne Empire* (New York 1966), p. 215.

5. Julius Beloch, *Die Bevölkerung der griechisch-römischen Welt* (Leipzig 1886).

6. No account has, however, been taken of Trajan's eastern conquests, in Mesopotamia and elsewhere, since they were relinquished by his successor, Hadrian.

7. E. S. Bouchier, *Spain under the Roman Empire* (Oxford 1914), p. 38; J. J. van Nostrand, "Roman Spain," *An Economic Survey of Ancient Rome*, ed. Tenney Frank (Baltimore 1938), III, 148.

8. R. Menendez Pidal, *Historia de España*, II, 317-18, cited by Josiah C. Russell, "Late Ancient and Medieval Population," *Transactions of the American Philosophical Society*, XLVIII (1958), p. 74.

9. V. M. Scramuzza, "Roman Sicily," in Frank, *op. cit.*, III, 334.

10. In a letter of 22 March 1967, to William C. Wedley, cited by the latter in "Manpower Policies for Development Planning in Libya," unpublished doctoral dissertation, Columbia University, 1971, p. 32.

11. *Op. cit.*, see calculations and table on p. 75.

12. Abdalla Laroui, *L'histoire du Maghreb* (Paris 1970), pp. 44-45.

13. For example, Allan Chester Johnson, "Roman Egypt," in Frank, *op. cit.*, II, 245.

14. Josiah C. Russell, "The Population of Medieval Egypt," *Journal of the American Research Center in Egypt*, V (1966), pp. 69-82; also *idem*, "Late Ancient and Medieval Population," pp. 78-80.

15. T. Walek-Czernicki, "La population de l'Égypte ancienne," *Démographie historique, Congrès international de la population* (Paris 1937), II, 7-13; and *idem*, "La population de l'Égypte à l'époque saite," *Bulletin de l'Institut d'Égypte*, (1940-41).

16. F. M. Heichelheim, "Roman Syria," in Frank, *op. cit.*, IV, 158.

17. Henri Lammens, *La Syrie* (Beirut 1921), p. 11.

18. Russell, "Late Ancient and Medieval Population," pp. 82-83.

19. T. R. S. Broughton, "Roman Asia," in Frank, *op. cit.*, IV, 812-15.

20. Russell, "Late Ancient and Medieval Population," pp. 81-82; part of the discrepancy is accounted for by the fact that Russell excludes some of the islands and eastern and southern areas at present in Syria and Iraq, whereas Broughton includes them.

21. Tenney Frank, "Rome and Italy," in Frank, *op. cit.*, V, 1, 140.

22. Russell, "Late Ancient and Medieval Population," pp. 71-73.

23. Albert Grenier, "La Gaule romaine," in Frank, *op. cit.*, III, 455.

24. *Idem, Les Gaulois* (Paris 1945), pp. 225-31.

25. F. Lot, *La Gaule* (Paris 1947), pp. 66-69.

26. R. G. Collingwood, "Roman Britain," in Frank, *op. cit.*, III, 7, 9, 276.

27. E. Cavaignac, "Notes de démographie antique," *Journal de la Société Statistique de Paris*, LXXVI (1935).

28. M. I. Finley, *Aspects of Antiquity* (New York 1968), pp. 155, 199.

29. *Ibid.*, p. 199.

30. E. Ashtor, "The Number of Jews in Mediaeval Egypt," *Journal of Jewish Studies*, XVIII, XIX. Ashtor believes that "the total of the Jewish population of Egypt at the end of the twelfth century cannot have exceeded the number of 10,000 to 12,000 souls."

31. This naturally raises certain difficulties. Thus Arab rule in North Africa went further south than Roman. On the other hand, the Arabs failed to subjugate the northwestern corner of Spain, which the Romans held, though for some time this was partly offset by their conquests in France. Sicily has been excluded from Group A, since it was not conquered by the Arabs until the ninth century.

32. This impression is shared by Professor S. D. Goitein, who knows more about economic conditions in medieval Islam than anyone.

33. Russell, "Late Ancient and Medieval Population," pp. 75, 91-92, 113-18.

34. R. M. Haywood, "Africa," in Frank, *op. cit.*, IV, 115-16.

35. "Late Ancient and Medieval Population," pp. 75-77, 89.

36. See *Initiation à l'Algerie* (Paris 1957), pp. 141-42; *Initiation à la Tunisie* (Paris 1950), p. 136; Louis Chevalier, *Le Problème démographique nord-africain* (Paris 1947), *passim*; Evans Pritchard, *The Sanusi of Cyrenaica* (Oxford 1949), p. 39. See also Braudel's estimates of 2 to 3 million for the sixteenth century, in the section entitled "Ottoman Empire, Sixteenth Century," in this chapter. Lucette Valensi, *Le Maghreb avant la prise d'Alger* (Paris 1969),

p. 20, gives the following figures for the beginning of the nineteenth century: Tunisia, "a little over one million"; Algeria, 3 million in 1830; Morocco, "more."

37. On this subject see Ibn Khaldun, *Al-Muqaddima*, ed. E. M. Quatremère (Paris 1858), II, 246-47; trans. Franz Rosenthal, as *The Muqaddimah*, 2nd ed. (Princeton 1967), II, 282-83. The impression of a sharp decline after 1050 is strongly reinforced by the excellent article of Claudette Vanacker, "Géographie de l'Afrique du Nord," *Annales*, XXVIII (1973), pp. 659-80.

38. See Russell, "The Population of Medieval Egypt," and sources cited therein.

39. Gabriel Baer, "Urbanization in Egypt, 1820-1907," *Beginnings of Modernization in the Middle East*, ed. William R. Polk and Richard L. Chambers (Chicago 1968), pp. 155-58.

40. H. A. R. Gibb and Harold Bowen, *Islamic Society and the West* (Oxford 1950), I, i, 209.

41. André Raymond, *Artisans et Commerçants au Caire* (Damascus 1974), pp. 204-5.

42. Charles Issawi, *The Economic History of the Middle East* (Chicago 1966), p. 209.

43. Russell, "Late Ancient and Medieval Population," p. 90.

44. Nicola A. Ziadeh, *Urban Life in Syria under the Early Mamlukes* (Beirut 1953), pp. 97-98.

45. Some figures kindly provided by Dr. Hassanein Rabie may be given here. In the late Mamluk period, the number of soldiers in Egypt was 42,000 and in Syria 31,000—of whom 15,000 were in Damascus, 8,000 in Aleppo, 5,000 in Tripoli, 2,000 in Safad, and 1,000 in Gaza; Khalīl al-Ẓāhirī, *Kitāb zubdat kashf al-mamālīk*, ed. Paul Ravaisse (Paris 1894), p. 104. This may suggest that the population of Syria was about three-quarters that of Egypt, or about 3.5 to 4 million at its peak.

46. *EI²*, s. v. "Djazīrat al-'Arab."

47. Great Britain, Admiralty War Staff, *A Handbook of Arabia*, p. 18.

48. Russell, "Late Ancient and Medieval Population," p. 89.

49. Robert McC. Adams, *Land Behind Baghdad* (Chicago 1965), p. 115.

50. G. Le Strange, *The Lands of the Eastern Caliphate* (Cambridge 1930), Chaps. II-VII.

51. Russell, "Late Ancient and Medieval Population," p. 9; see also E. Ashtor, *Histoire des prix et des salaires* (Paris 1969), pp. 550-51.

52. Muḥammad Salmān Ḥasan, *Al-Taṭawwur al-iqtiṣādī fī'l-'Irāq* (Beirut n. d.), p. 41.

53. Charles Issawi, *The Economic History of Iran* (Chicago 1971), pp. 12-13, 20, and sources cited therein.

54. Ashtor's opinion may be quoted in support: "We have every reason to suppose that the conquest of the countries of the Near East by the Arabs and the establishment of the Caliphan Empire resulted in a considerable

growth in the population of these countries . . . [i.e., Egypt, Syria, and Iraq] . . . It would seem that the demographic upswing came to an end in the course of the tenth century" (*Histoire*, p. 544). In Iran, it may have continued until the eleventh or twelfth century.

55. Russell, "Late Ancient and Medieval Population," pp. 92-93, 99-100; Speros Vryonis, *The Decline of Hellenism in Asia Minor* (Berkeley and Los Angeles 1971), pp. 25-30; P. Charanis, "Observations on the Demography of the Byzantine Empire," *Thirteenth International Congress of Byzantine Studies, Oxford, 1966* (London 1967), pp. 445-63. See also the review article by A. P. Kazhdan, "Novye issledovaniya po vizantiiskoi demografii," *Vizantiiskii Vremennik*, XXIX (1968), pp. 307-10.

56. Cited in Russell, *op. cit.*, p. 93.

57. See map in Nina Garsoian, "Later Byzantium," *The Columbia History of the World*, ed. John A. Garraty and Peter Gay (New York 1972), p. 442.

58. Comment on Charanis' paper, *Thirteenth International Congress . . .*, p. 474.

59. E. Stein, "Introduction . . . ," *Traditio*, VII (1949-51), cited by Charanis, p. 446.

60. Russell, "Late Ancient and Medieval Population," p. 148.

61. Josiah Russell, "Recent Advances in Mediaeval Demography," *Speculum*, XL (1965), pp. 84-101.

62. Charanis, *op. cit.*, p. 461; Vryonis, *op. cit.*, p. 26.

63. Ömer Lutfi Barkan, "Essai sur les données statistiques des registres . . . ," *JESHO*, I (1957), pp. 9-36.

64. Actually, Tunisia was not conquered until after Sulaymān's death, in 1574.

65. The question of the number of persons per hearth is a vexed one—both larger and smaller figures than 5 have been found. See Josiah Russell, "Recent Advances"; *idem*, "Late Medieval Balkan and Asia Minor Population," *JESHO*, III (1960), pp. 265-74; T. H. Hollingworth, *Historical Demography* (Ithaca 1969), and the figures quoted in Kazhdan, *op. cit.*

66. The figures for Syria suffer from another defect: they greatly underestimate the number of Christians and omit the Jews. See Charles Issawi, "Comment on Professor Barkan's Estimate . . ." *JESHO*, I (1958), pp. 329-33, and Barkan's reply.

67. Fernand Braudel, *La Méditerranée et le monde méditerranéen à l'époque de Philippe II* (Paris 1949), p. 137.

68. M. A. Cook, *Population Pressure in Rural Anatolia* (London 1972), p. 17.

69. Enver Ziya Karal, *Ilk Nüfus Sayimi, 1831* (Ankara 1943); F. Akbal, "1831 . . . Taksimat ve Nüfus," *Belleten*, XV (1951); these figures, and other census returns and estimates, are discussed in Charles Issawi, *Economic History of Turkey* (Chicago, 1980).

70. Simon Kuznets, "Economic Growth and Income Inequality," *American Economic Review*, XLV (1955), p. 26.

3

The Contribution of the Arabs to Islamic Civilization

For many centuries, in fact from the time Europeans first came in contact with the Islamic civilization in Spain and Sicily, they have been accustomed to designate the products of that civilization as "Arab" or "Arabian." Thus many historians refer to "Arabian medicine," "Arab science," "Arab philosophy," "Arab architecture," and so on.

In recent years a powerful reaction has set in against this view. Critics have pointed out that many, perhaps most, of the great figures in the realm of science and philosophy were not Arab by descent, but Syrians, Turks or, more frequently, Persians. Many of these critics have, consequently, been inclined to underestimate the role played by the Arabs in the creation and development of the Islamic civilization, or even to ignore it altogether. An extreme version of this latter view was put forward, not long ago, by the young Egyptian philosopher Abder Rahman Badawi, an admirer and follower of Spengler and Rosenberg. Talking of Salman the Persian he says, "He was a harbinger of the leading part which his race was to play in the spiritual life of Islam. We said the 'leading' part; it would have been more accurate to say the only part. For the truth is that this spiritual life owes almost everything to that many sided, talented and fertile Aryan race which—alone of all the peoples who embraced Islam—was capable of producing it."[1]

In view of such conflicting opinions, it is worth-while to enquire into the exact part played by the Arabs[2] in the creation and development of Islamic civilization.

In this paper an attempt has been made to evaluate the contribution made by the Arabs to Islamic civilization and to compare it with that made by another imperial people, the Romans, to "Roman" civilization. For this purpose a *list* has been compiled of those non-Arabs who distinguished themselves in the various fields of culture. This

Reprinted with permission from *Muslim World*, vol. XXXVIII-3, July 1948.

is followed by a list of those Arabs who similarly distinguished themselves. After that, the Arabs' contribution to the fundamental *institutions* of the Islamic civilization are enumerated and discussed. An
attempt is then made to discover the reasons which determined the
particular nature of the contribution of the Arabs. Finally an *analogy* is
drawn between the part played by the Arabs and that played by the
Romans in their respective civilizations.

In this article we shall confine ourselves to the eastern half of the
Arab Empire, viz., Egypt, Syria, Iraq, the Arabian peninsula, Persia
and Central Asia, for in Spain and North Africa genealogies are
even more confused than in the eastern countries, and it is even more
difficult to distinguish between Arabs and non-Arabs. We shall also
confine ourselves to the first five centuries of the Muslim era, which
witnessed practically all the creative achievements of the Islamic
civilization.

Within those spatial and temporal limits, there is no doubt that a
very impressive list can be made of those *non-Arabs* who distinguished
themselves in the various fields of culture.

There are first of all the *translators*, whose work laid the foundations
for all future developments. Most of those who translated Greek
texts into Arabic were Nestorian Christians from Syria or Iraq. Thus
Qusta Ibn Luqa was a Damascene, while Hunain Ibn Ishaq came from
Hira. Other translators from the Greek included the Jewish Masawaih
family and the pagan Thabit of Harran. Similarly Persian texts were
translated by Persians, such as Ibn al-Muqaffa' and the Naubakht
family, and Sanskrit texts by Indians.

Again, the leading *philosophers* were non-Arabs, notably al-Farabi
(died A.H. 339), Ibn Sina (d. 428), Ibn Miskawaih (d. 421) and al-
Ghazali (d. 505). The only Arab philosopher was al-Kindi (3rd century A.H.), who can claim to be the founder of Islamic philosophy
but whose stature is not comparable to that of his successors.

Theology too, in its various branches, was worked out largely by non-
Arabs, such as al-Bukhari (d. 265), the great compiler of the *Ḥadīth*
(Sayings of the Prophet), al-Baqillani (d. 403) and many of the
Mu'tazilite school. Al-Ghazali, the philosopher, must also be men-
tioned here, since his *Iḥyā' 'Ulūm al-Dīn* is rightly regarded as the
counterpart of Aquinas' *Summa*.

Ghazali's influence was largely responsible for the acceptance by
orthodox theology of *mysticism*. Here too the leading figures were
non-Arabs, notably Junayd (d. 297), and al-Hallaj (d. 309). In the

7th century A.H., Islamic mysticism produced what was perhaps its greatest figure in Jalal al-Din al-Rumi, a native of Bactria.

In the natural sciences, the predominance of the non-Arabs is marked. Thus in *medicine*, we have such distinguished figures as al-Razi (d. 320), with Ibn Sina the leading physician of the Middle Ages, and Ali ibn Abbas al-Majusi (d. 384). In *chemistry* there is the enigmatic Jabir ibn Hayyan (8th century A.D.?) whose philosophical views also display much originality. In *mathematics, physics* and *astronomy* practically all the leading men were non-Arabs, e.g., al-Khwarizmi (d. *circa* 230), Al-Farghani (d. *circa* 240), Abder Rahman al-Sufi (d. 376), Abu'l-Wafa (d. *circa* 390) and, although he falls outside our period, Omar al-Khayyam (d. 518), the astronomer poet. Perhaps greater than all these is al-Biruni equally eminent in the fields of philosophy, mathematics, astronomy and geography, a Sanskrit scholar, and the author of what is probably the greatest work on India ever written by a foreigner.[3] Non-Arabs also figured prominently in the fields of *historiography* and *geography*. Thus al-Tabari (d. 310), "the Livy of the Arabs," and the geographers al-Balkhi (d. 322), and al-Istakhri (middle of 4th century) were almost certainly non-Arabs, and other names might be added of persons who were probably of non-Arab descent, such as Ibn al-Nadim (d. 385), the author of the *Fihrist*, the first biographical bibliography of the sciences, and Ibn Hauqal, the geographer. In the *Shari'a*, or Canon Law, Abu Hanifa (d. 150), the first and greatest of the Jurists, was a non-Arab.

Most of the *grammarians*, too, were recruited from among the non-Arab population, notably Sibawaihi (d. 183) and al-Zajjaj (d. 311).

Even in *literature*, the contribution of the non-Arabs is marked. Some of the greatest of the prose writers, such as Ibn al-Muqaffa', the translator, al-Jahiz (d. 255) and al-Hamadhani (d. 398) were non-Arabs, as were also some of the most distinguished of the poets of the first Abbasid period, notably Bashshar ibn Burd (d. 167), Abu 'l-'Atahiya (d. 211), Ibn al-Rumi (d. 283) and Mihyar al-Daylami (d. 428).

Finally, apart from music,[4] which was intimately connected with poetry and in which the pre-Islamic Arab tradition was further developed by the Arabs after their conquests, the Arab *artistic* contribution was negligible. The conditions of life in the Arabian peninsula, except in Yemen, precluded the development of any architecture, and after the conquest the Arabs relied on the subject populations, especially the Copts, Syrians, Armenians and Persians, in all their buildings. The same was true of the decorative arts where, in the words of one authority, "Arabic script (was) the sole Arab contribution to Islamic art."[5]

No attempt has been made, when compiling the above list, to sort out the non-Arabs into their various ethnic groups. One general warning must however be given, viz., that the part played by the Persians is usually overrated, at the expense of the Turkish and other inhabitants of Central Asia, owing to the fact that the Arabic word for "non-Arabs" (*'ajam*) is often used to designate the Persians. Thus, whereas it is usually admitted that al-Farabi was a Turk, it is held that Ibn Sina was a Persian. This, however, has been strongly disputed.[6] Similarly Abu Hanifa is usually stated to be a Persian but there seems to be good evidence for holding that he was an Afghan.[7] Again Abu Nuwas, the poet, is generally claimed by Persians, but the fact is that while his mother was a Persian his father was a soldier in the Umayyad army, stationed in Damascus and sent to Iraq by the caliph Marwan— and may therefore have been of any nationality.

Confronted with such a bright galaxy, the student may well be inclined to admit that Islamic civilization was wholly the work of non-Arabs. Such a judgment would, however, be at least as erroneous as the opposite one which equates Islamic with Arab culture, and could be as easily refuted.

One might, for instance, make a list of all the Arabs who made their contribution to Islamic civilization and such a list would include all the greatest *poets*; the theologian al-Ash'ari; all the *jurists* except Abu Hanifa (i.e., Malik, al-Shafi'i and Ibn Hanbal); most of the *philologists*; many *prose writers*; such *grammarians* as Khalil Ibn Ahmad (d. 180), the teacher of Sibawaihi, and al-Mubarrad (d. 285); the great historian of literature Abu 'l-Faraj al-Isfahani (d. 356) whose name has usually caused him to be mistaken for a Persian but who was in fact a descendant of the Umayyad caliph Marwan Ibn al-Hakam; finally the geographer al-Maqdisī (d. 375), a native of Jerusalem.

Such a list is the more impressive in view of the very small proportion formed by the Arabs to the total population of the Empire. It is most unlikely that the number of Arabs who came in at the conquest could have exceeded 300,000, and subsequent infiltrations, though continuous, were never on a large scale. As against this must be set the 7,000,000 inhabitants of Egypt, the 4,000,000 of Syria and the large Persian, Turkish and other populations. Proportionately to their numbers, the cultural contribution of the Arabs was very great.

But such an approach does not get to the root of the matter. The real contribution of the Arabs to Islamic civilization lay not so much in the geniuses they produced as in the social institutions with which they provided the Islamic world.

There is, first of all, the *political framework*. Arab armies conquered a vast empire with a maximum of speed and a minimum of destruction, and Arab dynasties ruled over this empire. But it was not only the caliphs who were Arab. Until the Abbasids removed the capital to Baghdad and surrounded themselves with Persians, the great bulk of the ruling class was recruited from among Arabs. For at least the first 150 years of its existence, the Muslim empire could claim to be an *Arab* empire. And thanks to the peace prevailing in that Empire for two centuries, many peoples who had not previously had a chance now made their contribution to culture, notably the Persians and the Turks.[8]

Even more important was *religion*. Islam has undoubtedly been developed and enriched by many non-Arab theologians, but its most essential ingredient remains the Qur'an, a purely Arabian product.

And with religion came *language*, since in Islam as in perhaps no other great faith, language and religion are inseparably connected. The necessity of reading the Qur'an in the original—since translation was not permitted by some—meant that a very thorough grounding in Arabic had to be acquired. The fact that Arabic was the official language, without which employment in the higher government posts was extremely difficult, also gave it a great stimulus.

Finally the intimate connection between literature, especially poetry, and the Court, made Arabic, rather than Persian or Syriac or Coptic or Turkish, the literary language. Hence we see the following phenomena:

a. All the greatest poets were Arabs. Thus, under the Umayyads, we have al-Akhtal, the Christian Arab, al-Farazdaq and Jarir. In the so-called first and second Abbasid periods (132-334 A.H.) come Abu Tammam (d. 231) and al-Buhturi (d. 284). Finally in the great flowering of the fourth century we find al-Mutanabbi (d. 354), Abu Firas al-Hamdani (d. 357) and, greatest of all, Abu 'l-Ala al-Ma'arri (d. 449).

b. Most of the men of thought listed above as non-Arabs wrote and spoke Arabic at least as well as—and often considerably better than—their native tongues. It is only rarely that we learn that one of them spoke Arabic imperfectly, as did for instance Ibn Sina.

c. Arabic became not only the language of religion, literature and philosophy, but also that of science. Almost all the great scientific works were written in Arabic (the first scientific work in Persian dating from the second half of the 10th century), and Persian, Turkish and Urdu still contain a very large number of Arabic words in their scientific vocabularies—in fact one might say that their scientific vocabularies are still predominantly Arabic.

This political, linguistic and religious unity formed the basis of the Islamic civilization. Until about the 14th or 15th centuries, there was no part of the Islamic world where a Muslim did not feel at home. The career of the historian, Ibn Khaldun, offers the best illustration of this, since he occupied leading posts in Spain, Morocco, Algeria, and Egypt and was even offered a post by Timur Lank. Earlier, the historian, al-Mas'udi (d. 346), and the geographer Ibn Battuta had traveled freely from the Atlantic Ocean to China.

After about the 15th century the Muslim world began to split into two halves, which A. J. Toynbee[9] has called the "Iranic" and the "Arabic," the former including Turkey, Persia, Afghanistan, Central Asia and North India, the second what is known today as "the Arab world," i.e., the area lying between Iraq and Morocco. In the former, Persian was the predominant language; in the latter, Arabic. After the Shi'a revolution of Shah Ismail Safavi, in the 16th century, the cultural unity of the Iranic civilization was broken, but that of the Arabic has remained to this day, a lasting monument to the constructive work of the Arab conquerors of the 7th century.

Still, when all is said, the fact remains that the contribution made by Arabs to Islamic thought, science and art was relatively small. This relative sterility in the field of thought and art has not passed unnoticed, and more than one attempt has been made to explain it.

Thus there is the explanation given by Lassen,[10] which bases itself on the national character of the Arabs. According to him, Arabs are characterized by a marked predominance of the will over the emotions, while the latter are in turn much more developed than the intellect. This means that the Arabs are a courageous, active and practical people who are, however, incapable of long sustained or purposely directed action and who are deficient in the deeper kind of imagination. Hence their incapacity to produce any really great works of the imagination such as epics or tragedies; hence too their failure to excel in speculation, whether philosophical or scientific. But hence, also, their great contribution in such practical activities as religion and law.

Lassen's account may be accepted in its general outlines, though many of his deductions and the illustrations are certainly erroneous. In particular his view of the Arab as a being in whom will predominates over intellect and emotions seems to contain an important truth.[11]

But national characteristics are not immutable, and can often be traced to some sociological factor. This is why the explanation given by Ibn Khaldun, five centuries ago, seems to us nearer the mark. In a chapter entitled "Most of the learned men in Islam have been Persians,"[12] Ibn Khaldun discusses the reasons why "the men of learning in Islam . . . have been, with but a few exceptions, Persians, those of them who were Arabs by race being foreigners in their language, their environment and their teachers. And this has occurred in spite of the fact that Islam originated as an Arab sect with an Arab founder."

His answer is that learning can develop only in a sedentary society, where the crafts enjoy a long and uninterrupted tradition and attention. Now the Arabs could not be expected to produce any learning as long as they remained nomads. "Those Arabs, however, who forsook a nomadic for a sedentary life concentrated all their *energies on politics, rulership, and war*. This bred a disdain for the pursuit of learning as a profession, since it had become one of the crafts; for the ruling classes always look down on the crafts and professions and all that pertains to them."

It was, therefore, only the non-Arab sedentary populations who could produce any learning or scholarship, such as "the Persians, or those who were politically and culturally subject to them and had, therefore, developed a skill in the sciences and crafts owing to a long tradition of civilization."

Ibn Khaldun's contention seems to be fundamentally correct. For a century and a half the Arabs were a ruling class, occupied mainly in politics and warfare. The only other activities deemed worthy of such a class were the teaching and spreading of Islam, which demanded a knowledge of language and philology, the administering and developing of the Law of the Prophet and, last but not least, poetry, which occupied in post-Islamic society as exalted a position as it had done in pre-Islamic times and which was intimately connected with the Court, often serving as a vehicle for political propaganda. Hence it was that the Arabs excelled in the above mentioned branches of activity.

Ibn Khaldun's contention may be tested by studying the position of the Roman or Latin ruling class toward the provincial populations of the Empire, after the time of Augustus. Even if the term Roman be extended so as to denote all the inhabitants of the Italian peninsula, one cannot but be struck by the predominance of non-Romans over Romans in most fields of culture.

Speaking of the last years of the Republic, Rostovtzeff states: "The Romans paid little attention to the exact and minute discoveries of Greece in mathematics, medicine, physiology, astronomy, geography and the natural sciences. But," he adds, "grammar, rhetoric, archeology, jurisprudence, philosophy, the history of religion and law—all these became favorite subjects of study with educated Romans."[13]

The first part of his statement holds true of the four or five following centuries. Wherever we look we find the only valuable work being done by non-Romans, and almost always in the Greek, not the Latin, language.

Thus in *mathematics*, there were Nicomachus of Gerasa, Menelaus of Alexandria, and in the 3rd century, the great Diophantus of Alexandria, all of whom wrote in Greek. In *astronomy*, the scene is dominated by Ptolemy (d. *circa* A.D. 160), whose work constituted the basis of all studies during the next millenium or more. Ptolemy lived in Alexandria and wrote in Greek. In *medicine*, ignoring minor figures who were practically all non-Romans from the Eastern provinces, we find Rufus of Ephesus, Soranus of Ephesus, the great Galen of Pergamum and Aretaos of Cappadocia, all of whom lived in the second century and wrote in Greek.

Finally, all the great *geographers* were non-Romans who wrote in Greek, notably Strabo of Pontus, Ptolemy and Pausanias of Lydia. The only Romans who can be said to have distinguished themselves in the sciences were Pliny, Varro and the encyclopedist-physician Celsus—and all of these are relatively minor figures.

Our contention may be supported by two quotations taken from Roman writers. Thus Cicero complained that "the Greek mathematicians lead the field in pure geometry, while we limit ourselves to the practice of reckoning and measuring";[14] while Pliny reveals clearly the attitude of the Roman ruling class toward medicine. "Medicine," he says, "in spite of lucrativeness, is the one art of the Greeks that the serious Roman has so far refused to cultivate. Few of our fellow-citizens have been willing even to touch it, and if they do they desert at once to the Greeks."[15]

But even in the fields mentioned by Rostovtzeff as having interested the Romans, the contribution of the other peoples was often greater. This comes out most clearly in *philosophy*, where the only outstanding Roman name is that of Marcus Aurelius (who wrote in Greek), whereas the non-Romans include Philo the Jew, Seneca the half-Spaniard, Epictetus the Greek, Plotinus the Egyptian and Porphyry the Syrian.

The Romans on the other hand, made important contributions which almost coincide with those which were later made by the Arabs. The Roman contribution to *law* was immense, and needs no stressing. It is worth mentioning, however, that at least two of the "Five Great Jurists," Ulpian and Papinian, were Syrians connected with the law-school of Beirut.

In *literature*, especially in poetry and rhetoric, the Roman contribution was overwhelming. There were absolutely no equivalents outside Italy of Virgil, Horace and Ovid, to mention only these. The non-Roman men of letters, whether writing in Latin or in Greek, were all second-rate figures, with the possible exceptions of Lucian of Samosata (Syria) and Apuleius of Madura (North Africa).

But, unlike the Arabs the Romans produced some great *historians*, notably Sallust, Livy, Tacitus and Suetonius. The Greek Plutarch and Arrian of Bithynia are there, however, to testify to the fact that historiography was not a Roman monopoly.

In *architecture*, too, the Roman contribution was much greater than the Arab. The work of Roman engineers and architects still stands and arouses admiration. Nor was it only in execution that the Romans excelled: they gave some original ideas of their own notably as regards the arch and vault. But here, too, much that goes under the name "Roman" must be credited to other peoples. Thus to take only one example, Apollodorus of Damascus, the architect who built Trajan's forum and triumphal arches, was a Syrian.

From this very brief sketch it will be seen that there is a close analogy between the part played by the Arabs and that played by the Romans in their respective Empires. Both supplied the political framework, the ruling class (for a century or two, after which the subject populations took over) the laws and the dominant language and literature. Latin, however, never conquered the eastern part of the Roman empire in the way Arabic conquered Egypt, Syria and Persia, and Greek remained the language of science of the eastern half of the Mediterranean until it was supplanted by Arabic. The reason for this difference is that the Arabs made one very great contribution to their Empire which the Romans had failed to make to theirs: *religion*. For whereas the Arabs supplied the dominant religion the Romans imported their religions from the East. It is hardly necessary to point out that not only Mithraism and Manichaeanism but also Christianity were purely oriental products. As regards Christianity, of all the Church Fathers up to the time of St. Augustine, only St. Ambrose and St. Jerome could be said to be Roman in any sense, and only they wrote in Latin.

It is this religious contribution which makes the work of the Arabs in a way more impressive than that of the Romans. True, the Romans welded their Empire into a unit which was incomparably tighter and more homogeneous than the Arab Empire. But it is doubtful whether even the excellence of the Roman roads and administration, as well as the spread of the Latin tongue, would have allowed that unity to survive the barbarian invasions had it not been for the spread of Christianity. Christianity preserved the unity of the West just as Islam preserved that of the East. But, once more, Christianity was not a Roman product while Islam was an Arab product.

It only remains to point out, in conclusion, that the comparison of the part played by the Arabs and Romans does not give an answer to the question as to whether it was racial or sociological factors that determined the nature of their roles. For, on the one hand, it may be claimed that the Romans, like the Arabs, founded and maintained an empire because they were a practical, unimaginative and unspeculative race; while on the other hand it may be claimed with equal justice that the Romans, like the Arabs, constituted a ruling class and, therefore, engaged only in those activities which were directly connected with government, leaving speculation to the subject populations. The problem involved is a very deep and complex one, whose solution does not seem within sight at the present stage of knowledge.

The answer to the question set out at the beginning of this article is now clear. Islamic, like western and unlike Greek, civilization was not the work of one single people, but rather the result of the combined efforts of many. Of these the Arabs played a leading part, which is best compared to that of the Romans after the first century B.C. We can speak of "Arab civilization" with more justice than of "Roman civilization," but the term "Islamic civilization" seems better, even though non-Muslims played an important part in it, being more comprehensive and indicating more clearly the link that held that civilization together.

NOTES

1. *Shakhsiyyat Qaliqah fi 'l-Islam*, Cairo, 1946.

2. Throughout this paper the word Arab is used in a very restricted sense, to indicate a racial not a linguistic group. In normal usage "Arab" denotes all those whose mother language is Arabic, i.e., the inhabitants of the "Arab World." Here, however, it denotes only the inhabitants of the Arabian peninsula and their descendants.

It is hardly necessary to add that the classification of persons into "Arabs" and "non-Arabs" can only be highly tentative. For the Arabs were scattered widely, though thinly, over the various parts of their empire and mixed very freely with the other peoples, who in turn intermarried on a large scale.

3. Ibn al-Haytham (d. *circa* 430), the greatest Muslim physicist has not been included in this list. He was born in Basra and worked in Egypt, but it is difficult to ascertain his origin.

4. For the part played by the Arabs in the development of music see the article on Music in the *Legacy of Islam,* especially page 360.

5. A. H. Christie in *The Legacy of Islam*, p. 113.

6. A. M. Sayili "Was Ibn Sina an Iranian or a Turk?" *Isis,* volume XXXI, 1.

7. Charles C. Adams, "Abu Hanifah, Champion of Liberalism," *Moslem World*, July 1946.

8. It may be objected that whereas the Turks had not produced anything worthwhile before entering the Islamic civilization, the pre-Islamic Persians had evolved an architecture, literature and art of their own and had produced many noteworthy religious leaders such as Mazdak and Mani. Nevertheless it is a fact that after Islam Persian creativity seems to have been greatly stimulated.

9. *A Study of History*, 6 vols., Oxford University Press (1935-39).

10. Quoted by Abder-Rahman al-Badawi in *Al Ilhad fi 'l-Islam*, Cairo 1945.

11. It is not by accident that volition is so heavily stressed in Islamic thought. Thus according to al-Ghazali "the essential element of the soul is not the intelligence which is concerned with the bodily frame but the will: just as God is primarily known not as thought or intelligence, but as the volition which is the cause of creation" (D. O'Leary, *Arabic Thought and its Place in History,* p. 221).

12. *Prolegomena*, Part VI, Chapter 35.

13. *History of the Ancient World*, Vol. II, p. 173.

14. *The Legacy of Rome*, p. 297.

15. *Ibid.*, p. 286.

4
The Historical Role
of Muhammad

As de Tocqueville so well put it: "Historians who write in aristo-cratic ages are wont to refer all occurrences to the particular will or temper of certain individuals; and they are apt to attribute the most important revolutions to very slight accidents. They trace out the smallest cause with sagacity, and frequently leave the greatest un-perceived. Historians who live in democratic ages exhibit precisely opposite characteristics. Most of them attribute hardly any influence to the individual over the destiny of the race, nor to citizens over the fate of a people; but, on the other hand, they assign great general causes to all petty incidents."[1]

During the last hundred years, the mass of historians have tended to discount the influence of Great Men on the course of history, seek-ing rather to explain the latter in terms of population pressures, economic development, class struggles, climatic changes, racial or national characteristics and the like. And, generally speaking, it is true that close examination reveals the part played by the Great Men of history to be much smaller than appeared to their contem-poraries. Thus, a century after his death, we can see clearly that Napoleon's historical mission was the taming of the Revolution within France and at the same time the spreading of its equalitarian doctrines around Western Europe. We can also see that both these processes were well under way before Napoleon appeared on the scene. Al-ready in 1794 the Coup d'État of Thermidor marked the beginning of counterrevolution in France, and by 1795 the French armies had crossed the Rhine into Germany and the Low Countries.

The same analysis may be applied to several other leading historical figures, with similar results. But there are some men who do seem to have diverted history from the course it would otherwise have taken and who may, therefore, be classed among the great historical forces. One such man was the Arabian prophet, Muhammad. Per-haps the best way of measuring the historical significance of Muham-

Reprinted with permission from *Muslim World*, vol. XL-2, April 1950.

mad is first to describe the main events attributed to him and then
to evaluate his own contribution to those events.

The immediate effect of Muhammad's preaching was to found
the religion which inspired the Arab conquest of all the lands lying
between the Pyrenees in the West and the steppes of Central Asia
in the East. Its long-term effects were:

The establishment of Islam as a world religion;

The emergence of a specific Arab-Islamic culture;

And the permanent Arabization of the southern half of the
Mediterranean world.

The Spread of Islam. With an estimated total of over 300,000,000
followers,[2] ranging from Morocco to China and from Turkestan to
South-East Africa, Islam is undoubtedly one of the three or four
leading religions of the world. It has been said that the name Muhammad (or one of its derivatives such as Ahmad, Mahmud, Hamed, etc.)
is borne by more persons than any other masculine name in the world,
a fact which perhaps more than any other illustrates the sway of Islam.

Islam is moreover not only a widespread but a very living religion.
Not only does it retain its hold on its followers but it is steadily gaining
ground. Its missionary activities have never slackened, even when
the political power of the Muslim states was weakest, as in the eighteenth and nineteenth centuries[3] and it has scored, and is still scoring,
signal triumphs in equatorial Africa and South-East Asia.

The Emergence of Arab-Islamic Culture. The combined effect
of the Arab conquest and the rapid Islamization of what is now known
as the Middle East was to bring into being a new civilization, the Arab-
Islamic, stretching from Spain to Central Asia. Between the 8th
and the 13th centuries, this civilization led the world in most fields
of activity. Today, its cultural heritage provides the intellectual and
artistic background of nearly 200,000,000 Arabs, Turks, Iranians,
Afghans, Indians, Uzbeks and others.

The Arabization of the Southern Mediterranean. In the perspective
of world history this phenomenon is probably less important than the
two mentioned above; nevertheless it has considerable present-day
political and cultural significance.

Between Morocco and Iran live over 60,000,000 Arabs, the overwhelming majority of whom are Muslim but among whom Christians
have played, and continue to play, an important part. These Arabs
control some of the largest oil resources of the earth and occupy a

strategic position in the center of the Old World. They are rapidly moving toward political unity and will doubtless make their weight increasingly felt in international affairs.

Muhammad's Role. Such then is the balance sheet of Islam and the Arab conquest. It now remains to ask whether the three phenomena described above can be directly attributed to Muhammad.

Islam. That Islam was created by Muhammad as perhaps no other religion was created by any single man is not a matter for controversy. Judaism evolved very slowly, through many centuries, before assuming a shape at all resembling the one it now bears. St. Paul has been called the "Second Founder of Christianity." But although Islam underwent considerable development—although it has not in fact even yet finally crystallized—its characteristic features were undoubtedly stamped upon it by its founder, Muhammad.

This bare statement does not, however, convey the full significance of Muhammad's achievement, which can be appreciated only by realizing in what a state of spiritual poverty seventh century Arabia lay. A brief survey of Arabian Judaism, Christianity and paganism shows that none of them was a likely seedbed for a new world religion.

Judaism. This religion had been established in the Arabian peninsula for several centuries, but it had made relatively little headway. The Jews do not seem to have proselytized very actively, their only notable triumph being the conversion of the King of Yemen, Dhu Nuwas, ensuing in a persecution of Christians. Nor do the Arabian Jews seem to have been in that state of spiritual fermentation which precedes the birth of a new religion or the transformation of an old one. No important new ideas are known to have been contributed by the Arabian Jews to the development of Jewish theology. Except for the fact that the proportion of craftsmen was higher among them, the Jews did not differ greatly from their Arab neighbors, and the one literary portrait of an Arabian Jew which has come down to us— that of the hero As Samaw'al—does not bear any marks distinguishing him from the surrounding Arabs.

It therefore seems reasonably safe to say that Judaism in Arabia could not have provided the seeds of a new world-religion.

Christianity was in a somewhat different position. Supported by the prestige—and sometimes the arms—of Byzantium and Abyssinia it had undoubtedly made considerable progress in the northern and western parts of the peninsula, as witness the contemporary descriptions of Christian basilicas and the persecutions of Najran.[4] The very development of Muhammad's thought shows to what an extent Christian ideas—sometimes in an extremely distorted form—were current in Mecca and other parts of Arabia. There is then nothing to warrant the affirmation that Christianity could *not* have spread in Arabia, perhaps eventually converting the whole population of the country.

But, equally, there is not the slightest reason to believe that this Arabian Christianity would have made any startling contribution to world history either by creating a radically new form of Christianity or by spurring the Arabs to world conquest, which is precisely what Islam succeeded in doing.

There is even less justification for thinking that **Arab Paganism** had evolved to the stage where it was ready to produce a new, superior, world religion, in the way the Hellenistic world had been ripe for a new religion and had produced Mithraism, Christianity and other creeds.

Central Arabian paganism at the time of Muhammad was a poly-daemonism evolving toward the higher forms of polytheism.[5] One can go even further and notice, in the subordination of the main goddesses to the god Allah, an emerging monotheism. The trend itself is significant, and it is irrelevant for the purposes of this paper to enquire whether it was due to Christian or Jewish influence or to other causes.

There is also evidence that the old fetishism no longer "satisfied the religious emotions and insights of many of the Arabs."[6] In all the biographies of Muhammad mention is made of certain Arabs, such as Waraqa ibn Nawfal, who were seeking a higher religion, generally turning toward Christianity.[7]

All this is important, as showing that, to a certain extent, the ground had been prepared for Muhammad to come forward with a new message. It is also true that Muhammad incorporated much of the old Arabian religions in his system.[8] But this "does not alter the fact that the religious attitudes expressed in and mediated by the Qur'ān constitute a new and distinctive religious structure."[9]

Moreover, Muhammad created not merely a new tribal or national religion but a new *world-religion*. He was able to do this because he united in himself not only the religious intuition of a prophet but also the power of expression of a poet and the shrewdness and political sense of a statesman. This combination is probably unique in history and nothing short of it could have launched Islam on its career of world conquest.

Confirming the above contentions is the fact that, to the best of our knowledge, no prophets or seers *preceded* Muhammad, in the way that John the Baptist preceded Jesus Christ or that Wycliffe and Huss preceded Luther. The "false prophets" (of whom Maslama is the best known) who arose during Muhammad's lifetime and after his death were most probably inspired by his remarkable success, and must therefore be regarded as imitators, not forerunners.

To emphasize the importance of Muhammad's personality in the foundation of Islam does not, however, imply ignoring the historical conditions which enabled his religion to sweep the Near East. Islam's success seems to have arisen mainly from its attractiveness to the religious and national sentiments of the peoples living in the Fertile Crescent and Egypt.

There is considerable evidence that the Semitic world, which had been brought under Greek rule by Alexander's conquest and subjected to an intense process of Hellenization, was becoming increasingly restless and striving to liberate itself from both Roman political and Greek cultural domination.[10] The revolts of the Jews were the most spectacular, though not the most enduring, manifestation of this discontent. The renaissance of Aramaic literature was another pointer in the same direction. But perhaps the most significant, because the most widespread, sign of revolt was the emergence of one Christian heresy after another, the consequent sects engendered and the ceaseless struggle between the sects and the Orthodox Church centered on Byzantium. Historians are becoming increasingly aware that the religious struggles of the 4-6th centuries contained a very large, if not predominant, political element, viz., a nationalist revolt of Syrians and Egyptians against Byzantine rule.[11]

Judging from the results, Islam presented itself to those peoples as a Semitic religion which had transcended Jewish particularism into a world-wide view and at the same time had eliminated most of the Greek elements in Christianity. Islam's appeal was greatly reinforced by the fact that it had itself been greatly influenced, both in fundamentals and in details, by Nestorian Christianity,[12] which had been precisely a product of that revolt against Greek Christianity.

As a result, not only did the Muslim invaders get much help from the local populations[13] but within two centuries they had converted the bulk of the inhabitants to their own faith.

Islam's great advantage over the competing Christian heresies which were attempting to supplant the Church lay in the simplicity of its dogma; its social equalitarianism; and the prestige which it enjoyed as the religion of a conquering group.

The simplicity of Islamic dogma is well known and recognized. All that it demands is a belief in the Unity of God, in his Revelation to Muhammad, and in the Day of Judgment, as well as some simple observances. As a result, Islam readily appeals to all types of mind, the most sophisticated as well as the most primitive, and to all types of temperament, the laxest as well as the strictest. (It should, however, be remembered that some Christian sects were also striving after the same simplicity of dogma.)

No sect born in the Fertile Crescent or Egypt during the sixth or seventh centuries, however, had the social equalitarianism of Islam. Muslim equalitarianism was a product of desert tribal society, not of the caste-ridden ancient civilizations.

The same may be said of the prestige enjoyed by Islam as a conquering religion. And there is no doubt that the political power enjoyed by Islam greatly helped its diffusion. For while it is, with few exceptions, true that the Muslims did not try to convert others at the point of the sword,[14] it is equally true that the temporal success of Islam, its position as the State religion and the great social advantages to be gained by becoming a Muslim, were all potent factors in swelling the stream of converts.

Thus the spread of Islam must be attributed partly to the qualities it derived from its desert environment and partly to the state of mind of the contemporary Near East. But the fact that outside conditions helped him in no way detracts from Muhammad's achievement.

Arab-Islamic Civilization. The rich and complex entity known as Arab, Saracenic, or Islamic civilization contained many ingredients and was the product of many forces. Here it is sufficient to distinguish four main factors:[15]

First, a universal state ruled, for about a century and a half, by an Arab dynasty and an Arab ruling class. This gave the political framework in which the different elements could blend.

Secondly, the diffusion of Islam, the acceptance of Muslim religion as the underlying social and political ideology and the regulation of social life by Muslim law.

Thirdly, the universal use, for at least four or five centuries, of Arabic as the language of theology, philosophy, science and even literature throughout the vast expanse of the Muslim world.

Finally, the immense intellectual and esthetic contributions made by the non-Arab subjects (whether Muslims, Christians, Jews, or pagans) such as the Persians, Turks, Copts, and Syrians.

This brief sketch brings out the central fact on which this civilization was built, viz., a conquest by *Muslim Arabs*. And this brings out, in turn, Muhammad's contribution to that civilization. For while there is considerable divergence of opinion as to how far the conquest was due to Muhammad's preaching and how far to other factors, there can be no doubt that the fact that the Arab conquerors had already embraced Islam fundamentally changed the character of their conquest. This fact has not been sufficiently stressed by historians and deserves some elucidation.

The Arab conquest was due not only to religious factors, important as they were, but also to economic and demographic factors.[16] In fact the Arab conquest was merely the last of a long series of Semitic invasions from the desert to the sown. In the four millennia preceding Islam successive outbursts from the Arabian peninsula had resulted in the emergence of the Babylonians, Canaanites, Phoenicians, Hebrews, Aramaeans, Nabataeans and other Semitic peoples.[17] Whenever the power that controlled Syria or Mesopotamia showed any sign of weakening, a pressure from the desert would make itself felt. And the powers that controlled these countries in the 7th century, the Byzantine and Sasanian empires, were definitely showing signs of exhaustion. Perhaps the most eloquent proof of this is that, in their wars, both came to depend heavily on their satellite Arab forces; the Byzantines on the Syrian Arab kingdom of Ghassan and the Sasanians on the Mesopotamian Arab kingdom of Hira. In fact the last great Perso-Byzantine war was practically fought out and decided by the armies of the two rival Arab kingdoms.[18]

It will therefore be seen that the Persian and the Eastern Roman Empire had, like the Western Roman Empire, entrusted the keeping of their marches to allied "barbarians." In these circumstances, it is difficult to believe that sooner or later the Eastern barbarians, like the Western, would not have sought to conquer and take over the territories they were supposed to be guarding. With or without Muhammad, an Arab conquest of Syria and Mesopotamia would not only have been possible but even highly probable.

But, and this is the vital difference, such a conquest would have had consequences very different from those that actually took place. But for Islam, the Arab conquerors would have been—as their Semitic predecessors had been, or as their Western counterparts were— simple, raw, uncivilized barbarians. In such circumstances there is no reason to doubt that, like their eastern predecessors and western contemporaries, they would have succumbed to the civilization and religion of the peoples they had conquered. They would have been Persianized and Romanized. Above all they would have been Christianized.

Those are not mere speculations but a deduction, by analogy, from the fate of the Ghassanids of Hauran and, to a lesser extent, the Lakhmids of Hira, as well as the fate of those earlier Arab invaders who had founded the states of Palmyra and Petra. The Ghassanid ruins of Bosra and other places in the Syrian desert show how deeply Roman civilization had been assimilated; and Christianity too had struck deep roots, claiming both the ruling dynasty and the subjects. There is no reason to believe that any pagan Arab conquerors would have reacted to the impact of Romanism and Christianity differently from the way the Ghassanids had reacted.

Instead the 7th century Muslim conquerors came not only as raw barbarians seeking loot and conquest but also as missionaries of a new faith. They came committed to a religion, a law and, since the language of the Qur'ān was sacred, a language. The 14th century Arab sociologist and historian, Ibn Khaldun, well understood the spirit of these early Arab conquerors: "Hence it was the noblest and proudest members of the [Islamic] community who undertook to teach the Book of God and the Laws of His Prophet. . . . For the Book was revealed to a Prophet chosen from among *themselves* to serve as a guide to *them*. And Islam was *their* religion, for which they had fought and died, which had been given to them among all the nations and in which they gloried."[19]

As a result of all this, the Arabs entered with an attitude very different from that of, say, the Franks or the Goths—not to mention the Huns or Tatars.[20] They came to *teach*, not to learn. And although they learned an immense amount from their subjects, what they took over had either no connection with their religion, law and language (for example the natural sciences and technics) or else was absorbed in amounts sufficiently small and was adapted and transformed so as to harmonize with the basic requirements of the Muslim religion. The fact that Muslim civilization was hardly, if at all, influenced by Greek art, drama, poetry, mythology, historiography, and political life and thought, clearly shows how deeply Islam had affected its adherents and how greatly their outlook was conditioned by the framework of ideas they had taken from Muhammad.

The Arabization of the Southern Mediterranean. Muhammad was not only the founder of Islam and of Islamic civilization. He was also the founder of modern Arab nationalism, which is in some ways different from the nationalism of western or central European peoples such as the French, the Italians or the Poles. This is because the Arab world, stretching from the Atlantic Ocean to the Taurus and Zagros mountains, is not just another nation-state. It covers a group of peoples of widely different racial stocks (Berber, Punic, Egyptian, Aramaic, Phoenician, etc.) and very different historical pasts. These peoples have been *racially* Arabized only to a limited extent, an extent that decreases the further west one goes. On the other hand they have been completely Arabized in a linguistic and cultural sense. The last pre-Arabic languages (Coptic, Aramaean, etc.) spoken in the Eastern half of the Arab world died some centuries ago, and today are represented by only two small villages near Damascus and some others in Kurdistan, which continue to speak different forms of Aramaic.

In the Western half of the Arab world the only surviving language is Berber, which is spoken by about half the inhabitants of Morocco and a third of those of Algeria.[21] In the religious field, on the other hand, the process of adoption of the Arabian faith has been carried to an even greater degree in the West than in the East, for in North Africa, unlike Egypt, Syria, and Iraq, there are no Christian enclaves, though relatively large Jewish communities are to be found.

The present day Arab world is, therefore, the product of a cultural and historical process, a process of cultural diffusion carried out by the Muslin conquest of the 7th century and subsequent Bedouin invasions such as that of the Banu Hilal in North Africa in the 11th century. Its members are bound together by a common past, common memories, a common language and a common heritage. Professor H. A. R. Gibb has well defined the Arabs as "a people clustered round an historical memory." He goes on to say: "To the question 'who are the Arabs?' there is—whatever ethnographers may say—only one answer which approaches historic truth: all those are Arabs for whom the central fact of history is the Mission of Mohammad and the memory of the Arab Empire, and who in addition cherish the Arabic tongue and its cultural heritage as their common possession."[22]

One other characteristic of the Arab world remains to be noted: it is in many ways the vanguard of the Islamic world, and as such enjoys both the moral and political support of the non-Arab Muslims. This is due to the fact that, as the people among whom Muhammad was born and in whose language the Qur'ān was written, the Arabs have continued to enjoy a special prestige and position in the world of Islam. As E. F. Gautier[23] put it: "It is true that the Arabs have lost, since centuries, political domination over Islam, but they have kept moral domination. Islam is their creation. The human language which God employed, once and for all, in the Quran is the Arabic language. Today, as thirteen centuries ago, the holy cities of Arabia are the Holy Cities."

In the light of what has preceded, it does not seem too much to say that if any one man changed the course of history that man was Muhammad.

NOTES

1. A. de Tocqueville, *Democracy in America.*

2. This total has been obtained by bringing up to date, wherever possible, the figures given in the *Handwörterbuch des Islam* (Leiden 1941, article Islam). These figures, which were based on censuses or estimates dating from the 1920s or early 1930s totaled about 270,000,000, but higher estimates of the total Muslim population are quoted in the same article.

3. See Sir Thomas Arnold, *The Preaching of Islam* and H. A. R. Gibb, *Modern Trends in Islam*, Chapter I. Since there is no organized church in Islam, there has not been any missionary activity comparable to that of the Christian churches. But, precisely because of the lack of distinction between churchmen and laymen, every Muslim trader, traveler or soldier living abroad was a potential missionary.

4. There is also some evidence that Christianity was spreading in the area around Qatif and Bahrain—see Peter Bruce Cornwall, "In Search of Arabia's Past," *National Geographic Magazine*, April 1948.

5. Tor Andrae, *Mohammad*. By the sixth century Yemen had "not only been thoroughly impregnated with Judaism and Christianity but had modified its ancient paganism, consolidating the old pagan gods . . . in the

person of dhu-Samawi, the lord of the heavens, who at an earlier period of the highland culture had shared the supreme power with Talab Riyam and other deities." H. St. J. B. Philby, *The Background of Islam*, p. 114. As the same author goes on to say "in the highly civilised south paganism had virtually gone down before the impact of the monotheistic creeds of the north and had, presumably about this time, withdrawn to its last defenses in the area of Mecca." Ibid., p. 119.

6. H. A. R. Gibb, "Muhammad and the Qur'ān," MUSLIM WORLD, April 1948.

7. See article HANIF in *Encyclopedia of Islam*.

8. H. A. R. Gibb, "The structure of religious thought in Islam," MUSLIM WORLD, January 1948.

9. H. A. R. Gibb, "Muhammad and the Qur'ān"; MUSLIM WORLD, April 1948.

10. See Arnold Toynbee, *A Study of History*, Vol. I.

11. See H. Lammens, *La Syrie*; Edmond Rabbath, "Querelles Byzantines avant l'Islam" in *Cahiers de l'Est*, Beirut, Vol. I, No. 5; and Gustave Neyron, "Foi catholique en Orient avant l'Islam," in *Cahiers de l'Est*, Vol. II, No. 1.

12. See Tor Andrae, *Mohammad*.

13. See A. J. Butler, *The Arab Conquest of Egypt*.

14. Sir Thomas Arnold, *The Preaching of Islam*. In India more coercion seems to have been used than elsewhere; see James D. Brown, "The History of Islam in India," MUSLIM WORLD, January, April and July 1949.

15. For a fuller treatment, see C. Issawi, "The role of the Arabs in Islamic Civilization," MUSLIM WORLD, July 1948.

16. See P. K. Hitti: *History of the Arabs*.

17. Ibid.

18. A close historical parallel is to be found in the last stage of the Achaemenid empire, where both the central government and the rebels against its authority (such as the Egyptians or the provincial satraps) relied heavily on Greek mercenaries, a fact which paved the way for Alexander's sweeping conquest. See A. T. Olmstead, *History of the Persian Empire*.

19. *Prolegomena*—Quatremère's edition, Volume I, p. 45.

20. As was rightly pointed out by J. Weulersse, in *Paysans de Syrie et du Proche Orient*, Islam is "the only world civilization which was founded by nomads."

21. Robert Montagne: *La Civilisation du Désert*, Chap. VIII.

22. *The Arabs*—Oxford Pamphlets on World Affairs.

23. *Moeurs et Coutumes des Musulmans*.

5

Arab Geography and the Circumnavigation of Africa

Several changes had to take place before the peoples of medieval Europe could begin to think of exploring the world. Some of these consisted of technical improvements, such as the use of the compass and the introduction of stern rudders and fore and aft sails.[1] Others were political or economic. But among the most important was a transformation in men's outlook, of the mental picture which they had of the world. For some of the greatest obstacles holding back man's exploration of the globe have been psychological, not technical. It was not so much men's inability to overcome natural barriers which prevented them from extending the range of their knowledge by new discoveries as the notions they had of the world around them. It is not impossible that the Phoenicians circumnavigated Africa; it is practically certain that the Vikings reached the North American continent; and the distances spanned by the Polynesians in their light canoes are amazing.[2]

In the world-picture prevalent among most thinking people before the Portuguese discovery of the sea route to India, Western Europe was a remote outpost, cut off from the heart of the civilized world. For this picture, inherited from CLAUDIUS PTOLEMY—or rather, to be more accurate, attributed to him—included a twofold barrier to any sea communication between Europe and the East: a continuous land mass separating the Atlantic and Indian Oceans; and a Southern hemisphere in which life was impossible because of the excessive heat. Until this mental picture of the globe had been changed, there could be no hope for Europe to emerge from its isolation. It is the purpose of this note to examine the extent to which Arab geographers and travelers may have contributed to modify European conceptions regarding the earth, and more specifically those of HENRY THE NAVIGATOR[3] and his circle, by their views on the

Reprinted with permission from *Osiris*, vol. X, 1952, pp. 117-128.

western, southern and eastern coasts of Africa and by their conception of the nature of the southern hemisphere.

The African Continent

Arabic geography, like that of Christendom in the late Middle
Ages, was based essentially on the works of PTOLEMY of ALEXANDRIA.
Nevertheless it should be noted that "from the outset Muslim scholars
treated this text much more independently than at a later date did
the Western European scholars. Already in MUHAMMAD AL KHU-
WARIZMI's Surat al-ard (c. 830-40) we find a new version of PTOLEMY,
partly corrected and completed, partly distorted."[4]

Perhaps the greatest disservice rendered by PTOLEMY to posterity
was his conception of the African continent. In his map of the world,[5]
Africa is shown as extending indefinitely to the west and as stretching
out into the east to join South East Asia, making of the Indian Ocean
a landlocked sea. This naturally implied that there could be no direct
sea communication between the countries bordering the Atlantic
Ocean and India and the East, unless one cared to venture on the
vast expanse of Ocean which lay "behind" the visible part of the world
and which covered by far the greater part of the globe.

PTOLEMY's conception was accepted by many Muslim geographers
including the one who exerted the greatest influence on Europe, AL
IDRISI. In IDRISI's world map, drawn in A.D. 1154,[6] the east coast of
Africa is shown extending indefinitely eastward, well beyond Malaya.
Its tip was known as the Land of Waq Waq, a name which covered
indiscriminately Madagascar and Sumatra. It is true that the west
coast of Africa is represented as curving in, eastwards, near the
Equator. But at this point the map ends, and no regions south of
the Equator are shown, except for the sources of the Nile, some
unnamed mountains and "deserts and sands."[7]

Clearly, such a view gave little promise of a sea route to India.
But it was not by any means predominant among Muslim geographers. Many of them harked back to the older, and sounder,
tradition of STRABO which represented a greatly reduced Africa
as surrounded by the Ocean.[8] Thus the ninth century geographer
IBN KHURDADHBIH[9] stated that the part of the globe lying beyond
24° S. is covered by the Great Ocean which encircles the dry land,
thus implying the existence of a relatively short sea route from the
Atlantic to the East. A more explicit, but less encouraging, view is

that of the tenth century historian and geographer AL MAS'UDI[10] who says that the Atlantic Ocean is "connected with the Sea of China beyond Java."

The picture of the Enveloping Ocean given by MAS'UDI's younger contemporary, IBN HAUQAL,[11] closely following AL ISTAKHRI[12] indicates a definite connection between the Indian Ocean and the Atlantic. "The Enveloping Ocean surrounds the earth like a ring; the Sea of the Romans [Mediterranean] and the Sea of Fars [Indian Ocean] communicate with the Ocean." That he thought of the Ocean as surrounding Africa is shown by the following sentence: "The [regions lying] between the wastes of the Sudan and the Enveloping Ocean in the *South* are desolate deserts. I have not heard of any inhabitants or animals or plants living in these parts, nor is the extent of these two wildernesses[13] as far as the Ocean known. For it is impossible to cross them, owing to the excessive cold, which prevents habitation and life in the north and the excessive heat, which prevents habitation and life in the south."[14]

AL MUQADISSI frankly confesses that he "does not know whether the two seas [the Mediterranean and the Indian] communicate with the Ocean or issue from it."[15] But AL HAMADHANI is very definite. "The Great sea, than which there is no greater in the world, goes from the West [i.e., the Atlantic shores], passing by Clyzma [Suez] until it reaches the Waq Waq of China [probably Sumatra]."[16]

One more quotation will suffice, from AL BIRUNI (died 1048), one of the greatest scientific spirits of Islam. After describing the mountainous nature of the southern coasts of Africa and the stormy weather prevailing there he says: "But this does not prevent its [i.e., the Indian Ocean's] junction with the [Surrounding] Ocean south of these mountains. For traces of such a junction have been discovered, even though no one has actually seen it. The inhabited land is, consequently, surrounded on all sides by water."[17]

Thus most of the Muslim geographers seem to have believed in the existence of some sort of sea route between the Atlantic Ocean and South East Asia. But as long as the Ptolemaic conception of an elongated Africa, stretching eastwards parallel to Asia, persisted, there was little chance that anyone would attempt to take such a route. This view of Africa, however, contradicted another belief firmly held by all Muslim geographers, viz., that the greater part of the Southern hemisphere was covered by water.[18]

Moreover, a new factor was undermining the traditional picture of East Africa: the gradual southern push of Arab traders along its coasts. By the ninth century Arabs were established in Madagascar, and in the following centuries there were several waves of new settlers from Arabia and Persia and some conversion of Malagasies to Islam.[19]

Arab navigation in the Indian Ocean developed considerably with the passage of time. Names of famous captains like LAITH IBN KAHLAN and SAHL IBN ABAN are met with at least as early as the 12th century.[20] A remarkably accurate and detailed description of the coasts, winds and sea routes between East Africa and India and Sumatra is to be found in the writings of SULAIMAN AL MAHRI, who lived in the first half of the 16th century but drew on SHIHAB AL DIN AHMAD IBN MAJID, whose own work was composed before 1462-89.[21]

It will be remembered that it was a "Moorish pilot" who in 1498 took VASCO DA GAMA from Malindi, on the East Coast of Africa, to Calicut.[22] In the opinion of the distinguished French scholar GABRIEL FERRAND,[23] this "Moor" was undoubtedly SHIHAB EL DIN AHMAD IBN MAJID.

News of this activity was gradually filtering into Europe. Already before the end of the 13th century MARCO POLO had heard of the "great island of Madagascar" and of Zanzibar, both of which he describes in detail, mentioning the fact that the inhabitants of Madagascar were "followers of the law of Mahomet," that both it and Zanzibar were "visited by many ships from various parts of the world" and that there was no navigation further south because of the "sea current that runs with such force towards the south that it renders their return impossible."[24] Many Italians traveled in the Near East, for pilgrimage or trade.[25] It is perhaps on such sources—the available evidence does not warrant any more definite conclusions—that cartographers like MARINO SANUTO drew for their maps of the world, maps which were well known in HENRY THE NAVIGATOR's circle. SANUTO's map, drawn in 1306, is very interesting because in it Africa is represented as surrounded by the ocean and with a greatly reduced eastern bulge.[26] And with the replacement of the Ptolemaic picture of Africa by such a picture, one of the two great mental obstacles preventing the circumnavigation of that continent was removed.

The Southern Hemisphere

The second obstacle was, however, perhaps even greater. It consisted of a belief that the further south one traveled the warmer the climate grew until, somewhere behind the Equator, the heat was so great that no human existence was possible. The following quotation, from the anonymous author of HUDUD AL ALAM, is typical: "As regards the region lying south of the Equator some parts of it are occupied by the sea, and moreover, great heat prevails there and the people of those regions are more removed from the character of humanity. They are Zangis, Abyssinians, and the like. And farther on, down to the South Pole, no one can live on account of the excess of heat. Assistance is from God."[27]

The same view is expressed, somewhat more vigorously and imaginatively, by AL IDRISI: "The whole population of the globe dwells in the northern part; the regions lying in the south are abandoned and deserted because of the heat of the sun's rays. These regions being located in the lower part of the orbit of this body, it follows that the waters dry up and that all kinds of living beings are absent. For animals, like plants, can live only where there is water and coolness."[28]

This belief was usually backed by PTOLEMY's authority.[29] In point of fact, however, PTOLEMY had not been as categorical as his Muslim followers. The two following quotations show clearly his point of view. "If the earth is supposed cut into four equal parts by the equator and one circle through its poles, the extent of the part inhabited by us is very nearly enclosed in one or the other of the northern quarters."[30] "And people say they believe there are human habitations under the Equator since it is very temperate because the sun does not turn in the zenith, such is the speed of its passage through the divisions of the Equator, and therefore the summer heat would be temperate. Nor is the sun very far from the zenith in the tropics, so that the winter would not be severe. But we cannot say with any conviction what sort of habitations they are, for they cannot be reached by people from the part of the earth inhabited by us, and one would consider what is said about them conjecture rather than true information."[31]

The Muslim geographers followed PTOLEMY in believing that human habitation was confined to one or the other of the northern quarters but, less cautious than he, were more categorical about the excessive heat of the southern hemisphere. It is only rarely that we find a doubt, such as the one expressed by MAS'UDI[32] who states that some scientists believe that in the southern hemisphere are to be found temperate regions similar to those of the northern hemisphere—a view which he seems to reject.

This view was taken over by the Europeans, and more particularly by those interested in the Western parts of Africa. It finally hardened into a belief that Cape Non (Cape Nun, not far from the southern end of the Atlas mountains) constituted the limit of navigation, for beyond it the "seas were always kept boiling by the sun."[33] As the old saying went: "He who passes Cape Non, must turn back or not (i.e., nevermore)."[34] Later, Cape Non was rounded, but Cape Bojador took its place as the farthest limit of navigation. On the map of MARINO SANUTO, to which reference has already been made, a zone "uninhabitable from the heat" is represented in the center of Africa.

Several factors were however combining to assail this view. First, there was a very significant passage in ARISTOTLE's Meteorologica. "There are two inhabitable sections of the earth: one near our upper, or northern pole, the other near the other or southern pole; and their shape is like that of a tambourine. If you draw lines from the center of the earth they cut out a drum-shaped figure. The lines form two cones; the base of the one is the tropic, of the other the ever visible circle, their vertex is at the center of the earth. Two other cones toward the south pole give corresponding segments of the earth. These sections alone are habitable; beyond the tropics no one can live: for there the shade would not fall to the north, whereas the earth is known to be uninhabitable before the sun is in the zenith or the shade is thrown to the south: and the regions below the Bear are uninhabitable because of the cold."[35]

This passage is discussed at length by IBN RUSHD (AVERROES) in his *Commentaries*, a work translated into Latin and widely known throughout medieval Europe. IBN RUSHD fully agrees with ARISTOTLE that the southern hemisphere contains the counterpart of the northern regions, the cold gradually increasing as the South Pole is approached. The only point on which he takes issue *not* with ARISTOTLE but with "mathematicians, followers of PTOLEMY" is whether the region around the Equator is inhabited. His conclusion seems to be that it is inhabited, but that the excessive heat makes life there "unnatural." From what IBN RUSHD says, one gathers that there was a quite extensive literature on this subject.[36]

The whole position was restated as follows by IBN KHALDUN:[37] "From this [i.e., owing to the increase of heat as one moves south] certain philosophers have deduced that the Equator and the lands lying south of it are deserted. Yet several eyewitnesses and travelers have reported that these regions are in fact inhabited. This objection may be met by saying that the philosophers do not maintain that no life can exist in these regions. Rather they have been led by their arguments to the conclusion that, owing to the excessive heat, living beings decay rapidly, so that the existence of a human population is barely, if at all, possible. And in fact the regions lying on the Equator and south of it are reported to be very sparsely populated. IBN RUSHD maintains that the zone along the Equator is temperate and that the regions lying south of it are similar to those lying to the north, and are therefore inhabited in a like manner. His view cannot be refuted on the ground of the decay of things; it does not, however, take into account the fact that the ocean covers, in the south, the area corresponding to the inhabited regions in the North. Temperate zones are therefore absent in the South owing to the extent of the ocean . . . "

These views, added to the information current in all Arabic geographic books regarding the regions of Central Africa, were bound to undermine the traditional belief in the continuous southward increase of heat. For all these geographers stated categorically that there were inhabited, and indeed populous, regions *on* or *immediately south* of the Equator. Thus the author of *Hudud Al Alam* lists one country (the Sudan) lying on the Equator and no less than five south of it. These include Zaba (Java?), Zanjistan (Zanzibar) and Abyssinia. IBN KHURDADHBIH declared that the earth was inhabited as far as 24° S., while MAS'UDI fixes the limit of habitation at 19° S. Later on, SULAIMAN AL MAHRI stated that the northern tip of Madagascar lay 8° 37' South and the southern 25° 51' (the correct figures are 11° 57' and 25° 38' respectively).[38]

But it was not only on East Africa that Muslim traders had provided information. Their activity in Western Africa was very great, but it was carried mainly overland. Caravans continually moved to and fro between Arab North Africa and the lands of Gogo, Mali, Takrur and Ghana, bringing back gold, ivory, and slaves, and spreading Islam among the Negro peoples. Perhaps the most striking evidence of the intimacy of the relations between Negro West Africa and Arab North Africa is the fact that the ALMORAVIDES (AL MURABITUN), whose rule came to cover Muslim Spain as well as North Africa, originated, in the middle of the eleventh century, as a group of warrior monks on an island in the Senegal river.[39] In the fourteenth century, West Africa was extensively visited and described by the Arab traveler IBN BATTUTA.

Europe took a keen interest in this West African trade. Thus in 1223 the Genoese established a trading house in Tunis, and in 1320 the Venetians secured from the ruler of Tunis the privilege of sending caravans from that city. Italian geographers drew on the knowledge thus obtained. For instance, the Portolan of GIOVANNI DI CARIGNANO contains data on South Eastern Morocco not to be found in previous European maps.[40]

What was known to the Italians, and perhaps more, was known to the Portuguese and Spaniards. As regards Prince HENRY himself, we know that during the expedition to Ceuta, in 1414, he showed much interest in this matter. "Both AZURARA, the chronicler of his voyages, and DIEGO GOMEZ, his lieutenant, the explorer of the Cape Verde Islands and of the Upper Gambia, are quite clear about the new knowledge of the coast now gathered from Moorish prisoners."[41]

Thus, according to DIEGO GOMEZ, he learned "of the passage of traders from the coasts of Tunis to Timbuktu and to Cantor on the Gambia, which led him to seek those lands by the way of the sea." Among the more specific details about which he was informed was "certain tall palms growing at the mouth of the Western Nile (Senegal), by which he was able to guide the caravels he sent out to find that river."[42]

Upon reflection "the vague knowledge of the Guinea coast already gained through the Sahara Caravan Trade was improved by the Prince himself, during his stay at Ceuta, into the certainty that if the great western hump of Africa beyond Cape Bojador could be passed, his caravels would come into an eastern current, passing the gold and ivory coast, which might lead straight to India, and at any rate would be connected by an overland traffic with the Mediterranean."[43] It is also known that Prince HENRY corresponded with a merchant in Oran who supplied him with information about the Negro states of the interior.[44]

When, some years later, HENRY established at Sagres his centre for navigation and exploration, he took into his service a certain "Master JACOME from Majorca . . . with certain of the Arab and Jewish mathematicians, to instruct the Portuguese."[45] This Master JACOME may or may not have been JAHUDA CRESQUES, the Catalan cartographer,[46] but coming from Majorca he must have been familiar with the work of Arab geographers and the relations of travelers. Thus we know, for instance, that the Catalan cartographers used IDRISI.[47] And it was perhaps through these cartographers that HENRY and his circle acquired an erroneous belief which may have played an important part in stimulating their voyages.[48] This was the belief that the Niger, or Nile of the Blacks as it was called by Arab geographers, issued from the same source as the Nile, and that the Senegal river was the mouth of the Niger. When, in 1440 DINIZ DIAZ came upon the Senegal he thought of ascending to its source and then descending down the other Nile to the Mediterranean. For DIAZ, like HENRY himself and his chronicler AZURARA "thought not only that the Senegal was the Niger, the Western Nile of the Blacks, but that the caravels of Portugal were far nearer to India than was the fact—were getting close to the Mountains of the Moon and the Sources of the Nile."[49]

Conclusion

The conclusion of the foregoing may be stated as follows: It cannot be proved that Prince HENRY was directly influenced by Arab geography in his attempt to circumnavigate Africa. But it has been shown that all the elements necessary to produce the belief that such an enterprise was possible existed, in a form which was probably accessible to him, in the Arab geographers. The view that the greater part of the southern hemisphere was covered by water; that Africa was surrounded by the ocean; that the southern hemisphere contained a temperate zone; that life was possible along and immediately south of the Equator—all this produced a world picture which seemed to justify the attempt to reach India by sea. The further knowledge that Arab caravans were busily trading with regions south of the seemingly impassable Sahara and Cape Bojador and that Arab ships had found their way far south along the East African coast provided additional grounds for optimism. The different pieces of the jigsaw puzzle were there, and they fitted perfectly. It only required a great mind, eager to seize upon all shreds of evidence favoring its design, to put them together and obtain a rough working picture of the outline of the African continent. This is what HENRY and his circle, to their undying glory, did at Sagres.

NOTES

1. The technical, and other, aspects of Arab navigation are discussed in a book by G. F. HOURANI, *Arab Navigation*, Princeton 1951.

2. A striking illustration of this fact was provided by the "Kontiki" expedition which sailed in a raft from Peru to Polynesia, a total distance of 4,300 nautical miles.

3. An up to date bibliography on HENRY THE NAVIGATOR is given in ELAINE SANCEAU, *Henry the Navigator*, New York 1947. An older book, which discusses the progress of geographical knowledge in the Middle Ages is CHARLES RAYMOND BEAZLEY, *Prince Henry the Navigator*, London 1923. GOMES EANNES DE AZURARA's *Chronica do descobrimento e conquista de Guiné* has been translated into English by CHARLES RAYMOND BEAZLEY and EDGAR PRESTAGE under the title *The Chronicle of the Discovery and Conquest of Guinea*, 2 vols., London 1896-99. It contains a valuable introduction.

4. Preface by V. V. BARTHOLD to V. MINORSKY, *Hudud al Alam*, London 1937, p. 9.

5. See *The Geography of Claudius Ptolemy*, translated by EDWARD LUTHER STEVENSON, New York 1932. Map. I. The date and authorship of these maps has been questioned, but this does not affect the present argument since they are closely based on the text.

6. KONRAD MILLER, *Die Weltkarte des Idrisi*, 2 volumes; maps and text. Stuttgart 1926.

7. MILLER neatly summarized the relations between the views of PTOLEMY on Africa and those of IDRISI as follows: "Das Bild von Afrika ist bei beiden augenfallig ähnlich, aber der Inhalt ist ganz verschieden." *Ibid.*, vol. 2, p. 50.

8. They were also familiar with ARISTOTLE's opinion in the Meteorologica which seems to imply the existence of a channel, albeit a narrow one, between Africa and the "Southern Continent": "The Red Sea (Indian Ocean) for instance, communicates but slightly with the Ocean outside the straits (Atlantic)." Book II.i.354a. (Translated by E. W. WEBSTER in *The Works of Aristotle*, edited by W. D. Ross, Oxford 1931, volume III.) In the ninth century, the Meteorologica was translated into Arabic under the title *Al athar al 'ulwia*.

9. *Kitab al masalik wal mamalik*, extract in R. BLACHERE. *Extraits des principaux géographes arabes*, Paris and Beirut 1932, p. 24.

10. *Kitab el tanbih*, edited by M. DE GOEJE, *Bibliotheca Geographorum Arabicorum*, Leyden 1873, volume VIII, p. 68.

11. *Kitab al masalik wal mamalik*, edited by DE GOEJE, vol. II, p. 13.

12. *Kitab al masalik wal mamalik*, edited by DE GOEJE, vol. I, p. 7.

13. The one lying north of the inhabited parts of Europe and Asia and the one lying south of the Sudan.

14. DE GOEJE, *op. cit.*, p. 12.

15. *Ahsan al taqasim fi ma'rifat al aqalim*, edited by DE GOEJE, vol. III, p. 16.

16. *Kitab al Buldan*, edited by DE GOEJE, vol. V, p. 7.

17. *Qanun al Mas'udi*. Extract in BLACHERE, *op. cit.*, p. 242.

18. References to this can be found in practically every Muslim philosopher. See the quotation from IBN KHALDUN, below.

19. Article *Madagascar* in *Encyclopedia of Islam*.

20. GEORGE SARTON: Introduction to the History of Science, vol. II, pt. i,

p. 221; J. SAUVAGET in *Sur d'anciennes instructions nautiques arabes pour les mers de l'Inde, Journal Asiatique*, vol. CCXXXVI, fascicule I, gives reasons for believing that these two sailors lived in the 10th century.

21. See articles *Sulaiman al Mahri* and *Shihab al Din* in *Encyclopedia of Islam*.

22. VASCO DA GAMA's first contact with Islamic civilization in the Indian Ocean was actually made at Mozambique where, he reported, the inhabitants were Mohammedan and spoke the "Moorish tongue."

23. *Ibid.* See also G. FERRAND, *Instructions nautiques et routiers arabes et portugais des XVe et XVIe siècles*, Paris 1928, vol. 3, p. 177 et seq.

24. *The Travels of Marco Polo*, Book III, chapters 33 and 34, Modern Library Edition.

25. SARTON, *op. cit.*, p. 102.

26. Reproduced in BEAZLEY, *op. cit.*, facing p. 114. Following GEORGE H. KIMBLE, *The Laurentian world map with special reference to its portrayal of Africa*, Imago Mundi, I, 1935, it has been assumed in this article that the Laurentian Portolan of 1351 (reproduced in BEAZLEY, *op. cit.*, facing p. 120) contains later interpolations. The outline of Africa shown in this map is remarkably accurate.

27. *Op. cit.*, p. 50.

28. From *Géographie D'Edrisi*, translated by P. AMÉDÉE JAUBERT; *Recueil De Voyages et de Mémoires*, vol. V, Société de Géographie, Paris 1836, pp. 2-3.

29. PTOLEMY's *Mathematical Composition* had been translated into Arabic under the title of *Almajisti*.

30. PTOLEMY, *Mathematical Composition*, translated by R. CATESBY TALIA-FERRO; *The Classics of the St. John's Programme*, 1939, p. 50.

31. *Ibid.*, pp. 58-59.

32. *Op. cit.*, p. 31.

33. BEAZLEY, *op. cit.*, p. 119.

34. AZURARA, vol. II, p. 3: Quem passar o Cabo de Não ou tornara, ou não.

35. *Op. cit.*, Book II.5.362b.

36. AVERROES, *Commentaries in Junta*, edition of *Aristotelis opera*, Venice 1573-76, vol. 5, fols. 438A et seq. I am indebted to Professor H. WOLFSON of Harvard for help on this passage.

37. Edited by QUATREMÈRE, Paris 1858, vol. I, p. 86.

38. See references given above.

39. See articles in *Encyclopedia of Islam* and *Relation de Ghanat* in *Recueil de voyages et de mémoires*, Société de Géographie, Paris 1825, vol. I.

40. G. SARTON, *op. cit.*, vol. 3, pt. 1, p. 182.

41. BEAZLEY, *op. cit.*, p. 157.

42. Introduction to AZURARA's chronicle, Vol. II, p. iv.

43. BEAZLEY, *op. cit.*, p. 141.

44. Azurara, vol. II, p. xxvi.

45. Beazley, *op. cit.*, p. 161.

46. Sarton, *op. cit.*, vol. 3, pt. 2, p. 1593.

47. Miller, *op. cit.*, p. 51.

48. There are several examples of important discoveries arising from fundamentally erroneous beliefs. Among the best known is Columbus's first voyage to America, based on Toscanelli's map which, by magnifying the size of Asia, led him to expect to strike Asia roughly where America stands. It is also possible that Magellan's undertaking to circumnavigate South America was based on the strength of a map in which the mouth of La Plata was represented as a strait.

49. Beazley, *op. cit.*, p. 221.

6

Al-Mutanabbi in Egypt
(957-962)

When, just over a thousand years ago, the poet Abu al-Tayyib al-Mutanabbi entered Egypt, he had good reason to hope that his hitherto unsuccessful and unhappy life was taking a turn for the better. Fate had not allowed him to play the part of gentleman-warrior-poet for which he had cast himself:

> Night knows me, and war-steeds, the desert and its men,
> And the lance, and the sword, and the scroll, and the pen.

Al-Mutanabbi was of humble birth, the son of a water-carrier, but his precocious intelligence was soon recognized and enabled him to move in some of the most interesting intellectual circles of his time. As a youth, he came under the influence of the Qarmatians (one of the few genuinely revolutionary groups in the history of Islam), who called for radical changes in economic, social, political and religious life. Al-Mutanabbi's one attempt at starting a revolution failed dismally. He tried to rouse an Arab tribe by posing as a prophet (hence his nickname "he who claims to be a prophet") and by "revealing" sayings closely modeled on, and designed to rival, those of the Koran. His movement was quickly suppressed, and he was put in jail for a couple of years.

Like many other disappointed revolutionaries, he decided to make his peace with the established order. Henceforth, his ambition was to become a prince, or at least a governor, and his poetic genius seemed to provide a means to that end. If he could not be a revolutionary prophet, he could be a successful court poet. He attached himself to one patron after another, finding most satisfaction and reward at the court of Saif al-Dawlah, prince of Aleppo, who had surrounded himself with a group of brilliant poets and scholars. But after a few years, relations between prince and poet became more and more strained; al-Mutanabbi considered that he was not

Reprinted with permission from *Medieval and Middle Eastern Studies in Honor of Aziz Suryal Atiya*, Leiden, 1952, ed. Sami A. Hanna, pp. 236-239.

getting his due and felt himself the victim of a court cabal led by his rival, the poet Abu Firas, who was a cousin of Saif al-Dawlah. Matters reached a point where he felt that his life was in danger, and he suddenly left for Damascus, going from there to Cairo.

Al-Mutanabbi had come to Egypt at the invitation of its ruler Kafur, an able Negro eunuch slave of the royal household who had usurped power from the legitimate king. Egyptian rule then included Hijaz and southern Syria and the ambitious poet imagined that he was at last within sight of achieving his dream and securing a principality.

Relations between king and poet were at first very satisfactory. Kafur was generous in his gifts and al-Mutanabbi responded with verses of adulation intended to secure further recompense for himself and, possibly, also to vex his former patron Saif al-Dawlah. The following verses, freely translated, are by no means the most extravagant:

> I wish that Fate youth would to me restore
> And that wisdom take back which long years bore;
> For youth and reason are not enemies,
> Ripeness in young as well as old heads lies;
> Since boyhood was Kafur with wisdom fraught,
> In all things learned ere he had been taught;
> Experienced, knowing, generous of heart,
> His breeding comes from nature not from art;
> That richest prize, a royal crown, he won
> Before his life's career had begun;
> His empire vast stretches to Nubia,
> Iraq, Byzantium and Arabia.

But as months, and years, passed it became increasingly clear that Kafur had no intention of satisfying the poet's political ambitions. Nor would he let al-Mutanabbi leave Egypt for fear of his sharp tongue. To add to al-Mutanabbi's troubles, he suffered from attacks of malaria, of which he has left a description remarkable both for its clinical accuracy and for its humorous imagery and conceits:

> In Egypt weak and miserable I lie
> My sick bed sick of me, and of it I,
> Few friends to comfort me, my body shrunk,
> And, without liquor, reeling like a drunk.
>
> My visitor, as though from modesty,
> Will only in the darkness come to me;
> She spurns the couches which for her I spread

And in my bones prefers to make her bed;
My skin's for her and for my breath too tight—
She stretches it with every sort of blight;
The dawning light drives her away, and lo
From every pore her streaming tears do flow;
Listless and weak for her each night I wait,
Like lover fearful lest his love be late;
And she, perversely constant, always true,
Has never yet once missed her rendez-vous.
Daughter of woe, all woes do dwell in me—
I had not thought they would make room for thee.

Eventually, in 962, the poet did succeed in getting away. His pent-up disappointment and anger expressed themselves in one of the most venomous satires in the Arabic language, from which the following passages are taken:

The eunuch now is of the vagrants lord,
The free are all enslaved, the slave adored;
For Egypt's guards were careless of their charge
And foxes with sweet grapes their bellies gorge.
Slaves are not freemen's brothers fit to be
Although born in the clothing of the free.
Remember when a nigger slave you buy
To get a stick—niggers are rascals sly.
I never thought I would witness the days
When slaves would lord it and receive such praise;
Nor had I dreamt that *men* had vanished quite
And that there were the likes of our Snow-white,[1]
Or that a black with pierced lips was obeyed
By craven knaves and hireling cowards paid.

A few lines later the poem reaches its paroxysm:

Who has the gelding nigger virtue taught?
His masters white, his fathers chased and caught?
The dealer's hand twisting his bleeding ear?
His price—at tuppence he was deemed too dear!
Of course for Kafur there is this excuse
(Excusing can be one form of abuse):
When virile whites often a sense do lack
Of gratitude, how much more eunuchs black!

Al-Mutanabbi was to make yet one more attempt for political recognition. Returning to his native Iraq, he attached himself to the vizier in Baghdad; then, finding he still got no preferment, he moved on to Shiraz, the residence of the sultan Adud al-Dawlah. But this phase of his career did not last long. In 965, while traveling from Shiraz to Iraq, he was set upon by some tribesmen and murdered. One version has it that his killer was seeking revenge for having been ridiculed by the poet in one of his satires. Another version is more poetic, and not out of character. According to it, al-Mutanabbi was preparing to run away from his attackers when a companion told him that flight was not becoming to the author of the lines:

> Night knows me, and war-steeds, the desert and its men,
> And the lance, and the sword, and the scroll, and the pen.

Al-Mutanabbi turned back and died fighting.

NOTES

1. Literally "the father of whiteness," Kafur.

7

The Decline of Middle Eastern Trade, 1100-1850[1]

The decline of Middle Eastern trade is one aspect of the economic and cultural decay of the region. From the 12th or 13th century until the 19th, a process of economic deterioration took place, interrupted only by such rallies as those in Egypt and southern Syria in the late 13th and early 14th centuries, Anatolia in the 15th and 16th, northern Syria in the 16th and Īrān in the 16th and early 17th. And, except in Īrān and very briefly in Turkey, this economic deterioration was accompanied by intellectual and cultural decline. By any economic criteria, the Middle East stood far lower in the 18th century than in the 10th or 11th.

What made this process still more disastrous was that, during the same period, the other major civilizations were on an upward course, with relatively brief set-backs. This was true not only of Europe, the closest neighbor and main rival. In China, following what has been called the "commercial revolution" under the Tang and Sung (8th-13th centuries) that made it "the most advanced country in the world,"[2] "from the fourteenth to the early nineteenth centuries, the Chinese economy seems to have grown in almost all its aspects—population, area of cultivated land, volume of foreign trade, production of handicrafts and industrial goods, and even, perhaps, in the use of money."[3] In Japan, the Ashikaga and Tokugawa periods (14th-19th centuries) saw an even more impressive growth, which laid the foundations for the country's remarkable modernization and development.[4] As for India, its history in this period is both too complex and too obscure to permit generalization. However, Moreland's careful and conservative description of conditions around 1600 suggests considerable prosperity—a population of about 100 million, agricultural production per head of rural population "probably not very different from what it is now" and very flourishing handicrafts, especially textiles.[5] Indeed, the latter not only supplied

Reprinted with permission from *Islam and the Trade of Asia*, Oxford, 1970, ed. D. S. Richards, pp. 245-266.

Middle Eastern and other Asian and African markets, but successfully competed in Europe and the Americas until the close of the 18th century. The breakdown of the Indian economy does not seem to have occurred until the latter part of the 17th century, or even during the 18th.[6]

I. Exports of Middle Eastern Goods

A country's export trade consists of its own produce and of re-exports of goods imported from other countries. For the Middle East, the latter category was very important, and this paper is accordingly divided into two parts, dealing with export trade and transit trade, respectively; carrying trade is studied under the latter heading.

Following the time-honored practice of economists, the first question will be examined under the two sub-headings of supply and demand; first the factors which diminished the supply of Middle Eastern goods (or, more precisely, shifted the supply curve upward), and then those that diminished the demand for those goods (or, more precisely, shifted the demand curve downward).

(A) SUPPLY

From the 12th century to the early 19th, several forces operated to reduce the Middle East's capacity to produce goods, and therefore to export. Among the more devastating wars mention may be made of the later Crusades and the "scorched earth" policy of the Mamluks against raids from Cyprus and Rhodes; the Mongol and Tatar invasions, which caused havoc in Īrān, 'Irāq and Syria; and the Ottoman-Persian wars which ruined much of north-eastern Anatolia, north-western Īrān and 'Irāq. Plagues were recurrent and took a heavy toll. According to al-Maqrīzī, the Black Death carried off one-third of Egypt's population, and other countries may have suffered as much. In the following centuries there were several, not so spectacular but nonetheless devastating, epidemics.[7] And then there was the breakdown of government. In Egypt, Mamluk rule weakened in the mid-14th century and Bedouin incursions began to disrupt agriculture; the deterioration continued until government control was re-established under Muḥammad 'Alī.[8] In Syria, the unrelenting pressure of the desert on the sown carried the Bedouins, in the 18th century, to the sea near Acre and north of Tripoli. In 'Irāq there was a steady, almost unbroken, decline until the second Ottoman conquest of 1831. In Anatolia, government control broke down in large areas at the beginning of the 17th century and was not restored until the time of Maḥmūd II. And in Īrān, the end of the 17th century saw the collapse of Safavid rule and devastating Afghan, Ottoman and Russian invasions, and even under the Qajars government hold over the country remained precarious.

Agriculture

Middle Eastern agriculture was more vulnerable to such shocks than was that of other regions. The Middle East has been aptly compared to an archipelago, with small islands of cultivation surrounded by enormous seas of deserts, and the islands have often been submerged by the desert. The region contains no large continuous stretches of thickly populated areas comparable to those of China, India or Europe. And where, as in 'Irāq or Īrān, cultivation was dependent on elaborate and rather fragile irrigation works, it was even easier to disrupt and much more difficult to restore. Hence, the result of the catastrophes enumerated above was a great shrinkage of population and area under cultivation, leading to a sharp drop in the region's capacity to export agricultural produce.

In 'Irāq, Adams[9] estimates that the population of Lower Diyāla reached a peak of 800,000 around A.D. 800, fell to below 400,000 by 1100 and then dropped sharply to around 60,000 after the Mongol invasion had destroyed the irrigation works, staying at that level for the next five centuries. By the beginning of the 19th century, systematic cultivation in 'Irāq was confined to a few small areas.[10]

In Syria, the contraction of population and cultivated area was not so drastic, since its rain-fed agriculture was more resilient than 'Irāq's, with its delicate irrigation network. But Volney, writing at the end of the 18th century, pointed out that in the pashalik of Aleppo, whereas early defters showed "upwards of three thousand, two hundred villages, at present the collector can scarcely find four hundred"; the continued deterioration is vividly described in the reports of British consuls in the first half of the 19th century.[11]

The same process can be traced in Egypt. According to al-Maqrīzī and other historians, the number of villages fell from 10,000 under the Fatimids to 2170 in the 15th century. Concomitantly, land-tax receipts diminished sharply, from 10.8 million dinars in 1298 and 9.4 million in 1315 to 1.8 million in 1517. These figures cannot be accepted uncritically. Thus, the 10,000 figure for the Fatimid period is probably greatly exaggerated.[12] Again, the unit of account used in land taxation may not have been constant, and the fall in receipts was probably not as great.[13] Moreover, the 1517 figure reflects the disruption caused by the Ottoman conquest, and land-tax receipts did in fact rise again in the 16th and early 17th centuries.[14] But the general decline was nonetheless real.

The evidence for Anatolia is less clear. According to Ö. L. Barkan, the 16th century seems to have witnessed a period of population growth, followed by a decline toward its end. "By 1653 Haci Halifa reports that people had begun to flock from villages to the towns during the reign of Süleyman, and that in his own day there were derelict and abandoned villages all over the Empire."[15] This does not necessarily imply that the total population of Anatolia was declining, since at least some of the major towns were growing, but one can accept the evidence of rural depopulation.[16] Conditions seem to have deteriorated further in the course of the 18th century.

For Īrān, by contrast, the effects of the crisis at the beginning of the 18th century on population and economic activity are only too clear from reports by eyewitnesses and travelers, such as Krusinski and Hanway. If the figures compiled by Lord Curzon are at all accurate, the silk production of the northern provinces fell to only a small fraction of its former size.[17]

A decline in population, even if accompanied by an equal shrinkage in cultivated area, does not necessarily imply a fall in the level of living. In fact, given diminishing returns and assuming that the least fertile lands are abandoned first, it may lead to higher average and marginal productivity per man. This allows real wages to rise, and shortage of labor may induce landlords to offer higher wages. This process occurred in Europe after the Black Death, and may well have done so in parts of the Middle East. But even so, such a shrinkage must lead to a decline in the surplus available for export or other uses, unless it is accompanied by an improvement in technology or greater use of capital (which obviously did not take place in the Middle East) or unless the marginal product of labor is lower than the consumption of the worker and his dependents, which is very unlikely to have been true of that period.[18] Such a hypothesis may partly explain why the Middle East, a large exporter of foodstuffs in Roman times, gradually ceased to be one and resumed its former role only with the expansion that began in the 19th century.[19]

Handicrafts

In both the Roman and early Muslim periods, the Middle East's exports of manufactured goods, westward and eastward, seem to have been at least as important as its exports of agricultural goods. The subsequent decline of the handicrafts, and hence of the Middle East's capacity to export, is clear. Thus, the number of weavers in Alexandria is said to have fallen from 14,000 in 1394 to 800 in 1434, and that of sugar mills in Fusṭāṭ from sixty-six in 1325 to only nineteen in working order around 1400.[20] Generally speaking, in the Arab countries the decline in both quantity and quality seems to have continued until the 19th century, with a few exceptions as in Syria. In Turkey, the influx of foreign workers in the 16th century (Jews, Iranians, Syrians, Egyptians) improved techniques, but this was followed by stagnation or retrogression in the 17th and 18th.[21] And in Īrān, even at the height of Safavid splendor, Chardin was struck by the softness and laziness of the craftsmen and their lack of desire to innovate or even to imitate.[22] The subsequent breakdown must have disrupted Iranian crafts very severely.

This general decline is partly attributable to the above-mentioned shocks, whose effect on the crafts was often even more adverse than on agriculture.[23] But there are several other factors which explain why Middle Eastern crafts failed to develop as did those of Europe. First, one must note the weakness of the resource-base of the Middle East, and its deficiency in wood, the basic material of the Eotechnic period; in navigable rivers and water-power; in minerals, which in Europe gave rise to very large enterprises in the late medieval period; and, in view of its use in China from the time of the Han and in Europe since the late medieval period, one is tempted to add, in coal. And secondly, there was the lack of mechanical inventiveness and the failure to develop non-human sources of energy; examples of this are the disappearance of the windmill, which seems to have been invented in Īrān; the limited number of watermills and the continued use of the "Greek" rather than the "Vitruvian" type; the failure to improve harnesses, etc.[24]

Thirdly, there was the structure and policy of the various governments—Mamluk, Ottoman and Safavid. In all of them control lay in the hands of the military, who were generally of alien stock, and the bureaucracy; the entrepreneurial bourgeoisie, consisting of merchants, craftsmen and their guilds, never had enough power or organization to force or persuade the government to take its needs and interests into consideration. As a result, private property was always more precarious than in Europe, and any developing enterprise was more liable to be taxed out of existence. The same considerations partly account for the almost uninterrupted debasement of the currency and rise in prices in the Middle East from the 14th to the 19th centuries, a trend which seems to have been much more marked than in Europe, which cannot be fully explained by the influx of American bullion, since Europe was even more exposed to its impact, and which must have caused severe injury to the economy.[25] And these considerations also help to account for the fact that the Middle East did not outgrow what Hecksher, describing medieval Europe, expressively termed "the policy of provision." The main objectives of government policy were not to promote local production but to ensure that fiscal needs would be met and that the principal towns, and in particular the capital city, would be adequately supplied.[26] Hence, long after such statesmen as Cromwell and Colbert had shown how far the state was prepared to go in backing national industry, shipping and export trade, the Middle Eastern governments continued to tax local enterprises heavily, to impose higher duties on exports than on imports, to let coastal shipping fall into foreign hands and even to exempt foreigners from certain internal duties (e.g. the *mürüriye*) paid by nationals.[27]

To what extent can this stagnation in technology, and this unfavorable government policy, be attributed, as has so often been done, to Islam, with its prohibitions on interest, its ban on speculation and its contemptuous attitude to agriculture? Maxime Rodinson, in his very interesting *Islam et Capitalisme* (Paris 1966), has argued convincingly that both the doctrines and the practice of early medieval Islam were favorable to economic activity in general, and capitalist forms in particular.[28] Nevertheless, three adverse effects on economic activity may be noted. First, following the development of rational and scientific thought in the 9th-12th centuries, which threatened to undermine the religious basis of society, there was a swing to Sufism. This gave much spiritual vitality but "intellectual standards declined first, as Sufi speculation more and more replaced the objective criteria of orthodox reasoning and Hellenistic science. Then moral standards. . . ."[29] One aspect of the decline in moral standards was the arrogance of Muslims toward other faiths and cultures, a quality which was of course by no means peculiar to them but which became fatal when it persisted long after their decline and Europe's upsurge. Their lack of curiosity and their parochialism, born of a feeling of superiority, may be measured by the tiny number of Muslim travelers to Europe in the 16th-18th centuries, and by noting that the Turks and Arabs did not think of going to infidel lands for trade, at most allowing the Europeans to come to them.[30] Lastly, the fusion of religious and secular authority in Islam may have been one of the factors inhibiting the development of independent centers of power checking the central government. Islam, like most other non-Western civilizations, never had bodies enjoying power comparable to those of European feudal landlords, the Church, city-states, universities and other corporate groups, even making allowance for the influence of such groups as the *'ulamā* and the *ashrāf*. More specifically, as noted before, its guilds and bourgeoisie failed to make their weight felt, and to have their interests recognized, as did their European counterparts.

(B) DEMAND

In the course of the centuries under review, European demand for many goods exported by the Middle East was successively deflected, in part or in whole, to other producers, who could supply cheaper or superior products. For agricultural produce, this came about through the opening of new areas, with more favorable soil, climate or economic organization, e.g., centrally managed estates in Europe and slave plantations overseas. For industrial goods, this was due to the transfer of technology to Europe or the development of new techniques in that continent and India.

First the situation in the Mediterranean area will be studied and then that in the Indian Ocean area.

Mediterranean Area

Demand may be examined for three broad classes of goods: (a) manufactured goods; (b) raw materials and foodstuffs; and (c) textiles and textile materials.

(a) Until the 10th century, papyrus was a major item exported by the Middle East to Europe, after which it was replaced by paper, exported directly or through Constantinople. However, by the 12th century, paper was being produced in Spain and in the following century in Italy.[31] By the 14th century the tiny city of Fabriano had "become the [Western] world's largest center for the production of paper."[32] And soon after that the Middle East began importing paper from Europe and has continued to do so until the present day.[33]

High quality glass was produced in Syria and elsewhere, and some glassware was exported to Europe, as well as to the East.[34] But after the Crusades, there is some evidence that Middle Eastern "workers moved westwards to revitalize the Western industry at Venice and elsewhere."[35] By the end of the Middle Ages, the Middle East was importing window glass and other glassware from Europe and continued to do so, while its own production went on deteriorating in quality.[36]

Sugar was exported in large quantities, especially from Egypt, Syria and Cyprus.[37] But the Crusaders introduced the sugar-cane to Europe, and soon it was grown in several Mediterranean countries.[38] However, the real blow came when sugar was raised in plantations in virgin lands in Madeira, Azores and Cape Verde in the 15th century, and a still harder blow when it was grown in Brazil, after 1550.[39]

Various chemicals were exported from the Middle East, as is clearly shown in the Geniza documents, but Europeans gradually began to make or mine their own. Thus, alum was an important item of export from Egypt. In the 13th century between 5,000 and 13,000 qinṭār were shipped each year, and large quantities were also exported from Anatolia.[40] But in 1461, the Papal Commissioner of Revenue discovered large deposits near Civita Vecchia and "predicted that the vast works set up under his direction for the Pope would assure the defeat of the infidel by freeing Europe from its long dependence on the Near East."[41] In the meantime, the Egyptian mines had dried up!

(b) As for foodstuffs and raw materials, in the early Middle Ages there were some exports of wine from the Middle East. Then, gradually, they disappeared, presumably because Islamic prohibitions and, perhaps still more important, taxation led to the shrinkage of vineyards in Syria, Cyprus and Anatolia.[42]

The grain trade showed violent fluctuations, depending on the size of crops. In good years, Egypt, Syria and Anatolia exported wheat to Southern Europe, and in bad years imported but, by and large, the Middle East seems to have been a net exporter.[43] But after about 1590 a new source of supply was opened: north European, especially Baltic, wheat entered the Mediterranean in Dutch, Hansa and British ships. This competition did not completely displace Middle Eastern wheat, but it must have cut into its markets and forced down its price. By the 18th century, Balkan, Danubian and Russian grains (including maize) offered further competition.

Coffee was another foodstuff that, much later, suffered from the opening of new sources of supply. By the mid-17th century, Europe was acquiring a taste for coffee and considerable quantities were being imported from Mocha or through Egypt.[44] However, the Dutch transplanted shoots to the East Indies and ended the monopoly enjoyed by the Middle East. In 1721 "90% of the coffee imported into Europe by the VOC [Dutch East Indian Company] still came from Mocha and only 10% from Java; but five years later the ratio was reversed."[45] Again, this does not necessarily mean that the volume of Middle Eastern exports declined, but the price must have been affected. And by the mid-18th century, foreign competition was so great that the Middle East was actually importing coffee from the West Indies.

Other raw materials, e.g., madder root and gall-nuts used for dyeing, and valonia for tanning, continued to be exported through the 19th century. But from the 13th century, Middle Eastern dyestuffs began to feel the competition of Italian workshops,[46] and from the 16th numerous articles were imported from Central America. However, from the end of the 18th century a new item figured in Middle Eastern trade—opium, which was taken, from Turkey and later from Īrān by European and American ships, for local use or for re-export to China.[47]

Mention should also be made of the trade in pearls. During the Middle Ages the Middle East exported to Europe pearls drawn from both the Persian Gulf and Ceylon. For nearly a hundred years, from 1508 to 1602, the Portuguese held Bahrein, and with it presumably the main pearl fisheries, but then control reverted to the Arabs and Persians, and trade resumed. However, by then Europeans had direct access to Indian and Far Eastern pearls. In the course of the 19th century, exports of pearls from Bahrein increased greatly, but most of this seems to have been directed to India. And after the First World War, the competition of Japanese cultured pearls dealt the industry a crippling blow.[48]

(c) Textiles and textile materials continued to be the leading export of the Middle East until the recent discovery of petroleum. However, in the course of the centuries, there were great changes in their composition, and a shift from the export of manufactured goods to that of raw materials. The trade can be studied under three sub-headings: linen, silk and cotton. Exports of raw wool were minor and woollens were imported from Europe from the early Middle Ages, or from Tunis where a flourishing industry was established by Moriscoes.

Egypt was for long the major exporter of both linen and flax.[49] Gradually, exports of linen fell off, presumably because of the decline of the handicrafts and the growth of European competition; by the 17th century the French were no longer buying any linen. However, Egypt continued to export small amounts elsewhere, until the end of the 18th century.[50]

As for flax, new and far richer sources of supply were being developed. First in Romagna then, and on a much larger scale, in the Low Countries, France and the Baltic region.[51] In his book on the 17th century, Paul Masson mentions flax as an item of trade,[52] but not in his book on the 18th century,[53] although in fact a small amount was still exported. And it is significant that in his analysis of costs and returns on the fourteen major Egyptian crops around 1800, Girard does not include flax.[54]

Silk remained, until the 18th century, the leading export staple. Much more information is available on it than on most goods and the main outlines of the silk trade are clear.[55]

In the early Middle Ages high-quality silk fabrics were exported from the Middle East to Europe. These were made partly of local silk, grown in Īrān, Syria, Morea and elsewhere, and partly of silk imported from Spain and Sicily, as is shown in the Geniza documents.[56] But by the 13th century the virtual monopoly enjoyed by the Muslims in Europe had been broken and by the 15th Italian silk fabrics were selling in the Levant. This, however, did not mean the decay of the local silk industry which—in Īrān, Bursa, Syria and even 'Irāq—continued to meet most of the needs of the Middle Eastern market and exported to some adjacent areas such as the Sudan and India. But exports to Europe practically ceased, and in the 19th century, Middle Eastern silk weavers were hit very hard by the influx of European machine-made goods.

Instead raw silk became the main export item to Europe. The chief source was Īrān, exporting through Aleppo, Izmir or, more seldom, the Persian Gulf. Īrān's production was increasingly supplemented by the region around Bursa and other parts of western Anatolia, northern Syria and Lebanon; this made it possible to maintain the volume of silk exports from the Middle East during the collapse of the Iranian silk industry, early in the 18th century, and until its recovery in the 19th. But although the volume was maintained, the price must have been affected by increased competition, particularly since the quality of the Middle Eastern product was inferior. At first the main rivals were Italy and France, then increasingly China and India. "In 1636 the third silk producing area, Bengal, comes into the picture, and by the end of the century the Bengal silk trade surpassed that of Persia and China."[57] Late in the 19th century, Japanese competition was even more severe but Middle Eastern output nevertheless grew substantially, thanks to both foreign and government initiative, and it was estimated that in 1914 the Middle East was still producing 10% of the world's output.[58] It was the disruptions of the First World War, in Lebanon, Anatolia and Īrān, and the competition of rayon that practically wiped out Middle Eastern production.

As for cotton, in the Middle Ages Europe imported raw cotton from Egypt and still more from Syria, as well as from Cyprus and Greece, but not, apparently, significant amounts of cloth or yarn.[59] By the 17th century exports of raw cotton from the Middle East, to France, England and other countries, had become very important, and in the 18th they surpassed those of silk.

But the taste for cotton goods was growing in Europe; Indian cloth began to gain ground in the 17th century and the French started to buy yarn and cloth from Egypt.[60] This alarmed the wool industry, and for a time imports of cotton were prohibited within England and France. The removal of those prohibitions, early in the 18th century, led to a large increase in exports of cotton cloth from Aleppo, which drew on the production of northern Syria, southern Anatolia and northern 'Irāq, and from Egypt, as well as Greece.[61] But from the 1780s Indian competition became keener. And in 1761, heavy duties were imposed on imports of yarn to France, to protect French spinners and West Indian growers. All of this made it increasingly profitable to export Middle Eastern cotton in its raw form, and in fact in the second half of the 18th century raw cotton became by far the leading Middle Eastern export item.

The trend was accentuated in the 19th century. From the 1820s, thanks to the industrial revolution and steam navigation, machine-made textiles flooded the Middle East and ruined its handicrafts. At the same time the demand for raw cotton soared, to the great profit of Egypt. The American Civil War led to a short-lived expansion of cotton growing in Anatolia, Syria and Īrān, but it was only in the present century that the Middle East became once more one of the world's major suppliers of cotton.[62]

This decrease in the Middle East's capacity to export, and the decline in the demand for its goods, naturally affected its capacity to import. In the 18th century there are clear signs of shrinking markets for European or Indian goods in Egypt, Īrān and, a little later, in 'Irāq and parts of Syria.[63] In the 19th century, Middle Eastern trade with Europe generally showed a large import surplus, which seems to have been covered partly by import of capital and partly by shipping abroad a large part of the bullion that had been accumulated in previous centuries.

Indian Ocean Area

In the early Middle Ages, Middle Eastern exports to East Africa seem to have consisted mainly of cloth, glassware and weapons. To India and the Far East, the region probably exported "costly fabrics of linen, cotton or wool, including rugs; metal-work, iron-ore and bullion."[64] A list of Middle Eastern exports in the 11th-12th centuries, compiled from the Geniza documents, reads as follows: textiles and clothing, metals and metal ware, glassware, household goods, chemicals, medicaments, soap, paper and books, corals, foodstuffs and bullion. In return, the Middle East imported from East Africa timber and ebony and from India spices, iron and steel, and metal ware, silk and cotton textiles, leatherwork, porcelain, fruits and timber.[65] But by far the most important branch was probably the slave trade: "Though its output in any single year can never have reached the highest figures of the European trade, the total number of Africans it exported . . . must have been prodigious."[66] Some of these slaves were sent to various parts of the Middle East and others were shipped to India or further east.

One gets the impression—it is little more than that—that while Middle Eastern crafts were declining, those of India were improving.[67] At any rate, by the 16th-18th centuries, there seems to have been a marked shift in the trade pattern; it seems clear that the Middle East was importing large amounts of Indian cotton textiles and some silks, and sending in return pearls, dates, fruits, grains, horses, carpets and much bullion.[68]

The flourishing slave trade was, for some time, interrupted by Portuguese control over East Africa. But after about 1650 the 'Umānī took back the northern half of the east African coast and resumed the traffic, in which Europeans and a few Americans joined. In the course of the 19th century the slave trade was gradually suppressed, thanks mainly to British efforts, but even now it is not quite extinct.

II. Transit and Carrying Trade

For convenience, the following discussion will be centered on the spice trade, which for about a thousand years—until the 18th century—was the most valuable item in international trade. It will also be confined to the Red Sea route, which from the 10th or 11th century was far more important than either the Iranian route to the Black Sea or the Persian Gulf route to the Mediterranean.[69] Throughout this period, the price paid by consumers in Europe was many times that received by producers in the Indies. This meant large incomes for the intermediaries, i.e., the merchants and carriers in the Mediterranean, the merchants and rulers of the land bridge between the Indian Ocean and Mediterranean, and the merchants and carriers in the Indian Ocean.

Mediterranean

During the struggle for supremacy in the Mediterranean between the Arab and Byzantine fleets (650-1050), the Italian merchants began to capture the trade of that sea. From the middle of the 9th century they came to Egypt and Syria, in their own ships, and afterwards took over the trade with Byzantium as well. On the other hand, there is no evidence of Muslim ships trading with European ports.[70]

In the 11th century, seapower shifted to the Italians, who were thus enabled to transport and supply the Crusaders. The trade they developed survived the Latin states because considerable numbers of European merchants remained in the seaports of Egypt, the Levant, Cyprus, Cilicia and Constantinople. Moreover, the Europeans never lost their predominance in the Mediterranean, except briefly to the Ottomans in the 16th century, and, even when most harassed by the Barbary Corsairs, they retained the carrying trade. By the 17th and 18th centuries, much of the coastal trade of the Eastern Mediterranean had also passed into their hands.[71] And from the 1820s on, European steamers took over the bulk of the trade. In other words, from the early Middle Ages, the profits made in the Mediterranean trade on both domestic and transit goods accrued to Europeans.

Naturally the Europeans, particularly the Italians, were not content with domination of the Mediterranean. One of the most important aspects of the Crusades, particularly the later ones, was their endeavor to seize the land bridge between the Mediterranean and the Red Sea. The most successful of these attempts was Renaud de Chatillon's expedition in the Red Sea in 1181. The danger posed by this incursion to both the Muslim Holy Places and the spice trade was quickly realized by Saladin, who not only defeated and executed Renaud but pursued a policy, which was followed by his successors, designed to ensure Muslim control. Jewish, Byzantine and European merchants were forbidden to trade in the Red Sea area; their place was taken by the *Kārimī* traders, all of whom were Muslims, including a few converts.[72] Europeans, who had previously been allowed to set up factories in Cairo, were now confined to Alexandria and Damietta, Egypt's two main Mediterranean ports.

The Europeans tried hard to break through this new barrier by attacking the Egyptian seaports, but their bitter rivalries made concerted action impossible and prevented them from exploiting some initial victories, such as the capture of Damietta in 1219 and again in 1249, and of Alexandria in 1365. Attempts to circumvent the barrier, by opening up overland routes to the East, met with only temporary and partial success, during the Mongol period, when the Italians dominated the Black Sea and the Genoese sailed across the Caspian to "bring from thence [Īrān] the kind of silk called *ghellie*."[73] And the attempt by the Vivaldi brothers, in 1291, to sail to the East through the Atlantic ended in disaster.

A *modus vivendi* was therefore reached, which allowed Egypt to earn a very large income. Heavy taxes on spices formed the main item of government revenue. Hence, to quote Labib:[74] "it is not surprising that the price of Eastern goods [spices] should rise to three or four times its original level. Nor is it surprising to learn that the Egyptian government received the equivalent of one ship's cargo for every three or four ships." It can be presumed that European demand for spices was price-inelastic and that higher prices were passed on to consumers, and that, therefore, the Italian and other traders continued to make profits.[75]

This state of precarious but mutually profitable equilibrium lasted until the reign of Barsbāy (1422-38). By that time the combined results of depopulation, decline in agriculture and industry, deterioration of trade, high military expenditures and inflation and exchange depreciation, began to present the rulers of Egypt with a major economic crisis. Barsbāy's solution was to convert the spice trade into a government monopoly, channeling it through Egypt to the exclusion of Syria, and then, for good measure, to extend that monopoly to other branches of trade and even production, e.g., sugar.[76] The result may be judged from the following figures. A load of pepper which cost, at most, 2 dinars at the Indian ports of export was sold in Mecca for 10 dinars. But Barsbāy forced the European merchants to pay 80, 100 or even 120 dinars. Prices in Europe rose accordingly. It would seem that, in one form or another, the monopoly of the spice trade continued until the Portuguese irruption into the Indian Ocean.[77]

Attempts by both the European and *Kārimī* merchants to loosen this strangle hold proved fruitless. The *Kārimīs*, the largest and most promising section of the Middle Eastern bourgeoisie, were dispersed and ruined. The Europeans were, however, stimulated to renewed efforts to find a way round the Muslim land barrier. These efforts were crowned with success when the Portuguese sailed round the Cape of Good Hope and wrested from the Muslims control over the Indian Ocean.[78]

Indian Ocean

The main objective of the Portuguese was control over the spice trade. This they sought to achieve by seizing strategic islands and ports and by regulating navigation in the Indian Ocean. Thus after capturing Hormuz in 1508, they forbade any native vessel to trade in the Gulf without a pass.[79] And in 1515 Albuquerque told the ambassador of Shāh Ismā'īl: "Should any merchant from Persia be found in any other district of India save the port of Goa, they should lose their merchandize and be made subject to the greatest penalties which we could inflict."[80] The result was twofold: a decline in local navigation, discussed below, and a drop in the amount of spices going through the Middle East.

However, it is now clear that trade between Egypt and Venice continued on quite a large scale and that around 1550 the Portuguese attempt to monopolize spices broke down. For, on the one hand, the Portuguese never managed to control the sources of supply in the East Indies, and, on the other, the Ottomans denied them access to the Red Sea and, together with the Indian Marakkars, weakened their grip on the Arabian Sea. Furthermore, Portuguese officials were corrupt, and entered into various open and illicit agreements with local merchants and shippers in the Persian Gulf area.[81] As a result, Braudel estimates that in 1554-64 the Egyptian spice trade reached about 3-4,000 tons *per annum*, an amount equal to that of the Mamluk period.[82] To this should be added a much smaller amount passing through Syria. But even so, the existence of an alternative source of supply, to which even the Venetians could and did occasionally turn, had the effect of breaking the Egyptian monopoly, and forcing down prices.[83]

It is now generally admitted that the flow of spices through the Middle East was finally shut off not by the Portuguese but by the Dutch, who acquired much firmer control over the sources of supply and disposed of greater naval power.[84] By 1638 Mandelslo could write that the Dutch "furnish all Persia with Pepper, Nutmegs, Cloves and other Spiceries" and in 1677 Fryer, again talking about Persia, mentions the "Spice trade, which the Dutch engross."[85] European purchases of spice in the Middle East tapered off in the 17th century, and by the 18th the region was obtaining most of its spices through Europe.

It only remains to trace the decline of the Muslim carrying trade, and with it the other forms of coastal trade, in the Indian Ocean. Until the 16th century, the Muslims dominated the western Indian Ocean. In the 12th and 13th centuries Chinese shipping challenged the Muslim monopoly (thus, Ibn Baṭṭūṭa sailed on a Chinese junk and reports the presence of Chinese merchants in Malabar) and in the early 15th there were the famous expeditions which reached the coast of East Africa.[86] But this Chinese interest was short-lived, and after that few junks sailed west of Malacca, and few traders went beyond Bengal.[87]

The initial effects of the Portuguese irruption were catastrophic. Barros could say without much exaggeration, "This busy trade [to Malacca] lasted until our arrival in India, but the Moorish, Arabian, Persian and Gujarati ships, fearing our fleets, dared not in general now undertake the voyage and if any of their ships did so it was only by stealth, and escaping our ships."[88]

However, Portuguese power began to weaken early in the 17th century, and the Dutch and British, unlike the Portuguese, did not try to wipe out native shipping. The result, as mentioned before, was the revival of the slave trade from East Africa. But other forms of trade also recovered and continued to flourish until what has been called the maritime revolution of the mid-18th century. Until then, "The transport of goods between India and the Gulf was carried partly by vessels owned by Muhammedan merchants of Surat, and partly by vessels belonging to Arab merchants of Masqaṭ [Muscat]."[89]

To which may be added the following: "The preoccupation of the leading Bombay agency houses and 'country' captains with the expanding trade to China gave a freer field in the Arabian voyages to Armenians, Mohamedans, and Parsis. The flow of German crowns, 'Venetians' and other Levantine gold and silver into Cochin aboard Arab 'dhows' and Indian 'bombaras' does not seem to have slackened in the 1770's."[90]

But the steady growth in size, and improvement in quality, of European sailing ships, and the rapidly increasing capital at the disposal of European merchants, began to squeeze local shippers and traders more and more.[91] By the 1840s steamers were beginning to ply in Indian waters and in 1862 a regular service was inaugurated between India and the Gulf.[92] At the same time the suppression by the British navy of piracy in the Gulf must have further weakened the maritime basis of Arab trade, since, to quote Mephistopheles:

> Krieg, Handel und Piraterie
> Dreieinig sind sie, nicht zu trennen.

A British trade report for 1905 on Muscat, the former center of trade and piracy,[93] noted that: "Quite four-fifths of the trade of Muscat is with India, and in the hands of British Indian subjects working through partners or agents in Bombay."[94]

In the Red Sea a similar set of causes brought about a similar decline, particularly after the opening of the Suez Canal. Again to quote a British trade report for 1898:

"A century ago, however, Jeddah was no doubt the queen of the Red Sea, a very considerable center for trade, and managing a large coasting trade on both coasts. . . . Steam and the development and increasing ease and rapidity of sea communications entirely changed this aspect of affairs though the coasting trade in sailing vessels continued to prosper well beyond the middle of the century. . . . But most of their carrying trade has naturally been absorbed of late years by the Khedivié Company, and by two or three smaller steamers under the British flag. Arab merchants of this town now own only two large vessels of about 2500 tonnage (one steam and one sailing) as it may be concluded that they were unable to withstand the competition of organized companies, and not strong or wealthy enough to combine among themselves for establishing a local company."[95]

To sum up, the disintegration of Middle Eastern trade may be, *very tentatively*, traced to:

(1) The decline in the productive power of the region in agriculture and handicrafts, which reduced its exporting capacity and to a corresponding extent its capacity to import.

(2) The reduction in foreign demand for its goods, due to the development of alternative sources of supply.

(3) The loss of seapower in the Mediterranean, which handed over most of the carrying trade in that sea to Europeans, from the 9th century on.

(4) The loss of seapower in the Indian Ocean, which resulted in the diversion of the spice trade from the 16th century on.

(5) The growing competition in the Indian Ocean of, first, larger and better European sailing ships and then steamers, backed by capital and credit well beyond the power of the Middle Easterners to match.

(6) All of which was aggravated by the weakness and incompetence of the Middle Eastern governments and the ineptitude of their economic policy, factors that were probably connected with the social structure of the region.

NOTES

1. I am indebted for valuable comments and criticisms to Professors Robert S. Lopez, Aziz S. Atiya, Gerson D. Cohen, Jeanette Wakin, Thomas Goodrich and A. Abu Hakima.

2. Edwin O. Reischauer and John K. Fairbank, *East Asia: The Great Tradition* (Boston 1958), p. 220. For further details, see Robert Hartwell, "Markets, Technology and The Structure of Enterprise in the Development of the Eleventh-Century Chinese Iron and Steel Industry," *Journal of Economic History* (March, 1966), where it is pointed out that, by 1078, *per capita* production of iron was 3.1 lbs.; in Western Europe as late as 1700 it was only 3.5-4.3 lbs.

3. Reischauer and Fairbank, op. cit., pp. 333, 393.

4. Ibid., pp. 557-63, 626-42. See also M. Miyamoto, *et al.*, "Economic Development in Pre-Industrial Japan," *Journal of Economic History* (December, 1965) and Thomas C. Smith, *Agrarian Origins of Modern Japan* (Stanford 1959).

5. W. H. Moreland, *India at the Death of Akbar* (London 1920), pp. 22, 136, 180-84. This judgment is confirmed by Irfan Habib, *The Agrarian System of Moghul India* (Bombay 1963), p. 23: "Taking the area of the Moghul Empire as a whole, and assuming that cultural practice has not changed, the average acre sown cannot be as productive now as in Moghul times."

6. See Irfan Habib, op. cit., chapter ix, W. H. Moreland, *From Akbar to Aurangzeb* (London 1923), Ashin Das Gupta, *Malabar in Asian Trade*

(Cambridge 1967), N. K. Sinha, *Economic History of Bengal* (Calcutta 1956) and Shiva Chandra Jha, *Studies in the Development of Capitalism in India* (Calcutta 1963).

7. To take two examples from the end of this period. In the plague of 1773, according to the representatives of the East India Company in Baṣra, "for near a month the daily deaths in the town alone amounted from 3000 to 7000," and it was left "almost destitute of inhabitants." Their estimate of the loss of life on the Arabian coast was 2,000,000, an improbably high figure—see Ahmad Abu Hakima, *History of Eastern Arabia* (Beirut 1965), p. 87. And in Cairo, an outbreak of plague started in November 1783 and continued throughout the winter, causing up to 1,500 deaths per day—see C. F. Volney, *Oeuvres* (Paris 1825), vol. II, p. 152.

8. Following the Ottoman conquest, there was a short reprieve from about 1530 to the beginning of the 17th century, when government control increased and an effort was made to "restore to cultivation the lands which had been devastated during and immediately after the Ottoman conquest." See Stanford J. Shaw, *The Financial and Administrative Organization and Development of Ottoman Egypt* (Princeton 1958), p. 68.

9. Robert M. Adams, *Land Behind Baghdad* (Chicago 1965), graph on p. 115. Even if one does not accept Adams's figures, there can be no doubt about the trend he indicates.

10. For details see Charles Issawi, *The Economic History of the Middle East, 1800-1914* (Chicago 1966), p. 130.

11. Ibid., pp. 258-61. For the history of Syria in the medieval and early modern periods see Ira M. Lapidus, *Muslim Cities in the Later Middle Ages* (Cambridge, Mass. 1967), Jean Sauvaget, *Alep* (Paris 1941) and Philip K. Hitti, *History of Syria* (London 1957).

12. Ahmad Darrag, *L'Egypte sous le règne de Barsbay* (Damascus 1961), pp. 64-65. It is worth pointing out that the number of villages in Egypt today, on a larger cultivated area and with a far bigger population, is only 4,000.

13. Ibid., pp. 59-60.

14. Shaw, loc. cit.

15. Bernard Lewis, *The Emergence of Modern Turkey* (London 1961), pp. 32-33.

16. The population of Istanbul probably rose from about 500,000 in the middle of the 16th century to 600,000-750,000 toward the end of the 17th. See Robert Mantran, *Istanbul dans la seconde moitié du XVIIe Siècle* (Paris 1962), pp. 44-47. Bursa also seems to have been prosperous in this period, see *Encyclopaedia of Islam* (2nd ed.) s.v. "Bursa." For the general growth in urban population, see Ömer Lufti Barkan, "La Mediterranée de Fernand Braudel," *Annales*, vol. IX (January-March 1954).

17. George N. Curzon, *Persia and the Persian Question* (London 1892), vol. I, p. 367.

18. To illustrate, suppose 5,000,000 men farm 5,000,000 acres and pro-

duce 10,000,000 bushels, giving an average output of 2 bushels per man; then assuming household consumption is 1 bushel per year, the surplus is 10,000,000 *minus* 5,000,000, i.e. 5,000,000 bushels. Now suppose population shrinks to 3,000,000, cultivated area to 3,000,000 acres and production to 7,000,000. Average output per man has risen to $2^1/_3$ bushels, but the surplus is only 7,000,000 *minus* 3,000,000, i.e. 4,000,000 bushels.

19. "Sifting the available evidence, one must conclude that the Ottoman Empire was a state enjoying agricultural surpluses until the last quarter of the sixteenth century. In the decade following the death of Sultan Suleimān (d. 1566) there are numerous reports of drought and famine. Shortly thereafter, the long wars with Persia (1578-90) and with Austria (1593-1606) placed a tremendous burden on all of the productive resources of the Empire." Carl M. Kortepeter, "Ottoman Imperial Policy and the Economy of the Black Sea Region in the Sixteenth Century," *Journal of the American Oriental Society*, vol. LXXXVI (April-June, 1966).

20. Subhi Y. Labib, *Handelsgeschichte Ägyptens im Spätmittelalter* (Wiesbaden 1965), pp. 420-21.

21. Mantran, op. cit., pp. 420-21; H. A. R. Gibb and H. Bowen, *Islamic Society and the West* (London 1950), vol. I, pp. 295-96; Traian Stoianovich, "The Conquering Balkan Orthodox Merchant," *Journal of Economic History*, vol. XX (June, 1960).

22. *Voyages du Chevalier Chardin en Perse* (Amsterdam 1735), vol. III, pp. 97-99.

23. Thus the plague was more devastating in the cities than in the villages, and craftsmen were more difficult to replace than peasants; Alexandria never recovered from the Crusaders' raid of 1365, and the deportation of its craftsmen by Tamerlane was a severe blow to Damascus; the breakdown of government, although far less complete in the towns than in the countryside, was also a major blow.

24. For a fuller treatment, see Issawi, op. cit., pp. 4-6.

25. Traian Stoianovich, "Factors in the Decline of Ottoman Society in the Balkans," *Slavic Review* (December 1962), estimates that between 1550 and 1790 grain prices increased more than sevenfold, the rise in 1605-1700 being particularly sharp. Wages of unskilled labor rose only half as much, a fact to which the author attributes much of the social disorders of this period. See also Issawi, op. cit., pp. 520-24, Labib, op. cit., pp. 423-38, Darrag, op. cit., pp. 91-107 and Mantran, op. cit., Book II, chapter ii.

26. See Kortepeter, op. cit.; S. Ülgener, *Iktisadi Tarihimizin Ahlak ve Zihniyet Meseleleri* (Istanbul 1951); Bernard Lewis, "Some Reflections on the Decline of the Ottoman Empire," *Studia Islamica* (1958); and W. Hahn, "Die Verpflegung Konstantinopels durch staatliche Zwangswirtschaft," *Beihefte zur Vierteljahrschrift für Sozial- und Wirtschaftgeschichte*, vol. VI (1926).

27. Mantran's authoritative study may be quoted in support. "Personne dans le gouvernement Ottoman ne s'intéresse directement à la production 'nationale,' encore moins à la conquête des marchés extérieurs" (p. 214). "Il n'est donc pas question d'un integral capitalisme d'état, mais plutôt

d'un dirigisme qui a pour but d'assurer à la capitale de l'empire son ravitaillement et ses moyens de vivre mais aussi de fournir au trésor des rentrées d'argent" (p. 287). "En Turquie le gouvernement semble se désinteresser de ces questions et ignorer les conséquences de la stagnation économique" (p. 423). To which of course should be added the power of vested interests (p. 510). See also Issawi, op. cit., pp. 38-40. The insecurity and depopulation of the countryside made it impossible to escape the power of the guilds and other conservative forces by setting up workshops in the rural areas, as was done in Europe. (This last point was suggested by Ervand Abrahamian, a graduate student at Columbia University.)

In the 16th century, Ottoman economic policy had been somewhat more enlightened, aiming at extending trade with the West, at reserving the Black Sea for Ottoman ships, and at building new towns and reviving those that had declined. But the main beneficiaries of this proved to be the Balkan Christians, the Jews and the Armenians. See, for example, Cecil Roth, *The House of Nasi* (Philadelphia 1948); Stoianovich, "The Conquering Balkan Orthodox Merchant," loc. cit., and Kortepeter, op. cit.

For the economic policy of the Mamluks, see Labib, op. cit. and Lapidus, op. cit.; for the Safavids, see V. Minorsky, *Tadhkirat al-Mulūk* (London 1943).

28. See also S. D. Goitein, *Studies in Islamic History and Institutions* (Leiden 1966), chapters xi-xiii.

29. H. A. R. Gibb, "The Community in Islamic History," *Proceedings of the American Philosophical Society*, vol. CVII (April 1963).

30. Mantran, op. cit., p. 604. A very few Turks did go to Vienna for trade, see Stoianovich, op. cit., and a few Moroccans to Marseilles and Genoa, see Jean-Louis Miège, *Le Maroc et L'Europe* (Paris 1961), vol. II, p. 28.

31. Philip K. Hitti, *History of the Arabs* (London 1943), p. 564; Thomas F. Carter and L. Carrington Goodrich, *The Invention of Printing in China* (New York 1955), pp. 137, 247-50.

32. Robert S. Lopez, "The Trade of Medieval Europe: The South," *The Cambridge Economic History of Europe* (Cambridge, 1952), vol. II, p. 299.

33. Morris S. Goodblatt, *Jewish Life in Turkey in the XVIth Century* (New York, 1952), p. 51; Paul Masson, *Histoire du Commerce français dans le Levant au XVIIe siècle* (Paris, 1896), pp. 505-6. It is worth noting that the list of crafts in Istanbul in the 17th century given by Evliya Çelebi does not mention papermaking, see Mantran, op. cit. p. 412. Papermaking seems, however, to have continued in Bursa.

34. Aziz S. Atiya, *Crusade, Commerce and Culture* (Bloomington, 1962), vol. I, p. 185; A. H. Christie, "Islamic Minor Arts," in *The Legacy of Islam*, eds. Sir Thomas Arnold and Alfred Guillaume (London, 1931), pp. 129-30; W. Heyd, *Histoire du Commerce du Levant au Moyen Age* (Leipzig, 1923), vol. I, p. 180, vol. II, pp. 710-11; and Adolf Schaube, *Handelsgeschichte der Romanischen Völker* (Munich, 1906), p. 16.

35. D. B. Harden, "Glass and Glazes," in *A History of Technology*, ed. Charles Singer (Oxford, 1957), vol. II, pp. 327-8.

36. Fernand Braudel, *La Mediterranée et le monde mediterranéen à l'époque de Philippe II* (Paris 1949), p. 336; Mantran, op. cit., p. 407; Gibb and Bowen, op. cit., p. 305.

37. Labib, op. cit., p. 320; Heyd, op. cit., vol. II, pp. 9, 680-93.

38. Hitti, op. cit., p. 351; Lopez, op. cit., p. 352.

39. Braudel, op. cit., p. 470.

40. Labib, op. cit., p. 314; Heyd, op. cit., vol. II, pp. 565-70.

41. John U. Nef, "Mining and Metallurgy, etc.," *The Cambridge Economic History of Europe,* vol. I, p. 471.

42. Heyd, op. cit., vol. II, p. 10; Xavier de Planhol, *The World of Islam* (Ithaca 1957), pp. 50-53.

43. Labib, op. cit., p. 323; Braudel, op. cit., pp. 452-70; Kortepeter, op. cit.

44. Masson, op. cit., p. 415; Kristof Glamann, *Dutch-Asiatic Trade, 1620-1740* (The Hague 1958), pp. 183-95. The first coffee houses were opened in Oxford in 1650, in London in 1652, in Marseilles in 1671 and in Paris in 1672.

45. C. R. Boxer, *The Dutch Seaborne Empire, 1600-1800* (London 1965), p. 199.

46. Lopez, op. cit., p. 388.

47. Frank E. Bailey, *British Policy and The Turkish Reform Movement* (Cambridge, Mass. 1942), p. 94; N. A. Khalfin and A. A. Muradian, *Yanki na Vostokye* (Moscow 1966), pp. 35-6. In the early 1890s, Īrān's opium crop (about half of which was exported) was estimated at 70,000 puds (about 1,150,000 kilograms), worth 6,000,000 rubles (about £600,000), see M. L. Tomara, *Ekonomicheskoye Polozheniye Persii* (St. Petersburg 1895), pp. 12-13. For figures for earlier years see Baring's "Report on Trade and Cultivation of Opium in Persia," Great Britain, *Accounts and Papers 1881*, LXIX.

48. See Heyd, op. cit., vol. II, pp. 648-51; Issawi, op. cit., pp. 312-13.

49. Labib, op. cit., p. 312; Goitein, op. cit., p. 322.

50. Masson, op. cit., p. 409; Gibb and Bowen, op. cit., pp. 304-7. By the 14th century, Europe was exporting linens east, as far as China. Lopez, op. cit., p. 332.

51. Ibid., pp. 298, 311.

52. Op. cit., p. 503; so does A. C. Wood, *History of the Levant Company* (London 1935), p. 77.

53. Paul Masson, *Histoire du Commerce français dans le Levant au XVIIIe siècle* (Paris 1911).

54. Issawi, op. cit., p. 378.

55. See the excellent article "Ḥarīr," in *Encyclopaedia of Islam* (2nd ed.).

56. Goitein, op. cit., p. 320.

57. Boxer, op. cit., p. 200; for further details see Glamann, op. cit., pp. 114-27 and 282-84, and Holden Furber, *John Company at Work* (Cambridge, Mass. 1948), pp. 161-65.

58. *Encyclopaedia of Islam* (2nd ed.) s.v. *Ḥarīr.*

59. Labib, op. cit., pp. 311-12; Heyd, op. cit., vol. II, pp. 611-14.

60. Masson, *Histoire du Commerce français dans le Levant au XVIIe siècle* (Paris 1896), p. 409.

61. Ibid., p. 456; Stoianovich, op. cit.

62. For details see Issawi, op. cit., *passim.*

63. See Masson, *Histoire du Commerce . . . au XVIIIe siècle* (Paris 1911); Wood, op. cit., pp. 162-65; Furber, op. cit., p. 167; Glamann, op. cit., p. 165.

64. George F. Hourani, *Arab Seafaring* (Princeton 1951), p. 75.

65. Goitein, op. cit., pp. 339-43.

66. Sir Reginald Coupland, *East Africa and Its Invaders* (Oxford 1938), p. 35. The Atlantic slave trade is estimated to have carried at least 12 million slaves in the 15th-19th centuries. The slave trade from West to North Africa is believed to have averaged "at least two million per century." See sources cited in Leon Carl Brown, "Color in North Africa," *Daedalus* (Spring, 1967).

67. It is worth noting that the needs of urban markets in both the Middle East and South-East Asia had a very strong influence on the development of cotton production in Gujarat and on the east coast of India (information kindly supplied by Dr. Ashin Das Gupta).

68. See Moreland, op. cit., p. 209; Radhakamal Mukerjee, *The Economic History of India* (n.d.), p. 88; Mantran, op. cit., p. 587; Masson, op. cit., p. 520; Furber, op. cit., p. 167; Glamann, op. cit., chapter vii; J. G. Lorimer, *Gazeteer of the Persian Gulf* (Calcutta 1908-15), vol. I, p. 165; Muhammad Salmān Ḥasan, *al-Taṭawwur al-Iqtiṣādī fi 'l 'Irāq* (Beirut, n.d.), chapters ii and iii.

69. Part of this section has been taken from the writer's "Crusades and Current Crises in the Near East: A Historical Parallel," *International Affairs* (London, July, 1957).

70. Robert S. Lopez, *The Birth of Europe* (London 1967), pp. 284-91; Hélène Ahrweiler, *Byzance et la Mer* (Paris 1966); Ekkehard Eickhoff, *Seekrieg und Seepolitik zwischen Islam und Abendland* (Berlin 1966); and Armand O. Citarella, "The Relations of Amalfi with the Arab World before the Crusades," *Speculum* (April, 1967).

71. Mantran, op. cit., p. 491; Issawi, op. cit., p. 37. There was also a sharp increase in Greek, Albanian and Ragusan shipping, see Stoianovich, op. cit.

72. On the *Kārimī*, see Labib, op. cit., *passim*, Goitein, op. cit., chapter xviii and Gaston Wiet, "Les marchands d'épice sous les sultans mamlouks," *Cahiers d'histoire égyptienne*, vol. VII (1955).

73. *The Travels of Marco Polo* (New York, Modern Library, 1926), Book I, chapter iv.

74. "*al-Tujjār al-Kārimīya,*" *Majallat al-Jāmi'a al-Miṣrīya li'l-Dirāsāt al-Tārikhīya* (Cairo, May, 1952).

75. At the same time there was a shift in interest, as exemplified by Genoa.

"At the beginning of the fourteenth century, it still favored Persia, India, China and other countries along the spice and silk routes; but as these routes became clogged, it turned increasingly to the coarser wares and less sophisticated markets of freshly emerging countries in Eastern Europe, from Valachia to Poland," Robert S. Lopez, "Market Expansion: The Case of Genoa," *Journal of Economic History* (December, 1964).

76. Darrag, op. cit., chapter vi and Labib, *Handelsgeschichte, etc.*, chapter ix.

77. Ibid., pp. 333, 391 and 397.

78. A similar, short-lived, attempt to earn huge profits on the transit of goods between producers in the Indian Ocean and European consumers was made in the 18th century. The Pasha of Egypt, "inspired by the large transits of coffee in 1699," raised the duty by 12½%, in violation of existing treaties. But as "the European market provisionally was saturated, the European merchants could therefore refuse taking the dearer coffee." Similar attempts were made by the governor of Mecca and Jidda. And in 1719 the Sultan "sent several envoys to Yemen in order to obtain a prohibition of export by the Europeans. However, they received the answer that if the Sultan wanted to acquire all coffee from his countries, such a monopoly must be secured by the Turkish merchants if they guaranteed the Arabs an annual amount in cash which at least corresponded to that introduced into Yemen by the Europeans." See Glamann, op. cit., pp. 191-92.

79. Sir Arnold T. Wilson, *The Persian Gulf* (London 1928), p. 116.

80. Hadi Hasan, *A History of Persian Navigation* (London 1928), p. 147.

81. Auguste Toussaint, *History of the Indian Ocean* (London 1966), p. 114.

82. Op. cit., p. 428.

83. Braudel, op. cit., p. 421, Labib, *Handelsgeschichte, etc.*, pp. 470-76; see also F. C. Lane, "Venetian Shipping," *American Historical Review*, vol. XXXVIII (1933).

84. See Glamann, op. cit., Boxer, op. cit., J. C. Van Leur, *Indonesian Trade and Society* (The Hague 1955) and M. A. P. Meilink-Roelofsz, *Asian Trade and European Influence in the Indonesian Archipelago* (The Hague 1962).

85. Wilson, op. cit., pp. 163, 166; see also Glamann, op. cit., pp. 92-110, and Das Gupta, op. cit., pp. 12-18.

86. See T. Yamamoto "On Tawalisi described by Ibn Batuta," *Memoirs of the Research Department of the Toyo Bunko* (1936).

87. Das Gupta, op. cit., pp. 6-7; Jung-Pang Lo, "The Emergence of China as a Sea Power during the late Sung and early Yüan Periods," *Far Eastern Quarterly* (August, 1955).

88. Quoted by Hasan, op. cit., p. 146. On the Portuguese passport system, see Das Gupta, op. cit., pp. 9-12.

89. Lorimer, op. cit., vol. I, p. 166; Abu Hakima, op. cit., chapter vi; see also Das Gupta, op. cit., pp. 90-92.

90. Furber, op. cit., pp. 167-68.

91. Das Gupta, op. cit., pp. 135-36 and 168-69, Toussaint, op. cit., pp. 169-70.

92. The tonnage of vessels from the Persian Gulf entering British Indian ports rose from nearly 100,000 tons a year in the late 1850s to over 200,000 in the early 1900s and fell back below its original level by the First World War. Since these figures include British and other steamers, one may assume that the decline in Arab, Persian and Indian ships was quite sharp; figures compiled from *Statistical Abstract Relations to British India, 1841-1911* by Pelis Thottathil, a graduate student at Columbia University.

93. The following contemporary description of Muscat is worth quoting: "Muscat is a place of very great trade, being possessed of a large number of ships which trade to Surat, Bombay, Goa, along the whole coast of Malabar, and to Mocha and Jedda in the Red Sea. It is the great magazine or deposit for the goods which they bring from those parts . . ." Abraham Parsons, *Travels in Asia, etc.* (London 1808), p. 207, quoted in Ahmad Abu Hakima, op. cit., p. 175.

94. Issawi, op. cit., p. 310.

95. Ibid., p. 319.

8

Europe, the Middle East and the Shift in Power:
REFLECTIONS ON A THEME BY MARSHALL HODGSON

Suppose there are two lines on a graph, close together and moving in the same general direction and that at one point one of them begins to diverge from the other. After some time the gap between them will have widened very considerably. This simple image would command general agreement as an illustration of the different paths taken by Western and Middle Eastern or Islamic civilizations in the course of the last thousand years. Consensus would go further: by any acceptable criterion in the ninth to tenth centuries the Middle East was far more "advanced" than the West in economic development, urbanization, literacy, science, philosophy, scholarship, architecture, craftsmanship, and so on. By the same criterion the West was far more "advanced" than the Middle East in the eighteenth to nineteenth centuries. The question at issue is at what points in time and in what fields the West overtook and surpassed (*dognat i peregnat,* as the Russians say) the Middle East.

A fashionable view today is that this did not happen until the seventeenth century. One obvious reason for this belief is the fact that until well into that century the military power of the Islamic empires was clearly superior to that of the European. The Spaniards might conquer the New World and the Portuguese and Dutch control the Indian Ocean and the shores of Africa from a few strategically placed islands and fortified ports. But the Ottomans fully held their own against Austria, besieged Vienna in 1683 and defeated Peter the Great at Pruth in 1711; the Crimean Tatars sacked Moscow in 1571

Reprinted with permission from *Comparative Studies in Society and History,* vol. 22:4, 1980. I am indebted to A. H. Hourani, Bernard Lewis, Roy Mottahedeh, Avram Udovitch, and Constantine Zurayk and an anonymous referee for many useful comments.

and defeated Golitsyn's large army in the Ukraine in 1689; the North Africans expelled the Spanish and Portuguese in the sixteenth century and raided the south of England and Ireland in the seventeenth; the Safavis, with English help, expelled the Portuguese from Qishm and Hormuz; and the British and French could not even have dreamed of establishing a base of power in India before the eighteenth century. And Muslim military power did not rest only on superior numbers but on keeping abreast of current advances in European military technology.

But it is by no means only a matter of military power. Until around 1500, to quote Marshall Hodgson—whose monumental, illuminating and thoroughly idiosyncratic *The Venture of Islam* (3 vols., Chicago, 1974) is one of the most successful attempts to study Islamic civilization in its world context—"This international Islamicate society was certainly the most widely spread and influential society on the globe."[1] And again,

By this period, however, Islamdom had expanded so fast that, though probably less than a fifth of the world's population were Muslims, yet the Muslims were so widely and strategically placed that the society associated with them did embrace in some degree the greater part of cited mankind.[2]

And, of course, cities meant both trade and culture.

But in his eagerness to counteract the Eurocentrism and Western bias of Orientalists and other scholars, Hodgson goes much further than this.

In the sixteenth century on the whole, as we have seen, the parity of the cited societies of the Oikoumene still prevailed . . This occurrence in world history reflects European history in that the Renaissance florescence did not yet, in itself, transcend the limitations of agrarianate-level society. But the crucial changes were clearly under way by the end of the sixteenth century. And, by the end of the eighteenth century, they were all of them completed, at least as regards some particular field in some particular place, for example as regards astronomical physics throughout the Occident, or cotton cloth production in England.[3]

Hodgson bolsters his argument in three ways. First, there is a glowing account of "The greatness of the sixteenth century: the Persianate Flowering," with an enthusiastic description of its painting, philosophy and mysticism, the culture and institutions of the three great empires that drew their inspiration from it, Safavi, Ottoman and

Moghul, and their "relatively high degrees of order and prosperity."[4] Second, there is a drastic downgrading of the Renaissance: "But in itself the Renaissance did not exceed, in its creativity or in its basic institutional novelty, a number of other great florescences that had occurred in the Agrarian Age of Oikoumenic history: in particular it was no more remarkable than the flowering of Sung China or even than the startling cultural renovations and initiatives of the High Caliphal Period in Islamdom."[5] Third, the unique characteristics that enabled Western Europe to surpass other cultures are explained thus:

The shift therefore from reliance on custom and continuity, to reliance on calculation and innovation, although it occurred only in a limited measure, was not in itself what was specific to the Modern Western Transmutation. It was not this that set the Westerners apart from both their ancestors and the rest of the world. It merely accompanied and facilitated a change in the patterns of investment of time and money. This, as we shall see, occurred only in a special form, one that I shall call technicalistic, so that *specialized technical considerations tended to take precedence* over all others. Indeed in that form—rather than in other forms—the shift went to unprecedented lengths.[6]

Hodgson's argument has two flaws. First, he is too concerned with levels and not sufficiently with trends; in mathematical terms, he does not pay enough attention to the sign of the first derivative. This leads him into a serious error of timing and prevents him from seeing that Europe started to catch up with the Middle East long before the sixteenth century. Secondly, he does not realize that this advance took place because at a very early date Europeans began to apply their minds to those fields in which, because it can work on a large amount of empirical data, human reason seems to operate most efficiently and to yield cumulative results: technology, the natural sciences, economics, statistics. If Kant had not preempted the term for a very different use, one could have called this activity Practical Reason. It should be sharply distinguished from inquiries into questions of theology, metaphysics, ethics, law, politics or esthetics, which are in many ways more profound and important but in which, at an early date, the human mind came up against barriers that have, so far, proved insurmountable; hence, the insights of men like Zoroaster, Gautama, Isaiah, Aeschylus—not to mention Plato and Aristotle— have never been surpassed and seldom equalled.

The technological advance of Europe began at a very early date. It was propelled partly by borrowings from other cultures; for example, paper and a number of crops from the Middle East, breast harnessing and horseshoes from Central Asia. The ultimate source of many of these borrowings was China,[7] but mainly they were due to native ingenuity. A leading authority, Lynn White, sums up the situation as follows:

. . .from about the sixth century Europe began to show innovations in technology more significant than those found in the more elaborate, neighbouring, and kindred cultures of Byzantium and Islam. By the middle of the fourteenth century, after the invention of the mechanical clock had increased the number of artisans skilled in making metal machines, Europe surpassed China and seized global leadership in technology.[8]

In agriculture, White mentions such innovations as the heavy wheeled plough; breast harnessing of horses[9]; horseshoes; the common use of scythes and the improvement of the harrow; the consequent development of the three-field system; and in Mediterranean Europe the introduction of many tropical or Far Eastern crops that had earlier been brought into the Middle East and North Africa, for example, mulberries, sugar, rice, hardwheat, cotton and numerous vegetables.[10]

Agricultural progress may be illustrated by the rise in the yield-to-seed ratio of the four main grains, wheat, rye, barley and oats. In England in the period 1200-1249 they averaged 3.7, but by the fourteenth century they had risen to 4.7, and by the sixteenth century to 7; for France the corresponding figures were 3.0, 4.3 and over 6.[11] The latter figures are low compared to some Middle Eastern ones for wheat: 15 in Egypt around 1800 and 5 to 6 in Anatolia in the middle of the nineteenth century, by which time English and French yields were much higher.[12] But once again, the direction of change is important, and there is no reason to believe that the degree of progress achieved in Europe had its counterpart in the Middle East. An interesting contrast in this respect is provided by the very different responses of Europe and the Middle East to the drastic reduction of the rural population caused by the Black Death. In the Middle East it "does not seem to have aided the long-term improvement of agrarian technology"—as in Europe.[13] And the evidence gathered by Andrew Watson indicates that, after reaching a peak in the eleventh or twelfth century, Islamic agriculture both shrank in area and declined in quality.[14]

In the handicrafts, water mills were far more widespread in Europe than in other civilizations. "By 1086, William the Conqueror's Domesday Book records that the 3,000 settlements in England [whose total population was about 1,100,000]—most of them very small— averaged nearly two mills apiece."[15] In the next three centuries watermills were put to an unprecedented variety of uses, in the textile, metallurgical, wood and other industries, and their presence, in turn, stimulated a number of inventions or borrowings, such as the cam and the crank. The windmill was almost certainly taken from the Middle East—it is mentioned in the celebrated conversation between 'Umar ibn al-Khattāb and Abū Lu'lu'a in A.D. 644[16]—but was developed beyond recognition and diffused widely throughout Western Europe. The difference the large-scale use of water and wind power made may be judged from the fact that whereas the working rate of a man is about 0.1 horsepower, an ox 0.66 and a camel 2, that of an overshot water mill is 2 to 5 and of a post windmill 2 to 8.[17] Perhaps even more important, machinery was brought into almost every village and the whole population had a demonstration of its workings and uses.

White also, rightly, dwells on innovations in shipbuilding, navigation and weaponry, although it does not seem that European ships became distinctly superior to Chinese junks until well into the fifteenth century. And thanks to extensive borrowing and full use of European experts, the Ottomans managed to keep abreast of European armaments throughout the sixteenth century.

But there are three inventions that deserve fuller notice: clocks, spectacles and printing. The influence of clocks on men's work habits and patterns of thought has been immense. But in addition clocks are among the first complex modern machines, and Cipolla is right in seeing in the consignment of a clock from Italy to the Middle East in 1338 a harbinger of the export of European machinery overseas.[18] By considerably prolonging people's working lives, spectacles also constitute a significant step forward, and they too were soon exported to the Middle East. As for printing, of course thousands of books had been printed in China and Japan in earlier times, but Europe made a huge leap forward: "By about 1500, when twelve countries already knew the secret, forty thousand editions of books had been printed."[19] Or, to give another example, "At least 750,000 copies of his [Erasmus's] books, not including his translation of the New Testament, were sold during his lifetime," that is, 1469-1536.[20]

All this does not, of course, mean that European technology surpassed Middle Eastern technology in all branches. In some branches—for example, in pottery, ceramics and some textiles—the opposite remained true for some centuries. In some branches of hydraulics, Middle Eastern engineers showed great skill and inventiveness.[21] In others there is clear evidence of deterioration in late medieval and early modern times. Indeed, Professor Ashtor sees a direct connection between European technological progress and Middle Eastern stagnation, the latter due mainly to the replacement of free enterprise under the Abbasids and Fatimids by various forms of control, monopoly and extortion under the Mamluks. As a result, "most Near Eastern industries were [by the fourteenth century] no longer able to compete with Western manufactured goods, imported by Italian and other merchants,"[22] which caused them to deteriorate still further.[23]

Technological advance, which was sustained even during the dark fourteenth century, was not accompanied by corresponding scientific progress. In mathematics, astronomy and certain other sciences, Europe was not ahead of Islam in the later Middle Ages. But here, too, by the fifteenth century something new had emerged, perhaps best exemplified by Henry the Navigator (1394-1460) and Leonardo da Vinci (1452-1519). Henry's research institute at Sagres was certainly not the first of its kind—the museum in Alexandria, Bayt al-Hikmah in Baghdad and others come to mind. What is new about it is its dedication to one specific and highly practical objective: maritime exploration. For this purpose Henry drew on all relevant branches of knowledge—geography, astronomy, shipbuilding and navigation—and, in spite of his deep religious and indeed crusading bent, on all cultures and creeds, enlisting the service of Jewish and Muslim scientists. As for Leonardo, one has only to study his sketches and notes on machinery (for both production and military operations), on hydraulics, on geological formations, on anatomy and on the vast world of plant and animal life, to realize that a new scientific spirit, using observation to a hitherto unequalled extent, had arisen. As usual, Sigmund Freud was only partly right in saying of him, "He was like a man who awoke too early in the darkness, while the others were all still asleep."[24] In fact, a new age had dawned. And it is facts like these that make Hodgson's comparison of the Renaissance to Sung China or Caliphal Baghdad somewhat absurd. It would be fruitless to argue whether Aquinas was a deeper thinker than Averroës, St. Francis a more profound mystic than Ibn al-'Arabī, the

Divine Comedy a greater poem than the *Shāhnāmeh*, Botticelli a finer painter than Bihzād, or St. Peter's a nobler structure than the Sulaymānieh. But it would be equally vain to search for the counterparts of Henry and Leonardo outside Europe. And if a further contrast be desired, one can recall Bayāzit II's prohibition of printing in Arabic and Turkish in 1485[25] and the impossibility of setting up a Turkish press in Istanbul until 1727, on the one hand, and, on the other, the flow of Arabic books from Italian presses.

In economics, no less than in technology and science, Europe also took an early lead. Three aspects should be clearly distinguished: economic thought, economic practice and economic policy. In economic thought, as in the other social sciences, Ibn Khaldūn (1332-1406) towers above his contemporaries, whether Muslim or European. He has clear and coherent theories of value, price and production and excellent insights into such matters as the role of gold and silver in international trade, the function of government expenditure and other questions.[26] In many important aspects it took European economics a couple of centuries or more to catch up with his thought. His student al-Maqrīzī (1364-1442) also shows an understanding of economic phenomena and in his *Ighāthat al-umma bi-kashf al ghumma*[27] gives a very good analysis of the currency debasement and inflation that Egypt was undergoing. Al-Maqrīzī's student, Ibn Taghrī Birdī, was also interested in prices and other economic matters.

Medieval Europe had no one comparable to Ibn Khaldūn. But already by 1360, Nicole Oresme in his *Traictie de la Première Invention des Monnaies* reveals a clear understanding of bimetallism and Gresham's Law and the harm caused by currency debasement. Copernicus (1473-1543) adumbrated the Quantity Theory of Money and in 1569 Jean Bodin expressed the theory very clearly and gave a good analysis of the causes of the great rise in prices.[28]

In the Middle East, soon after al-Maqrīzī, interest in economic affairs seems to have disappeared. This can be illustrated from the writings of two of the most distinguished historians of the Ottoman period, Naima (1665-1716) in Istanbul and al-Jabartī (1753-1825 or 1826) in Cairo. Naima had read Ibn Khaldūn, of whom he says, ". . . its author—a marvellous man—has surpassed all historians . . . into his preface he introduced the whole of his learning."[29] But among the many things he did not learn from Ibn Khaldūn was curiosity about economic matters. A perusal of his account of the years A.H. 1000-1026 (A.D. 1591-1617), 467 pages in the English translation, reveals one solitary example: the rectification by Muhammad pasha in A.H. (A.D. 1607) of the tax abuses from which Egypt was suffering and his attempt to. regulate its coinage.[30] From the point of view of this essay, al-Jabarti is more interesting than Naima. One can hazard the guess that, but for the French invasion of Egypt in 1798, which turned his world upside down, he would have been a rather pedestrian chronicler. His account of the period A.H. 1171-1187 (A.D. 1757-1773), which covers the rise and fall of 'Alī Bey al-Kabīr,[31] is barren of economic or social information: five cases of confiscation, imposition of a new tax, the abrogation of the coins issued under 'Alī Bey and the livestock owned by a rich 'ālim.[32] But the dislocations caused by the French invasion quickened his perception, and his account of the year A.H. 1213 (A.D. 1798-99)[33] contains many interesting observations: for example, the extravagant prices offered by the French for foodstuffs, their strange habit of paying owners and drivers of camels and donkeys for their services, and similarly their habit of giving laborers wages instead of just forcing them to work, a detailed account of the kind and rates of taxes imposed, the difficulties landowners had in establishing their title deeds, as required by the authorities, the reduction of food prices by decree, the effects of the British blockade on the local market, and so on.[34] And by the time he reaches Muhammad 'Alī, his intense dislike of the pasha's policies, which had adverse effects on the *'ulama* class to which he belonged, made him chronicle in vivid detail some of the important measures, e.g., the abolition of the *iltizām* (tax farms) and confiscation of the *rizaq* (endowments).[35] But Jabarti's book was suppressed until 1870 and lack of interest in economic matters continued until the last quarter of the nineteenth century.[36]

If a small digression may be allowed, Naima and al-Jabartī illustrate a major flaw in the intellectual structure of the Middle East.

. . . the Ottomans as leaders of the Muslim world and Muslim civilization, had grown to be so self-contained, so sure that they themselves embodied the good and the true, that they failed to pay the indispensable minimum of attention to the 'heathen.' Naima apparently knows practically nothing of contemporary Europe, and very little of the Europe of the past. He is a liberal in Ottoman terms, open minded and inquisitive within the framework of the Ottoman's Muslim civilization. Yet, he sees nothing incongruous in comparing eighteenth-century Europe—the Europe of Prince Eugene, Marlborough, and Louis XIV—with the Europe of the Crusaders. Each had many Nemçe [Germans], and they had an emperor! Certainly Naima was well educated, in terms of his own world. It is equally certain that that education did not equip the individual to defend his world against the new challenges that a new Europe was already pressing home.[37]

But it was not just a question of Eugene and Marlborough—Naima was a contemporary of Newton and Leibniz. Yet, after listing a set of not very exciting Ottoman scholars, men learned in the religious sciences and literature, he concludes: "This much is sufficient to awaken the envy of Christians.

> If this does not please you—
> Turn away your face: never mind it."[38]

Al-Jabartī showed himself equally impervious to Western culture, even when it was brought to his doorstep by Napoleon's army. The Institut d'Egypte invited him, along with some other *'ulamā*, to attend some chemical experiments, but this seems to have aroused a mixture of amazement and amusement, as did the attempt to impress the Egyptians by launching balloons.[39] All this forms a striking contrast to Japan, where interest in Western learning developed in the eighteenth century to the point where a few scholars had a clear understanding of the Copernican system and the circulation of the blood.[40]

Returning to the point under discussion, interest in economics goes along with interest in numbers[41] and here too Europe very soon surpassed the Middle East. Although Egypt, for example, was regularly surveyed for cadastral purposes, nothing as detailed as the Domesday Book (A.D. 1086) seems to have survived before the Ottoman fifteenth century *defters*.[42] Medieval Islam made a notable contribution to mathematics but statistics was not its *forte*. One would look in vain in the works of Arab or Ottoman historians or adminstrators for the kind of mentality evident in Giovanni Villani (1276-1348):

. . . From the amount of bread constantly needed for the city, it was estimated that in Florence there were some 90,000 mouths, divided among men, women and children. . . It was reckoned that in this period [1336-1338] there were some 80,000 men in the territory and district of Florence. From the rector who baptized the infants—since he deposited a black bean for every male baptized in San Giovanni and a white bean for every female in order to ascertain their number—we find that at this period there were from 5,500 to 6,000 baptisms a year, the males usually outnumbering the females by 300 to 500. We find that the boys and girls learning to read [numbered] from 8,000 to 10,000, the children learning the abacus and algorism from 1,000 to 1,200 and those learning grammar and logic in four large schools from 550 to 600 . . .

The workshops of the *Arte della Lana* were 200 or more, and they made from 70,000 to 80,000 pieces of cloth, which were worth more than 1,200,000 gold florins. And a good third [of this sum] remained in the land as [the reward] of labor, without counting the profit of the entrepreneurs. And more than 30,000 persons lived by it. [To be sure] we find that some thirty years earlier there were 300 workshops or thereabouts, and they made more than 100,000 pieces of cloth yearly; but those cloths were coarser and one half less valuable, because at that time English wool was not imported and they did not know, as they did later, how to work it . . . .[43]

To document adequately the difference in economic practices between Europe and the Middle East would require the writing of the economic history of the two areas over several centuries. Here, only two contrasts need be noted: first, the great superiority of European methods of accounting, acquired at the very latest after the introduction of double-entry bookkeeping in the late thirteenth or early fourteenth century[44] (the same may be said about insurance[45]); second, the capacity among Europeans to build larger, more complex and more durable economic structures than the Middle Easterners built. Many examples could be given but four will suffice. First, European and Middle Eastern guilds (which may or may not antedate the Ottoman period) have many features in common but the former seem to have been more structured and permanent, as well as more autonomous and politically powerful, than the latter.[46] Second, Europe surpassed the Middle East in maritime matters. One can admire the organization of the thirteenth- and fourteenth-century convoys of merchant ships sent by Venice to various parts of the Mediterranean, which outshone their Middle Eastern counterparts; European shipbuilding, map-making and navigating techniques were better.[47] Third, one can contrast the Hanse with their contemporaries and counterparts the Kārimī merchants.[48] The latter operated over a vaster area; and considering the wealth of the Indian Ocean region and the high price of the spices and other articles in which the Kārimī merchants traded, may have had a turnover as large as or larger than that of the Hanse. But the very absence of records and the scattered information available about them suggest that the Kārimī did not have the organization, the power, nor, presumably, the aspirations of the

Hanse. And in later periods the position of the bourgeoisie seems to have been even worse.[49] Lastly, banking methods and organization varied. Several recent works have shown that the medieval Middle East had both the legal instruments for credit operations (*mudāraba, qirād, muqārada*) and partnerships (*mufāwada*), as well as the organizational methods for carrying out large and far-flung commercial operations. The words *jahbadh* and *sarrāf* (moneychangers) and *saftaja* and *sakk* (promissory notes) occur frequently. Money was exchanged and transferred, checks were drawn and cashed, funds were deposited, loans were made and interest was charged by means of various subterfuges. Kings and ministers borrowed from bankers and authorized the latter to collect taxes.[50] But here again the size, organization and the scale of business of such Florentine banking firms as the Bardi and Peruzzi in the thirteenth to fourteenth centuries, and the Medici and Pazzi in the fifteenth, dwarfs anything available in the Middle East until the nineteenth century. Several other banks in Genoa, Bruges and elsewhere, could also be cited.[51]

Lastly, there is the question of economic policy. This can be introduced by a quotation from David MacPherson, writing in 1805: "No judicious commercial regulations could be drawn up by ecclesiastical or military men (the only classes who possessed any authority or influence) who despised trade and consequently could know nothing of it."[52] MacPherson had medieval European governments in mind, but his judgment applies even more to Middle Eastern governments. In these, the dominant elements were bureaucrats and soldiers, whose interest in economic matters was limited to taxation and provisioning. Taxes supplied the revenues needed to defray the expenses of the court, the army and the bureaucracy, and it is not surprising that almost the only statistics available in Arabic and Turkish writings are army lists and tax returns. Provisioning applied to the cities, whose inhabitants could be troublesome in times of shortage. Hence, elaborate measures were taken to ensure adequate supplies of grain and other necessities to the capital and large towns, and when goods were scarce maximum prices were often imposed.[53] Of course, the rulers realized that a minimum of order and justice was necessary if the peasants were to produce the surplus on which they drew, and exhortations to apply both were frequent. But that seems to have been the sum total of interest in economic development. A

few illustrations may be given from the excellent study by Bernard
Lewis, "Ottoman Observers of Ottoman Decline."[54] In the mid-
sixteenth century the former Grand Vizier Lutfi Pasha reviewed
the state of the empire in his *Asafname* and made recommendations.
His remarks on economic matters are confined to the following:

> The control of prices is an important public responsibility, and the Grand
> Vizier must devote special care to it. It is not right if one high Official is a
> rice merchant or if the house of another is a drugstore. The fixing of prices
> is in the interests of the poor.

On taxes he remarks, "The Sultanate stands on its treasury. The
treasury stands by good management. By injustice (*zulm*) it falls."
He goes on to say that tax revenues should be assigned to government
commissioners rather than to tax farmers and that the amounts
should be fixed by the chief treasurer. Extraordinary taxes levied
on the peasantry, he says, should be neither too heavy nor too frequent, and steps should be taken to prevent the depopulation of
the countryside. In 1630, Koçu Bey's *Risale* is penetrating and
eloquent on the ills of the empire, but on economic matters he
merely deplores government waste and corruption and the raising
of poll taxes to intolerable levels.[55] Around 1653, Katib Çelebi,
an official in the Ministry of Finance, wrote a detailed and informative
treatise containing army lists and figures on revenue and expenditure.
But he too merely recommends cutting government expenditures
and abolishing the sale of offices. Other reformers of the seventeenth and eighteenth centuries follow the same lines. Once more
Naima may be quoted. His recommendations include:

> First, an attempt should be made subtly to get expenses and income to
> balance, perhaps through some means of reducing expenditures. But the
> people should not be irritated by having their names struck off the state
> payroll; no individual should be given cause to complain because his allow-
> ances have been reduced or his pay cut; nor should this make necessary any
> emergency levies or the levying of any new taxes [if this sounds like an
> American campaign speech, it should only increase our sympathy for the
> predicament of the Ottoman budget-balancers]. Fourth, the outlying
> provinces and the whole state should be exploited and administered so
> that the peasants will have security and the lands of Islam will be prosperous,
> and so that the government will get full revenue, and the governors and
> commanders will receive their profits and thus can maintain their local
> households at full strength and fully equipped.[56]

Before examining other aspects of Ottoman economic policy, a comparison with contemporary Europe is in order. Here too fiscalism and provisioning loomed large. Carlo Cipolla puts it very well:

The greatest concern of modern governments, in the field of economic policy, has been, in the last half-century, the "business cycle." The greatest bogey has been unemployment. Throughout the whole of the Middle Ages, the greatest concern of governments was the "crop-cycle." The greatest bogey was famine.[57]

But there was an additional, very important factor due to the relatively greater economic and political power of the traders and craftsmen, namely greater consideration for the interests of producers, often at the expense of consumers. In the Italian, German, Flemish and Dutch city-states, traders and craftsmen were in fact the predominant power, and shaped economic policy to suit their interests.[58] Again to quote Cipolla:

in the majority of cases there was a conscious effort to industrialize. At the beginning of the fourteenth century the conviction was widespread that industry spelled welfare. In a Tuscan statute of 1336, statements may be read which might have been written by the most modern upholders of industrialization in the twentieth century.[59]

But even such national monarchies as England and France also took commercial and industrial needs into account. By the fourteenth century both England and France were enforcing measures designed to secure a favorable balance of trade by curtailing the import of competitive goods and encouraging that of inputs into goods that could supply local needs or be exported; by expanding exports, especially those with a large "value added" component, for example, cloth rather than raw wool; and, more generally, by stimulating local production.[60] By the seventeenth century a full-fledged mercantilist theory had developed and in the 1660s Sir William Petty was expressing a very "modern" concern with production and employment as the basis of national prosperity.[61] Such views had a marked effect on government policy.[62]

A few striking contrasts may be noted. Like Europe, but with a lag, the Ottoman Empire participated in the Price Revolution, and its currency suffered accordingly. But whereas the main European currencies were soon stabilized and experienced little or no depreciation thereafter, the Ottoman *akçe* showed a great, almost uninter-rupted, decline beginning in the fifteenth century, well before the influx of American bullion, and continuing until the middle of the nineteenth century.[63] Stability was achieved in Europe not fortui-tously but through the arduous efforts of the governments, as the history of Elizabeth's reign clearly shows, whereas in Turkey (and Iran)[64] the currency was continually debased. It should be added that, until the end of the seventeenth century, the power and resources of the Ottoman Empire were greater than those of any European country except perhaps Spain and France, which presumably implies that it had the means, but not the will or skill, to reform its currency.

Also, we can again contrast attitudes to trade. Of course, the Middle Eastern rulers realized the importance of foreign trade, if only as a source of customs duties, and took some measures to stimulate it, for example, the building of caravanserais, upkeep of a few strategic roads and privileges granted to European merchants.[65] But whereas the Europeans thought of trade as a means of increasing national wealth and employment, as well as holdings of bullion, and took what they thought to be appropriate measures, the Ottomans were con-cerned only with revenues and supplies; duties were levied on exports as high as those on imports and the exporting of certain goods was prohibited. This is often attributed to the Capitulations, and was no doubt perpetuated by them until the very eve of the First World War, in spite of the Turkish desire to change the tariff.[66] But the orig-inal policies were adopted by the Ottomans at the height of their power of their own free will. Clearly, these policies must either have been regarded as favorable to the interests of the empire or, if not, the economic consequences must have weighed little against the political advantages sought.

Indeed, I have not come across a single reference to such general concepts as "exports," "imports" and "balance of trade" in either Arabic or Turkish sources before the nineteenth century. I have asked several scholars who have worked in the Ottoman archives, both central and provincial, whether they had ever seen such con-cepts used, and have not yet had a positive answer.

One particular aspect of this question deserves notice: shipping. The English Navigation Acts of 1651 are only the most conspicuous of the attempts made by European governments to protect and stimu-late their merchant marines.[67] By contrast, the Ottomans opened even their coastal trade to foreign ships. Here again the policy was perpetuated by weakness but originated in strength. And here again one cannot help surmising that in addition to those mentioned above, another factor may have operated. Most Ottoman shipping, like foreign trade, was in the hands of Greeks and other non-Muslims, a fact of which the government was fully aware.[68] This must have greatly decreased its desire to promote shipping and trade, the benefits of which would have accrued mainly to communities of dubious loyalty. But this consideration cannot have been important before the second half of the eighteenth century, and does not explain the previous centuries of neglect.

The judgment of an eminent historian is worth quoting:

> Even at the times of the greatest Ottoman power, the Turkish provinces never achieved anything like Western propserity. No attempt was made to husband human or natural resources. Wasteful farming methods exhausted the soil and consumed what little the tax collectors left.[69]

The first conclusion that can be drawn from this analysis is that the image of two lines, or rays, crossing at a point is inadequate. What we have in fact are two broad spectra, intersecting over a wide range. In military power and military technology, Europe did not surpass the Muslim empires until the seventeenth century. In astronomy, painting, architecture, philosophy and mysticism, it can be argued, with greater or less cogency, that the Middle East remained level with Europe until well into the sixteenth century. But in technology, most branches of science, economic activity and economic policy, the point of intersection came much earlier—possibly as early as the thirteenth century, more probably in the fourteenth, certainly by the fifteenth century. The same applies to certain other very important aspects not dealt with in this essay, such as scholarship and political institutions—one has only to think of city-states, juries, parliaments and the linking of taxation and representation. In other words, in almost all aspects of power except the military aspect, Europe was preponderant by the fifteenth century at the latest. And since that power was derived from mental activity working on a broad base of natural and human resources, it was capable of almost indefinite expansion. This was to become painfully evident to the rest of the world in the eighteenth and nineteenth centuries.

Of course, there was nothing genetically preordained, inevitable or eternal about the predominance of the West. Once more to quote Hodgson:

Such Europeans have wondered why in recent years, after many centuries (so they suppose) of static quiescence, the various backward peoples are now stirring. They have overlooked the wonder of how it could be that, for what was in fact a rather brief period of little more than one century [*sic*], the Europeans could have held so unique a position in the world.[70]

And since different epochs require different qualities, it may well be that in the coming decades or centuries those characteristics which gave Europe and America their leadership—restlessness, individualism, skepticism, an arrogant attitude towards nature—may prove to be their undoing. But the account given here does perhaps suggest that a long time may elapse between the moment a civilization begins to stir and the moment when it catches up with the leading civilization of the period.

NOTES

1. Hodgson, vol. 2, p. 3.

2. *Ibid.*, vol. 3, p. 11.

3. *Ibid.*, vol. 3, p. 180.

4. *Ibid.*, vol. 3, pp. 46-133. Hodgson quite rightly draws attention to the "Arabist" bias of Western Orientalists, which makes them equate "Middle Eastern" or "Islamic" civilization with "Arab." Needless to say, this particular bias is shared by the Arabs themselves, who tend to think that after about A.D. 1200 the Middle East entered into a prolonged decline. Perfectly correctly, Hodgson stresses the immense importance of the Persian and Turkish contributions from the thirteenth to the seventeenth centuries. This fact inevitably complicates the analysis in this paper, since Europe has to be compared and contrasted with two rather different entities, the "Arab" world of the seventh to twelfth centuries and the "Iranian-Ottoman" world of the eleventh to eighteenth centuries.

Since both Europe and the Middle East consisted of regions with vastly different degrees of development, throughout this essay comparison has been between best and best, the highest points in the Middle East being compared to the corresponding ones in Europe.

5. *Ibid.*, vol. 2, p. 571; see also p. 176.

6. *Ibid.*, vol. 3, p. 182; italics in original.

7. As Joseph Needham, *Science and Civilization in China* (Cambridge, 1954-   ) has reminded us, China's contribution to technology and science has been immense. The argument developed in this paper is not intended to apply to it.

8. "The Expansion of Technology," in Carlo M. Cipolla (ed.). *The Fontana Economic History of Europe* (London, 1972) vol. 1, p. 144; see also Lynn White, *Medieval Technology and Social Change* (Oxford, 1965); Charles Singer (ed.),

A History of Technology (Oxford, 1956, 1957), vols. 2 and 3; Maurice Daumas (ed.), *Histoire générale des techniques* (Paris, 1962, 1965), vols. 1 and 2; and the *Cambridge Economic History of Europe* (hereafter cited as CEHE), vols. 1-4.

9. Lefebvre des Noëttes, *La force motrice animale à travers les ages* (Paris, 1924).

10. Andrew Watson, "The Arab Agricultural Revolution and its Diffusion," *Journal of Economic History*, vol. 34, 1974, pp. 8-35, and a forthcoming book by the same author; Watson points out, however, that the Europeans were rather slow in adopting many of these crops.

11. B. H. Slicher van Bath, *Yield Ratios, 1810-1820* (Wageningen, 1963), p. 16 ff.

12. Charles Issawi, *Economic History of the Middle East 1800-1914* (Chicago, 1966), p. 377; *idem.*, *Economic History of Turkey, 1800-1914* (Chicago, 1980), pp. 214-15.

13. M. W. Dols, *The Black Death in the Middle East* (Princeton, 1977), p. 271.

14. Watson, *op. cit.*

15. White, *op. cit.*, p. 155.

16. Al-Tabarī *Ta'rikh*, ed. M. J. de Goeje *et al.* (Leiden, 1879-1901), vol. 1, p. 2,722.

17. A. R. Ubbelohde, *Man and Energy* (London, 1963), pp. 50-51. Tower windmills, which gradually replaced post windmills in Europe, were much more powerful. The Edinburgh Museum has a huge waterwheel built in 1826 and used until 1965 for barley milling, cotton spinning and ragbreaking for paper. It had a capacity of up to 150 horsepower. On the other hand, windmills seem to have disappeared at an early date in the Middle East, and al-Jabartī mentions the ones put up by the French in Cairo in 1798-1799 as an unfamiliar phenomenon. 'Abd al-Rahmān al-Jabartī, *'ajāib al āthār fi al-tarajim wa al-akhbār* (Beirut, 1978), vol. 2, p. 231. Earlier some seven or eight windmills had been set up in Alexandria by Europeans. P. S. Girard, cited in Issawi, *Economic History of the Middle East, op. cit.*, p. 377. Al-Jabartī also mentions wheelbarrows as something unfamiliar. *Op. cit.*, vol. 2, p. 232.

18. Carlo M. Cipolla, *Clocks and Culture* (London, 1967), preface.

19. Hermann Kellenbenz, "Technology in the Age of the Scientific Revolution," in Cipolla, ed. *Fontana Economic History, op. cit.*, vol. 2, p. 180.

20. George Faludy, *Erasmus* (London, 1970), p. 257.

21. For a very good recent account, see Donald R. Hill, *The Book of Knowledge of Ingenious Mechanical Devices* by Ibn al-Razzāz al-Jazarī (Dordrecht, 1974), an edition of an early thirteenth century manuscript.

22. Eliyahu Ashtor, "L'apogée du commerce venitien," *Venezia Centro di Mediazione* (Florence, 1977), vol. 1, pp. 318-21.

23. At this point it might be of interest to speculate on whether the technological advances of the Middle East and Europe were in any way connected with their population trends. The Arab Agricultural Revolution of the seventh to eleventh centuries may well have been stimulated by, and certainly

made possible an appreciable growth in, population, and so was the corresponding European upsurge. The Black Death drastically reduced the populations of both regions, but recovery came much earlier in Europe than in the Ottoman Empire; as for the Arab countries, no long term upward trend seems discernible in them until the nineteenth century. It is therefore possible that Europe's greater technological inventiveness may have owed something to its population pressure. See Charles Issawi, "The Area and Population of the Arab Empire: An Essay in Speculation," in A. L. Udovitch (ed.) *The Islamic Middle East, 700-1900: Studies in Economic and Social History* (Princeton, 1981).

24. Quoted in Ladislao Retti, *The Unknown Leonardo* (New York, 1974), p. 6. This book based on two notebooks discovered in Madrid in 1965, gives an idea of the breadth and depth of Leonardo's observations.

25. Permission was given to print books in Hebrew, Greek and Western scripts, and many were produced.

26. See M. A. Nashaat, "Ibn Khaldun, Pioneer Economist," *L'Egypte Contemporaine*, vol. 38, 1944; Charles Issawi, *An Arab Philosophy of History* (London, 1950), introduction and chs. 3 and 4; Jean David Boulakia, "Ibn Khaldun, a Fourteenth Century Economist," *Journal of Political Economy*, vol. 79, no. 5 (Sept.-Oct. 1971).

27. Ed. Gamal al-Shayyāl (Cairo, 1940).

28. See lengthy extracts from Oresme and Bodin in A. E. Monroe, *Early Economic Thought* (London, 1924).

29. Lewis Thomas, *A Study of Naima*, ed. Norman Itzkowitz (New York, 1972), p. 112.

30. *Annals of the Turkish Empire*, trans. Charles Fraser, vol. 1 (London, 1832), pp. 371 and 377.

31. *Op. cit.*, vol. 1, pp. 307-440.

32. *Ibid.*, vol. 1, pp. 316, 320, 363-4, 385, 387, 399, 416.

33. *Ibid.*, vol. 2, pp. 179-287.

34. *Ibid.*, vol. 2, 193, 196-97, 209-210, 216-218, 231-32, 246, 249.

35. See translation of relevant passages in Charles Issawi, *Economic History of the Middle East*, pp. 380-383.

36. For the Turks, see Şerif Mardin, *The Genesis of Young Ottoman Thought* (Princeton, 1962); for the Arabs, Ra'if Khūrī, *al-fikr al-'arabi al-hadīth* (Beirut, 1943), translation forthcoming; see also B. Lewis and P. Holt, *Historians of the Middle East* (London, 1962).

37. Thomas, *op. cit.*, pp. 82-93.

38. Naima, *op. cit.*, p. 98.

39. Al-Jabartī, *op. cit.*, vol. 2, 230-44.

40. Donald Keene, *The Japanese Discovery of Europe, 1720-1830* (Stanford, California, 1968), *passim*.

41. The connection was clearly grasped by Sir William Petty, who has

been called by Marx "The founder of political economy." In his *Political Arithmetic*, written probably in 1672, he says, "Instead of using only comparative and superlative Words, and intellectual Arguments, I have taken the course . . . to express myself in terms of *Number, Weight* or *Measure.*" Quoted in Eric Roll, *A History of Economic Thought* (London, 1961), p. 100.

42. Of course this argument from silence is by no means conclusive. The fact that no documents have survived does not prove that they did not exist. But in a society whose literary output was so enormous and those historians were so numerous and prolific and often close to official circles, it is difficult to believe that if significant information on such matters as population or production or foreign trade had existed, some of it would not have been picked up by scholars like Ibn Khaldūn, al-Maqrīzī or al-Qalqashandī. On the questions that did interest medieval Middle Eastern governments, taxation and the army, much information and quite a few figures are available. A clear idea of the extent and limitations of economic data available for what was the most advanced and most tightly governed Middle Eastern country is given by Hassanein Rabie, *The Financial System of Egypt, A.H. 564-741/ A.D. 1169-1341* (London, 1972); see especially chapter 1, "A Critical Survey of Sources."

43. See the long extract in Robert S. Lopez and Irving W. Raymond, *Medieval Trade in the Mediterranean World* (New York, 1955), pp. 71-74; compare with a similar one for Milan in 1288, pp. 62-66 and contrast with the Arabic description of Fez in the fourteenth century, pp. 74-75.

44. *Ibid.,* pp. 359-77.

45. *Ibid.,* pp. 255-65.

46. For Europe, CEHE, vol. 3, pp. 230-80; for the Middle East, *The Encyclopedia of Islam*, sv. "Sinf"; Claude Cahen, "Y a-t-il des corporations professionelles dans le monde musulman classique?" in A. H. Hourani and S. M. Stern (eds.), *The Islamic City* (Oxford, 1970), pp. 51-64; Gabriel Baer, *Egyptian Guilds in Modern Times* (Jerusalem, 1964); *idem.*, "Administrative, Economic and Social Functions of Turkish Guilds," IJMES, vol. 2, no. 1 (January, 1970); *idem.*, "Guilds in Middle Eastern History," in M. A. Cook (ed.), *Studies in the Economic History of the Middle East* (London, 1970); B. Lewis, "The Islamic Guilds," *Economic History Review* (1937); C. Issawi, *Economic History of Iran* (Chicago, 1971), pp. 284-92.

47. Contrast S. D. Goitein, *A Mediterranean Society* (Berkeley and Los Angeles, 1967), vol. 1, pp. 301-53, with F. C. Lane, *Venice, a Maritime Republic* (Baltimore, 1973), pp. 118-34; see also an unpublished paper by A. L. Udovitch (presented to Spoleto Conference, 1977).

48. *The Encyclopedia of Islam*, new ed., sv. Kārimī."

49. The most detailed study is that of André Raymond, *Artisans et Commerçants au Caire*, 2 vols. (Damascus, 1974) covering the seventeenth and eighteenth centuries; it brings out very clearly the stagnation, or even retrogression, of the handicrafts and the low income and status of the craftsmen (pp. 206-42). The merchants were much more prosperous and were linked

by marriage and partnerships not only among themselves (pp. 411-15) and with the 'ulamā (pp. 423-24), but also with the Janissaries (pp. 587-808). But this did not lead to the fostering of trade or promotion of commercial interests: "Les maîtres de l'Egypte se bornèrent en général à en exploiter au jour le jour les ressources sans paraître soupçonner l'intérêt qu'il pouvait y avoir à en favoriser le développement" (p. 710). Some of the sixteenth-century pashas built bazaars, but this soon stopped. The *Ocaks* of the Janissaries offered the merchants some protection, while greatly exploiting them, but by the eighteenth century power had passed to the Beys, whose extortion was unaccompanied by any protection or other benefits (pp. 783-85). For a different interpretation, see Afaf Lutfi al-Sayyid Marsot, "The Political and Economic Functions of the 'ulamā in the 18th Century," *Journal of the Economic and Social History of the Orient*, vol. 26, pp. 2-3, and Peter Gran, *Islamic Roots of Capitalism, Egypt 1760-1840* (Austin, Texas, 1979); I am impressed, but not convinced, by their arguments.

50. Goitein, *op. cit.*, pp. 229-66; A. L. Udovitch, *Partnership and Profit in Medieval Islam* (Princeton, 1970), pp. 77-82, 170-172 and *passim*; E. Ashtor, *A Social and Economic History of the Near East in the Middle Ages* (Berkeley and Los Angeles, 1976), pp. 144-47; 'Abd al-'Azīz, al-Dūrī, *Tārikh al-'Iraq al-iqtisādī fi al-qarn, al-rābi' al-hijri* (Baghdad, 1948), pp. 158-79; Sobhi Labib, "Geld und Kredit," *Journal of the Economic and Social History of the Orient*, vol. II, 1959; for a recent survey that covers the Islamic world, see *The Dawn of Modern Banking* (New Haven, 1979).

51. CEHE, vol. 33, pp. 75-97.

52. Quoted in CEHE, vol. 3, p. 281.

53. For eighteenth and early nineteenth century Istanbul, see Charles Issawi, *The Economic History of Turkey, op. cit.*, pp. 24-33, which includes a translation of an article by Lütfi Gücer on grain supply; see also the very informative article by W. Hahn, "Die Verpflegung Konstantinopels durch staatliche Zwangswirtschaft," *Beihefte zur Vierteljahrschrift für Sozial und Wirtschaftsgeschichte*, vol. 7, 1926.

54. In B. Lewis, *Islam in History* (London, 1973), pp. 199-213; this article contains numerous references to European and Turkish sources on price fixing and regulation.

55. Actually Koçu Bey was being unfair to the government. Poll taxes were fixed in gold and remained constant, but the amount actually levied, in silver coins, was raised in proportion to the debasement of the currency and the relative fall in the price of silver.

56. Thomas, *op. cit.*, p. 88.

57. CEHE, vol. 3, pp. 399-400.

58. This difference in attitude may be attributed to differences in social structure. In Europe the state broke down with the fall of the Roman Empire, leaving room for the growth of city-states, guilds, feudal powers and an independent church. In the Middle East central government did not collapse, and its presence inhibited the emergence of other centers of power.

59. *Ibid.*, p. 413, and more generally pp. 408-19.

60. *Ibid.*, vol. 3, pp. 281-361.

61. Roll, *op. cit.*, pp. 61-111; J. Schumpeter, *History of Economic Analysis* (New York, 1952), pp. 210-15.

62. CEHE, vol. 4, pp. 566-75.

63. See graph in *ibid.*, p. 458; O. L. Barkan, "The Price Revolution of the Sixteenth Century," IJMES, 1975; Issawi, *The Economic History of Turkey, op. cit.*, ch. 7.

64. Issawi, *The Economic History of Iran, op. cit.*, pp. 343-50.

65. Halil Inalcik, *The Ottoman Empire in the Classical Age* (London, 1973), pp. 121-166; *idem.*, "Capital Formation in the Ottoman Empire," *Journal of Economic History* (1960); Carl M. Kortepeter, "Ottoman Imperial Policy and the Economy of the Black Sea Region in the Sixteenth Century," *Journal of the American Oriental Society*, vol. 86, no. 2 (April-June, 1966).

66. Issawi, *The Economic History of Turkey, op. cit.*, ch. 3.

67. " 'Navigation laws' were also common, and they appeared as early as the fourteenth [*sic*] century (see, e.g., the orders of Jaime I to Barcelona of 1227 and 1286)." CEHE, vol. 3, p. 415.

68. See note of Porte to British Minister, 1802 (PRO/FO 78/36).

69. Franz Babinger, *Mehmed the Conqueror and his Time* (Princeton, 1978), p. 454.

70. Hodgson, *op. cit.*, vol. 3, p. 178.

9

Crusades and Current Crises
in the Near East

Inference by analogy is rightly frowned upon by historians; if comparisons are odious, how much more so must analogies be? And yet, in many fields of human experience, as Samuel Butler wisely pointed out, "Though analogy is often misleading, it is the least misleading thing we have." For, although history does not, of course, repeat itself, we are surely justified in assuming that like causes should give rise to like effects and that the continued presence of certain constant factors will probably produce similar situations.

No student of the Crusades can fail to be struck by the similarities presented by some of their aspects with the contemporary Near Eastern scene. In the opinion of the present writer, this parallelism is not fortuitous but represents the similarity in the effects arising from the repetition of a common process—the impact of an alien Western society on the Moslem Near East—acting on a situation characterized by certain basically unchanged common features.

Near Eastern Constants

Of these constant features of the Near Eastern scene, four may be pointed out: one of physical geography, one of combined physical and human geography, and two of culture.

The first constant is the fact that Egypt and "greater" Syria form the natural bridge—or barrier—between the Mediterranean and the Indian Ocean, i.e., between the European and Far Eastern centers of economic activity. True, alternative routes exist; but they are longer, harder, more hazardous, and considerably more expensive. The overland route through Central Asia, with its terminus on the Black Sea, was economic for the import of silk from China, but not for Indian spices or cloth, or for the heavier goods sent back in return by Europe. The overland route across Persia to Trebizond, on the Black Sea, though shorter, crosses very rough and perilous lands. The sea route round the Cape of Good Hope, probably discovered

---

Reprinted with permission from *International Affairs,* vol. 33, 1957.

by the Phoenicians in the sixth century B.C.,[1] is so long and slow that it is economic only if it carries a large and steady flow of traffic; but it too cannot in normal times compete with an all-sea route through the isthmus of Suez.

The importance of Egypt and Syria as a potential bridge or barrier has manifested itself and been widely recognized whenever Europe has flourished. This first took place on a large scale in the Hellenistic and Roman period; after some centuries of decline, the economic revival of Europe in the eleventh century once more emphasized the importance of the Near East. The rapid growth of the seventeenth and eighteenth centuries brought out the inadequacy of the recently rediscovered Cape route, and gave rise to a set of projects for piercing the isthmus of Suez. The exploitation of Persian Gulf oil in this century has added a vital commodity to the list of goods passing through the Near East, and brought into being a network of pipelines and tanker routes.

The second constant is one of physical and human geography: Egypt is the center of gravity of the area under consideration. A study of the long history of Syria shows that, unless countered by a very prosperous and dynamic Mesopotamia (e.g., in the ninth to sixth centuries B.C. and the eighth and ninth centuries A.D.), the attraction of Egypt has been overwhelming. In the periods when both countries were not part of a foreign empire—Persian, Roman, Byzantine, Ottoman—Syria was much more often ruled from Egypt than locally. This occurred with but few significant interruptions between A.D. 878 and 1516. Egypt's desire to control Syria has been largely, though never solely, motivated by the wish to hold all the Mediterranean exits of the land-bridge. Its power to do so was due, first, to its having a firmer agricultural base, and one capable of supporting a much larger population, and secondly to the fact that it has in historical times almost always been a unified country, in marked contrast to Syria; this latter factor has in turn been due to its compactness, the flatness of its land, and the excellence of its internal communications—in all of which respects Syria presents a marked contrast. As for the agricultural base, Syrian rain-fed cultivation has never been a match for Egyptian irrigation. Nor in the long run has Mesopotamian agriculture been able to compete with Egyptian. For although Mesopotamian perennial irrigation, based on an elaborate system of dykes and canals, was more productive than Egyptian basin irrigation, which merely relied on the annual flooding of the Nile, it was always much more fragile and more liable to be destroyed. As the great irrigation engineer, Sir William Willcocks, pointed out, "Of all the rivers of the world, the Nile is the most gentlemanly," and Egypt's economic stability and political influence have always rested on that foundation.

The third constant has been cultural—the social cohesion produced in the Near East by Islam. This has been the dominant cultural factor in the southern and eastern Mediterranean since the seventh-century Arab conquest split that sea into two halves, a Christian and a Moslem. The effects of this cleavage on Europe have been penetratingly analyzed by Henri Pirenne in his *Mahomet et Charlemagne*,[2] and his views have been revised, corrected, and supplemented by several distinguished scholars. Here, it is sufficient to point out that this cleavage has introduced a cultural and social factor previously unknown in the Mediterranean world: a powerful and profound, though occasionally latent, hostility between its northern and southern halves. One result of this hostility has been that disputes between the northern and southern Mediterranean States were no longer mere family quarrels, as were, for instance, clashes between Moslem States or between Christian States; a greater degree of bitterness and relentlessness was to be expected in such disputes. Moreover, an attack by one of the two cultures on the other was likely to have widespread repercussions on the latter. Thus Christians from many lands came to the help of the Spanish and Portuguese Kingdoms in their wars against the Moors, and fought at Nicopolis and Vienna against the Turks. Similarly, Moslems from many lands rushed to the defense of Palestine and Egypt against the Crusaders.

The last constant factor may be briefly dealt with; it is the immense religious significance of Jerusalem, first for Jews, then for Christians, and finally for Moslems. Any conflict centering on or near Jerusalem automatically acquires an additional dimension and a further degree of intensity.

The Parallelisms

It is against this setting that the two parallel dramas of the Crusades and their aftermath, and of modern Western penetration in the Near East, will be considered. Two episodes and an interlude will be examined: the establishment of the Crusader states and a modern parallel, the establishment of the State of Israel; Egypt's attempt to secure a monopoly of the spice trade and the similar contemporary attempts to control the petroleum trade; and the Crusaders' attack on Alexandria from Cyprus and the recent Anglo-French attack on Port Said.

The Crusader States. "Tout mouvement commence en mystique et finit en politique," observed Charles Péguy. Both the Crusades and Zionism drew their original impetus from a yearning for Jerusalem and both resulted in the establishment of a state in Palestine. Both intrusions were successful mainly because the great disunity among the numerous Arab states in Egypt and Syria more than offset their numerical superiority. The title of the first volume of René Grousset's massive history of the Crusades, *L'anarchie musulmane et la monarchie franque*, accurately describes the situation. "C'est un spectacle bien curieux que celui de cette énorme masse musulmane qui aurait pu écraser vingt fois le corps expéditionnaire aventuré en Asie et qui, faute d'union, se laissa démoraliser et paralyser par l'irruption franque."[3] Or, to quote Steven Runciman: "It was, above all, the disunion of the Arabs that permitted the small intrusive state to be established within their lands."[4]

In addition to disunity, there was failure to assess correctly the power and dynamism of the newcomers. When the Crusaders approached Syria, the Fatimids saw in them potential allies against the Seljuks. Emissaries were sent and negotiations took place near Antioch, the Fatimids offering to cede northern Syria to the Franks provided they received Palestine as their share. These negotiations failed, but the Fatimids took advantage of the general confusion caused by the irruption of the Crusaders to seize southern Palestine, and when the Crusaders reached Jerusalem, it was from the Fatimids that they had to capture it.[5] One cannot help comparing this episode with the part played by some Arab leaders before and during the Arab-Israeli war.

But, both times, once the implications of the presence of a hostile state in their midst sank in, a coalescence of the Arabs began to take place. This process was, however, very slow, and for a long time the Crusaders remained in a position to attack any of the neighboring countries; indeed, the Crusaders were able to reach Cairo and the outskirts of Damascus and to range widely in the Hauran. However, when some eighty years after the initial Frankish conquest Salahuddin succeeded in unifying Egypt, Syria, and Yaman under his rule, he definitely put an end to any Crusader hopes of further expansion, although reinforcements from Europe and disunity among his successors enabled the Latin states, now greatly shrunk, to survive for almost another century. The end came at the hands of the Mamelukes, who firmly ruled over Egypt, Syria, and most of the Red Sea coast of Arabia. The similarity, however, is not confined to broad outlines but extends to details, such as the following:

(1) From the earliest stages of the Crusades, the Latins established their superiority as fighters; man for man, there seems little doubt that they were more than a match for their foes. But this was by no means enough to compensate for the great inferiority in numbers. Hence, they remained dependent on Christendom for men and money, endured as long as Christendom retained enough interest to continue supplying them, and withered and collapsed when that interest was lost.

It is again appropriate to quote Runciman:

Outremer was permanently poised on the horns of a dilemma. It was founded by a blend of religious fervor and adventurous land-hunger. But if it was to endure healthily, it could not remain dependent upon a steady supply of men and money from the West. It must justify its existence economically. This could only be done if it came to terms with its neighbors. If they were friendly and prosperous it too would prosper. But to seek amity with the Moslems seemed a complete betrayal of Crusader ideals; and the Moslems for their part could never reconcile themselves to the presence of an alien and intrusive state in lands that they regarded as their own. Their dilemma was less painful, for the presence of the Christian colonists was not necessary for their trade with Europe, however convenient it might be at times.[6]

In the end, Europe lost interest in the Crusader states. "Among the lesser folk who had contributed so largely to the ranks of the earlier crusades all interest in the movement died out. The *non-croisé* bested the *croisé* as in Rutebeuf's dialogue; men stayed home, tended their gardens and secured the spiritual benefits of crusading through the acquisition of indulgences."[7] A comparable dialogue is going on today between Zionist and non-Zionist Jews in Europe and America, but its outcome is still in doubt and it would certainly be premature to say that outside interest in Israel has waned.

(2) Another similarity is provided by the contrast between newcomers and old-timers. To quote Runciman once more: "Wise Frankish statesmen in the East followed Baldwin's tradition, adopting local customs and forming local friendships and alliances, while newcomers from the West brought with them chauvinistic ideas

that were disastrous for the country."[8] The way this contrast struck contemporaries is well expressed by Usamah ibn Munqidh, an Arab nobleman of the twelfth century: "Among the Franks are those who have become acclimatized and have associated long with the Moslems. These are much better than the recent comers from the Frankish lands. But they constitute the exception and cannot be treated as as rule."[9] Similar sentiments have often been expressed regarding Mr. M. Sharett and other Israelis born in Palestine and able to speak Arabic and get on with their Arab neighbors. But needless to say, such general mutual antipathy has never prevented individual friendships between some members of the hostile groups. The same Usamah thus describes his relations with a Frankish knight: "He was of my intimate fellowship and kept such constant company with me that he began to call me 'my brother.' Between us were mutual bonds of amity and friendship."[10]

(3) In both periods, strenuous efforts were made by the Palestinian state to break out to the Red Sea, through the Gulf of Aqaba, in order to open a way for trade with the Far East. In both periods such efforts were equally strenuously resisted by the rulers of Egypt. Renaud de Chatillon's break-through, in 1181-2, was swiftly and successfully countered by Salahuddin who, in a letter to the Caliph in Baghdad, said that the Crusader fleet, if victorious, could "cut the pilgrim route (to the Hijaz) . . . and capture the merchants of Yemen, Karim and Aden."[11]

(4) The next point of similarity is more fundamental. It was pointed out that, under the shock of the Crusader intrusion, the Arab states in Egypt and Syria coalesced under Salahuddin. This process was not, however, a mere dynastic union; it was part of a far-reaching social change. It involved the replacement of the luxury-loving, cultured, easygoing, tolerant Fatimids by stronger, more coarse-grained, more single-minded successors. The change was consummated under the Mamelukes, a military caste whose primary interest was warfare. The Mamelukes succeeded in their main military objective, the expulsion of the Crusaders, but in the process they over-strained the economy of their country, sacrificing first agriculture and industry and then, as will be seen below, international trade. The last few years of their rule were marked by inflation, a decline in rates of exchange, and a fall in the standards of living and of culture. A similar change has taken place in Egypt from the supine, polished,

luxury-loving society of the 1930s and 1940s to the rougher, healthier, less easy-going, more militaristic society of today.

Moreover, in both cases, popular hostility to foreign intrusion was largely responsible for the change. Disgust with the Fatimids for their failure to take effective measures against the Crusaders reached its height after the massacre of Bilbeis in 1168, when Amalric "spared neither age nor sex, says the Latin chronicler, in the devoted town. This barbarous act at once ranged the Egyptians on the side of Nur-ed-din."[12] The beneficiary of this revulsion was the latter's lieutenant, Salahuddin: "The result of these successes against the 'infidels' was such a measure of popularity in Egypt that Saladin felt himself strong enough to take a decisive step," the dethronement of the Fatimids.[13]

The hostility engendered by the Crusader invasion smouldered on for generations. Thus, when Salahuddin's nephew, al Kamil, signed a treaty with the Emperor Frederick II by which Jerusalem was demilitarized and ceded to the Crusaders, his action provoked "une tempête d'indignation," which broke out even in his court and which was fully exploited by his rival the King of Damascus.[14] The same popular hostility to any understanding with the Crusaders caused the breakdown of the negotiations between Louis IX and the Mamelukes and forced the latter to settle their outstanding differences with the Ayyubids of Damascus.[15]

(5) No less important is the deterioration in the position of Christians and Jews in the period of the Crusades. In spite of their wars with the Byzantines, the Fatimids had treated their minorities remarkably well. The constant wars in Palestine, however, led to a Moslem reaction under Salahuddin and his successors. His nephew, al Kamil, "was recognized by the church of Egypt as the most generous and beneficent sovereign they ever had"; but this improvement was cut short by the crusade of Louis IX, which "exasperated the Saracens, and it is said that 115 churches were destroyed in consequence of the conquest of Damietta."[16] Under the Mamelukes conditions deteriorated still further. Eventually, by a common process of chain reaction, this deterioration affected the Jewish community as well, although its sympathies had always lain wholly with the Moslems in their struggles with the Franks. A similar process is taking place today; the position of the Jews in Egypt, which until recently was quite satisfactory, has been finally made impossible by the recent Israeli invasion of that country, and it is likely that the

hostility thus generated will spread to other foreign or minority groups as well.

(6) The last parallelism is the most dramatic of all. While the Moslems were fighting the Crusaders, a new and far greater danger began to loom on the horizon, the Mongol invasion. This danger was first perceived by the ruler of Iraq, the Caliph Al Musta'sim who, in 1253, sent a message to the rulers of Damascus and Cairo urging them to make peace and "unite to fight the Tatars."[17] His appeal was partly successful, in that the two Moslem rulers did settle their differences, but nothing could turn their attention away from the Crusaders. As Runciman put it: "But had it not been for the Crusades the Arabs would have been far better able to meet the Mongol aggression. The intrusive Frankish State was a festering sore that the Moslems could never forget. So long as it distracted them they could never wholly concentrate on other problems."[18] As a result, although in desperate battles the Mamelukes later on preserved Egypt from the Mongol invasion, they could not save Iraq or Syria. Al Musta'sim was slaughtered, together with scores of thousands of his subjects; his capital was ruined, and Iraq was so thoroughly devastated that it did not recover for over six centuries. Syria was wrecked only comparatively less. One wonders whether, in this respect, history will repeat itself.

An Interlude: The Capture of Alexandria in 1365. The story of this interlude can be briefly told, in the words of the leading authority on the subject, Aziz Atiya.[19] An expedition, prepared with great secrecy, set sail from Cyprus, landed in Alexandria and, after a brisk siege, captured the city, slaughtering, according to a Frankish chronicler, some 20,000 inhabitants. "Alexandria was the terminus of the Oriental trade routes and the beginning of the Occidental," and the booty was immense. After seven days, however, the Crusaders judged it prudent to withdraw, and the Egyptians allowed them to do so "undisturbed."

"The news of the success of the crusade had a mixed reception in Europe. The Pope and the curia at Avignon were much gratified," and similar enthusiasm was aroused at the courts of France and Savoy. But "in one quarter the news of the capture of Alexandria was badly received and bitterly criticized. Venice, which cared little for the holy cause and much for its trade interests in the Sultan's dominions, was alarmed on hearing the news and at once charged its diplomatic agents with the difficult task of mending the damage wrought by the crusade. Its envoys hastened to the Sultan's court to protest against the recent events, to assure the victim of aggression that they had no hand in the matter, and to beg for the re-establishment of peace and amity and the resumption of trade intercourse so beneficial to both parties. The Sultan refused to come to any definite understanding with a Christian nation while he was still in a state of war with Cyprus. Peace, he argued, must be made first with the King of that island. The envoys then sailed to Cyprus and persuaded Pierre to open negotiations with the Sultan. Exchange of embassies between the two courts was begun with a view of arriving at an amicable solution and healing old and new wounds, but before any treaties were signed or even the real intentions of the Sultan were made known, the Venetians hurried to the West to announce that peace was concluded between Cyprus and Egypt. This premature announcement put an end to the preparations on foot in Europe for the crusade and weakened the position of King Pierre in his negotiations."

Peace was eventually concluded, after protracted negotiations, but in the meantime Egypt "was impoverished by the loss of trade with the Christians and the state funds were depleted. . . . The Sultan was the loser by his obstinate procrastination."

The similarities with the recent Suez Canal crisis and the Anglo-French attack on Port Said are too obvious to need pointing out. One melancholy footnote may, however, be added. "Indirectly, the Latin warriors of the Cross only plundered the fortunes of their Eastern co-religionists; for, as soon as the campaign came to an end, the Sultan issued a decree whereby all the property of the Christians in Egypt and Syria was confiscated and used to pay for the damage done to Alexandria." In the same way, the damage done to Port Said is being paid for by the Jewish community and the British and French subjects resident in Egypt.

In conclusion, one cannot but quote Atiya's summing up of the campaign. "It failed in its chief aim, that is, a permanent land base for the Christians, and it did not solve the problem of the reconquest of the Holy Land. . . . It did not weaken the Sultan to the extent contemplated as a preliminary measure toward the abolition of Egyptian independence." It merely accelerated the deterioration of relations between Islam and Europe.

The Monopoly of the Spice Trade. The third parallelism arises out of Egypt's attempt to gain control over, and monopolize, the most valuable commodity in international trade. In ancient times this was frankincense from southern Arabia; today it is Persian Gulf oil; in the Middle Ages—and indeed until the eighteenth century[20]—it was spices from the Indies. In all three periods the commodity had to be shipped from a Syrian or Egyptian Mediterranean port, and at all times Egypt has sought to obtain control over these ports and so to regulate the trade.

In the early Middle Ages, trade between Europe and the East was carried on by polyglot Jews whose far-flung commerce, extending from Europe to China, has been described, in a frequently quoted passage, by the ninth-century geographer Ibn Khurdadhbeh.[21] Under the Fatimids, Jews played a leading part in the economic life in Egypt, while, in the twelfth century, European penetration had reached the point where the Pisans were allowed to establish a trading "factory" in Cairo.[22] Under Salahuddin, however, a conscious reaction set in and a successful attempt was made to reserve the spice trade for Moslems. Jewish, Byzantine, and European traders were forbidden to trade in the Red Sea area; their place was taken by the Karimi traders, all of whom were Moslems, including a few converts to Islam. Salahuddin realized the need for preserving good relations with Europeans, since Moslem traders seldom operated in the Mediterranean, owing to European supremacy in that sea, but he confined them to Alexandria and Damietta, Egypt's main Mediterranean ports.

The result of these measures was that Egypt, with its control over Syria, acquired a great bargaining power. On the other hand, Europe was disunited: Venetians, Genoese, Catalans, Marseillais, and Florentines competing bitterly with each other. As the Venetians put it concisely, "Siamo Veneziani, poi Cristiani"—"we are first of all Venetians, then Christians."[23] The extent to which Venice was prepared to break the European front in defense of its interests came out clearly during the attack on Alexandria described above. A still more striking example was provided a century later. In the 1440s and 1450s, during a war between Rhodes and the Mamelukes, the Hospitallers raided the Egyptian shores and, as a result, the Sultan heavily fined European traders in Egypt. Thereupon Venice offered its mediation and, in 1464, sent its fleet to Rhodes and after a fight forced the Hospitallers to restore the Egyptian goods and prisoners.[24]

The Europeans did not, however, submit tamely to Egypt's monopoly. They made repeated, but unsuccessful, attempts to break it by force, in a series of Crusades of which that of Louis IX is the best known. They also tried to open an overland route to the Far East, sending expeditions such as that of the Polos as far as China; here, however, they were frustrated by the geographical factors mentioned above. A *modus vivendi* was therefore reached, which allowed Egypt to reap a fabulous income. Heavy taxes on spices formed the main item of government revenue. Hence, to quote Labib, "it is not surprising that the price of Eastern goods (spices) should rise to three or four times its original level. Nor is it surprising to learn that the Egyptian Government received the equivalent of one ship's cargo for every three or four ships." It may be noticed in passing that, in 1955, the amount received by Middle Eastern governments in oil royalties and taxes was about a third of the value of the petroleum exported from the region.

This state of precarious but mutually profitable equilibrium lasted until the reign of BarsBay (1422-38). By that time, a high level of military expenditure, coupled with a decline in agriculture and industry and resulting in inflation and exchange depreciation, began to present the rulers of Egypt with a major economic crisis. Bars-Bay's solution was to convert the spice trade into a government monopoly. He acted by quick successive measures: traders were forbidden to buy spices without a licence; all the spice trade was channelled through Egypt, leaving Syria out; Europeans were allowed to buy only in Alexandria; no Moslem trader was allowed to sell until the Sultan had disposed of his own stock of goods; finally, Karimi traders were forced to sell their goods to the Sultan. Having thus become the sole monopolist, BarsBay was able to raise the price of spices by 50 dinars.[25] A cargo of pepper that cost 50 dinars in Cairo was sold at Alexandria to Europeans for 130 dinars.[26]

These measures were, naturally, resented by both Moslem and European traders. The former tried to organize alternative centers of trade in Aden and Jidda, but could not escape the Egyptian stranglehold. The latter tried boycotting, but were equally unsuccessful. However, this further twist of the screw, which was maintained by BarsBay's successors, brought home the imperative necessity for Europe to escape from the grip of the Egyptians. Italian attempts to find a sea route to India were taken up more systematically by the Portuguese. More intensive study of Arabic and other sources[27] and improvements in shipbuilding went hand in hand. Finally, in 1498, Vasco da Gama reached India and Egypt's monopoly was shattered. Mameluke and Ottoman attempts to destroy Portuguese sea power in the Indian Ocean were unsuccessful and the Venetian proposal for a canal across the isthmus of Suez received no serious consideration in Cairo. And although there was a revival of the spice trade through Egypt and the Levant in the sixteenth century, this was soon followed by another collapse.[28] It was not until the nineteenth century that trade began once more to flow in abundance through Egypt.

It would seem that Europe is once more facing a similar crisis. Egyptian control over the canal, coupled with Syrian control over the oil pipelines, is once more threatening Europe's jugular vein. So far, Western disunity has prevented the formation of a common bloc of oil consumers. The dangers of the situation have, however, been realized and countermeasures are being taken. These include not only the development of substitutes for Middle Eastern oil, such as atomic energy, the production of oil from shale, the expansion of Western hemisphere oil production, and, possibly, the laying of pipelines from the newly discovered field near Teheran, across Turkey and from the Red Sea to the Mediterranean across Israel, but also the building of supertankers which can repeat da Gama's exploit and circumnavigate Africa, bypassing the Suez Canal and existing pipelines. Whether the mere existence of such countervailing power will suffice to check the emerging Arab monopoly and produce a *modus vivendi* acceptable to both sides, or whether a more violent outcome will ensue, is for the future to decide.

In conclusion, it may be once more stressed that these analogies should not be pressed too hard. Almost the only sure statement about history is that it does not repeat itself. It is certainly not the intention of the present writer to suggest that study of the past makes it possible to predict the future, nor even to assert that the similarities between the contemporary situation and that prevailing at the time of the Crusades outweigh the important differences that distinguish them. On the other hand, if history does have any meaning, the existence of such close parallelisms cannot be without significance for an understanding of present moods and attitudes in the Near East. It may even have some bearing on the problems being faced by both the peoples of the region and those of the West who have dealings with them.

NOTES

1. The details given in Herodotus' account seem to provide conclusive evidence regarding the Phoenician circumnavigation of Africa—see Herodotus, *Persian Wars*, Book IV, Chapter 42.

2. English edition, *Mohammed and Charlemagne* (London, 1939).

3. René Grousset, *Histoire des Croisades* (Paris, 1936), Vol. III, p. iv.

4. Steven Runciman, *A History of the Crusades* (Cambridge, 1951), Vol. I, p. 305

5. Ali Bayyumi, *Qiam ad dawlah al ayyubia fi misr* (Cairo, 1952), p. 45, quoting Muhammad Mustafa Ziada. The purpose of the negotiations is still the subject of controversy among historians; for the opposing views of Sir Hamilton Gibb and Steven Runciman see pp. 95 and 315-16 respectively, of Kenneth M. Setton (ed.), *A History of the Crusades*, Vol. I (Philadelphia, 1955). It should perhaps be added that even more obscurity envelops the relationships between some Arab and Zionist leaders.

6. Runciman, *op. cit.,* Vol. III, p. 365.

7. John L. Lamonte, "Crusade and Jihad," in Nabih Amin Faris (ed.), *The Arab Heritage* (Princeton, 1944), p. 183.

8. Runciman, *op. cit.*, Vol. II, p. 101.

9. *An Arab-Syrian Gentleman and Warrior.* Memoirs of Usamah Ibn-Munqidh. Trans. P. K. Hitti (New York, 1929), p. 169.

10. *Ibid.,* p. 161.

11. Quoted by Subhi Labib, "At tujjar al Karimia wa tijarat misr fil 'usur al wusta," in *Majallat al jam'ia al misria liddirasat at tarikhia* (Cairo, May 1952).

12. Stanley Lane-Poole, *A History of Egypt in the Middle Ages* (London, 1925), p. 184.

13. *Ibid.,* p. 192.

14. Grousset, *op. cit.,* Vol. III, pp. 309-10.

15. Joseph Nasim Yusuf, *Louis at tasi' fil sharq al awsat* (Cairo, 1956), p. 163.

16. Lane-Poole, *op. cit.,* p. 241.

17. Nasim, *op. cit.,* p. 163.

18. *Op. cit.,* Vol. III, p. 472.

19. Aziz Suryal Atiya, *The Crusade in the Later Middle Ages* (London, 1938), Chapter XV.

20. Fernand Braudel, *La Méditerranée et le Monde méditerranéan à l'époque de Philippe II* (Paris, 1949), p. 429.

21. See, among others, Henri Pirenne, *op. cit.,* p. 258.

22. Labib, *op. cit.;* the following account draws heavily on Labib's pioneering work.

23. Atiya, *op. cit.,* p. 114.

24. Ibn Tighri Birdi, *annujum azzahira* (Cairo, 1928-49), Vol. III, p. 478.

25. Labib, *op. cit.*

26. Lane-Poole, *op. cit.,* p. 340.

27. Charles Issawi, "Arab Geographers and the circumnavigation of Africa," in *Osiris*, Vol. X (Bruges, 1952).

28. F. C. Lane, "The Mediterranean Spice Trade," in *American Historical Review*, April 1940.

10

Reflections on the Study of Oriental Civilizations

In the last analysis, one's view on the study and teaching of the history and civilization of the Orient, and one's understanding of the relationship between Oriental and Western cultures, depends on one's philosophy of history. Or, if one wants to avoid grandiloquent terms and use instead the jargon of the economist, it depends on the simple model in terms of which one interprets the historical process. And, whether he is aware of it or not, everyone who is engaged in studying a foreign culture and consciously or unconsciously relating it to his own, uses such a model, just as everyone has some kind of metaphysics. As M. Jourdain learned from his teacher, we must all speak either verse or prose—that is unless we speak gibberish. And, if we try to represent the prevailing models graphically, we find that they fall into two groups: the linear, or continuous, and the circular, or closed-in. For the sake of completeness, one should add a third group, the equivalent of gibberish; this can be represented by scattered dots and really amounts to saying that history is just "one damn thing after another," one event alongside or following the other, with no necessary connection between them; I might add that this is a very widespread view at the present time.

The linear model represents the unity and continuity of civilization. It states, essentially, that there have been not several different civilizations but one Civilization, with a capital "C," which manifested itself in different peoples at different times. This view is generally associated with the doctrine of progress: the line moves upward on the chart, though it is admitted that its slope is not uniform, that there may be cycles around the trend, and that some very sharp drops have occurred. Further refinements are possible; for example, the line may be twisted around one's finger to form a spiral, the symbol chosen by Vico.

So much for the forms of the process; as for its content, there are several versions. There is the view of the eighteenth-century En-

Reprinted with permission from *Approaches to Asian Civilization*, 1964, eds. Theodore de Bary and Ainslie T. Embree.

lightenment. There is Hegel's majestic picture, in which the world spirit expresses itself in a dialectical process, finding its final resting place in the Prussian monarchy, and its very different offspring, the Marxist dialectic. And there is the liberal view of history as the story of Liberty: here the culminating point is political democracy, of the British or the American type, according to the predilection of the author.

Now, all these linear theories are open to grave objections. And most of these objections arise from the fact that they were all devised by Westerners and explicitly or implicitly assume that European or, at best, Western civilization is the culmination of history and the consummation of the work of the ages.

This view is arrogant and parochial, and as such offends our susceptibility in this mid-twentieth century, with our "One-World" ideas. It is obvious that Chinese, Indian, and other civilizations are not merely preparations for Western civilization. They stand in their own right and would make sense even if Western civilization had never come into being—or if it were to disappear tomorrow. So, indeed, stands all the past. As a conservative nineteenth-century Russian writer, Leontiev, put it, we can hardly believe that "The Apostles preached, the martyrs suffered, poets sang, painters painted and knights glittered in the lists simply in order that the French or German or Russian bourgeois in his horrible and ludicrous clothes might live an individual and collective life complacently on the ruins of all the greatness of the past."[1] Nor is the suggestion less ludicrous if we substitute "working class man" for "bourgeois."

Another objection is that, almost inevitably, any linear theory tends to be optimistic: the line moves up. But in this age of neo-barbarism, concentration camps, and thermonuclear bombs, we tend to be skeptical of all optimistic views and of theories of progress. We are more inclined to agree with Rivarol that "The most civilized empires will always be as near to barbarism as is the most polished iron to rust." Or with Ranke that "All generations are immediate to God."

It is therefore not surprising that, in reaction to such linear theories, circular theories of civilization should have been evolved. The most uncompromising of these is the theory of Spengler, for whom each civilization forms a closed circle. And, for those who find Spengler too repulsive—or merely too rigid—there are more appealing models. Thus Toynbee's theory may be represented by clusters of circles, since some civilizations are related to others by affiliation.

Another possible variation is that of interlocking circles stretching out in a chain—provided it is made perfectly clear that the chain is not "leading anywhere," is not registering "progress." This picture is drawn to take account of the influence which some civilizations have, at certain times, exerted on others. But, whatever the variations, one essential feature remains: each civilization is self-contained, each is "philosophically equivalent" to the others.

Circular theories seem to have been widely accepted, explicitly or implicitly. They fit well with the cultural relativism preached by anthropologists. And they appeal to those who are trying, for the best of motives, to transcend Western egocentricism.

But, in fact, they also raise grave objections. The first of these comes from the religious believer, or at least the believer in a revealed religion; for him, history is ultimately one because all men share in its crucial events. Thus, for the Christian, all men participated in the Fall, and all were equally redeemed by Christ. The message of the Gospel is addressed to the whole of humanity, whom it will one day reach. And the Final Judgment awaits all equally. Similar beliefs are held by Islam and Judaism.

Secondly, and at the opposite pole, there are the objections of those who stress the predominant influence of technology on history. For them, too, history has a fundamental unity, based on similarity of technological development. When mankind gave up food gathering and hunting as its main occupations and took up agriculture and handicrafts, it closed the first chapter in history and began the second. As for the third chapter, it opened with the Industrial Revolution, which is rapidly spreading all over the globe. Compared with the difference between food gatherers and farmers or craftsmen, differences between various societies of farmers or craftsmen are insignificant, and the same holds for differences between industrialized and pre-industrial societies.

And in between these two groups, and participating in the nature of both, come the Marxists, with their belief that technological development is one of the most important causes of change in the economic structure—which in turn determines the social, political, and cultural superstructure—and their conviction that the gospel of Marx is addressed to the whole of humanity, which will embrace it in the not too distant future.

None of these three views, the religious, the technological, and the Marxist, is fashionable in academic circles, but all three, nevertheless, carry considerable weight. They should at least make us pause and consider whether the reaction has not been pushed too far.

It is at this point that the social scientist may have a small contribution to make. Surveying the work of historians and humanists engaged in the study of Oriental cultures, he cannot but be struck by the emphasis they put on differences rather than similarities, on what is peculiar to each civilization rather than what it has in common with others. Of course, they are right. Of course, they should try "to penetrate in all its individuality and uniqueness the development of one society, or one civilization, the behavior not of men and women in general, but of one particular group in a given period of time."[2] But in doing so, they are in danger of forgetting an even more important truth, namely that "The simplicity of man is great, despite his diversity."[3] They are liable to forget that the members of other civilizations were, and are, men like themselves, with the same passions, facing the same or similar problems, using the same reasoning process. And, by passions, I do not mean so much the individual passions, such as love and hate, awe, fear, and so forth. These are too clearly depicted in the classics of the Orient—the *Ring of the Dove* by Ibn Hazm, the *Tale of the Genji,* the Chinese and Persian poems, and others—for anyone to have any doubts. I mean rather the social passions; the resentment of oppression, the craving for justice, the feeling of solidarity within a social group, the tensions between groups and classes, and the consequent struggles for power. Similarly, the reasoning process I have in mind is best exemplified in science and technology and in constructing, analyzing, and reflecting on social institutions—that is, man's reason applied to natural or social phenomena. One can illustrate this point from the study of Islamic history and contemporary civilization.

Islamic studies were sired by classical philology out of theology. We should, therefore, be duly grateful to these two disciplines, which were the only available parents. But it seems fair to say that they have kept their offspring too long in leading strings, that they have shut it off from contact with other disciplines. As a result, Islamic studies suffer from two great weaknesses: first, they have neglected some very important aspects of Islamic history and culture; and, second, their approach to many fundamental problems is often inadequate.

As regards the first point, much work has been done by scholars on such subjects as literature, theology, law, and, to a lesser extent, philosophy. But other, at least as important, fields have hardly attracted any attention. Take, for example, economic history. As a distinguished scholar put it, "Of all varieties of history the economic is the most fundamental. Not the most important: foundations exist to carry better things. . . . But economic activity with its tools, fields, trade, inventions and investment is the basement of man's house."[4] Moreover, Islamic economic history is varied, complex, interesting, and quite rich in sources. Yet, singularly little has been done on this subject. And until more work is done, our knowledge of the Islamic world is bound to be very imperfect. Incidentally, this also seems to apply to the other Oriental cultures, with the conspicuous exception of Japan. The same is true of the history of technology. Here, too, the Islamic world has some important inventions, or improvements, to its credit, but the history of Islamic crafts has yet to be written. And one cannot but suspect that when it is written it will raise some very interesting questions. Thus, to take one example, it is generally believed that the presence of abundant slave labor impeded technological progress in Greece and Rome. Did the fact that Islam relied to only a small extent on slave labor, then, stimulate its technological development? This and many other questions have not yet been raised, much less answered, And also waiting for an answer are several questions in the natural sciences, another field in which much work remains to be done.

Now, these neglected fields have two things in common, apart from their intrinsic importance. First, they deal with activities which cut across cultural borders. Literature, law, and theology are usually specific to a particular group, but methods of trading, navigating, weaving, and observing the stars have much in common in spite of differences of time and place. Their study therefore may lead to a less particularistic view, to more emphasis on universal characteristics. And, second, the study of such fields can be carried out only by people who have mastered the corresponding discipline. Only one with a thorough knowledge of medicine can write medical history and only an engineer can most usefully study the irrigation works of a past age. As another distinguished economic historian put it: "This relation of theory to the study of history is not peculiar to the field of economics. On the contrary, it is necessary to historical study to base itself all along the line upon what has been found with regard to the general character of those phenomena which are studied: to take a parallel as remote from economics as possible, the study of the history of war has always been found to stand in need of a knowledge of tactics and strategy . . . . And this essential unity in the treatment of warfare has been found to exist in spite of the fact that war has from some points of view been revolutionized through the use of powder and steam.

"As to economics, this necessary unity in the problem, irrespective of time and space, is considerably greater than is the case with war. It is here, if anywhere, a question of *necessités permanentes;* for the basis of economic life and consequently of economic theory is practically universal and all-embracing; it is the necessity for making both ends meet."[5]

For this reason, it seems particularly important to touch on these subjects in any course on Oriental civilization. For this may well stimulate some student of engineering, chemistry, or economics to seek at some future date to apply his knowledge to exploring the history of that subject in some Oriental civilization.

So much for the neglect. The inadequacy of the approach is also due to the failure to apply some of the findings of the social sciences to the study of Islamic history. We know, for instance, that Islam contained huge cities—in the tenth century, Baghdad may have had a population of 1.5 million,[6] and Cairo was probably not very much smaller. We know that there were vast differences between the rich and the poor; we know that the city dwellers belonged to very diverse ethnic and cultural groups; we also know that important economic and social changes were taking place. Does not this suggest that we ought to reexamine the history of medieval Islam in the light of the working of pressure groups, group conflicts, and class struggles? If we can trace such movements in Greece, Rome, and medieval Europe, is it not *a priori* likely that they had their counterparts in Islam? And, if so, is it not worth looking more closely at such movements as the Khariji, Ismaili, and Qarmati, to name only the more conspicuous ones?

As an example, consider the story of the poet Al-Mutanabbi, who is traditionally believed to have posed as a prophet, "revealing" verses modeled on the Koran to simple Bedouins, in the hope of establishing his rule over them. As related, the whole episode is rather puerile and whatever his defects, Al-Mutanabbi—by any reckoning one of the three or four greatest Arabic poets—was not puerile. But a French scholar has made the whole matter look much more sensible by showing that the poet was a Qarmati, that is, he belonged to "one of those social movements which develop, as always in the Orient, under the cover of a religious reform,"[7] a revolutionary movement which tried to reduce "the reality of all the rites and even all the cults claimed to be of divine institution sheltered by the Islamic state, to a certain number of human laws—to social, rational, rules designed to give happiness to all on earth—by the fusion of all religions, regarded as simple, selfish castes."[8] And a similar explanation seems to be applicable to that other great Arabic poet, Al Ma'arri. "Those who have read the recently discovered *Majalis* of his teacher and friend Muayyad Salmani of Shiraz, who was no other than the Grand Dai of Ismaili propaganda, know that the bitter skepticism of the *Luzumiyat* and the *Ghufran* can no longer be considered as an individual singularity but testifies to the development, in favorable psychological ground, of the germs of methodic doubt and insurrectionary sarcasm contained in the initiatory teaching of the societies based on Ismaili doctrine."[9]

These very brief allusions to Al-Mutanabbi and Al Ma'arri suggest another point. Among the most important sources for the history of the movements and ideas of Islam are the works of the poets. For in many ways, Arabic poets fulfilled in their society the function of editorialists and columnists, advocating or combatting ideas, supporting or attacking different groups. A politico-sociological approach to Arabic poetry may therefore often prove very rewarding. Or consider a much more prosaic subject—inflation. The last four hundred years have shown what havoc a prolonged rise in prices can wreak in the most diverse societies, what dislocations it can cause, what tensions provoke, and what new ideas generate. Now, we know that there were several inflationary periods in Islamic history, and we have evidence that at least some of them caused considerable concern to those who lived through them.[10] Should we not, then, use our painfully acquired knowledge not only to study the course of price movements in Islamic history but also attempt to trace their political, social, and other consequences?

Or take yet another social science—demography. There is no doubt that the findings of contemporary demographers cast much light on one of the main driving forces of the history of all civilizations, population movements. Any historian or student of a culture who fails to make the fullest use of the methods and conclusions of demography does so at his peril. Thus, to take only one example, recently a very distinguished historian, basing his study on the Ottoman archives, published some figures on the population of the Ottoman Empire in the sixteenth century. In the main, his estimates seem very reasonable and are in line with other available information. However, they include subtotals for the Syrian provinces, broken down by religion, and I was able to show that the figure for the Christian population was much too low. For, given our knowledge of emigration, immigration, and conversion in Syria, these figures would imply, between the sixteenth and twentieth centuries, a rate of population growth which, as far as we know, has never occurred in pre-industrial societies. They also, incidentally, would imply that in the sixteenth century, Christians formed a much smaller fraction of the total population than they do at present, a conclusion which contradicts what we know from other sources.[11]

Another point where social scientists may have a small contribution to make is in stressing the more universal aspects of the doctrines of some of the great Oriental thinkers. Of course this approach can be very dangerous. As C. S. Lewis put it: "When we select for serious consideration those doctrines which 'transcend' the thought of his own age and 'are for all time,' we are assuming that the thought of *our* age is correct; for of course by thoughts that transcend the great man's age we really mean thoughts that agree with ours."[12] And in this same conference, three years ago, a particularly well-qualified scholar stated that: "It will be found in general that the peculiar obstacle in the way of understanding Ibn Khaldun's thought is not its alien or singular character, but an assumed similarity, if not identity, between it and modern thought."[13]

But these objections, though weighty, are not conclusive. Our knowledge of natural laws, social phenomena, and human psychology *is* much greater than that of our predecsssors, and in this subject at least it would be foolish to let ourselves be unduly inhibited by false modesty. Similarly, although it is essential to remember that, say, Ibn Khaldun was a medieval Muslim thinker and not a Professor in the Columbia Business School, and therefore to relate him to the thought of his time, preoccupation with what is peculiarly Muslim and medieval must not be carried so far as to obscure what is human and universal. After all, Plato was a disgruntled Athenian aristocrat, but that is not the most interesting or enduring aspect of his thought. And, in these matters, the bias of the social scientist may act as a useful corrective to that of the Orientalist.

But it is above all in the study of the contemporary East that this corrective is most needed. The professional Islamicist, Sinologist, and so forth, often tends to be so fascinated by the peculiar character of "his" civilization—which he has apprehended after long and arduous study of its past—that he forgets the equally important common elements which it shares with the rest of humanity. And he also tends to ignore, or underemphasize, the great changes that are taking place in it—and indeed its very capacity for change. Thus a most distinguished Islamic scholar assured me that, in the Middle East today, "plus ça change, plus c'est la même chose." I replied that, compared to the deep and many-sided revolutionary changes sweeping through the Middle East today, North America and Europe seemed almost stagnant! Another eminent Orientalist declared that what was happening in China was nothing new: China had witnessed many previous revolutions in which the landlords had been liquidated and so on. I pointed out as mildly as I could that this was the first time in its history that China was producing 12 million tons of steel (the present figure is higher) and that that fact made some difference. Again, some scholars have interpreted the present regime in Egypt as a reincarnation of the Mamelukes, and have sought to study it accordingly. And yet, more light can probably be shed on this regime by studying such phenomena as nineteenth-century German nationalism, and contemporary Peronism, Chinese Communism, and Titoism than by studying the history of fifteenth- or eighteenth-century Egypt.

In a word, the Oriental societies are being subjected to two sets of forces. On the one hand are those historical ties binding them to their past and preserving their own peculiar culture. On the other are those world-wide trends drawing them into the mainstream of twentieth-century history. The Orientalist tends to overemphasize the first, the social scientist the second, and it would be futile to argue who is nearer the truth. What is essential is that both kinds of approach be used.

And this brings us back to the starting point of this paper and may suggest yet another working model to represent the relation between the major civilizations since the beginning of recorded history: a series of roughly parallel lines, one or the other of which sometimes pulls away from one of its neighbors, or draws a little closer to it and may even touch it. This represents the distinctiveness, independence, and philosophic equivalence of all the major civilizations. In the last few hundred years, however, one of the lines, the Western, changes its course quite sharply and moves away from the others, in what I believe to be an "upward" direction, though the value judgment implied in that last point is not essential to the model. What is essential, however, is the fact that the other lines, as though drawn by the first, are now moving, at a greater or slower speed, in the same direction. In other words, the scientific, technical, organizational, and other changes which started in Europe some three centuries ago, and made it so much more different from other civilizations, are sweeping over the rest of the world at an accelerated rate, and bringing huge cultural changes in their wake. And it does not seem too fanciful to suggest that, in some not so distant future, the lines may gradually converge and humanity may see an increasingly rich layer of common civilization superimposed on the age-old diversity of cultures which it has known since the beginning of history.

NOTES

1. Quoted by Nicolas Berdyaev, *The Origins of Russian Communism* (London, 1937), p. 103.

2. Alan Bullock in Hans Meyerhoff, ed., *The Philosophy of History in Our Time* (New York, Doubleday Anchor Books, 1959), p. 298.

3. Karl Jaspers in Hans Meyerhoff, ed., *The Philosophy of History in Our Time*, p. 336.

4. John Harold Clapham, *A Concise Economic History of Britain from the Earliest Times to 1750* (Cambridge, Cambridge University Press, 1949), Introduction.

5. Eli Heckscher, "A Plea for Theory in Economic History," *Economic Journal* (Economic History Series, No. 4, London), January, 1929.

6. *Encyclopedia of Islam*, 2d ed., article Baghdad (Leiden); this figure seems much too high, but one of 500,000 is reasonable.

7. R. Blachère, *Un Poète arabe du IVe siècle de l'Hégire* (Paris, 1935), p. 4.

8. Louis Massignon cited in R. Blachère, *Un Poète arabe du IVe siècle de l'Hégire*.

9. Louis Massignon, "Mutanabbi, devant le siècle ismaelien de l'Islam," in *Al Mutanabbi* (Mèmoires de l'Institut français de Damas) (Beyrouth, 1936), p. 2

10. See, for example, the interesting and remarkably penetrating study by the fifteenth-century Egyptian historian, Al Maqrizi, *Ighathat al umma bi kashf al ghumma* (Cairo, 1940).

11. Those interested can find the original estimates, the criticism and a

rebuttal in the first volume of the *Journal for Economic and Social History of the Orient* (1957-58).

12. C. S. Lewis, *The World's Last Night,* p. 96

13. Muhsin Mahdi, "Ibn Khaldun," in Wm. T. de Bary, ed., *Approaches to the Oriental Classics* (New York, Columbia University Press, 1959), p. 70.

11

Middle Eastern Economic Development, 1815-1914:

THE GENERAL AND THE SPECIFIC

In the century between the Napoleonic and First World Wars a world economy, based on Western Europe, was built. Two aspects of this process may be distinguished. On the one hand, the various regions were successively integrated in a world-wide economic and financial system, through mechanical transport, mass migration, vast capital flows and a huge expansion in international trade. And on the other, the economy of the non-European countries was profoundly transformed. Thanks to the spread of security, the introduction of modern hygiene and the reduction of famine, death rates fell and population increased severalfold. In response to rising European demand for raw materials and helped by a sharp reduction in transport costs, agricultural output greatly expanded and export of cash crops multiplied; this in turn had deep repercussions on systems of land tenure, generally resulting in a shift from communal or tribal ownership to individual property rights. Handicrafts, exposed to the competition of European machine-made goods, were for the most part eliminated; and since, for a variety of economic, social and political reasons, modern factories did not rise to take their place, a process of de-industrialization occurred in many parts of the world. Social systems were also transformed and the already great inequality prevailing in these countries increased. For although the level of living of the masses probably rose in most places over the greater part of the period, the income and wealth of the upper strata grew much more rapidly. Lastly, the active agents of change were mostly foreign—either Europeans or Americans or immigrants from neighboring countries, e.g., the Chinese and Indians in south-east Asia.

Reprinted by permission of the Oxford University Press from *Studies in the Economic History of the Middle East,* London, 1970, ed. M. A. Cook, PP. 395-411. For fuller and more accurate details on the topics dealt with in this chapter, see Charles Issawi, *Economic History of Iran* (Chicago, 1971), *idem., Economic History of Turkey* (Chicago, 1980), and *idem., Economic History of the Middle East and North Africa* (in press).

The above description fits the Middle East very closely for the period under review. The purpose of this paper is to examine whether and in what respects the region diverged from the prevailing patterns and trends. For this purpose four topics that lend themselves to quantitative analysis will be examined in some detail: population growth, foreign capital investment, mechanical transport and foreign trade. Five other topics will also be briefly discussed: agriculture, industry, levels of income, educational progress and agents of economic change. Wherever possible, comparison will be made with world totals and with figures for two other regions with sharply contrasting experiences, India and Japan; Japan was chosen as the most successful example of development in recent history while India, on the contrary, represents a country that failed to develop rapidly in spite of a promising start in several fields. Lastly, an attempt will be made to determine whether the Middle East had its own distinctive pattern of development.

It goes without saying that this paper represents only a tentative first approach to a field that has received very little study. Essentially, it raises questions rather than providing answers. Its main purpose is to stimulate discussion and suggest topics for further research.

Population

In the nineteenth century population growth occurred in almost all parts of the world, but its extent varied considerably. The following table gives some crude estimates made by Carr-Saunders and Wilcox, respectively.[1]

For India, the population has been guessed at about 120 million in 1800. The 1872 census gave a total of 206 million, the 1911 census of 315, and the 1921 census of 319 million; about half the increase

	Compound Annual Rate of Increase per 1,000					
	1800-1850		1850-1900		1900-1920	
Africa	1.1	0.0	4.7	6.9	7.7	-0.4
N. America	29.8	29.8	23.0	23.0	18.6	18.6
Latin America	11.1	7.2	13.0	13.0	18.6	18.6
Asia	4.3	2.0	5.4	2.8	2.8	6.1
Europe and USSR	7.1	7.0	8.7	7.0	7.0	7.0
Total	5.1	3.4	7.3	5.9	5.9	7.1

in 1872-1911 is attributable to improved methods of enumeration and additional areas covered[2] and the negligible growth in 1911-21 is due to the influenza epidemic. The "real increase in population (allowing for the inclusion of new territory) in 50 years has been 88.6 million, i.e., 34.9 per cent,"[3] giving a compound rate of growth of 6 per thousand. Accepting the 1800 guess of 120 million would imply a rate of growth of 7 for 1800-72, which may err on the side of exaggeration. Japan's population in 1800 was probably around 30 million. The 1872 census showed a figure of 33 million (which should probably be raised to 35 or 36 million) and that of 1920 of 56 million,[4] indicating rates of growth of 1 and 11 per thousand, respectively; however, the first figure should be slightly raised and the second reduced.

For the Middle East estimates are of the very roughest. Egypt's population in 1800 is usually put at 2.5-3 million, but good reasons have been given for raising the figure to at least 3.5 million.[5] The first reliable census, that of 1897, put the total at 9.72 million and the 1917 census at 12.75 million, indicating rates of growth of 11 and 14 per thousand, respectively. For Iraq, where the first census was taken in 1947, Hasan's estimates show annual rates of growth of 13 between 1867 and 1890, 18 in 1890-1905 and 17 in 1905-19.[6] No reliable figures are available for Syria—which term is used throughout this paper to cover "geographical" or "greater" Syria. British consular estimates in the 1830s ranged from 1,000,000 to 1,864,000, but most of them fall between 1,250,000 and 1,450,000. Estimates for 1910-15 cluster around 3.5 million.[7] Assuming a figure of 1,350,000 for 1835 and 3.5 million for 1914 would suggest a rate of growth of 12 per thousand; putting the figure at 1,864,000 would reduce the growth rate to 8. If these figures are at all correct, they would indicate that the rate of growth of the population of the Arab countries was distinctly higher than those of Asia and Africa in general and India and Japan in particular. If this is so, it would mean that a large share of the increment in income achieved during the period under review was swallowed up by population growth.

Available data on Algeria point in the same direction.[8] However, it should be remembered that not even an indication of the trend of population in Arabia is available, while that of the Sudan is believed to have fallen during the Mahdist period, following an earlier growth under Egyptian rule.[9]

Data for Turkey and Iran are even more fragmentary. The 1831 Ottoman "census" put the number of males (*erkek*) in Anatolia at

2,384,000. If one assumes this to refer to adult males, a population of some 10 million is indicated—a figure of the same order of magnitude as other very rough estimates given by various European sources.[10] On the eve of the First World War, the population of the territory of what became the Republic of Turkey was put at 14,549,000.[11] Accepting these two figures at their face value would indicate the low growth rate of 4 per thousand in 1831-1914 (but see footnote 15, below). For Iran it is not even possible to say whether the population in the latter half of the nineteenth century was larger or smaller than it had been at the beginning of that century. Thus Rawlinson put the total in 1850 at 10 million but in 1873 "after two desolating visitations of cholera and famine" at 6 million.[12] Other estimates for the 1880's range between 5 and 10 million, the two least unsatisfactory showing 7,654,000 for 1884 (by Houtum Schindler) and 6 million for 1888 (by a Russian scholar, Zolotarev). A later estimate by Houtum Schindler put the population in 1897 at 9 million, while Lorini gives a figure of 9,332,000 for 1899.[13]

As a very rough check on these figures, one can attempt some backward extrapolation. In 1956, when the first nation-wide Iranian census put the population at 18,955,000, that of Egypt was 23,532,000 and that of Turkey 24,771,000.[14] Assuming the same ratio to have prevailed in 1890 would indicate a figure around 7 million for Iran, compared to about 9 million for Egypt. However, it seems highly unlikely that in 1890-1956 the Iranian rate of growth was as high as the Egyptian. This might indicate that the higher estimates given by Sir A. Houtum Schindler—a British-German general in the Iranian army, who knew the country well—are nearer the mark, a conclusion that tallies with Curzon's and Lorini's.[15]

As for Iran's rate of growth, for what it is worth, one can quote Curzon's guess, presumably based on the India Office records on which he drew so heavily, that at the time of his journey, a period "free both from war and famine," the population was growing at ¾ percent per annum.[16] And for what they are worth, most of the estimates of town populations quoted by him show some increase in the period 1800-90, often following sharp declines in the eighteenth century; however, there were some important exceptions, e.g., Isfahan and Meshed, whose populations seem to have declined.

Capital Investment

A United Nations study, *Capital Movements during the Interwar*

Period, has put the total long-term foreign investment outstanding in 1914 at $44,000 million. Of this over $2,000 million, or as much as one-twentieth, was in the Middle East.

Total investment in Egypt on the eve of the First World War was over £E. 200 million, of which 94 million represented the outstanding public debt and the rest investment in the private sector.[17] For Turkey, the outstanding government debt at the time of the Lausanne conference was 161 million Turkish gold pounds, a figure not too significantly different from the one for 1914. Private foreign investment in 1914 was £66.4 million.[18] In Iran the only important private investment was that of the Anglo-Persian Oil Company, whose capital was raised to £4.2 million in 1914; the addition of the few Russian, British and other enterprises (banks, mines, transport, telegraphs, fisheries, etc.) would bring the total to well over £10 million.[19] As for the public debt, at the outbreak of war some £2 million was owed to Britain and the equivalent of about £4.8 million to Russia.[20]

The magnitude of foreign investment in Turkey and Egypt may be gauged by comparing it with the following figures, which represent total foreign investment in both the private and public sectors in 1913: India about £360 million, Japan about £200 million, China about £150 million, Brazil a little over £150 million, Mexico a little over £100 million. Relative to their population, the Ottoman Empire, and still more strikingly Egypt, had received an enormous amount of foreign capital. In Iran the scale of foreign investment was much smaller. It may be added that hardly any of the investment in the Ottoman Empire percolated to the Persian Gulf-Red Sea area; the exceptions were the Hijaz railway and some railway and irrigation construction in Iraq. Similarly the Sudan was only just beginning to attract foreign capital at the outbreak of war.

When, however, attention is turned to the *use* made of this foreign investment, the picture looks much less favorable. For whereas the bulk of the Indian and Japanese public debts helped to finance economic development, most of the Ottoman, Egyptian and Iranian public debts was either taken up in commissions and charges, or was used to repay earlier debts or to finance wars, or for indemnity payments, or was spent by the monarchs in various unproductive ways.[21] As a result these countries found themselves saddled with debt charges that absorbed one-eighth of the Iranian budget, nearly a third of the Ottoman and almost half the Egyptian, and yet had very little to show in return.

Transport

Three factors shaped much of the development of transport in the Middle East: the region's location, the pattern of growth of steam navigation and the rivalries of the Great Powers. The high fuel consumption of steamships confined them to rivers and narrow waters for many decades; it was not until the 1870's that the greater part of international trade was carried by steamers rather than sailing ships. But within such waters steam navigation spread rapidly and by the 1830s the Mediterranean was criss-crossed by several lines. In the late 1830s British, French and Austrian lines provided regular services to Egypt, Syria and Turkey. After that progress was swift. Describing the situation around 1860, Farley reported: "The mails leave London for Syria every Friday via Marseilles and every Monday via Trieste; while English steamers run regularly between Beirut and Liverpool"[22]—to which he could have added the Russian Black Sea line, which started operations in 1845 and served the Levant and Alexandria. And by 1870, there were three Egyptian, three British, five French, four Austrian, two Italian, one Russian and one Turkish steamship lines maintaining regular services to Egypt, and many others with ships calling at irregular intervals.[23] In the meantime, regular steamer services betwen India and Suez had been established in 1834, and between India and the Persian Gulf in 1861. It may be added that the opening of the Suez Canal not only attracted a vast volume of traffic to the Eastern Mediterranean but also strongly stimulated the development of steam navigation in general, by greatly facilitating fuelling on the Europe-Far Eastern route.[24]

Thus one may say that the Middle East was very adequately served by steamship lines connecting it with the outside world. It also had commercial steamboats on its navigable rivers at fairly early dates: the Nile in Egypt by 1841 and in the Sudan by the early 1860's,[25] the Tigris-Euphrates in 1862 and the Kārūn in 1888.

As regards railways, the other principal means of transport in the nineteenth century, the Middle East, with the definite exception of Egypt, was far less well-equipped. In 1913 total railway track in the world was over 1,100,000 kilometers; of these 4,300 were in Egypt, 3,500 in the Ottoman Empire and 2,500 in the Sudan, i.e., less than 1 percent of the world total, a figure commensurate with neither the region's area nor its population. By that date India had 56,000 kilometers of railway and Japan 11,000. Two further facts stand out: the high development of railway transport in Egypt (which accounted for nearly half the regional total) and its absence in Iran.

By 1913 Egypt had a higher railway mileage per unit of *inhabited* area than almost any country in the world, and per unit of population than most countries.[26] It owed this position to an early start: Egypt had its first railway before Sweden or Japan, and it was not until the 1870's that the *total* railway mileage of Argentina and Brazil surpassed that of Egypt, while Japan did not catch up until the 1890's and China until after 1900. This in turn was largely due to the British desire for swift connections between Alexandria and Suez, the two steamship terminals on the route to India. A combination of factors made it possible for the British to push their railway scheme, against French opposition—just as the French were later to carry out the Suez Canal project, much more slowly and laboriously, a-gainst British obstruction. And after that the rulers of Egypt—first the viceroys and then the British—had enough freedom of ac-tion and sufficient resources to build a large network.

The completion of the trans-Egyptian railway greatly reduced the attraction of the rival route, through Mesopotamia, which also had its supporters in Britain. Other factors holding up railway develop-ment in Turkey, Syria and Iran were the weaker financial positions of these countries and the intensity of Great Power rivalries. One has only to read the diplomatic history of the Baghdad railway, or to follow the various projects and counter projects for railways in Iran drawn by the British and the Russians, to realize what an im-portant impediment this constituted. Here, too, except for Egypt and the Sudan, the contrast with India and Japan is striking.

Foreign Trade

International trade grew rapidly in the period under review. Rough estimates put the total (exports plus imports) in current prices at £320 million in 1800, £560 million in 1840, £1,450 million in 1860, £2,890 million in 1872-3 and £8,360 in 1913. Since prices were much higher in the period 1800-40 than in 1880-1913, the increase in real terms was greater than the twenty-five-fold rise reg-istered in the above figures.[27]

Taking the Middle East as a whole, the expansion of foreign trade did not match the general advance. The Egyptian figure may indeed have been higher than the world average. The first reliable statistics

put total trade in 1823 at £E. 2.1 million; by 1860 the total stood at
£E. 5.1 million; by 1880 at £E. 21.8 million and by 1913 at £E. 60 million, a thirty-fold increase; moreover, the 1823 level was probably
higher than that of any of the previous fifty years or so.[28] But Ottoman
trade almost certainly did not rise as fast, though comparison is vitiated
by the fact that the area covered shrank steadily. In 1829 Ottoman
trade with Britain and France amounted to £2.6 million, and total
trade may be guessed to have been around £4 million. In 1876 the
total was estimated at £54 million and in 1911 it stood at £63.5 million—perhaps a fifteen-fold increase[29]—and for the other parts of
the region the growth in trade was surely much smaller.

The only available series for Iran, compiled by Entner, refers
to that country's trade with Russia and shows a drop from an average
of 10 million gold roubles in 1830-1 (a figure higher than that of
previous years and reflecting the effects of the Treaty of Turkman-
chai of 1828) to 6.9 million in 1860 and a recovery to 10.4 million
in 1880; after that there was a rapid rise to a peak of 101.3 million
in 1913.[30] In fact, however, Iran's total trade must have risen much
less than ten-fold over the whole period. First, because the figures
are in gold (1896) roubles, and therefore deflate the value of the
1830-1 totals, when prices were higher. (The figure for 1830-1 in
account roubles was 25.2 million.) Secondly, because Russia's share
of total trade probably rose appreciably over this period—it grew
from 45 per cent of the total in 1901-2 to 63 per cent in 1912-13,[31]
and in the late 1880's Curzon had estimated it at about £2 million
(a figure that agrees fairly well with the Entner series) out of a total
Iranian trade of some £7-8 million,[32] or say 30 percent.

The few available data on Arabia and the Sudan also indicate
that the rate of growth must have been rather slow.[33]

Both India and Japan showed faster growth in their foreign trade
than did the Middle East. Following the abrogation, in 1813, of
the monopoly hitherto enjoyed by the East India Company "the
increase in trade with India [in 1814-32] has been enormous."[34]
By 1835-9 total trade averaged £18.7 million per annum (or about
twice the 1814 level)[35] and in 1909-14 slightly over £250 million,
a more than twenty-five-fold increase in one hundred years. In Japan total trade rose from an average of 36.0 million yen in 1868-70
to 1,511.4 million in 1913, a more than forty-fold increase.[36]

But although Middle Eastern foreign trade grew more slowly
than did that of India and Japan, it played a relatively larger part
in the economy of the region. Thus, *per capita* trade in Egypt in

1913 amounted to $24.3, in the Ottoman Empire to $15.2, and in Iran to $10.3; the corresponding figures for India were $4.3 and for Japan $12.6. As a proportion of gross national product, trade must have been far higher in the Middle East than in Japan and India.[37]

No less important is the difference in the composition of trade. By 1913 the Middle East's exports consisted almost entirely of agricultural produce, with some minerals from Turkey and a very small amount of oil from Iran. The same was true for India, except for some textiles. But Japanese exports already contained an appreciable proportion of cotton and silk textiles and other manufactured goods.

Agriculture

This large population growth and increase in exports presupposes an expansion of agricultural output, and all available evidence points to such a trend in most parts of the region. Generally speaking this was accomplished within the framework of peasant farming rather than plantation farming, and by extension of cultivated area rather than by intensification.[38] Hardly any attempts were made to improve methods of cultivation other than the foundation of the Ottoman Agricultural Bank in 1888 and one or two irrigation projects such as the Konya and Hindiyya dams, and there is no evidence of a rise in yields per acre.

The major exception to this statement was of course Egypt. Here, extension of cultivation was impossible without irrigation works, which became steadily more elaborate and expensive in the course of the century. Conversion from basin to perennial irrigation naturally increased total annual yield per acre, since more than one crop could be grown on the same patch of land in a year and there was a shift to more valuable cash crops, especially cotton. But there is also evidence of a sharp rise in yields *per crop* per acre.[39] And at the turn of the century systematic efforts at intensification by means of selective breeding and application of chemical fertilizers were begun.[40]

India's experience recalls both that of Egypt and that of the rest of the Middle East. In most regions there was simply an extension of the cultivated area, with a switch to cash crops unaccompanied by a rise in yields. But there was also an enormous expansion of irrigation, and by 1913 government irrigation works watered an area of 25 million acres while private works accounted for a further

22 million. And starting around 1900 systematic research and experimentation was undertaken.[41]

Japan's development was completely different. Since most of the cultivable land was already under cultivation, growth could come only by raising yields, through intensification. This began as early as the 1870's and has been sustained to a remarkable degree ever since.[42]

Industry

"In India there was a much more definite hiatus than in the West between the decay of the handicrafts and the establishment of factories, during which certain types of demand were largely met by imports."[43] In the Middle East the hiatus was even greater. For, on the one hand, the decline of some handicrafts, under the impact of European competition, began as early as the eighteenth century and was sharply accelerated from the 1830's on. And, on the other, the advent of modern industry was greatly delayed—indeed it was only just beginning to appear at the outbreak of the First World War, and did not really gain a foothold until the 1930's.[44]

India, on the other hand, continued to export handicraft textiles to Europe and elsewhere until early in the nineteenth century—it is worth recalling that Alexander Hamilton's report of 1791 demanded protection as much from Indian as from British goods; the decline of its handicrafts started around 1820 and modern industrialization began earlier than in the Middle East, in the 1860's, gathered strength in the last quarter of the nineteenth century and reached large proportions by 1914, in spite of a slackening after the 1890's.[45] As for Japan, there was practically no hiatus. For the handicrafts were immune to foreign competition until the opening of the country in the 1850's, and after that were greatly helped by the government to modernize and play an important part in the economy. And, on the other hand, as early as the 1850's, and much more so after the Meiji restoration in 1868, modern industries were set up by the government or private enterprise, making of Japan a significant industrial power by 1914.[46]

Levels of Living

Only the most tentative statements are possible regarding trends in levels of living. In Egypt it is possible that there may have been a fall in levels of living (but surely not in *per capita* income) under

Muḥammad ʿAlī, followed by a rise under his immediate successors. In the 1860's the cotton boom seems to have appreciably raised levels of living and during the British occupation there is also evidence of a distinct improvement.[47] For Syria, two scholars believe that there was a general impoverishment in the 1840's-50's,[48] but the decline in levels of living, if any, may well have been confined to the towns. It seems probable that from the 1860's until the First World War a steady, if slow, rise in *per capita* incomes and levels of living occurred. As for Iran, "in periods of peace before the mid-nineteenth century the peasants were apparently better off than they are today."[49] Clearly, one cannot draw conclusions for the region as a whole.

The course of events in India is at least as obscure. The most recent and authoritative survey of the state of knowlege in this field observes: "It is dismaying to realize that even within very broad ranges of error we do not know whether during the past century-and-a-half the economy's performance improved, stagnated, or actually declined," and adds, "This is true whether we attempt to measure performance in terms of *per capita* income or by any reasonable combination of qualitative-quantitative elements."[50] As for Japan, "some advance in living standards is evidenced in the decline of mortality rates, in increased *per capita* consumption of food and clothing supplies, and in the growth of public services of various kinds—especially in the cities," but most of the increase in national product was absorbed by population growth, capital investment, and armaments.[51]

Educational Progress

Here one can be much more definite. Both in mass and in higher education the Middle East—which had started at a very low level in 1800—lagged behind other regions with distinctly lower *per capita* incomes. Thus Egypt's illiteracy rate in 1907 was 93 per cent, a figure equal to that of India but well above Burma's 71 per cent, Ceylon's 69 per cent and the Philippines' 51 per cent—not to mention Japan where already in the 1850's a male literacy rate of 40-50 per cent had been achieved and by 1914 "virtually the entire population had attained functional literacy, and compulsory school attendance was as close to 100 per cent as it could be."[52] Illiteracy among the Turks (though not among the minority groups) must have been still higher, since the 1927 figure was 92 per cent (by which time Egypt's had fallen to 85 per cent) and in Iran higher still. As for higher education, by 1914 Egypt had only an embryonic university in Cairo, and Turkey a young and anaemic one in Istanbul,[53] in contrast to the small but far superior Indian universities (three of which were by then over sixty years old) and technical institutes, not to mention the excellent Japanese universities.

The one exception to the above statement is Lebanon, where illiteracy rates were almost certainly not below 50 per cent and which had two good foreign universities.

Agents of Economic and Social Change

Here too the main facts are clear, and very significant. In Japan the impetus for economic development came from the ruling circles, who kept a firm hold over the whole process. Foreign capital investment in the private sector was negligible, and although foreign skills played an important part they did so under Japanese supervision and control.[54] In India, by contrast, the main impetus was British—not only through the goverment, which built the railways, ports, and irrigation works, but also in the private sector: in foreign trade, plantations, finance, and several industries. But much of the development was carried out by Indians, e.g., the cotton textile industry and other branches. In this process Parsees played a leading part, but Hindus, notably the Marwaris, also had their share. The role of the Muslims was negligible.[55]

In the Middle East the development that took place before 1914 was achieved almost entirely by foreigners or members of minority groups—Armenians, Greeks, Jews, Christian Lebanese, and Syrians. The lack of interest of the Muslim majority—whether Egyptian, Turkish, Arabian, or Iraqi—is striking, and has often been commented upon. Only in Syria, Iran, and Hadramaut is there any evidence of commercial entrepreneurship among Muslims.[56] It may be added that the only country to receive any appreciable immigration was Egypt, which by 1914 had nearly a quarter of a million Europeans and somewhat fewer Armenians, Lebanese, Syrians, and Jews, all of whom played a dominant part in the economy; mention should also be made of Jewish immigration to Palestine.

Conclusion

In drawing conclusions from the foregoing analysis, to see whether there was a specific pattern of economic development in the Middle East, an initial distinction should be made between the Mediterranean portion and the Persian Gulf-Red Sea portion of the region. The latter, which includes Iran, Iraq, Arabia, and the Sudan, was relatively little affected by the changes taking place in the world until the exploitation of oil made of it, suddenly, the center of the Middle East economy. Until the First World War, the impact of the world upon it had been mainly negative since European competition had severely hurt its shipping trade[57] and handicrafts without developing commensurately its other resources.

As for the Mediterranean region, here too there was much diversity, the trends observed being far more advanced in Egypt than in Syria or Turkey; the result of the foregoing discussion may be summarized as follows:

Population—growth probably started earlier than in other underdeveloped regions (including India and Japan) and therefore, even assuming that rates of increase were no higher than elsewhere, may have reached greater overall dimensions; this was certainly true of Egypt and possibly of Syria and Iraq.

Foreign Capital Borrowing—this was extemely high, and the proceeds were largely used unproductively, in contrast to India and Japan.

Transport—regular steamship connections with Europe were established very early; railways were highly developed in Egypt, much less so in Syria and Turkey.

Foreign Trade—growth was rapid, though slower than in Japan and, except for Egypt, slower than in India; however, both in *per capita* terms and as a percentage of gross national product, foreign trade was far greater than in India or Japan.

Agriculture—expansion of output was obtained by the extension of the cultivated area, not by intensification as in Japan. In Egypt even more than in India, irrigation played a leading part.

Industry—Middle Eastern crafts seem to have suffered more from foreign competition than did those of India and Japan; in addition, modern industry came much later.

Education—remarkably little progress was made in this field, probably less than in India, not to mention Japan.

Agents of Growth—these were drawn almost solely from foreign or minority groups, in sharp contrast with Japan and, to a far lesser extent, India.

Underlying the pattern formed by these trends are three basic, and partly interrelated, factors: the region's proximity to Europe and its strategic location, its social and political backwardness, and the nature of foreign economic and political control. To them should be added a fourth: the scarcity of those resources on which industry was based until the end of the nineteenth century, notably water-power, wood, coal, and iron. Almost the only raw material available for industrialization was cotton.

Proximity accounts for the early date at which Europe began to impinge on the economy of the Middle East. It helps to explain the forging of transport links with Europe, the exposure of Middle Eastern handicrafts to devastating foreign competition, the ex-pansion of Middle Eastern agricultural output in response to for-eign demand, and the consequent rapid growth of foreign trade. Proximity may have impelled Europeans to help in establishing quarantines and other hygienic controls in the Middle East, to pre-vent the spread of epidemics, and in this way may have stimulated population growth.[58] It facilitated the migration to the Middle East of European entrepreneurs and technicians, who made an impor-tant contribution to the region's development and imposed on it a certain direction and pattern. And proximity certainly facilitated European economic and political control over the Middle East.[59]

The social and political backwardness of the region helps to ac-count for the nature of its response to the impact of European eco-nomic expansion. Three aspects of this may be distinguished. First, the educational and cultural level of the Middle East was very low, even compared to other underdeveloped regions such as Japan and India, not to mention southeastern Europe and Latin America.[60] Secondly, its social structure was unfavorable for development. For various historical reasons, it had failed to produce a vigorous bour-geoisie and lacked autonomous bodies, such as city states, guilds, and other corporations which could express, and defend, the inter-ests of classes or groups interested in economic development; in-stead, control remained firmly in the hands of the military and ci-vilian bureaucracy. Thirdly, and no doubt at least partly as a con-sequence, the economic ideas and policies of the government were singularly unenlightened. In Europe, the basic tenet of the Mer-cantilists was the need to promote exports in order to increase the output of local industry, and various measures were used to achieve this end. In the Ottoman Empire, however, exports were taxed at a higher rate than imports. Here prevailed a "policy of provision," to use Hecksher's expressive term describing the medieval European attitude. The main objectives were not to promote local production but to meet the fiscal needs of the government and to ensure that the principal towns, and in particular Istanbul, would be adequately supplied. Some signs of a more enlightened policy appeared under Selim III but little came of it. And after that Middle Eastern statesmen, such as Reshid Pasha, swallowed the liberal prescription for economic growth and did little to help the economy until the latter part of the nineteenth century.[61]

The very low educational and cultural level of the Middle East, its social structure, and the form of its political institutions, meant that it had neither a half-way efficient government nor a native bourgeoisie that could take the country's economic development in hand and help to guide its course along the desired path. Hence when it was struck by the Industrial Revolution, with its demand for the exploitation of its raw materials, markets, and transport possibilities, development had to be carried out by Europeans assisted by minority groups—if it was to be achieved at all. But development through such an implanted bourgeoisie had four fatal defects. First, a very large share of the fruits of progress went to foreigners or members of minorities; to take an extreme case, just before the First World War these two groups may have owned 15-20 per cent of Egypt's wealth and absorbed well over 10 per cent of its income. Secondly, the presence of educated foreigners or minority groups weakened the main pressure on the governments for the spread of education and the development of human resources in these countries. Thirdly, the existence and power of this bourgeoisie inhibited the growth of a native Muslim one. Lastly, because of this factor, the whole process of capitalist development in the region remained alien and was regarded as such by its inhabitants, a fact that helps to explain the measures taken against foreigners and minority groups in Turkey in the 1920's and in Egypt in the 1940's-50's. It should be added that in Syria and Lebanon foreigners played a different and far smaller part and development was much more indigenous.

Lastly, as regards foreign economic and political control, in a way the Middle East had the worst of both worlds. Japan, never having lost its full independence, was able to carry out the 1868 revolution and thereafter to guide the economy in the direction demanded by the national interest, as interpreted by the ruling group. India, by contrast, was subjected to outright British control. This had many drawbacks, which have been rightly stressed since the time of Adam Smith. But it had some advantages, which were strikingly foretold by Marx (see his brilliant "The Future Results of British Rule in India," published in the *New York Daily Tribune,* July 1853) though carefully ignored by his followers. After the initial plunder and dislocation, British rule provided honest and efficient administration. It also ensured that the foreign debt was used productively, to build the largest irrigation system in the world and the third largest railway network, and to provide some education, and it transformed the land tenure system. And while not encouraging, and indeed often positively impeding, industrialization it "laid down the material premises" for it.

In the Middle East, however, there was no complete foreign *political* control, except in Aden and in the Sudan after 1896. In the rest of the region there was much influence by rival powers, which jealously watched and checked each other. This led to the abortion of Muhammad 'Ali's attempt at development and of two promising revolutions, the Egyptian in 1882 and the Iranian in 1908-9, and to the stultification of much progress that might otherwise have taken place in Turkey, Iran, and Syria. Even in Egypt the Capitulations and Caisse de la Dette thwarted many of Cromer's reforms.[62] Yet foreign *economic* control was overwhelming and led not only to the buttressing of the existing social order and to the creation of a deep feeling of discouragement but also to the sucking out of vast sums from the region in the form of payments of interest and dividends. This drain, together with the rapid population growth, wars, royal extravagance, and possibly the rise in consumption levels, left little for investment in physical and human capital. The disastrous results of such a situation showed themselves most clearly in Egypt after the First World War, when the limits of cultivation had been reached and terms of trade deteriorated. Fortunately for the Middle East, it got a second chance, in the form of the discovery of the oil resources and a huge amount of foreign aid, and this is enabling it today to carry out a new program of industrialization and modernization of its economy and society.

NOTES

1. *Cambridge Economic History of Europe,* vol. vi, Cambridge 1965, p. 58.
2. *Ibid.,* p. 64.
3. Vera Anstey, *The Economic Development of India,* London 1957, p. 605.

4. *Cambridge Economic History*, p. 65.

5. Gabriel Baer, "Urbanization in Egypt 1820-1907," in W. R. Polk and R. L. Chambers (eds.), *The Beginnings of Modernization in the Middle East*, Chicago 1969.

6. M. S. Hasan, "Growth and Structure of Iraq's Population, 1867-1947," *Bulletin of the Oxford University Institute of Statistics*, xx, 1958.

7. For sources see Charles Issawi, *The Economic History of the Middle East*, Chicago 1966, p. 209.

8. For a fuller discussion see Charles Issawi, "Economic Growth in the Arab World since 1800," *Middle East Economic Papers* (Beirut), 1964.

9. See Issawi, *Economic History*, pp. 332, and 469-70, respectively.

10. See *ibid.*, p. 17.

11. Elliot G. Mears, *Modern Turkey*, New York 1924, p. 580, quoting *Statesman's Yearbook*. This figure is not necessarily incompatible with that of the census of 1927, viz., 13,648,000, in view of Turkey's huge war losses and the exodus of Greeks, Armenians, and others.

12. George Curzon, *Persia and the Persian Question*, London 1892, vol.ii, p. 492.

13. *Ibid.* p. 493, *Encyclopaedia Britannica* (Eleventh Edition), s. v. Persia, and Eteocle Lorini, *La Persia economica*, Rome 1900, p. 378. L. A. Sobotsinskii, *Persia* (St. Petersburg, 1913), p. 12, quotes a "contemporary" (1909) estimate by Medvedev of 10 million.

14. United Nations, *Monthly Bulletin of Statistics*.

15. The corresponding figure for Turkey would be about 10 million in 1890, which would imply a rate of growth of over 15 per thousand between 1890 and 1914; this figure seems too high, and it is therefore probable that the 1890 figure was well above 10 million. By the same token, the 1831 figure may have been somewhat below 10 million.

16. *Op. cit.*, p. 493.

17. See A. E. Crouchley, *The Investment of Foreign Capital in Egyptian Companies and Public Debt*, Cairo 1936, and L. A. Fridman, *Kapitalističeskoye razvitiye Yegipta*, Moscow 1963, p. 13.

18. For details see Issawi, *Economic History*, pp.94-106.

19. For details see Muhammad 'Alī Jamālzāde, *Ganji-i Shāygān*, Berlin A.H. 1335, pp. 98-117. The Russian Discount Bank's capital was 64 million gold roubles and the total value of the Russian property to which the Soviets renounced all claims in 1921 has been put as high as 600 million gold roubles. However, the latter figure includes various military installations and the basis of the valuation is not clear. See S. G. Gorelikov, *Iran*, Moscow 1961, p. 153, citing M. V. Popov, *Amerikanskiy imperializm v Irane*, Moscow 1956, p. 5.

20. See Jamālzāde, *op. cit.*, p. 155, and Sir Percy Sykes, *A History of Persia*, London 1921, vol. ii, p. 523.

21. Issawi, *Economic History*, pp. 94-106, 430-8.

22. J. Farley, *The Resources of Turkey*, London 1862, p. 209.

23. A. E. Crouchley, *The Economic Development of Modern Egypt*, London 1938, p. 142. See also Aḥmad al-Ḥitta, *Tārīkh Miṣr al-iqtiṣādī*, Cairo 1957, and N. Verney and G. Dambmann, *Les Puissances étrangères dans le Levant*, Paris 1900.

24. See Max E. Fletcher, "The Suez Canal and World Shipping," *Journal of Economic History*, 1958.

25. See Richard Hill, *Sudan Transport*, London 1965.

26. See Charles Issawi, "Asymmetrical Development and Transport in Egypt, 1800-1914," in Polk and Chambers (eds.), *op. cit.*

27. Albert H. Imlah, *Economic Elements in the Pax Britannica*, Cambridge, Mass., 1958, pp. 189, 94-8.

28. For details see Issawi, *Economic History*, pp. 363-4.

29. *Ibid.*, p. 30. For Syria the rise may have been of the same order, from say, £500,000 a year, in the 1820's to about £10 million in 1911—both figures referring to sea-borne trade, which rose far more rapidly than land-borne—see *ibid.*, pp. 208-9. For Iraq, Hasan puts average total trade at £438,000 in 1864-71, £1,760,000 in 1880-7, and £6,428,000 in 1912-13— see Muḥammad Salmān Ḥasan, *Al-taṭawwur al-iqtiṣādī fī al-'Irāq*, Beirut n.d., pp. 95 and 223.

30. Marvin L. Entner, *Russo-Persian Commercial Relations, 1828-1914*, Gainesville, Fla., 1965, p. 8.

31. *Ibid.* p. 63.

32. Curzon, *op. cit.*, vol. ii, pp. 562, 582. An earlier estimate had put the Russian share much lower. Even after doubling the figure for Persian imports from Russia, to take account of smuggling, total trade between the two countries in 1852-7 was put at 4.4 million thalers, out of a total Persian trade estimated at 42 million, or £6.3 million; however, the latter figure, which includes estimates for trade with Central Asia, may be somewhat too high. See Ernst Otto Blau, *Commerzielle Zustände Persiens*, Berlin 1858, pp. 164-5.

The League of Nations, *International Statistical Yearbook, 1928*, Geneva 1929, put Iran's imports in 1913 at $55 million and its exports at $38 million, or a total of $93 million (about £19 million). This would imply a three-fold increase in current prices in the sixty years preceding the First World War. Since price levels in the 1850's were close to those prevailing in 1913, the increase in real terms must also have been about three-fold.

Some increase must also have taken place in the first half of the nineteenth century. This is suggested by the fact that in 1831-56 trade through Trabzon, almost all of which was in transit to or from Iran, multiplied twelve-fold (Blau, *op. cit.*, pp. 235-6). In the early 1850's Trabzon accounted for almost half of Iran's imports and a sixth of its exports.

Earlier figures are contradictory. In 1834 J. B. Fraser estimated Iran's total trade with Europe, including Russia, at £1 million (*ibid., p. 165*). In 1836, W. Stuart put Britain's exports to Iran at just over £1 million and stated that Russia's were two-thirds higher (Curzon, *op. cit.*, vol. ii, p. 564).

33. See Issawi, *Economic History*, Part V, Introduction, and Part VII, Introduction.

34. Liverpool East India Committee, quoted in I. Durga Parshad, *Some Aspects of Indian Foreign Trade, 1757-1893*, London 1932, p. 132.

35. *Ibid.* p. 215.

36. Bank of Japan, *Historical Statistics of the Japanese Economy* (1966).

37. See Issawi, "Asymmetrical Development"; the foreign trade and population figures were taken from the League of Nations *Statistical Yearbook*, 1928.

38. For details see Issawi, "Economic Growth"; also Hla Myint, *The Economics of the Developing Countries*, London 1964, chapter 3.

39. See A. E. Crouchley, "A Century of Economic Development," *L'Egypte Contemporaine*, (Cairo) 1939, and E. R. J. Owen, "Cotton Production and the Development of the Egyptian Economy," D. Phil. Thesis, Oxford University, 1965.

40. See Robert L. Tignor, *Modernization and British Colonial Rule in Egypt*, Princeton N. J., 1966, Chapter 7.

41. See Anstey, *op. cit.*, chapter 7.

42. See chart in U. S. Department of Agriculture, *Agriculture in 26 Developing Nations, 1948 to 1963*, Washington D. C., p. 45. The most recent discussion of this question is in James I. Nakamura, *Agricultural Production and the Economic Development of Japan, 1873-1922*, Princeton, N. J., 1966.

43. Anstey, *op. cit.*, p. 207. However, the following judgment by a highly qualified scholar should be noted. "The vast expansion of British cloth exports to India skimmed off the expanding demand. The handloom weavers were at least no fewer in number and no worse off economically at the end of the period than at the beginning. . . The traditional sector, generally speaking, did not decline absolutely in economic significance," Morris D. Morris, "Towards a Reinterpretation of Nineteenth-Century Indian Economic History," *Journal of Economic History*, 1963.

44. See Issawi, *Economic History*, pp. 38-59, 542-60. For Muhammad 'Ali's attempt at industrialization see *ibid.*, pp. 389-402.

45. See Anstey, *op. cit.*, chapter 9. *Cambridge Economic History*, pp. 908-19, and Krishan Saini, "Some measures of the economic growth of India, 1860-1913," unpublished paper, Columbia University.

46. See *Cambridge Economic History*, pp. 875-99, and William W. Lockwood, *The Economic Development of Japan*, Princeton N.J., 1954.

47. See Owen, *op. cit.*, and Issawi, *Economic History*, p. 365.

48. I. M. Smilianskaya, "*Razloženiye feodalnikh otnoshenii. . .* ,"translated in *ibid.*, pp. 226-47, and Dominique Chevallier, "Western Development and Eastern Crisis in the Mid-Nineteenth Century," in Polk and Chambers (eds.), *op. cit.*

49. Nikki R. Keddie, *Historical Obstacles to Agrarian Change in Iran*, Claremont Asian Studies, Claremont, California, 1960, p. 4. See also A. K. S. Lambton, *Landlord and Peasant in Persia*, London, 1953, pp. 143-5.

50. Morris, *op. cit.;* see also Anstey, *op. cit.,* chapter xvi. However, there is evidence of distinct progress in the forty or fifty years preceding the First World War—see Saini, *op. cit.*

51. Lockwood, *op. cit.,* pp. 34, 138-50.

52. Herbert Passin, *Society and Education in Japan,* New York 1965, p.11— for details see Issawi, "Asymmetrical Development."

53. At that time Robert College drew its students almost solely from minority groups—see Mears, *op. cit.,* chapter 5.

54. Only one field was at first dominated by foreigners, the export trade. But even here, "by 1913 the bulk of overseas commerce was handled by Japanese firms, and half of it already moved in Japanese ships," Lockwood, *op. cit.,* p. 329.

55. See Morris, *op. cit.,* pp. 109-17, and D. H. Buchannan, *The Development of Capitalistic Enterprise in India,* New York 1934, chapters vii-xiii.

56. See Issawi, *Economic History,* pp. 114-25, 505-13, Jamālzāde, *op cit.,* pp. 93-117.

57. Thus the total tonnage of vessels from the Persian Gulf entering Indian ports rose from nearly 100,000 tons per annum in the late 1850's to over 200,000 in the early 1900's and then fell well below its original level by the First World War—see *Statistical Abstract Relating to British India.* Since these figures cover not only Arab and Persian craft but British and other steamers plying between India and the Gulf, the fall in the former must have been very great. The same occurred in the Red Sea region.

58. For a detailed study see Robert Tignor, "Public Health Administration under British Rule, 1882-1914," unpublished doctoral dissertation, Yale University, 1960. Rudimentary quarantines were established in several Ottoman ports in the first half of the nineteenth century.

59. The following judgment deserves consideration: "Had Japan been situated in closer proximity to the great industrialized nations of the West, her pattern of growth and structural change after 1868 would probably have been somewhat different. Both the pressure to industrialize, and the opportunity to do so, might have been somewhat diminished. She would have enjoyed more favorable access to large external markets for her coal, marine products, and high-value farm crops. Western consumer manufactures might also have competed more strongly in Japan than was the case, delaying the progress of industry." Lockwood, *op. cit.,* p.353.

60. See Issawi, "Asymmetrical Development."

61. *Idem, Economic History,* pp. 52-3.

62. Another important factor was the restrictions imposed on the Middle Eastern governments by international commercial conventions, which prevented them from giving tariff protection to their industries. But these restrictions had their counterpart in India and, until 1899, in Japan.

12
The Bases of Arab Unity

The unity of the Arabs, like that of most other national groups, is that of a people inhabiting a definite stretch of territory, bound by ties of kinship, speaking a common language, sharing common historical memories, and practicing a common way of life, expressed in the form of religion and other cultural traits. As Sir Hamilton Gibb put it, the Arabs are "a people clustered around an historical memory." He goes on to say: "To the question 'who are Arabs?' there is—whatever ethnographers may say—only one answer which approaches historic truth: all those are Arabs for whom the central fact of history is the mission of Mohammad and the memory of the Arab Empire, and who in addition cherish the Arabic tongue and its cultural heritage as their common possession."[1]

The Islamic Society

The Arab World—to use a grandiose but widely current, useful, and revealing term—is a segment of a wider cultural area designated by Professor Toynbee as the Islamic Society, and its nature and unifying bonds can be best understood by first examining those of the larger unit. Briefly put, the unity of Islamic Society is the result of a long historical process operating on a broadly homogeneous physical environment.

The outstanding characteristic of the physical environment is its aridity. A glance at the maps prepared by Unesco[2] shows that the bulk of the Islamic Society falls within the huge arid area stretching from the Atlantic Ocean to China.[3] And within this region, the Arab world occupies the driest of all. Over two-fifths of the total area of the Arab world is classified as "extremely arid," defined as areas in which "at least twelve consecutive months without rainfall have been recorded;" another two-fifths is "arid," i.e., "rainfall is not adequate for crop production"; and the bulk of the remaining part is "semi-arid," i.e., "rainfall is insufficient for certain types of crops and grass is an important element of the natural vegetation unless overgrazing has replaced it with brush." The only parts of the region which receive adequate rainfall are generally too hilly

Reprinted with permission from *International Affairs*, vol. XXXI, No. 1, January 1955.

to be suitable for large-scale cultivation, viz., the Alawite, Lebanese, and Palestinian mountain ranges, the highlands of Yemen, and the Atlas mountains and their foothills in North Africa.

The aridity of the region has important economic, social, and political consequences. In the first place, agriculture, and consequently the formation of large and stable societies, is confined to relatively exiguous strips of land lying on the windward sides of mountains or in river valleys or oases; and, whereas in humid zones agriculture and animal husbandry are integrated in a system of "mixed farming," in the arid zone shortage of water and population pressure have made it essential to devote available land to raising food crops—or, exceptionally, high value industrial crops—rather than fodder crops which, when converted into meat, have a much lower calorific content than have grains. Between the islands of cultivation lie large stretches of steppe or desert where rainfall is inadequate for agriculture but where the existence of scrub makes it possible to raise sheep and camels; this has brought into being no-madic shepherd tribes whose complex relations with the sedentary cultivators constitute one of the main *leit-motifs* of the region.

Another important aspect is the uncertainty of rainfall and its heavy concentration in the short winter season.[4] The resulting great variability in crop yields makes the position of the smaller cultivators highly precarious. In addition, a series of droughts, not uncommon in the region, may easily result in ruin or even famine for thousands of peasants. Hence the smaller cultivators, who are chronically indebted to landlords or city merchants, tend to lose their land and to be reduced to the status of tenants. In other words, aridity is one of the main factors making for unequal distribution of land.[5]

The historical forces which, originating in the Middle East, have shaped the Islamic Society go back to the very dawn of history. From the earliest times, the river valleys of the Nile and Tigris-Euphrates[6] radiated their culture to surrounding lands, especially Syria. Later Egyptian, Hittite, Assyrian, and Babylonian conquests led to an interchange of customs and ideas which was greatly accelerated by the large-scale deportations and exchanges of population carried out by the Assyrians and Babylonians.

Iran brought the whole of the Middle East under its sway and gave it a common administration and an excellent system of roads. The Greek conquest gave it a common tongue which it used for 1,000 years, and a common basis of philosophy and science. Rome provided the western half of the region with a remarkably efficient administration and an incomparable system of law. After overcoming its rival, Mithraism, Christianity swept over the Ancient East, west of Iran, and established itself as the dominant religion with an organized and centralized hierarchy.

The unifying effect of Christianity can hardly be overestimated, for it was the first popular force to arise in the region, the first which struck deep roots in the masses. And, because of that, it was able to give the death blow to such old and moribund civilizations as the Egyptian and Babylonian, thus clearing the ground for the emergence of a new civilization.

The final form of this new civilization, which had been slowly emerging from underneath the layer of Greco-Roman culture which for 1,000 years covered the Middle East,[7] was provided by Islam. Pushing East, Islam once more united the destinies of Iran to those of the Fertile Crescent, and penetrated to Central Asia. But Islam did more: it finally split the Mediterranean into two halves, the northern Christian and the southern Muslim, each with its own distinctive civilization. For many centuries Asia Minor lay in the Christian half, but the Ottoman conquest brought it into the Islamic orbit; indeed it made of it, for a few centuries, the center of Islam.

The first unifying factor, then, is the Islamic religion, the faith of the overwhelming majority of the inhabitants of the Middle East. Even the Shi'i national revolution in Iran, in the sixteenth century, did not quite succeed in splitting the unity of the Islamic world.

The second connecting link has been the Arab caliphate and later the Ottoman Empire. The latter never included Iran or Afghanistan, but, for nearly four centuries, it kept the rest of the Middle East under a single rule. Moreover, the Ottoman Empire took over most of the administrative and social structure built by its predecessors, as they had done with the work of their predecessors. Hence the political, social, and even administrative continuity in the Middle East countries.

Particularly noteworthy is the existence of a legal code common to all the Islamic countries, the Shari'a or Muslim Canon Law. The Shari'a has colored the Islamic Society at least as deeply as English Common Law has colored the Anglo-Saxon world and of all the unifying forces it is perhaps the most powerful.

The Islamic countries have another important heritage: a common scholastic culture. This culture, in which are to be found Greek,

Persian, Aramaic, and other elements, was elaborated between about A.D. 800 and 1200, mainly in Damascus, Baghdad, and Cairo, and diffused throughout the Muslim world. Until less than a hundred years ago it formed the sole equipment of the educated classes, and it is still the basis of the culture of the masses. Together with religion and law it has given the Islamic world its unity and its unique character.

The medieval scholastic culture was diffused through the Arabic language, until about the twelfth century the sole medium of science, literature, and thought. The rise of Persian, and subsequently Turkish, national literatures broke up this linguistic unity, but Arabic continued to be the language of religion and law, and abstract and scientific terms have continued to be taken from Arabic roots. It is not too fanciful to say that, if Persian has been the French or Italian of one half of the Islamic Society,[8] Arabic has been the Latin of the whole. As Sir Hamilton Gibb put it: "It is a strange phenomenon that while Islam began as a protest against Arab culture and tradition as a whole, by the end of this [early Abbassid] period the literary heritage of ancient Arabia was indissolubly linked up with Islam, to be carried with it to the ends of the old world."[9]

Cultural Unity of the Arab World

The mark which distinguishes the Arab world from other segments of the Islamic Society is the fact that, within the former, Arabic is a living language. The reason why only part of the Islamic Society has been Arabized is—in addition to the fact that religion is less earthbound and more mobile than nationalism—to be found in a combination of geographic and historical factors. A glance at the map shows that the Arab world is bounded by well defined natural frontiers:[10] the Sahara and Indian Ocean, the Atlantic Ocean, the Mediterranean, and the Taurus and Zagros mountains.[11] Most of these frontiers have formed very effective barriers to the permanent expansion of Arabism, though they have not prevented frequent raids and even short-term conquests. There is little Arabism, though much Islam, south of the Sahara, except along the East coast of Africa, where direct access by sea from southern Arabia was possible. Anatolia resisted all Arab assaults and was later Islamized by the Turks. Iran, although conquered by the Arabs, was not assimilated by them and soon reasserted its individuality and shook off their political as well as cultural domination while evolving its own peculiar form of Islam.

The two most porous frontiers of the Arab world have been the Nile Valley and the western Mediterranean. In the first, the boundaries of Arabism are very difficult to draw, since a gradually shading continuum unites Egypt to the Negro Southern Sudan, passing through Nubia and the Arab-speaking Muslim Northern Sudan. The western Mediterranean witnessed the establishment across its narrow straits of two flourishing centers of Arab civilization in Sicily and Spain—a phenomenon further discussed below.

Another physical feature of the Arab world may be noted—its flatness. It is worthy of note that its only non-Arabic speaking inhabitants, the Kurds and the Berbers, dwell in its mountainous extremities and that the Syrian and Lebanese mountains shelter religious minorities whose attachment to Arabism is not completely unqualified. It is significant that Ibn Khaldun entitled one of the chapters of his *Prolegomena* "Arabs Conquer only Plains."[12]

The historical process which eventually led to the Arabization of this huge region may be described as its filling up with the sediments left by the successive Semitic waves which have broken over it during the last five or six millennia. It is believed that, in the fourth millennium B.C., a Semitic people from Arabia amalgamated with the indigenous population of the Nile Valley to form the Egyptian civilization while another migration of Semites merged with the Sumerians of Mesopotamia to produce the Babylonian civilization. During the next millennium the Canaanites occupied Palestine and Syria and the Phoenicians settled on the Lebanese coast. In the second millennium B.C. the Hebrews and Aramaeans conquered Palestine and Syria and during the following millennium the Nabataeans installed themselves in those two countries.[13] And in between the more spectacular conquests and mass migrations there were constant infiltrations from the desert into the Fertile Crescent and Nile Valley.

Some of these Semitic peoples migrated farther afield, spreading their culture to a large part of the Mediterranean. The outstanding example is the Phoenicians who, either directly or through their daughter colony of Carthage, established trading ports and cities in Malta, Sicily, and southern and eastern Spain, and closely controlled the North African coast from Sirte to beyond the straits of

Gibraltar.[14] Another factor was the migration of Jews all over the Mediterranean. And, still more important, was the spread of Christianity, a Semitic religion which in some countries, for example Egypt, dissolved the old cultures and prepared the ground for more purely Semitic Islam. The importance of these factors was revealed by the help given to the Arab invaders by the heretical Christians of Egypt, by the Maltese, and by the Spanish Jews.

It is surely not fortuitous that, at its height, the Arabic-speaking Islamic civilization coincided almost exactly with the limits of Semitic culture. Its north-eastern borders were the Taurus-Zagros mountains, which had always formed an effective barrier to Semitic expansion, and its north-western frontiers were those Mediterranean lands, Sicily, Malta, and south-eastern Spain, which had been most deeply impregnated with Semitic influences.[15] Its spread along the eastern African coast was preceded by extensive trading between that region and southern Arabia in pre-Islamic times, accompanied by some migration.

The Arab conquest, the latest of the Semitic invasions, was facilitated by a long period of infiltration which led to the establishment of the Arab Kingdoms of Ghassan in Syria and Lakhm in Iraq. It was followed by innumerable migrations of tribes into these and other neighboring countries. As a result, Syria, Iraq, Transjordan, Palestine, and, to a lesser extent, Lebanon were, over the course of centuries, markedly Arabized in race and completely Arabized in language. Egypt was much less affected ethnically, since the Arab conquerors either lived in the cities or camped on the fringes of cultivation; moreover the extreme aridity of the Egyptian desert (even judged by Middle Eastern standards) makes it incapable of supporting a large nomadic population: nevertheless, Egypt has been linguistically and culturally Arabized. In North Africa, conditions vary, Libya and Tunisia being much more Arabized than Algeria and Morocco. In the latter, the Berber language and Berber culture are still very powerful,[16] and it is possible that they would still be dominant but for the eleventh-century invasion of the Banu Hilal and Banu Sulaim, who caused much havoc and set North Africa back in its cultural development but printed it on a deep Arabic stamp.[17]

The degree of cultural unity attained by the Arab world in the Middle Ages may be judged from the career of Ibn Khaldun, who passed with the utmost ease from North Africa to Spain, Egypt, and Syria, occupying in each place an important political or judicial position. Similar examples could be quoted by the dozen.

Political Disunity of the Arab World

The political disunity of the Arab world is no less evident than its cultural unity. Following the breakdown of the Omayyad Empire, it rapidly disintegrated into separate and hostile entities. For four centuries the Ottoman Empire imposed a large measure of unity but this was succeeded by total disintegration brought about by the Treaty of Versailles. Today, there are no less than eight sovereign Arab States and, including the Sudan, the two zones of Morocco and Tangier, twelve protected areas or colonies.

This disunity is to be explained by geographical, historical, socio-economic, and political factors. First of all, there is the great length of the Arab world. From the western corner of Morocco to the eastern tip of Arabia it stretches across seventy degrees of longitude and has a maximum length of over 4,300 miles. This length is not matched by corresponding depth since the vast desert spaces are mainly empty. In terms of population—a more significant criterion than area—the Arab world takes the shape of a very long, extremely thin, sprawling band.

To these defects of structure must be added those of texture. The Arab world has been aptly likened to an archipelago, and a glance at a vegetation map[18] shows by what vast barren spaces the small islands of cultivation and settlement are separated. Now an archipelago can be held together, but only by a power which commands the seas,[19] and similarly the Arab world was held together only by such a strong State as the Omayyad Empire, which drew upon the enthusiasm and energy of the initial Arab conquest. At best of times, a series of discrete centers such as those inhabited by the Arabs is much more difficult to unite than a continuum of habitation, such as France or England.

The difficulty is aggravated by inadequate communications. Not only are the density of roads and railways, and the relative number of motor cars, radios, and telephones, lower than in more advanced countries[20] but existing road and railway networks are not always adapted to local needs. As in other underdeveloped areas, much of the transport system was built by foreigners and was designed primarily to facilitate export trade; in doing so it undoubtedly advanced the development of the region, but did not do much to draw together its constituent parts. In spite of the progress of the last fifteen years, communications between most Arab countries are either poor or roundabout or non-existent. It should be added that the facts mentioned in the two preceding paragraphs stand in the way of the development of the transport system. For, other things being equal, it is easier to provide a compact area than an equal elongated area with an adequate rail and road network. And, secondly, it is expensive, and sometimes prohibitive, to build a railway (or even a road) between two productive centers separated by a large empty space: a good example is the absence of the often mooted Baghdad-Damascus railway.

These geographical factors only partly explain the lack of economic and social integration. Two different aspects may be distinguished: lack of integration within each Arab country, and lack of integration between different Arab countries. As regards the first, low production, inadequacy of transport, and general underdevelopment mean that a large proportion of the population lives in a subsistence economy, retaining the bulk of its produce for its own consumption and resorting to the market very seldom, whether for purchase or sale. In other words division of labor—one of the most powerful sources making for social integration—has been carried out to only a limited extent. It may be added that in recent years economic development has been drawing the inhabitants of the Arab world into the market economy at an accelerating rate.

Three other social factors may be mentioned in this context. In the past, the distinction between town and country was sharper in the Middle East than in Europe and relations between the two were looser.[21] Although this state of affairs is also changing, it has left its mark on the mentality of the Middle Eastern peoples. Secondly, there remains the great gap between the nomadic and settled populations. In all Middle Eastern countries nomads continue to lead a life separate from that of the rest of the community. Attempts are being made to integrate the nomads, by enforcing the authority of the State, by providing some health and educational services, and by encouraging settlement, but so far only a limited measure of success has been achieved. Lastly, there are the deep cleavages between religious communities. Owing to the intensity of the religious and denominational feeling of Middle Easterners, this factor has a more divisive effect than in Europe or the United States.

As regards the second aspect, namely, the lack of integration between Arab countries, it may be attributed to inadequacy of communications, low level of production, the large part played by foreigners in the economic development of the region and the political history of the last seventy years. The first two factors need no elaboration; the lack of a surplus for exchange and of the means to transport this surplus largely account for the low level of trade between Arab countries. Less obvious, but hardly less important, has been the fact that the economic development of the region was largely carried out by foreign capital and enterprise. The economy of each Arab country was thus geared to that of the industrial complex of Western Europe. Each concentrated on one or two agricultural or mineral raw material exports, receiving in exchange the manufactured goods, raw materials, and foodstuffs which it needed. One effect of this phenomenon was that economic progress remained strictly localized within countries, such as Egypt; or even within subdivisions of countries, for instance the palm groves of Iraq and the mining districts of North Africa. The only important exception has been the petroleum industry of Iraq and Arabia. This generated a huge income in countries with very few complementary resources capable of absorbing that income; it also involved the laying of pipelines to the Mediterranean coast; as a result some income has spilled over into neighboring countries, particularly into Lebanon.

The general development and the improvement of transport following the First World War should have led to a greater measure of exchange between the Arab countries. But, precisely at that moment, formidable barriers made themselves felt, in the shape of new political frontiers. The British, French, Spaniards, and Italians divided among themselves Arab Africa and the British and French, Arab Asia. Different currencies, linked to those of the Metropolitan Powers, circulated in the various Arab countries and customs barriers impeded trade between these countries. Nor did matters improve with the attaining of independence by the eastern Arab States since, for a long time, they continued to practice economic nationalism. Indeed, in certain respects, there was further disintegration. "As each country gained political independence, it sought to promote its economic well-being through policies designed to develop its own resources as fully as possible. Preoccupied with its own economic problems, no government has modified either its course of action or its plans in the light of developments in other parts of the region. This tendency continued after the Second World War. Under the mandates there were no tariff barriers between Lebanon, Palestine, Syria, and Transjordan, but the achievement of independence broke the monetary and fiscal ties holding some of these areas together. In 1950 the customs union between Lebanon and Syria was brought to an end."[22]

The economic disintegration brought about by foreign rule was accompanied by political and cultural disintegration. Each country, absorbed in its own struggle against a specific foreign government, tended to isolate itself from the others. In each, different foreign traditions and methods began to implant themselves—French in Syria and Lebanon, British in Iraq and Palestine, Italian in Libya, Spanish in Morocco. Education in foreign schools and universities produced very different values, prejudices, and ways of thought. Not least important, in each country dynastic, political, and administrative vested interests arose, whose position stood to suffer from a merger of their country in a bigger whole.

As a result of all these natural and man-made barriers and partitions when, both under the influence of European ideologies and in obedience to its own laws of development, the Arab world began to experience nationalism that feeling took two forms. On the one hand there was pan-Arabism, a movement aiming at uniting all Arab countries. And on the other hand there were various local movements, which sprouted wherever there was a sufficiently large physical basis and population for them to take root. The most noteworthy of the latter are Egyptian, Iraqi, Moroccan, and Tunisian nationalism, all of which correspond to old and well defined units. In the Levant, nationalism is more ambiguous and complex, because of the broken nature of the area and of the various cross-divisions within it; four main trends may be discerned: Syrian nationalism in its narrowest sense, corresponding to the present borders of the Syrian Republic; its counterpart, Lebanese nationalism; Greater Syrian nationalism, which aims at the union of geographical Syria, i.e., Syria, Lebanon, Jordan, and Palestine; and the Fertile Crescent movement, which seeks to unite geographical Syria and Iraq. It may be mentioned that, up to the present, local nationalisms have been more vigorous than pan-Arabism. This is not suprising in view of the fact that they have a more solid historical base, correspond to strong traditional parochial sentiments, are backed by powerful dynastic, political, and economic vested interests, and offer to aspiring statesmen and reformers an outlet for immediate practical work.

Prospects of Arab Unity

At this point it might be concluded that the centrifugal forces in the region are so strong that Arab unity is a dream impossible to fulfill. But such a judgment would be erroneous, since it ignores the no less powerful centripetal forces.

Of these the first, and most binding, are the cultural factors mentioned above, the community of language, religion, and way of life. It is doubtful whether the pull of religion within the Arab world has appreciably weakened in recent times. That of language has, if anything, increased; for with the spread of literacy the number of those who have access to classical Arabic, the *lingua franca* of the Arabs, is rapidly growing. And as more people read the Arabic classics, as well as contemporary works published in other Arab countries, their sense of kinship with the inhabitants of other parts of the Arab world becomes stronger and stronger. This is being reinforced by the speedy development of transport and communications between Arab countries, especially the radio and cinema.

The impact of recent economic and cultural development on the Arab way of life has been more complex. Its initial effect was that some parts of the Arab world, notably Egypt and Lebanon, pulled so far ahead of the rest that they came to feel that they lived in different worlds. More recently, however, the situation has begun to change. The main factor has been the discovery of oil, which is enabling Iraq and the Arabian peninsula States to draw abreast of the more advanced countries. Another factor which may eventually work in the same direction is the heavy capital investment now taking place in North Africa.

Economic development is also acting in another way to draw the Arab countries together. As they advance beyond the level of a subsistence economy, the diversity of their resources stands more clearly revealed, and with it the possibility of complementarity and the necessity of cooperation. Thus, to take only the eastern Arab countries, the oil producers can offer fuel and capital; Iraq, Syria, and the Sudan have vast land and water resources; Egypt has industrial and agricultural skills; and Lebanon can provide unmatched business enterprise, as well as the most pleasant climate to be found

in the region. The realization of the possibilities offered by cooperation has, very recently, resulted in the taking of some noteworthy
measures, notably a payments and preferential customs agreement
which, having been ratified by four States, entered into force in 1953.
Other very important proposals include an Arab Development Bank,
whose capital would be subscribed to by all Arab States, an Arab
Navigation Company, the reconstruction of the Hejaz railway, and
the building of an Arab highway linking Kuwait, Saudi Arabia, Iraq,
Jordan, Syria, and Lebanon.

Lastly, there are the political factors. Arabs have begun to realize
that, although their individual states are insignificant, a combination of well over 60 million persons, controlling the southern half
of the Mediterranean and both its eastern approaches, as well as
almost half the world's oil deposits could—provided it developed
its natural and human resources—come to count in world affairs.
This realization led, in 1945, to the establishment of the Arab League.
So far, the League has impressed outsiders more with its weaknesses
than its strength, but its very survival is a triumph for pan-Arab
public opinion, which carried with it the reluctant governments
of the Arab countries. And it must not be forgotten that, although
its political achievements have not been brilliant and its real interest
in economics is very recent, it has done some good work in the cultural field. The latter includes much interchange of teachers as well
as the holding of inter-Arab congresses of lawyers, doctors, engineers, educators, etc., all of which is helping to bring the countries
closer together.

It is not the purpose of this essay to predict whether the centrifugal forces will overcome the centripetal. On the one hand, political and economic self-interest—in some countries even survival—
call for integration in a larger unit.[23] On the other hand there are
well-entrenched vested interests and strong parochialisms—fo-
mented, wherever possible, by foreign Powers. And with every day
that passes local vested interests gain in strength; to take only one
example, the establishment of identical industries such as cotton
textiles and sugar refineries in Egypt, Lebanon, Syria, and Iraq has
brought into being one more opponent of integration. It is thus
clear that the unification of the Arab countries, if it is to come, will
have to be brought about by the conscious and sustained efforts of
the Arab governments and peoples. The blind forces of geography,
the impetus of history, and even the cohesive ties of language and

culture do not, by themselves, automatically ensure unity. This is not the place to discuss the measures required for unification, but it may be repeated that what is needed is not only integration between the various countries but also integration within each country. In other words unification requires, among other things, a far-reaching transformation designed to democratize Arab society, develop its natural resources, and raise the economic, social, and intellectual level of its members.

In may be pointed out, in conclusion, that unification is not necessarily an either-or choice. Between the two extremes of complete unity, which at the present time is not practical, and complete independence for each State, which is clearly undesirable, lie several possibilities. Some of the smaller countries may band together in a federation and the units so established may enter into confederal relations with other Arab units. For, to return to the starting point of this essay, although the term "Arab World" is rather grandiose it does reveal the fact that the entity so designated is vast and complex. And it is unlikely that the solution appropriate for such an entity is a simple cut-and-dried formula borrowed from foreign cultures with a vastly different political experience.

Afterword, 1981

More than twenty-five years have passed since the foregoing essay was written, and the central problems posed in it still remain unchanged: the push and pull of centrifugal forces. Four sets of events, however, profoundly affected the balance of forces at work: the independence of the remaining Arab colonies; the huge increase in oil revenues; the spread of education and the mass media; and the relative decline of Egypt. The sheer passage of time has also reinforced the factors making for the perpetuation of the *status quo*, by strengthening loyalties and entrenching vested interests still deeper.

The achievement of independence by Morocco, Tunisia, Algeria, Sudan, and the smaller countries of the Arabian peninsula—and one might add Libya, even though its independence dates from 1951—more than doubled the number of Arab states. In addition, Mauritania and Somalia have joined the Arab league. Some of these countries, notably Algeria, Tunisia, Libya, and Kuwait, have played a very active role in inter-Arab politics. And several of them have brought with them new concerns, for example with sub-Saharan

Africa, and different approaches to international problems. As regards the centrifugal and centripetal forces at work, this increase in numbers works both ways. On the one hand, the multiplication of protagonists has complicated the process and made a simple solution, such as unity, that much more difficult. But, on the other, it may now be easier for any given small state to envisage entry into a union consisting of numerous entities, since the probability of their combining against it is lower than if their number had been smaller and since the wider diversity of interests due to greater numbers means that there are more "cross-cutting" interests that prevent a line-up against any one state. More particularly, in 1955, Arab unity inevitably meant leadership, or even domination, by Egypt, which towered above all the other states. Today, however, several states equal or surpass Egypt in some of the main constituents of power. The rise of these countries increases the number of choices, and thus may make it somewhat easier for the Arabs to envisage some form of unity.

The huge increase in oil revenues, which has so greatly enhanced the importance of the Arab world as a whole, also works both ways. Since oil is produced mainly in what used to be the poorer and less socially developed parts of the Arab world—the Arabian peninsula, Iraq, and Libya—it has raised the economic level of those countries and partly bridged the gap between them and their more advanced neighbors, thus making it easier to envisage some kind of union between them. In addition, oil revenues have made such a union much more urgent—indeed some would say imperative—since the producing countries have an abundance of capital, which they cannot fully absorb because of the lack of complementary resources, while the others suffer from a great shortage of capital but are endowed with such factors of production as labor (Egypt, Jordan, Lebanon, Syria, Tunisia, Morocco) and land (Sudan, Iraq). But, against that, oil has created a discrepancy between rich and poor states in the region far wider than anything that ever existed before, and the prospect of rich states agreeing to pool their enormous wealth, as distinct from handing out small portions of it to carefully chosen recipients, is very remote. Perhaps the most that the "unifiers" can hope from oil is the following. First, the flow of funds from the oil producers to the other countries—in the form of government to government grants and loans, loans from various Arab funds, and private investment—runs into the tens of billions of dollars. Much of this has been productively invested, bringing the income of the recipients a little closer to that of the donors. Secondly, oil incomes have generated a demand for goods from other Arab countries, more particularly Egypt, Lebanon, Jordan, and Syria, and raised the level of inter-Arab trade, which, however, still constitutes under five percent of the combined foreign trade of the Arab countries. Thirdly, oil incomes and the shortage of both skilled and unskilled labor in the producing countries had, by 1979, drawn in some 2,000,000 Arabs: North and South Yemenis, Egyptians, Jordanians, Syrians, Lebanese, and Sudanese to the Gulf countries and Egyptians, Tunisians, and Moroccans to Libya. The remittances these emigrants send are a major item in the balance of payments of the recipient countries, and the services they provide cannot be dispensed with by the host countries; thus they are forging a strong economic link binding almost all the Arab states. Fourthly, oil wealth has enabled the Arabs to establish certain joint projects, like the Arab Monetary Fund, the Arab Petroleum Investments Company, the Arab Maritime Petroleum Transport Company, and the Arab Shipbuilding and Repairs Yard Company; it has also given the Arabs an opportunity to work together in such institutions as the Organization of Petroleum Exporting Countries (OPEC), the Organization of Arab Petroleum Exporting Countries (OAPEC), the Arab Fund for Economic and Social Development, the Islamic Development Fund, and the numerous national funds (Kuwaiti, Saudi, Abu Dhabi, Iraqi) that recruit their staff from many countries and cooperate with the nationals of the various states to which they have given loans. Lastly, the hope of tapping incomes generated by oil and obtaining access to the markets of the oil producers probably accounts for the—albeit very limited—success of the Arab Common Market, which grants tariff preferences to the participating states.

The third factor, the spread of education and the mass media, has strengthened the centripetal forces in three ways. First, it has greatly narrowed the formerly wide gap between the cultural level of the more advanced countries (Egypt and Lebanon, followed by Syria, Jordan, and Tunisia) and the other Arab lands. The remarkable educational progress of the more backward countries, notably Kuwait, Iraq, Libya, Algeria, and Saudi Arabia, has raised the proportion of their children attending school to equal, or exceed, that of the more advanced countries. Some of their universities compare very favorably with those of Egypt and Lebanon. Kuwait has also emerged as a publishing center that challenges the former monopoly of Cairo and Beirut. In other words, the cultural levels of most of the Arab countries are far closer today than they were twenty or thirty years ago, removing one of the bigger obstacles to unity. In addition, literacy has spread rapidly, from less than twenty percent of the total adult Arab population to not much below fifty. This has a special importance in the Arab world, where written Arabic is almost identical from Morocco to Oman but where the spoken language varies greatly and beyond a certain distance becomes unintelligible, e.g., to an Egyptian or Syrian in Algeria or Morocco. The spread of literacy is making it possible for a much larger proportion of Arabs to communicate with each other than ever before. This process of intercommunication is also being facilitated by the spread of newspapers, radio broadcasts, films, and television. And one may assume—without, of course, any conclusive proof—that closer contact will lead to a greater desire to draw together politically.

Lastly, there is the decline of Egypt. Egypt was, and perhaps still is, for many reasons the leader of the Arab world and until recently no other country was in a position to challenge it. It is located in the center of the community composing the Arab League, between the 46 million North Africans (inhabiting 2.2 million square miles), the 22 million Africans (inhabiting 1.2 million square miles), and the 45 million Asians (inhabiting 1.5 million square miles). Its population of over 40 million still constitutes over a quarter of that of the Arab League members—thirty years ago it formed two-fifths. It had been a modern going concern since the early nineteenth century and had developed the earliest and most efficient political and administrative organization and by far the largest army. Its Gross National Product probably exceeded the combined total of those of all the other members of the League, and its foreign trade almost equalled that of all the others. Except for Lebanon, whose level was high but whose scale was much smaller, it had a virtual monopoly of higher education, book publishing, journalism, and films, and its books, newspapers, and films were eagerly sought all over the Arab world. Again, except for Lebanon, it alone had a surplus of teachers and technicians, who were sent in large numbers to other countries. It alone had an élite that was experienced in government and international diplomacy. Its national identity was far more firmly established than that of any other Arab country. And, until the late 1960's, its position was further enhanced by the appeal of Nasser to the other Arabs, which persisted longer and to a greater degree than his appeal to the Egyptians themselves.

But even at its most powerful, Egypt was rather uneasy and clumsy in dealing with the other Arabs, and today its position is far weaker. First of all, it no longer towers above the others. Whereas in 1950, its population was nearly four times that of its closest competitor, Iraq, today it is little more than twice that of Morocco, Algeria, or Sudan. Its Gross National Product and foreign trade are far smaller than those of several countries: Saudi Arabia, Algeria, Iraq, and even Kuwait and Libya. Its per capita income is among the very lowest in the Arab League. As mentioned before, its cultural preeminence is now challenged not only by Lebanon but also by Kuwait and Tunisia. More successfully than in the 1950's, its rivals—Iraq, Algeria, Saudi Arabia, Libya, and Syria—are questioning its leadership and opposing many of its policies.

It is very difficult to judge whether this development will promote or impede Arab unity. On the one hand it may be argued that German and Italian unity was achieved through the overwhelming power of Prussia and Sardinia, and that, in the absence of Egypt, there is no other comparable candidate for the role, though countries like Iraq and Syria have certainly shown interest. On the other, it may be said, perhaps more plausibly, that Arab unity, if it should come, will not be achieved by force, since the potential components are too disparate and too evenly matched, to have it imposed on them. In these circumstances, the eclipse of Egypt may ultimately promote some kind of drawing together, by making the association one between equals or near-equals. As in 1954, one can only pose the question and say that no clear either-or solution seems in sight, and that if and when one is arrived at it will probably take a shape which at the moment we do not envisage. As Moltke told his staff one day: "In any given situation, the enemy has three courses of action open to him; of these he will choose the fourth."

NOTES

1. H. A. R. Gibb, *The Arabs*—Oxford pamphlets on World Affairs (Oxford University Press, 1940), p. 3. The present definition takes into account a very interesting point made by Professor Bernard Lewis in an unpublished lecture. According to him, Middle Eastern nationalism passed through three stages. In the first, which covers the greater part of their

history, Middle Easterners thought of themselves as an *umma*, a people sharing a common religion. In the nineteenth century, under the influence of French Enlightenment and the French Revolution, the concept of *watan*, or *patrie*, began to replace that of *umma*, i.e., the basic category was that of a territorial group. This concept later gave way, under the influence of Polish and Hungarian refugees in Turkey, to that of *qaum*, or *Volk*, in which the binding forces are those of kinship and language. It will be seen that each of these stages brought to the fore one of the main component elements of nationalism, i.e., propinquity and neighborhood; kinship—real or fancied—and common speech; and way of life, of which religion is the most important constituent. See also the article by Professor Lewis, "The Impact of the French Revolution on Turkey," in *Journal of World History*, vol. II (Paris, July 1953).

2. Peveril Meigs, *World Distribution of Arid and Semi-Arid Homoclimates*, Unesco mimeographed document NS/AZ/37, rev. (Paris, 28 December 1952). The classification takes into account both precipitation and temperature and is designed for the study of "agricultural potentialities."

3. At a relatively late stage in its history, the Islamic Society produced offshoots in jungle areas, notably Bengal, Indonesia, and Equatorial Africa. But these offshoots, in spite of their numerical importance, have played a minor part in Islam.

4. The mean annual rainfall in Beirut, about thirty-five inches, is slightly greater than that of London. But whereas in England rainfall is fairly evenly distributed throughout the year, in Lebanon as much as two-thirds of the total may fall in the course of six or seven weeks.

5. The contrast between the tenanted *latifundia* and the peasant farms of Italy and Spain is also partly due to variability or inadequacy of the rainfall. See Economic Commission for Europe, *European Agriculture, A Statement of Problems* (Geneva, 1954), p. 18.

6. These valleys were the two foci of the Ancient East and have continued to be the two main centers of the Arab world.

7. See A. J. Toynbee, *A Study of History*, vol. I (London, Oxford University Press, for R.I.I.A., 1933), pp. 72-82, and Oswald Spengler (trans. by C. F. Atkinson), *The Decline of the West*, vol. II (New York, Knopf, 1926), pp. 189-92.

8. The part designated by Dr. Toynbee as the Iranic Society, as distinct from the Arabic.

9. H. A. R. Gibb, "An Interpretation of Islamic History," in *Journal of World History*, vol. I, no. I (Paris, July 1953).

10. The doctrine of natural frontiers, viz., that each people has definite physical boundaries delimiting it from other peoples and presenting an obstacle to both its expansion and its invasion by others, is of course part of the mythology of nationalism. It can easily be shown that most nations have no such boundaries (e.g., the Germans, Poles, Russians), that other nations have used the doctrine as a pretext for conquest (e.g., the French in their effort to annex the left bank of the Rhine), and that in still other cases the natural frontiers were reached only after a long process of ex-

pansion and assimilation (e.g., the conquest of Wales and Scotland by the English who thus attained the natural frontiers of Great Britain). However, like most mythologies, this one contains an important core of truth, viz., the fact that great physical barriers, such as seas, mountains, deserts, jungles, and swamps (but not rivers) do tend to mark off the peoples living on either side and thus to facilitate the growth of national cultures and separate national consciousnesses.

11. It may be noted in passing that the north-eastern political frontiers of Syria and Iraq do not quite coincide with either the physical or the cultural frontiers of the Arab world. As a result, Arab minorities are to be found in Turkey and Iran and non-Arab minorities in Iraq and Syria.

12. Ibn Khaldun, *Prolegomena,* ed. by Quatremère (Paris, 1858), vol. I, p. 269.

13. P. K. Hitti, *History of the Arabs* (London, Macmillan, 1949), pp. 10-12.

14. Punic continued to be spoken in parts of North Africa until St. Augustine's time.

15. At the same time, it is worth remarking that, of all European countries, Malta, Sicily, and Spain have a climate closest to that of the main centers of Arab civilization. The only areas in Europe marked as "arid" on the above-mentioned Unesco map are in Malta and Spain, with the exception of a very small patch in eastern Greece.

16. Berber is spoken by about half the inhabitants of Morocco and a third of those of Algeria—see Robert Montagne, *La civilisation du désert* (Paris, Hachette, 1947), chapter 8.

17. See E. F. Gautier, *Les siècles obscurs du Maghreb* (Paris, Payot, 1942), Book IV.

18. See for example the vivid map reproduced at the end of E. B. Worthington, *Middle East Science* (London, H.M.S.O., 1946). Large barren steppes or deserts separate the following: southern from northern Arabia; northern Arabia from Syria and Iraq; Syria from Iraq; Palestine from Egypt; Egypt from the Sudan; Egypt from Cyrenaica; Cyrenaica from Tripolitania; and Tripolitania from Tunisia.

19. The analogy of sea power is used, in a different context, by Bernard Lewis, *The Arabs in History* (London, Hutchinson's University Library, 1950), p. 55.

20. See United Nations *Review of Economic Conditions in the Middle East, 1949-540,* tables 30-5 and *Research Memorandum No. 14.*

21. See H. A. R. Gibb in *Journal of World History,* op. cit.

22. United Nations, *Review of Economic Conditions in the Middle East, 1951-52,* p. 4.

23. Moreover, the climate of world opinion has changed and nation-States are giving way to *Grossräume*, or at least to closer associations of States. This can be seen even in the seed-bed of nationalism, Western Europe. And just as European nationalism had its repercussion on the Arabs, supra-nationalism may also be expected to have important consequences in the region.

13

The Transformation of the Economic Position of the *Millets* in the Nineteenth Century

The rise and decline of the *millets* is one small aspect of a vast process. In the nineteenth century a worldwide market was formed; it was made possible by the industrial and transport revolutions, the mass emigration of tens of millions of Europeans and Asians to other continents, the outflow of a large amount of European capital, and the establishment of an international network of trade and finance. In the countries thus affected by Europe's thrust, foreign or minority groups played a very important role as intermediaries between Western capital and the local population: Chinese in Southeast Asia, Indians in Burma and East Africa, Lebanese in West Africa and so on. The liquidation of the European empires, the ending of the predominance of Western capital and the intensification of local nationalism spelled the downfall of these groups, just as the rise of English, French, and other nationalisms in the late Middle Ages had led to the expulsion of the Jews and Lombards, who had played a similar part.

In the Middle East—Turkey, Egypt, the Levant and, to a lesser extent because of its late and slow development, Iran—the function of the *millets* was essentially that of middlemen between the Muslim masses and the forces that were transforming them, i.e., European capital and enterprise and modernizing Middle Eastern governments. More specifically, the *millets* performed three roles. First, they were an entrepreneurial petty bourgeoisie of traders, moneylenders, brokers, and commissioners, linking the large European importers, exporters, and banks with the indigenous farmers, craftsmen, petty traders, and other producers and consumers. Secondly, along with some Europeans, they staffed the liberal professions, whose skills are required by a developing society: physicians, phar-

Reprinted with permission from *Christians and Jews in the Ottoman Empire,* eds. Benjamin Braude and Bernard Lewis.

macists, engineers, architects, lawyers (in the Western-type courts set up in Turkey and Egypt) and stockbrokers. Lastly, they formed a large part of the salaried middle class employed by the government or by the large European enterprises such as banks, railways, public utilities, and industries; and a perhaps even larger part of the skilled urban working class.

Needless to say, in the performance of these functions, some members of the *millets* acquired great wealth and power as high government officials, merchants, bankers, industrialists, and even landowners, but the vast majority remained in the ranks of the petty bourgeoisie or lower.[1] Not surprisingly, their influence grew along with European economic and political power in the Middle East and the concurrent efforts of the Middle Eastern governments to reshape society on Western lines and began to decline—either immediately before, or more generally, just after the First World War—when Middle Eastern society began to produce Muslims capable of carrying out these middle class functions and when growing nationalism demanded the replacement of foreigners or members of minority groups by ethnic Turks, Egyptians, Iraqis, or Persians.

I

From the very beginning of Islamic civilization, Christians and Jews had been prominent in such urban activities as medicine, trade, moneylending, and handicrafts.[2] At times, one group had enjoyed a brief period of great influence and prosperity. Thus, in the sixteenth century Jewish immigrants from Spain and Portugal played a leading part in medicine, banking and occasionally, diplomacy. Their knowledge of European languages, their training in Iberian or Italian universities and their contacts with co-religionists and others in Western Europe gave them a decisive advantage over all other groups, Muslim or Christian. The books in Greek, Latin, Spanish, Italian, and Hebrew that poured out of the presses they set up, starting in 1494 in Istanbul, bear witness to their intellectual activity.[3] In Iran in the seventeenth century Armenians "dominated the Persian external trade and much of the internal commerce," their activity stretching from Europe to India.[4] But such prominence was exceptional; generally speaking, in most handicrafts Muslims were either the majority or a strong minority, most local or regional trade was in Muslim hands and the Eastern trade—

which until perhaps as late as the end of the eighteenth century was distinctly larger than the European—was dominated by Muslims.[5]

Developments in the late eighteenth and nineteenth centuries changed all this. A survey of the situation at the beginning of this century, when the influence of the *millets* was at its peak, reveals a very different picture. In most parts of the Middle East they played a leading role in the economy. In Turkey, the Greeks, Armenians, and Jews, in that order, dominated the urban sector and controlled a considerable part of the rural. The predominance of non-Muslims in finance is shown by the fact that of the 40 private bankers listed in Istanbul in 1912 not one bore a Muslim name. Of those that could be identified with a reasonable degree of confidence, 12 were Greeks, 12 Armenians, 8 Jews, and 5 Levantines or Europeans. Similarly, of the 34 stockbrokers in Istanbul, 18 were Greeks, 6 Jews, 5 Armenians, and not one was a Turk.

As for the provinces, in the European part there were 32 bankers and bank managers: of those identifiable, 22 were Greeks, 3 Armenian, 3 Jews, and 3 Levantines or Europeans. In the Asian parts (excluding the Arab provinces in which many Arab, particularly Christian, names were to be found) there were 90 bankers. Of those that could be identified, 40 were Greeks, 27 Armenians, 6 Levantines or Europeans, and 2 Turks (in Eskişehir and Harput).[6]

A similar situation prevailed in industry, though here one cannot be as precise since many establishments, especially the larger ones, were listed under the name of the firm, not the owner. Turkish Muslim names appear much more frequently than in finance, but still constitute a small minority. In the silk industry, Armenian names prevail and in the cigarette paper industry, Jewish. In the other branches of industry, the predominance of Greeks is very clear.[7] According to a calculation by Tevfik Çavdar, the capital of 284 industrial firms employing 5 or more workers was divided as follows: Greeks 50 percent, Armenians 20, Turks 15, Jews 5, and foreigners 10, and their labor force: Greeks 60, Armenians 15, Turks 15, and Jews 10 percent.[8]

In foreign trade the share of the *millets* was also overwhelming. A list of the large importers of textiles in Istanbul in 1906 shows 28 Armenian names, 5 Turkish, 3 Greek, and 1 Jewish. In 1910, of 28 large firms in Istanbul importing Russian goods, 5 were Russian, 8 Muslim, 7 Greek, 6 Armenian, and 2 Jewish, and almost all large traders with Russia in the eastern provinces were Armenians.[9]

A detailed breakdown for 1912, based on various yearbooks, is given by Indzhikyan,[10] whose totals are (in percentages):

	Number	Turks	Greeks	Armenians	Others
Internal Trade	18,063	15	43	23	19
Industry and					
Crafts	6,507	12	49	30	10
Professions	5,264	14	44	22	20

In agriculture Muslims—Turks in Anatolia, Arabs in the Asian provinces—were predominant but the *millets* also played an important part. Figures on shares of landownership or the output of different crops are lacking but the following remarks, by an acute observer, are suggestive:

Cereal cultivation in western Asia Minor is in large measure in Greek hands, in central Anatolia almost exclusively in Turkish, in Armenia predominantly in Armenian, and in other parts in Arab hands. In fruits and cash crops, the leading role in western Asia Minor is played by the Greeks, further east by the Armenians, and to a small extent in Palestine by the Jews. In the growing of mulberries [for silkworm breeding] the leading groups in western Asia Minor are the Armenians and the Greeks, in Syria the Christian Arabs.[11]

It may be added that in the most rapidly expanding sector of agriculture, cotton, the main thrust came from the *millets*. In the Izmir region, cotton farms belonged "mostly to Greeks, but also to Turks." While in Adana, of the large landowners using modern methods, "few are pure Turks, but rather Greeks, Armenians, Syrians, and so on."[12] Greek predominance was even more pronounced in cotton growing, spinning and weaving, and cotton oil pressing in Adana. Thus, whereas the Muslims accounted for the bulk of the traditional grain crops, the *millets* developed and controlled the more valuable cash crops exported to foreign markets.

Whereas in Turkey the two leading *millets*, the Greeks and Armenians, were even more indigenous than the Turks, in Egypt the oldest non-Muslim community, the Copts, played a minor part in the economy. That their average economic level was higher than that of Muslims is shown by the fact that, shortly before the First World War, although forming only 6 percent of the population, they claimed that they paid 16 percent of the Land Tax[13]—and land was by far the greatest source of wealth and income. Scattered data support this contention and indicate that during the second half of the nineteenth century Copts bought large amounts of land and invested in irrigation pumps, cotton gins and other machinery and, particularly in Upper Egypt, ranked among the largest land-owners.[14] Prominent Coptic landowning families included Khayat, Dos, Bushra Hanna, Wisa, Sarofim, and Bulus. Copts were also prominent among the directors of land development companies.[15] Their higher educational level (p. 221, below) explains the disproportionately large share of Coptic government officials, 45 percent of the total, particularly marked in such departments as Finance, Interior, and Railways.[16] Copts were also—and have continued to be— well represented in the professions and included many of Egypt's most prominent lawyers, physicians, engineers, scholars, and journalists.[17] In the first half of this century they supplied many leading politicians, such as Butrus Ghali, Sinot Hanna, Georges Khayat, Wasif Ghali, Makram Ebeid, and Saba Habashi. They also continued to pursue their traditional handicrafts, notably goldsmithery. But in modern industry and finance they played only a minor part: a list of 1,406 company directors in 1951 shows only 4 percent had Coptic names.[18] Overall, their economic position was distinctly better than that of Muslim Egyptians, as witnessed by the fact that of the over 1,000 persons who had the unwelcome distinction of being sequestrated in 1961, 6 percent bore Coptic names—a proportion relatively much larger than that of Muslims (55 percent) but far smaller than that of Jews (4), Syrians or Lebanese (22), Greeks or Armenians (9), and Europeans (4).[19] "During the 1940s, Copts became middlemen, entering the business of contracting or export-import. In recent years some Copts from the leading families have gone full cycle, becoming tradesmen, but on the level of the high-fashion couturier shop in Cairo's new Hilton Hotel."[20] But they were neither innovators in modern business nor in control of any important economic sector.

Second only to the Copts in antiquity and much less influential politically, the Jews played a far more prominent economic role.

Perhaps the most striking illustration of this is the fact that as late as 1951, after nearly thirty years of attempts to Egyptianize the economy and after the Arab-Israeli War of 1948 had severely shaken their position, Jews still formed 18 percent of company directors, a figure that had fallen to 5 by 1960.[21] Jewish families such as Cattaui, Mosseri, Menasce, Suares, Rolo, and Harari, most of whom had been resident in Egypt since the beginning of the nineteenth century or before, played an important part in the foundation and administration of Egypt's leading banks: National Bank, Crédit Foncier, and others. Although individual ownership of land by Jews was small,[22] they provided much of the capital and most of the directors of some leading land development companies, notably Kom Ombo Company.[23] Together with some more recent immigrants from Europe, such as Mandelbaum and Horowitz, they established industries like sugar refining and cigarettes.[24] Two of Cairo's three principal department stores, Cicurel and Chemla, were Jewish-owned as were several somewhat smaller ones. Jews constituted a large proportion of stockbrokers,[25] insurance agents, and the personnel of banks and leading business firms. They were very well represented in the professions, notably medicine, law, and the foreign language press. Lastly, in the period before the First World War, some had risen to high positions in the Egyptian civil service, e.g., Blum, Seligman, Harari, Adeh, and Biyalos.[26] But the majority of Jews were of modest means—petty traders and employees—and a small number were extremely poor.

The same was true of the Syro-Lebanese community, which was roughly equal in numbers to, but less affluent than, the Jewish. It included some very large landowners such as the Sidnawi, Sursuq, Lutfallah, Karam, Chedid, Sa'b, Zogheib, Khlat, Eid, Kahil, and other families, most of whom had acquired their land in the years 1882-1914.[27] In 1951 Lebanese and Syrians constituted 11 percent of company directors, a figure that had risen to 13 by 1960.[28] Starting in the 1920s, they founded some rather large firms in the textile and other industries (e.g., Rabbath, Tagher). They supplied a large number of professional people—lawyers, physicians, engineers, stockbrokers—though few of the very top rank. Many attained high posts in the Egyptian civil service while in the Sudan they formed an indispensable link between the highest British officials and the lower rank Sudanese, such families as Shuqayr, Atiyah, and Isawi contributing several top administrators.[29] But the greatest impact of the Syro-Lebanese was on the press. "Out of 166 papers published in Cairo between 1828 and 1900 about 36 were owned by men whose names were recognizably Syrian; out of 188 between 1900 and 1914, about 21 were Syrian. In Alexandria, there were 31 Syrian newspapers out of 61 between 1873 and 1900, and 7 out of 27 between 1901 and 1914." Similarly for periodicals, in Cairo 28 out of 130 started between 1848 and 1900 and 12 out of 161 between 1900 and 1914, while in Alexandria, "9 out of 23 periodicals started between 1881 and 1900 had Syrian editors and 6 out of 34 between 1901 and 1914."[30] It should be added that their publications included both the two leading newspapers, *al-Muqaṭṭam* and *al-Ahrām*, and the two most prestigious and influential journals, *al-Muqtaṭaf* and *al-Hilāl*.

The political and administrative power enjoyed by Armenians under Muḥammad 'Alī and his immediate successors, which culminated in the premiership of Nubar Pasha and the Cabinet or Undersecretary posts of Tigrane, Yacoub, Artin, Boghos Nubar, and others,[31] had disappeared by the First World War, no doubt helped by the substitution of Arabic for Turkish (which was spoken by many Armenians) as the official language. This was not offset by an increase in economic power. Some of the larger cigarette factories (e.g., Matossian) were owned by Armenians, as were several smaller factories and workshops in shoemaking, metal work, and other industries. They had few company directors—under 2 percent in 1951 and less in 1960.[32] The amount of land owned by Armenians was very small. In some professions, such as medicine, engineering, and pharmacy, they were quite well represented. But the enormous majority consisted of petty traders, small employees, skilled craftsmen, and industrial workers.

Unlike the Copts, Jews, and Syro-Lebanese, the Greeks were never in a position to influence Egyptian politics or contribute to Arabic culture, though they can boast of modern Alexandria's most distinguished son, the poet Cavafy, and did produce a large number of minor scientists as well as prominent physicians, engineers, and lawyers in the Mixed Courts.[33] But their influence on the country's economic development from the early days of Muḥammad 'Alī until the Second World War was probably the greatest and most widespread of any *millet*. More than any other community, they operated at every level of Egyptian society except the government bureaucracy, from high finance and large-scale cotton exporting to village grocers, petty traders, and moneylenders, and industrial workers. It may be added that they played much the same role in the Sudan, which they had first penetrated in the middle of the nineteenth century and reentered literally on the heels of the British army of reconquest, to Lord Cromer's amazement and slight amusement.[34] However, in the Sudan, Greeks were far less prominent in the upper layers.

Starting at the top, in 1951 Greeks constituted 7 percent of company directors;[35] fifty years earlier the ratio must have been still higher.[36] Greeks founded, or played a major part in establishing, many of Egypt's earliest banks: Anglo-Egyptian Bank, 1864; Banque d'Alexandrie, 1872; Banque Générale around 1880. Such leading families as Salvago, Benachi, Rhodonachi, Zervudachi, Zafiropoulo, Zarifi, and others were also instrumental in creating the National Bank and the Land Bank.[37] In cotton exporting Greeks, including, in addition to the above families, such firms as Choremi, Benachi, Gregusci, Andritsakis, and Casulli—some of them founded in the 1860s—accounted for nearly a quarter of the quantity shipped. Most of the balance was exported by British and other European houses.[38] Greeks were no less well represented in other branches of import-export trade and when, in 1883, the Alexandria General Produce Association was formed, 15 of the 24 founding members were Greeks, including names like Ralli and Sinadino.[39]

Greeks were also active in various branches of internal trade, more particularly in purchasing cotton from the smaller farmers and delivering it to the exporters in Alexandria. Indeed from the dissolution of the Muḥammad 'Alī monopolies, in the late 1840s, until after the turn of the century, they almost monopolized the business, but were gradually subjected to a double squeeze by the large banks on the one hand and small Egyptian and other traders on the other.[40] During the same period they aquired a good deal of land, by purchase or foreclosure for debt. Thus in 1899 Averoff willed 1,160 *feddans* to the Greek community,[41] and there were even larger landowners.[42] They played a leading part in the development of long staple cotton, commemorated by such varieties as Sakellarides, Zagora, Yannovitch, Pilion, and Casulli, introduced vine growing (Gianaclis), and were active in dairy and poultry farming.[43] In industry, they were prominent in cotton ginning, controlling one quarter of Egypt's gins in 1929 and introducing noteworthy improvement in the closely linked oil pressing, as well as in tanning, alcohol, beer, soft drinks, and various food processing industries. They also dominated both the manufacturing of cigarettes, which they introduced in the 1860s, and its export (Gianaclis, Kyriazi, Melachrino, etc.).[44] Lastly, mention should be made of their active part in construction work, hotels and Nile transport.[45] And Greeks were well represented among the employees and skilled workers not only of Greek but of other firms.

The peculiarity of Lebanon is that here alone Christians not only secured a commanding early lead in the nineteenth century but managed to keep it until the 1970s. Already in the eighteenth century their superior education and French connections (p. 220, below) had enabled them to move ahead in both the embryonic bureaucracy and the expanding trade with Europe. The collapse of the French trading network in the Levant, during the Revolutionary and the Napoleonic wars, left a vacuum into which they eagerly stepped and Muḥammad 'Alī's rule created further opportunities for both Europeans and Lebanese Christians. But the remarkable fact is that the latter soon took over in Lebanon's two main activities: silk production and foreign trade.

Silk in Lebanon was grown mainly by Maronite farmers and, starting in 1836, reeled by up-to-date French and British establishments. But already by 1846 there were five silk-reeling plants "à l'européenne" owned by Lebanese—almost certainly all Christians—"in the plains of Beirut and the lower reaches of the Mountain."[46] And in 1862 the French consul stated that of 44 silk-reeling plants, 33 belonged to natives—the vast majority Christians—who owned 1,350 out of the 2,200 pans in use.[47] It may be added that by the 1850s silk had come to account for over one half of Lebanon's gross agricultural output.[48] By 1870 foreign firms were only 15 percent of the total and by 1910 3 percent.[49] This local Christian lead was maintained until the demise of silk cultivation, following the destruction of mulberry trees during the First World War and growing competition from Japanese silk and rayon. In 1931 an observer could state: "Lebanese industrialists have set up improved (*perfectionnés*) establishments that produce a good quality silk bought by Lyon. We may mention, as a model of the kind, the filature of M. Naccache, in Beit Mery."[50]

The same was true of trade. In 1826 the French consul stated that out of 34 commercial firms dealing with Europe, 15 belonged to local Christians and 6 to Turks, i.e., Muslims. By the late 1840s, the Lebanese seem to have taken over much of the foreign trade from the British and French, and here too the Christians were an overwhelming majority. A list of the 29 firms engaged in direct trade with England in 1848 shows only 3 Muslim and no Jewish names; the others consisted of Maronites (e.g., Naqqash, Eddeh, Dahdah), Greek Orthodox (Sursuq, Bustros, Trad), and Greek Catholics (Medawwar, Misk). Lebanese Christians had also established agencies in London, Manchester, and Marseilles.[51]

This situation persisted during the next hundred years or more. The development of Lebanese trade after the First World War was accomplished mainly by Christians, as was the promotion of tourism (Sursuq, Qasuf, Jbeili),[52] the establishment of a far-flung financial network and, later, the laying of an industrial base (Cortas, Esseili, Tamer). Christians continued to be disproportionately represented in the civil service, the professions, and intellectual activities, all of which naturally resulted in their earning distinctly higher incomes than Muslims or Druzes. Thus according to the 1971 National Fertility and Family Planning Survey, the average annual family income of Catholics (80 percent of whom were Maronites) was LL 7,173, of non-Catholic Christians (65 percent Greek orthodox and 29 Armenian Orthodox) LL 7,112, of Sunnis 5,571, of Shi'is 4,532, and of Druzes 6,180, the national average being LL 6,247; the percentage of families in each group earning less than LL 1,500 was 6%, 8%, 15%, 22%, 11%, and 12% respectively.[53]

The situation was somewhat different in Syria. It is true that in the main commercial center, Aleppo, from the sixteenth century on, Europeans traded "chiefly through the intermediary of the native Christians and Jews," including Armenians.[54] In the late eighteenth century the role of minorities in Aleppo "as bankers and moneylenders was vital."[55] In 1840, speaking of geographical Syria, Bowring could state:

The Mussulman population are seldom associated with the progress of arts or industry, and, though possessing the influence which belongs to the ruling authorities, are rarely instrumental in the creation of capital or the diffusion of civilization. Most of the commercial establishments are either in the hands of the Christian or Jewish population

and, more specifically, "the principal moneylenders and traffickers in specie, throughout the East, are the Jews."[56] But the figures he gives on the firms engaged in foreign trade show that the Muslim share in Aleppo was not insignificant while in Damascus it was preponderant; they may be tabulated thus, keeping the original spelling:[57]

Denomination	Number of Firms	Capital (millions of piastres)	Main House
Aleppo			
Muslim	85	8.5-10.0	Agi Wosa Muaket
Christian	30	14.0-18.0	Fathalla Cubbe
Jewish	10	2.0- 2.5	
Damascus			
Muslim	66	20.0-25.0	Hadji Hussein Chertifchi, Abderachman Asim, Aga Bagdadi, Mahomet Said
Christian	29	4.5- 5.5	Hanah Hanouri
Jewish	24	16.0-18.0	Mourad Farhi, Nassim Farhi

Both Christians and Jews played a significant part in handicrafts, and a preponderant part in a few, but Muslims formed a large majority in most branches.

In the course of the next hundred years, the commercial power of the Jews declined and that of the Christians increased, but the Muslims continued to be very active in trade. And when after 1945 Syria began to industrialize it was Muslim traders rather than Christians who played the main part. The main group, the Khumasiyya of Damascus, consisted entirely of Muslim merchants, who also formed the majority in the second largest Damascene combine, although it was headed by a Christian, Sahnawi. The Aleppo industrialists were all Muslims: Mudarris, a large landowner, Hariri and Shabarek, both the latter being traders.

For Iraq, one fact is clear: trade and finance were dominated, to an extent unknown elsewhere, by Jews. Longrigg puts the matter bluntly: "In Baghdad, with a city community of some 50,000, they almost outnumbered the Sunni Arabs and exceeded the Christian, Persian, and Turkish minorities combined. With their agents in Manchester, Bombay, and Paris they had so far the supremacy in commerce and foreign trade that Muslims were often forced into partnership, while Christian merchants had been largely driven from the field."[58] This statement may be confirmed by some figures. A list of exporters in the United Kingdom in 1907 dealing directly with Persia and the Persian Gulf shows 12 Jewish names, 5 British, 2 Muslim, 1 Christian Arab, and 2 uncertain.[59] Similarly, a list of the main establishments in Iraq engaged in import-export trade around 1908 shows 7 foreign names, 5 Jewish, and 1 Muslim.[60]

A distinction must, however, be made between import trade, centered on Baghdad, and export trade, centered on Basra. The former soon passed into local hands. In 1839-40 two British firms were established in Baghdad and as late as 1857, in spite of the arrival of two Greek and one Swiss firms, "except the two British firms . . . there are no foreign merchants who are engaged in the direct trade with Europe."[61] But the business was soon taken over by local firms, at first Persian and Jewish and then almost solely Jewish.[62]

In 1879 "the Jewish Mercantile Community of Bagdad have nearly all the trade with England in their hands whereas the native Christian merchants trade mostly with France. There are only two English merchant firms in Bagdad."[63] Trade with Britain was many times as great as that with France. A few years later a British consul declared: "The wealth of Baghdad is rapidly passing from the Mohammedans to the Christians and Jews"[64] while another stated: "The Jews are the largest traders in Baghdad but there are also many native Christian and Muhammedan merchants."[65] Finally, in 1909, a list of importers who had branches in England showed 19 names, of importers who bought through Commission Houses 30, and of bankers 5; all were Jewish.[66] The Jewish business community included such internationally famous names as Sassoon, Zilkha, Haskiel, and Kadoorie.

In the provinces the situation was somewhat different. At Gumtara in 1891 the government put orders for grain with two Jewish and one Christian merchant, at Samawa with one Jewish and one Muslim, at Diwāniyya with two Muslims, and at Dighara with two Muslims.[67] At the Shi'i holy city of Karbala in 1882 there were no Christians except one or two government clerks; "a few families of Jews monopolize, as usual, the money-dealing of the place."[68]

The situation in Basra was also different, but then "Baghdad has a decided mercantile predominance over Basra which, apart from the date and grain export trade, is merely the ocean port of Baghdad."[69] In the 1870s, export of dates was carried out by 6 European and 6 local firms, most of the latter being Muslim, and the same was broadly true of grain and wool.[70] A petition of Basra merchants in 1891 was signed by 5 Britishers, 3 Muslims, 2 Greeks, and 1 Syrian, and in 1908 there were two Greek firms.[71]

This structure of export and import markets continued until the Second World War, except that in both the Muslim share increased.[72] Throughout the period landownership and agricultural production remained in the hands of Muslims.

II

An explanation of the economic ascent of the *millets* can start with two general remarks. First, as observed by various social scientists from Sir William Petty to Alexander Gerschenkron, a minority that is excluded from certain avenues of power, like the army, church, and politics, tends to concentrate on and excel in business and the professions—in other words, the Avis complex. Secondly, minorities are clannish. They help, hire, promote, and do business with each other, to the great annoyance of the surrounding majority. But these explanations are insufficient for the Middle East: firstly, because there were other minorities, such as the Shi'īs, Nusayrīs, Kurds, and others who did less well than the Sunnī Muslims: secondly, because the success of the *millets* was relatively greater than that of similar minorities in other parts of the world. Five further factors may be mentioned: participation in expanding sectors; foreign protection; a favorable situation following various reforms in the Ottoman Empire and Egypt; superior education; and help from coreligionists outside the region.

The *millets* participated actively in those sectors of the economy that expanded most rapidly in the nineteenth and twentieth centuries: foreign trade with Europe and the Americas, the various branches of finance, mechanized transport, export-oriented agriculture, and modern industry. By the last decades of the nineteenth century some 90 percent of Middle Eastern trade was with Europe and the United States, and the formerly predominant Eastern trade had dwindled to a trickle.[73]

This change had been accompanied and facilitated by a marked shift in trade routes, from caravans to steamships; particularly important was the diversion caused by the opening of the Suez Canal. All this seriously hurt such inland towns as Kayseri, Konya, Diyarbekir, Erzurum, Aleppo, Damascus, and Mosul, where Muslim traders had been predominant. Conversely, it greatly benefited such ports as Salonica, Izmir, Beirut, and Alexandria, where *millets* were an important minority, or even a majority, of the population. Even where caravan trade continued, it tended to shift its route to a closer port. Thus, the Tabriz trade from the 1830s on made for Trabzon rather than Aleppo, Izmir, or Istanbul and was soon captured by foreign or minority firms;[74] similarly the trade of Mosul turned away from Aleppo and toward Baghdad and Basra.[75]

Already by the eighteenth century many minority groups were active in the trade with Europe. A French report of 1784 states: "Formerly, the Armenian and Greek cloth merchants formed an association, through which they made all their purchases, thus imposing their terms on the French. The Grand Signor has destroyed this association by severe penalties."[76] In the 1820s Armenian merchants established their bases in European countries. "In the 1860s the Armenian colony in Manchester already consisted of 30 families; these firms opened branches in Istanbul and Izmir."[77] The Greeks were no less active, monopolizing certain branches. "One third of the members of the Ottoman Chambers of Commerce consisted of Greek firms and organizations. In the Commercial-Industrial Chamber, founded in 1884, Greeks retained a majority until the Balkan Wars." The role of Jews was far smaller, but quite significant.[78]

In Syria the Christians, starting as interpreters for the French and other consuls and merchants, soon struck out on their own and by the beginning of the eighteenth century Melkites controlled a large part of the trade and shipping between Syria and Egypt.[79] When the French commercial position in the Levant was ruined by the Revolutionary Wars and Napoleon's expedition to Egypt, Syrian Christian and Jewish firms took over part of its business.[80] The same trade established the basis of the Syrian community in Egypt, some of whose members also became middlemen between European importers and the Mamlūks.[81] Similarly, during the French Occupation and the first years of Muḥammad 'Alī's reign, the Greeks in Egypt both increased in numbers and engaged in shipping and trade with the Eastern Mediterranean—activities that prepared them to take full advantage of the subsequent expansion of trade with Europe.[82]

The result of these developments may be seen in a list compiled by Bowring of the seventy-two merchant houses in Alexandria in 1837.[83] Of the identifiable names, forty-three were European (British, French, Austrian, Tuscan, and Swiss), fourteen Greek, five or six Syrian, four or five Jewish, two Maltese and one Armenian. Of the twenty-seven in the last five groups, seventeen were protégés of European countries other than Greece. Only two were Muslims: a Tunisian and a Turk. The business of the minority firms was still very small compared to that of the big European houses, but the Muslims hardly entered the picture at all. And for a long time the process was cumulative: the profits made in foreign trade could be used to buy real estate in the expanding seaports, where values and rents were rising rapidly.

The *millets* were even better placed in finance. The famous Galata bankers were Levantines, Greeks, Armenians, and Jews, and during the first half of the nineteenth century they dominated the field. Most of the *sarrafs* came from the *millets*. In Turkey the Armenians were particularly influential,[84] but the Jews also played an important part until 1826.[85] All this led to important international contacts: "The Rayahs who lend their money secretly at an exorbitant profit, have no method of placing their fortunes when they retire from trade. This inconvenience has induced many rich Greeks, Armenians, and Jews to place money in the foreign Funds and even to follow it into Italy, Germany, France, and Russia."[86] In Egypt the *sarrafs* had been, since the Arab conquest, Copts. But the customs were held by Jews until the second half of the eighteenth century when they were replaced by Syrians[87] or Copts.[88] Under Muḥammad ʿAlī Greeks and Armenians joined their ranks.[89] In Syria and Iraq, Jews and Christians were also well represented among the *sarrafs*, and sometimes engaged in bitter rivalry.[90]

All this meant that the *millets* were well placed to found small private banks, some of which attained considerable importance in the second half of the nineteenth or first half of the twentieth century, e.g., Zilkha, Suares, Trad, Tepeghiosi. They were also able to serve as agents or employees of European banks, insurance companies, brokerage houses, and other institutions.

The other growing branches may be briefly examined. Minority members soon became local agents of the French, Austrian, Russian, British, and other shipping lines serving the eastern Mediterranean. Others, like the Sursuqs in Beirut, supplied the ships with coal. As regards the railways and river steamers, except for a few concessions in Syria and Palestine which were soon sold to foreign interests, the minorities had little part, but they supplied a large share of their technical and skilled personnel. Thus in Iraq the only large government enterprise, the Saniyya steamboats, was ably headed by a Jew, Sassoon. When he resigned in disgust he was succeeded by an Armenian, Sirop.[91] And it may be noted that the two engineers sent by the Baghdad Railway to northern Iraq in 1911 were Greek and Armenian.[92]

The decline of the handicrafts, due to European competition, ruined many members of the *millets*, but probably a far larger number of Muslims. In the founding of modern factories, however, the minorities showed much more enterprise and skill until the First World War. In addition to the data given above, mention may be made of the Armenians, notably the Dadians, who managed the various factories established by the Ottoman government in the 1830s, and some private entrepreneurs like the *sarraf* Jezairli (Jezairlian) who set up silk filatures in Bursa.[93] Greeks and Armenians also worked many coal mines in the Zonguldak area. Greeks, Armenians, and Jews, as well as Muslims, opened workshops for carpetmaking in the Izmir region. Such activities were often financed by capital accumulated in foreign trade, money-lending, or tax collecting.

Most of these developments could not have taken place without the foreign protection enjoyed by so many *millet* members. In the eighteenth century and much of the nineteenth, property was very insecure in the region, being subject to arbitrary taxation and high risk of confiscation. Some scholars have seen much merit in this situation, as a dispenser of rough justice, an accelerator of social mobility, and a provider of government revenues, but it was hardly conducive to private enterprise, innovation, and investment. Girard saw this clearly. Ottoman subjects had no protector for their trade in their own ports, but were subject to exactions which "n'avaient de bornes que celles de l'avidité des exacteurs." That is why almost all foreign trade was carried out by foreign nations.[94]

Quite a large number of Christians and Jews, but not Muslims, got around these obstacles by acquiring a *berat* from a foreign power. As shown so clearly by Robert Haddad[95] for the Christian Syrians, this enabled them to pay lower customs duties than unprotected Ottoman subjects, avoid part of the arbitrary taxes levied by local authorities, and in addition acquire much greater immunity from the Maltese and other corsairs who preyed on Ottoman shipping. In Turkey, *berats* had originally been issued to embassy interpreters recruited from the *millets*, but by the end of the eighteenth century each mission had begun "to rear up its own interpreters" and no longer needed Ottoman subjects. "Those invested with *berats* therefore turned the protection to purposes of trade. The most opulent among the Greeks, Armenians, Jews, etc., in Constantinople and in the provinces made it a point to obtain protection."[96] Hence although, as noted before, the Eastern trade, including that between Istanbul and Egypt, was in the hands of Muslims, some of whom were very rich, that with Europe, both maritime with England, Holland, France, and Russia, and overland with Austria, was dominated by Greeks and Armenians.[97] A note in 1802 from the Porte to the British Minister stated explicitly that Muslims traders were "a very small number" compared to the *rayas*.[98] Selim III tried hard to end the abuses arising from the excessive issuance of *berats* and to foster Ottoman trade and shipping but had no success.[99]

In Egypt it is worth noting that in 1837 all but one of the seventy-two Alexandrine merchants listed above had either foreign citizenship or protection. In Aleppo, nineteen Jews were granted British protection between 1848 and 1861, and by 1881 their number had risen to nearly forty; it may be presumed that most of them were engaged in trade.[100] Christian *protégés* of France, Austria, Russia, and other countries, also largely in trade, were probably much more numerous. In Damascus in 1863 the consul reported that "British subjects and their *protégés* were then the chief moneylenders there."[101] As for Iraq, in Baghdad in 1844 "a considerable proportion of the native merchants connected with the Indies, Syria, and Constantinople enjoy the protection of the English, French, and Russian governments."[102] Here, as in Aleppo, the British extended their protection mainly to Jews and the other Powers to Christians. In 1850 a list of British *protégés* in Baghdad showed seven Jews, all merchants trading with India and four Christians, one of whom was a trader.[103] By 1890, "with the exception of Sir Albert Sassoon, the whole of the Sassoons are British born subjects. Sir Albert Sassoon, by naturalization and Firman, is a British subject—he used to sit in the Legislative Assembly of Bombay."[104]

The mobility and security provided by foreign protection may be illustrated by the history of the Thaddeus family. Their ancestor, David, emigrated from Isfahan to India. His son Kevork, born in Surat in 1747, became in 1778 "linguist and broker of the English factory at Basra" and died in 1807. His son, Thaddeus, succeeded him in his post but in 1832 took his family to Bombay where he died in 1842. In 1843 Rawlinson brought Thaddeus' two sons, George and John, to Baghdad, to serve in the Residency where they were joined in 1845 by their brothers, Yaqub and Gabriel, who were still serving in the Residency in 1894. George died in 1892 and John, having become a landowner and a Turkish subject, had been dismissed but all other descendants were British subjects.[105] The obverse is illustrated by the following remark by the very knowledgeable Resident at Baghdad, Kemball, in 1862. Pointing out that the steamboat run by Lynch and Co. was in "constant occupation," had "full cargoes," and was "universally appreciated," he continues:

> the example set by Messrs. Lynch and Co. would be immediately followed by the Native Speculators were they not deterred by the curse of the Sukhreh which is in constant operation in this Province and which would subject their vessel to be at all times diverted from her commercial voyages whenever the Government might require her services to supply the place of a damaged bridge boat or to carry stores, fodder, grain, and troops from one point of the River to another. From this curse, experience has shown that a Foreign Flag could alone protect them.[106]

Ten years earlier his predecessor, Rawlinson, had stated that Turkish officials were so arbitrary that it was impossible for any native merchant to do a proper job as agent of a British firm unless he enjoyed British protection, and asked that such protection be granted to an Armenian in Basra.[107]

By the middle of the nineteenth century foreign protection of minorities had greatly widened. Not only holders of *berats* but all aggrieved members of *millets* within reach of a foreign consul looked to him for protection and redress. At the same time the Ottoman government was attempting to remove some of the disabilities from which its non-Muslim subjects suffered, and Muḥammad 'Alī carried this policy much further. Moreover, in their efforts at modernization, both governments needed every ounce of local talent available, and since the minorities were already much more educated and westernized their role in administration and policymaking greatly increased.

The result was an odd combination of privilege and discrimination. In Egypt Christians and Jews were treated remarkably well and so, on the whole, were Greeks and Jews in Anatolia—except, of course, for the atrocities commited by both sides during the Greek

War of Independence. In eastern Anatolia the Armenians were "ruthlessly exploited and oppressed" by the Kurdish Beys, sometimes with the connivance of the local authorities.[108] In the Fertile Crescent intercommunal relations were more tense. The struggle in Lebanon was more or less between equals, but the anti-Christian riots in Aleppo in 1850 were not; nor were the pillaging and killings at Ma'lula in 1850-51;[109] nor above all were the Damascus massacres of 1860, in which some 5,000 Christians died. But, under international pressure, these incidents were followed by severe punishments and nothing comparable took place even during the tense period of the 1875-78 wars, although the British consuls reported several incidents of killing and pillaging in Aleppo and its region (but not in Damascus), and the visit of a British naval squadron to Syrian waters was deemed salutory.[110] Except for the apprehension caused by occasional blood libels, such as the one in Damascus in 1840, the Jews in Syria were left undisturbed. In the Mosul region, however, the 8,000 Jews were "subject to tyranny of the worst kind"[111] while "the atrocities practised by the Kurds upon the Christians are revolting to humanity."[112] In 1867 Jews in Arbeel were killed and robbed with impunity,[113] and in 1899-1900 Christians in the region also suffered.[114] The attitude of the Muslims of Mosul toward Christians and Jews was described in 1909 as "that of a master toward slaves whom he treats with a certain lordly tolerance so long as they keep their place. Any sign of pretention to equality is promptly refused."[115] This attitude was not unknown in other towns, and on the whole the minorities learned to keep their place, thus avoiding major incidents.

But while the situation of the minorities was not enviable, their economic position was becoming much more favorable. First, their taxes were reduced, as shown by the following judgment on the effect of the *Tanzimat* on Erzurum, made in 1845:

The Armenian Agriculturist formerly often paid 20 per Cent, while the Mohamedan paid only 5, at most 10 per Cent; and it frequently happened, besides, that the latter, by favor, was exempted altogether from the Tax. This year, however, both classes have paid equally their legitimate 10 per Cent, and the Tax has been fairly levied. Free quarters on the Christians and forced labor are both prohibited by the Tanzimat; but, until Essat Pasha's time, the abuses continued; they probably will be abolished hereafter. The property of the inhabitants of the Town has been three or four times assessed, but always so unfairly, that the valuation has been rejected.

At last, it was asked what the Mussulmans could bear and what the Christians. The answer given was, that the former (consisting of 9,000 families) could contribute 75,000 piastres or £750; and the latter (1,000 families), 32,000 piastres or £320; this sum, the Armenians had usually paid for the Salian, while the Turks had never contributed at all. The Government, then, ordered that the Mussulmans should pay 75,000 piastres, and the Christians 35,000; but it abated from the two 10,000 piastres, and directed the Chiefs of the nations to distribute the tax justly and conscientiously among their coreligionists. The Turks here took, however, the whole abatement on their own contribution; so that they pay 65,000 piastres—£650, and the Christians 35,000—£350.[116]

Secondly, minority members were increasingly employed by the government. "The Egyptian government made the same use of Syrian Christians as it customarily made of Coptic Christians in Egypt, employing them all over Syria as tax collectors," and appointing the Bahri brothers to head the finance departments of Damascus and Aleppo.[117] This was a mixed blessing since tax gatherers are seldom liked. The same happened to Armenians, Greeks, and Jews in Turkey. In Lebanon, Volney had already noticed that, thanks to their higher literacy, the Maronites had become "what the Copts are in Egypt. I mean, they are in possession of all the posts of writers, intendants, and kiayas among the Turks."[118] Thirdly, the increasing modernization of Ottoman and Egyptian legislation and the establishment of courts based on Western principles helped the minorities, who were more at ease with them and able to take fuller advantage of their provisions. Particularly important was the Ottoman Land Code of 1858 and its counterparts in Egypt; allowing free transfer of land, it made possible the accumulation of vast holdings by Christians and Jews in Anatolia, Egypt, and Syria through purchase or foreclosure for debt.[119]

But the most important advantage resulted from the exclusion of the *millets* from the army, viz., their exemption (in return for payment of a special tax) from conscription to which Muslims were increasingly subjected. This, together with the removal of restrictions on land purchase and other forms of discrimination and oppression which had impeded them, put *rayas* in a very advantageous postion to compete with Muslims. A few examples from Anatolia are illustrative:

In Erzurum in 1848: "The Armenians have more hands, the Mussulman youth being taken for military service. The Mussulmans do not hire labor and they are unable to cultivate the extent of land they possess."[120] In Biga in 1860: "Their [Christians'] pecuniary means being larger than those of the Mussulmans, they are constantly purchasing property from the latter. I understand however that formerly Christians were restricted from so doing; but the prohibition as regards this province was abolished some years ago, mainly through the instrumentality of Mr. Consul Calvert."[121] In Izmir: "The Christian races are . . . buying up the Turks." Before the Decree of Gülhane, the large Turkish landlords "lived by a system of oppression and plunder which was put a stop to by the Hatt." The Turks, handicapped by conscription, "fall into the hands of some Christian usurious banker (Armenian, Greek, or occasionally European) to whom the whole property or estate is soon sacrificed."[122] Relative freedom from conscription also helped the Lebanese Christians under Muḥammad ʿAlī. "Financially, it is possible to observe them in the 1820s as serfs of such Druze Shaikhs as Abu Nakad and at the end of the Egyptian period as the chief moneylenders to the same shaikhs."[123] Muslims were fully aware of this factor: "The Mussulmans of Beyrout and I believe generally of Syria express an opinion that if they are to be treated on a footing of exact equality with their Christian fellow subjects, it is unjust that they alone as a class should give their flesh and blood for the conscription but that the Christians equally with themselves should furnish recruits for the army."[124] Conscription was not applied to non-Muslims until the eve of the First World War.

The matter was put succinctly by a British diplomat and scholar in 1900: "But when force does not rule, when progress, commerce, finance, and law give the mixed population of the Empire a chance of redistributing themselves according to their wits, the Turk and the Christian are not equal; the Christian is superior. He acquires the money and land of the Turk, and proves in a lawcourt that he is right in so doing."[125]

The help provided to the *millets* by their coreligionists abroad was twofold: business contacts and opportunities, and education. The Greeks, and to a lesser extent the Armenians, in Western Europe and Russia certainly facilitated the trade of their Middle Eastern coreligionists with these countries. The Jews of Livorno, and elsewhere, performed the same function and so, to a far smaller extent, did the Lebanese in America and the Parsees in India. But a still greater service was the opening of schools by these foreign groups for the local communities: the Greek and Armenian schools in Turkey and the Alliance Israélite schools in all parts of the region. The Syrian Christians were even more fortunate in having numerous Italian and French Catholic, American, British and German Protestant, and Russian Orthodox schools, starting in the early nineteenth century. The Copts also greatly benefitted from the mission schools opened in Egypt in the nineteenth century.

The use made by the *millets* of this opportunity, and the results achieved, may be illustrated by some figures. In the Ottoman Empire in 1896 there were 31,000 pupils in Muslim Middle (*rüşdiye*) schools, compared with 76,000 in non-Muslim and 7,000 in foreign (the vast majority being non-Muslims), and 5,000 in secondary *(idadiye)* compared with 11,000 and 8,000. It is true that in elementary (*ibtidaiye*) schools Muslims far outnumbered the others, but the education received in them was of very little value.[126] As early as the 1870s the Greeks in Istanbul alone had 105 schools with 15,000 pupils,[127] and the Armenians were not behind, frequenting in addition to their own schools those of the Catholic and Protestant missionaries.[128] In Egypt the Greeks opened their first school in 1843 and soon had a wide network.[129] Jewish schools, opened by immigrants from Europe, also date from the 1840s,[130] and the Syrians and Armenians had theirs, too. As a result, in the 1907 census the literacy rate for Jews was 44 percent, that for Copts was 10, and for Muslims only 4 percent. The contrast was even more striking in Iraq, where the Christians and Jews had their local missionary and Alliance schools—most of which were attended by members of the other religion as well—while the Muslims were almost unprovided for. In Mosul, for example, the 90,000 Muslims had "practically no education at all . . . even amongst the members of the great families there are very few indeed who can express themselves in Turkish and, so far as I am aware, there is only one Muslim in the whole city who knows a European language, viz., Daud Chelebi, Dragoman to the German Vice-Consulate. This gentleman is also the only one who has visited Europe." In contrast the 9,000 Christians had about 2,000 children (some no doubt from nearby villages) in missionary schools and the 4,000 Jews had an Alliance school.[131]

Two aspects of this educational headstart may be noted. First, the minorities learned European languages, which equipped them to deal with the new social structures that were coming into being. A search by the British consular authorities in Syria in 1878 for interpreters produced the following results: in Beirut, 53 persons were named as knowing at least Arabic and English, 10 knew French as well, and one in addition Italian and Turkish; of these four were foreigners, 6 Druzes, and all the rest Christians. In Damascus, 10 knew English and Arabic, and 4 also knew French, 1 Italian, 1 Spanish, and 3 Turkish; all were Christians. In Jerusalem, 9 persons— 6 Jews and 3 Christians—knew English and Arabic, and most of them knew several languages, including Turkish, French, Italian, and Greek. And in Aleppo, one of the dragomans knew English, French, Italian, Arabic, and Turkish, while the other was described as an even "better linguist"; both were Christians.[132]

The other aspect is concentration on professional education. "Although the Copts make up only 6 percent of the population, they produced 21 percent of the law graduates, 19 percent of the engineering, 15 percent of the medical, and 12 percent of the teaching graduates between 1886 and 1910."[133] The same was broadly true of other *millets* and explains their predominance in the professions and as employees of large enterprises. It is perhaps superfluous to add that the minorities felt much more affinity with Western culture than did Muslims and absorbed it with almost no reservations.

III

The downfall of the *millets* may be briefly described. Essentially, it was due to the fact that they had been too successful, absorbed too large a share of the fruits of economic progress and, to make matters worse, began to forget the traditional wisdom of their fathers and to take seriously the slogans "Liberty, Equality, Fraternity." In the latter they were abetted by foreign well-wishers, or interested parties, who naturally let them down in their hour of need.[134] Many were even more short-sighted and actively collaborated with the occupying powers, from whom they had in the past sought protection.

With his usual sweep, Berque states: "Who profited thereby, apart from the colonizers? Here and there we find partial indications: some middlemen—Jewish, Syro-Lebanese, Coptic, very occasionally Muslim, turning the import trade to their best advantage: some pashas, associated with the interests of those in power; an occasional landowner, acquiring mechanized pumps and setting himself up as a bourgeois lord of the manor; on a humbler level the village *umdas* and shaikhs."[135]

Of course this was not so—the level of living of the Egyptian masses rose,[136] education spread and a remarkable intellectual and social awakening took place. But to most Egyptians, squeezed between the rich foreigners on the one side and the Greek, Jewish, or Syrian moneylender on the other, the description would have seemed accurate. Eliot makes the same point about Turkey: "One may criticize the Turkish character, but given their idiosyncracies, one must admit that they derive little profit from such blessings of civilization as are introduced into their country. Foreign syndicates profit most, and after them native Christians, but not the Osmanli, except insofar as he can make them disgorge their gains."[137] This was a-chieved in the horrendous events of 1895-1923, which disposed of practically all the Armenians and Greeks. Many Jews left of their own accord, and the remaining minority members were finally finished off by the *Varlik Vergisi* of 1942.[138]

In Egypt the economic position of the foreigners and minorities remained strong until after the Second World War, as the figures given above indicate. But from the late 1930s the government tried to squeeze them out, by stimulating a local bourgeoisie and insisting, quite properly, that books be kept in Arabic (which most had not bothered to learn) and that preference be given to Muslims—and to a lesser extent Copts—in hirings. After 1946 many foreigners and minority members, seeing the storm signals, left the country. The 1948 Arab-Israeli war undermined the position of the Jews, and the 1956 war destroyed it, along with those of the French and British. The nationalizations and sequestrations of 1961, which crippled the Egyptian bourgeoisie, finished off foreign interests and those of the Syrians and remaining Jews. Copts have also come under great pressure.[139]

The development of Zionism in Palestine had increasingly adverse effects on the position of Jews in Iraq, and the 1948 war led to a mass exodus. The same occurred, to a lesser extent, in Syria. In the latter, Christians, who were disproportionately represented in business and the professions, suffered correspondingly from the upheavals, nationalizations, and sequestrations that have occurred since 1949. In Lebanon the current civil war, whatever its outcome, will probably end Christian predominance. The golden days of the *millets* are gone.

NOTES

1. In a memorandum of 27 February 1910, printed in Elie Kedourie, *Arab Political Memoirs*, London, 1974, p. 267, the dragoman of the British Consulate in Baghdad classified the Jewish community of that city as: 1) rich and well off—bankers merchants—5%; 2) middle class—petty traders, retail dealers, employees —30%; 3) poor—60%; 4) beggars—5%. My impression is that the Armenian, Jewish, and Syro-Lebanese communities in Cairo and Alexandria were somewhat better off (i.e., a larger proportion fell in the top two brackets), and the Jewish communities in Damascus and Istanbul worse off—for the latter, see A. Sussnitski, in *Allgemeine Zeitung des Judentums*, Berlin, 3, 12, and 19 January 1912. An indication of the condition of the Armenians of Istanbul in the 1860s is given by the fact that when an attempt was made to raise money for religious purposes only 3% were able to contribute 75 piastres (say $3.50), although such statements must be taken with a large pinch of salt, O. G. Indzhikyan, *Burzhuaziya osmanskoi imperii*, Erevan, 1977, p. 154.

2. And not only in Islam. "At the end of the [fifteenth] century, Joseph Bryennius sadly recorded that medical practice was entirely in the hands of Jews," Steven Runciman, *The Last Byzantine Renaissance*, Cambridge, 1970. p. 92.

3. Abraham Galante, *Turcs et Juifs*, Istanbul, 1932, pp. 94-101.

4. R. W. Ferrier, "British Persian Relations in the Seventeenth Century," Ph.D. Thesis, Cambridge University, quoted in Charles Issawi, *Economic History of Iran*, Chicago, 1971, p. 57. A monopoly in Persian silk in Aleppo was established in 1590-1632 by the Armenian Khocha Petik, whose commercial network covered Anatolia, Persia, and India, Avedis Sanjian, *The Armenian Communities in Syria under Ottoman Dominion*, Cambridge, Mass., 1965, pp. 48-49. See also Niels Steensgaard, *The Asian Trade Revolution of the Seventeenth Century*, Chicago, 1973, pp. 378-85.

5. In Egypt in 1783, trade with Europe was put at only 236 million *paras*, compared with 1,373 million for North Africa, the Ottoman Empire, and the Red Sea; except for some of the trade with Syria the latter was in Muslim hands, André Raymond, *Artisans et Commerçants au Caire*, Damascus, 1973, vol. 1, p. 193. In Iran, too, trade with Central Asia, Transcaucasia, the Ottoman Empire, and India in 1800 far exceeded that with India and Europe by the East India Company and other European groups and was mainly in Iranian hands, Issawi (cited n. 4), pp. 130-135, 262-267. In 1825, Damascus alone bought 18,500,000 piastres "worth of Asian goods, mainly brought by caravan from Baghdad, or more than twice as much as all Syria then bought from Europe. There was a brisk trade with Mecca . . . Thus, in the years before the Egyptian invasion such international trade as there was was primarily an Asian trade." William R. Polk, *The Opening of South Lebanon*, Cambridge, Mass., 1963, p. 162, citing Boislecompte. In Iraq, at the beginning of the nineteenth century, trade in Asian goods was almost certainly larger than in European, and most of the latter came to Baghdad by caravans from Syria and Turkey, Charles Issawi, *Economic*

History of the Middle East, Chicago, 1966, p. 136. For Muslim economic activity in the Ottoman Empire, see Kemal Karpat, *An Inquiry into the Social Foundations of Nationalism in the Ottoman State*, Princeton, 1973 and Halil Inalcik, "Capital Formation in the Ottoman Empire," *JEH*, 29(1969), pp. 97-140 and Ronald Jennings, "Loans and Credit in the Early Seventeenth century Ottoman Judicial Records," *JESHO*, 16(1973), pp. 169-217.

6. Marouche and Sarantis, *Annuaire Financier de Turquie*, Pera, 1912, pp. 137-140.

7. A. Gündüz Ökçün, *Osmanli Sanayi*, Ankara, 1970, *passim.*

8. Cited by Indzhikyan (cited n. 1), p. 166. This book is a rich source of information on the economic activity of the minorities.

9. Ibid., pp. 206-209.

10. Ibid., pp. 211-314.

11. A. J. Sussnitzki, "Zur Gliederung wirtschaftslicher Arbeit," translated in Issawi (cited n. 5), p. 117.

12. W. F. Brück, "Türkische Baumwollwirtschaft," *Probleme der Welwirtschaft*, No. 29, Jena, 1919.

13. Report of Coptic Congress, cited by Kyriacos Mikhail, *Copts and Moslems under British Control*, London, 1911, p. 29. Some estimates are even higher. Thus Ramzi Tadros, *Al-aqbāt fial-qarn al'ishrin*, Cairo, 1910/11, cited in Doris Behrens-Abouseif, *Die Kopten in der aegyptischen Gesellschaft*, Freiburg in Breisgau, 1972, p. 48, puts Coptic holdings at about one-fifth of the cultivated area and states that 26 families owned 20,000-30,000 *faddans.*

14. Gabriel Baer, *A History of Landownership in Modern Egypt*, London, 1962, pp. 63-64, 137-138.

15. Ibid., pp. 129-131.

16. *British Parliament, Accounts and Papers*, Egypt, no. 1, 1911, p. 8; in a few of the more technical departments, Copts were prominent until very recently: in the Department of Mechanical Power of the Ministry of Rural Affairs in 1959, Copts "comprise 20 percent of the personnel"; but in the Ministry as a whole they formed only 13 and in the Ministry of Foreign Affairs under 2 percent, Edward Wakin, *A Lonely Minority*, New York, 1961, pp. 41-44.

17. See two interesting autobiographies, Naguib Mahfouz, *The life of an Egyptian Doctor*, Edinburgh, 1966 and Salama Musa, *Tarbiat Salama Musa* (Cairo, 1947); both men began their activity before the First World War and continued it after the Second.

18. Charles Issawi, *Egypt in Revolution*, London, 1963, p. 89.

19. Ibid., pp. 89-90. This had also been true at the beginning of the century; speaking of the "bourgeoisie of businessmen" that was growing up in Cairo and Alexandria, Berque notes "a few" Muslims but "many Copts such as Bushtur, Hinaya Shinuda, Andraus Bishara, and others" Jacques Berque, *Egypt: Imperialism and Revolution*, New York, 1972, p. 243; see also p. 200 for the career of the of the merchant-industrialist Wisa Buqtur.

20. Wakin (cited n. 16), p. 28.

21. Issawi (cited n. 18), p. 89.

22. Berque (cited n. 19), pp. 227, 244.

23. Baer (cited n. 14), pp. 130-131.

24. Jacob M. Landau, *Jews in Nineteenth Century Egypt*, New York, 1969, pp. 13-15.

25. The first Chairman of the Cairo Stock Exchange, in 1872, was A. Cattaui, and the tradition proved durable, Berque (cited n. 19), p. 99.

26. Landau (cited n. 24), pp. 11-12.

27. A. H. Hourani, "The Syrians in Egypt in the Eighteenth and Nineteenth Centuries," *Colloque international sur l'histoire du Caire*, Cairo, 1964, pp. 226-227.

28. Issawi (cited n. 18), p. 89.

29. See biographical details in Richard Hill, *Biographical Dictionary of the Sudan*, London, 1967. In 1932, out of the total of qualified government personnel, 4,793, there were 913 British, 520 Egyptians, 164 Syrians, 2,913 Sudanese and 71 others. Anthony Sylvester, *Sudan under Numeiri*, London, 1976, p. 48. These figures reflect the massive retrenchment of non-Sudanese personnel; earlier the figure for Syrians was distinctly higher.

30. Hourani (cited n. 27), pp. 226-227.

31. Lord Cromer, *Modern Egypt*, New York, 1908, vol. 2, pp. 219-225.

32. E. I. Politi, *Annuaire des Sociétés égyptiennes par Action*, Alexandria, 1951; *Egyptian Stock Exchange Yearbook*, Alexandria, 1960.

33. Athanase G. Politis, *L'Hellénisme et l'Egypte moderne*, Paris, 1929-30, vol. 2, pp. 401-490.

34. Cromer (cited n. 31), vol. 2, p. 250.

35. Politi (cited n. 32).

36. See list for 1929 in Politis (cited n. 33), vol. 2, pp. 291-294.

37. Ibid., vol. 2, pp. 260-266; this list excludes branches of Hellenic banks operating in Egypt, e.g., Banque d'Athènes, Banque d'Orient, etc., see ibid., vol. 2, pp. 266-78.

38. Ibid., vol. 2, pp. 230-243.

39. Ibid., vol. 2, pp. 213-219.

40. Ibid., vol. 2, p. 223.

41. Ibid., vol. 1. p. 290.

42. See list in ibid., vol. 2, pp. 103-107 and Baer (cited n. 14), p. 121.

43. Politis (cited n. 33), vol. 2, pp. 97-159.

44. Ibid., vol. 2, pp. 304-374.

45. Ibid., vol. 2, pp. 56-68, 374-379.

46. Dominique Chevallier, *La Societé du Mont Liban*, Paris, 1971, p. 220; in previous centuries other communities had also grown silk on a large scale, information kindly supplied by Professors Bernard Lewis and Adnan Bakhit.

48. Charles Issawi, "Lebanese Agriculture in the 1850s," *American Journal of Arabic Studies*, 2(1973), pp. 66-80 and Chevallier (cited n. 46), chapter 14.

49. Toufic Touma, *Paysans et institutions féodales chez les Druzes et les Maronites du Liban du xvii siècle à 1914*, Beirut, 1971, p. 372, and more generally, pp. 366-373 and Ismail Haqqi, ed. *Lubnān: mabāhith 'ilmiyya waijtima 'iyya*, Beirut, 1970, vol. 2, pp. 487-530.

50. Raymond O'Zoux, *Les Etats du Levant sous mandat français*, Paris, 1931, p. 275.

51. Beirut, vol. 1, fol., 398 and see list in Charles Issawi, "British Trade and the Rise of Beirut, 1830-1860," IJMES, 8(1977), p. 98; also Chevallier (cited n. 46), p. 206.

52. For the period before 1914 see Haqqi (cited n. 49) pp. 521-544.

53. Joseph Chamie, "The Lebanese Civil War: an Investigation into the Causes," *World Affairs*, Winter, 1976/77. For a breakdown of businessmen by religion, see Yusif A. Sayigh, *Entrepreneurs of Lebanon*, Cambridge, Mass., 1962, p. 70.

54. Avedis Sanjian (cited n. 4).

55. Herbert Bodman, *Political Factions in Aleppo, 1760-1826*, Chapel Hill, 1963, p. VII.

56. John Bowring, *Report on the Commercial Statistics of Syria*, New York, 1973, pp. 7, 25.

57. Ibid., pp. 80, 94.

58. Stephen Longrigg, *Iraq: 1900 to 1950*, London, 1953, pp.10-11.

59. *Kelly's Directory*, quoted in FO 195/2243.

60. See Issawi (cited n. 5), pp. 184-185 for details.

61. Kemball to Redcliffe, 26 December 1857, FO 195/577.

62. Muḥammad Salman Ḥasan, *Al-tatawwur al-iqtiṣadī fī al-'Irāq*, Beirut, n.d., p. 263.

63. Trade Report 1878/79, FO 195/1243.

64. Plowden to St. John, 11 February 1881, FO 195/1370.

65. Trade Report 1884, FO 195/1509.

66. Ramsay, Note, FO 195/2308.

67. Muston to Consul General, 18 September 1891.

68. Tweedie, Diary, FO 195/1409.

69. Crow to Barclay, Memorandum, 8 January 1907, FO 195/2242

70. Hasan (cited n. 62), pp. 139-162.

71. Petition of 20 June 1891, FO 195/1722 and Crow to O'Connor, 18 January 1908, FO 195/2274.

72. Hasan (cited n. 62), pp. 139-152.

73. For figures on Turkey see Vedat Eldem, *Osmanli Imparatorluğun Iktisadi şartlari hakkinda bir tetkik*, Ankara, 1970, chapter 9; for Egypt see

Ministry of Finance, *Annuaire Statistique,* Cairo, 1910; for Iran see Issawi (cited n. 4), chapter 3.

74. Issawi (cited n. 4), pp. 92-116.

75. Hasan (cited n. 62), p. 262.

76. See Issawi (cited n. 5), pp. 31-32.

77. Indzhikyan (cited n. 1), p. 186.

78. Ibid., pp. 157-158. Greek migration to England began in the 1830s; by the 1850s there were 55 Greek firms in Manchester, including Ralli Brothers—see Issawi (cited n. 4), p. 104—and 14 in London and by 1870 there were 167 in Manchester, see S. D. Chapman, "The International Houses: the Continental Contribution to British Commerce, 1800-1860," *Journal of European Economic History,* 6(1977), 5-48. The Jews missed an earlier opportunity in the sixteenth and seventeenth centuries. As late as the 1670s a French visitor stated that there was no "noteworthy family or foreign merchant who did not have a Jew working for them, either to appraise merchandise and judge its quality, or to serve as interpreter or inform them of what was happening . . . . The other Oriental nations, like the Greeks, Armenians, etc., do not have this talent and do not attain their skill." But the reaction caused by the Messianic claims of Sabbatai Sevi (in 1666) caused the Jewish community to turn its back on modern learning and to reduce its participation in outside activities. See M. Franco, *Essai sur l'histoire des Israélites dans l'Empire Ottoman,* Paris, 1897, p. 115.

79. Robert Haddad, *Syrian Christians in Muslim Society,* Princeton, 1970, p. 40.

80. William Polk, *The Opening of South Lebanon,* Cambridge, Mass., 1963, p. 73, citing Boislecomte.

81. Hourani (cited n. 27), pp. 222-23.

82. Politis (cited n. 33) vol. 1, chapters one and two.

83. J. Bowring, "Report on Egypt and Candia," *UK Accounts and Papers* 1840, vol. 21, pp. 80-82. In Cairo, out of 55 large firms, 15 were European, 10 Greek Catholic (Syrian), 6 Greek Orthodox, and 24 "Turkish."

84. See Vartan Artinian, "A Study of the Historical Development of the Armenian Constitutional System in the Ottoman Empire, 1839-1863," Ph.D. Thesis, Brandeis University, 1969, pp. 18-19.

85. For the fierce struggle in 1815-26 between the Jewish *sarrafs,* who were linked to the Janissaries, and their Armenian rivals, and the tragic death of all the protagonists, see Franco (cited n. 78), pp. 133-140. By 1831 Slade could say "The Armenians are the chief bankers of European Turkey, having supplanted the Jews in that dangerous but lucrative employment in consequence of possessing superior honesty or rather inferior knavery." Adolphus Slade, *Records of Travel in Turkey, Greece, etc.* London, 1854, p. 434.

86. Ainslie to Carmarthen, 10 January 1786, FO 78/6.

87. Hourani (cited n. 27), pp. 222-223.

88. Stanford Shaw, *The Financial and Administrative Organization and Development of Ottoman Egypt*, Princeton, 1962, p. 103.

89. Politis (cited n. 33), vol. 2, p. 279.

90. See Polk (cited n. 5), pp. 134-135.

91. Newmarch to Stronge, 29 April 1904, FO 195/2218; despatch FO 195/2340.

92. Despatch November 1911, FO 195/2369; for the role of Greeks and Armenians in the Ottoman agricultural bureaucracy, see Donald Quataert, "Ottoman Reform and Agriculture in Anatolia," Ph.D. Thesis, UCLA, 1973, pp. 64-128.

93. For the Dadians, see Edward Clark, "The Ottoman Industrial Revolution," IJMES, 5(1974), pp. 65-76, 1974; for Jezairli and others, Indzhikyan (cited n. 1), pp. 160-171 and Report for 1851/52, FO 78/905.

94. Girard, "Mémoire," in *Description de l'Egypte,* Paris, 1809-22, vol. 17, p. 373.

95. Haddad (cited n. 79), pp. 32-49.

96. Report 24 April 1806, FO 78/50.

97. Board of Trade, 17 September 1790; Traian Stoianovitch, "The Conquering Orthodox Merchant," *JEH*, 20(1960), pp. 234-313.

98. FO 78/36.

99. Stanford Shaw, *Between Old and New*, Cambridge, Mass., 1971, pp. 177-179.

100. Note of 22 July 1876, FO 195/1113 and Wilson to Goschen, 11 May 1881, FO 78/3535. Perhaps even more important was the appointment of local consular agents. In a letter to the Minister of Foreign Affairs of 20 March 1836 (CC Beyrouth, 2), the French consul in Beirut, Guys, pointed out that this innovation had begun in Egypt and been introduced into Syria under Muḥammad 'Alī; the Ottoman government had forbidden and punished such practices. "Since the dearest wish a *raya* can have is that of becoming a consul, there is no doubt that in future everything will be done to secure such a place."

101. Cited by Polk (cited n. 5), p. 224.

102. Rawlinson to Aberdeen, 25 April 1884, FO 78/574.

103. List, 16 September 1850, FO 195/334.

104. Livingston to Tweedie, 15 August 1890, FO 195/1722.

105. Mockler to the Wali of Baghdad, 18 January 1894, FO 195/1841. Armenian connections with India and other parts of Asia were very old. Armenians had played an important part in the trade of India, Indonesia, and the Philippines in the seventeenth and eighteenth centuries—see Holden Furber, *Rival Empires of Trade in the Orient, 1600-1800*, Minneapolis, 1976, *passim*.

106. Kemball to Bulwer, 10 September 1862, FO 195/717.

107. Rawlinson to Redcliffe, 2 November 1853, FO 195/367.

108. M. S. Lazarev, *Kurdistan i Kurdskaya Problema,* Moscow, 1964, pp. 32-37.

109. See Antoine Rabbath, *Documents inédits pour servir à l'histoire du Christianisme en Orient,* Paris, 1910, vol. 2, pp. 167-185. Needless to say, the Syrian Christians often behaved foolishly when they felt protected against the Muslims. "The Christians of Damascus, who were horribly tyrannized by the Turks of this city and who now feel protected, are perhaps taking too great an advantage of the fortunate change that has taken place in their political existence. It is a fact that they miss no occasion to defy the Muslims and that this bluster has deplorable consequences for them in spite of the support of the authorities and the armed forces." Guys to Broglie, 3 June 1832, CC Beyrouth, 1 bis.

110. Various despatches in FO 195/1113.

111. Rassam to Ponsonby, 10 August 1841, FO 195/228.

112. Rassam to Canning, 29 July 1843, ibid.

113. Kemball to Lyons, 10 August 1867.

114. Agent Mosul to Consul General, 11 January, 24 February, and 1 July 1899, FO 195/2055 and 4 December 1900, FO 195/2074.

115. Notes on the City of Mosul, FO 195/2308. More generally, for the indignities and vexations, or worse, suffered by Christians, see Consular Reports from Aleppo, Beirut, Damascus, Jerusalem, and Mosul, FO 195 series.

116. Report on Trade, FO 78/654.

117. Polk (cited n. 5), p. 135; H. Lammens, *Syrie,* Beirut, 1921, vol. 2, p. 156.

118. C. F. Volney, *Travels Through Syria and Egypt,* London, 1788, vol. II, p. 32.

119. Issawi (cited n. 5), pp. 71-90; Baer (cited n. 14), pp. 7-12, 63-70.

120. Report on Trade, FO 78/796.

121. Reply to Questionnaire, FO 78/1525.

122. Ibid., FO 78/1533.

123. Polk (cited n. 5), p. 137.

124. Eldridge to Eliot, 7 February 1876, FO 195/1113.

125. Sir Charles Eliot, *Turkey in Europe,* New York, 1965, p. 153.

126. *Istatiskik umumi idaresi,* Istanbul, 1316/1898.

127. A. Synvet, *Les Grecs de l'empire Ottoman,* Istanbul, 1878, pp. 32-33.

128. Artinian (cited n. 84), chapter 3.

129. See Politis (cited n. 33), vol. 1, chapter 5, for details.

130. Landau (cited n. 24), p. 71.

131. Notes on the city of Mosul, FO 195/2308.

132. Various despatches in FO 195/1201. Already, around 1830, Slade (cited n. 85), p. 288, had noted: "Some of the Greeks here [Philippopolis] spoke German tolerably. The most useful European language in Turkey

is Spanish. All the Jews talk it, impurely certainly, but quite well enough for interpretation; indeed their Spanish, such as it is, is their household language, Hebrew being considered classical. Moreover, Spanish is the chief ingredient of the lingua franca."

133. Donald M. Reid, "Educational Career Choices of Egyptian Students, 1882-1922," IJMES, 8(1977), pp. 349-378; note also "In the late 1940s, the proportion of Copts in Egyptian schools above the elementary reached one in four"—Wakin (cited n. 16), p. 27.

134. An incident related by the British Consul in Baghdad illustrates an attitude that was becoming widespread among all the *millets*: "When a Jew (an Ottoman subject) named Salih bashi, who had been arrested for forcible resistance of the town authorities, was brought before the proper tribunal (or perhaps before H. E. the Wali) to be interrogated, he refused to answer unless the Foreign Consuls were present, an attitude on his part, as may easily be imagined, not calculated to mollify the Government." This and similar incidents led the United States Consul to say it was "the Baghdad Government rather than the Jews who stood in need of support." Tweedie to Ambassador at Constantinople, 17 November 1889, FO 78/4214. As against that, "The French Consul has been rather posing as the Protector of the Christians, but I think he would be much wiser if he told them that he was in no position to protect them, which is the truth, and advised them to be very careful in their behavior." Ramsay, Confidential Memorandum, 21 April 1909, FO 195/2039. As regards the painfully acquired wisdom of the fathers, the following story came to me from a highly trustworthy source. In 1943 General Catroux, feeling that France's position in Syria was becoming shaky, invited a delegation of Armenian notables in Aleppo. He explained that their situation would be perilous if France left and reminded them of the 1915 massacres and other horrors. A long silence followed, broken by the eldest and wisest Armenian: "If I understand you right, you are seeking our help. But if you need our help, you must be in a very weak position. And if you are in such a position, it would be very unwise of us to offer you our help."

135. Berque (cited n. 19), p. 190.

136. The most observant and scientifically minded of his time, 'Alī pasha Mubārak, writing in the early 1870s, had no doubts regarding both the population growth and the improvement in living conditions that had taken place since Muḥammad 'Alī. See *Kitab Nukhbat al-fikr fitadbīr nīl Miṣr*, Cairo, 1297/1880, p. 184. For the rise in mass consumption in 1885-89 to 1910-12, see Issawi (cited n. 5), p. 365, and the sources cited there.

137. Eliot (cited n. 125), p. 153.

138. See Bernard Lewis, *The Emergence of Modern Turkey*, London, 1961, pp. 291-296.

139. Wakin (cited n. 16), pp. 43-49.

14
The Arab World's Heavy Legacy

No observer of present trends in the Arab world can fail to be impressed by the strength of its revulsion against Western political and economic values and ideologies. To take one example among many, a recent book by a prominent Egyptian publicist starts with two propositions which he not only believes to be self-evident but obviously assumes are accepted as such by his readers: present-day capitalism does not work; and Western democracy is a sham, since all power is concentrated in the hands of the owners of the means of production. Judging from pronouncements at the recent Cairo conference of non-aligned nations, such views are widespread in Africa and Asia.

The revulsion of the Arabs is not difficult to understand in view of their grievances—many real, more fancied—against the Western peoples. But the matter is more complex. It is not just a question of a whole society turning against an alien civilization. It is also a process in which some parts of a society turn against other parts, and in doing so against certain alien values which the latter represent. In other words, the ideological changes taking place in the Arab countries today reflect deep structural changes in their society. The principles and institutions that held together the traditional Arab society have broken down; a desperate search is under way for new bases of integration; and it is felt that the traditional Western ideologies and institutions do not provide these bases.

Arab society in the eighteenth century had very few virtues. Its economy was not only stagnant but actually retrogressing. Its politics were characterized by venality, rapacity, insecurity, and oppression. Its intellectual and artistic life were barren. Worst of all, it lived in a smug, self-satisfied lethargy, completely isolated from the outside world—"we do not hear of a single Egyptian who had visited Europe in the sixteenth, seventeenth, and eighteenth centuries."[1] But it had one redeeming feature, the obverse of some of its defects: it was a stable, integrated society, i.e., practically all its members believed in the prevailing values and had a strong loyalty to a small group and at least passive acceptance of existing institu-

---

tions. An exception would have to be made for the bedouins, who lived in the steppes and deserts. Although always willing, and generally able, to raid the sedentary folk and to pillage or extort "protection money" from them, they were seldom in a position to overthrow the government, much less to change the existing order.

Of the sedentary population, perhaps four-fifths consisted of peasants, whose condition was hardly idyllic. Their exploitation by the tax-farmers cannot but have aroused deep resentment. The constant feuds between village factions added their share of misery. Bedouin raiders, famine, and plagues were frequent visitors. But the prevailing communal systems of land tenure (*musha*, *dira*, and *ard al-fallah*) provided both security and a rough measure of equality, since the land of the village was periodically redistributed among its members in more or less equal shares. This meant that there were no landless peasants. It also meant that within the community there were no great differentiations of wealth. Lastly, it meant that each individual knew that he belonged to two closely knit units, the family and the village, which would stand by him in case of need.

The handicraftsmen, who probably constituted the majority of the urban population, were bound together by guilds (*asnaf*) and religious brotherhoods (*turuq*). The former regulated production and doubtless formed strong barriers against technological and economic progess. But, in alliance with the brotherhoods, to which they were closely tied, they did provide the craftsmen with security and an object of loyalty. A further integrating factor was the tie of kinship binding the inhabitants of each quarter, which often constituted a self-contained unit with its own gates, baths, and place of worship.

The merchants, who in Europe were for several centuries a dynamic and even revolutionary class, certainly did not constitute a threat to the existing order. For one thing, their wealth was small and political power very limited—the Islamic world never had city-states with independent, self-reliant bourgeoisies. For another, they had practically no contacts with the outside world which might have inspired them with new ideas. Lastly, in many areas and branches their activity was largely regulated by custom, which meant that the driving force of competition was greatly attenuated.[2]

Another group which in the West and Russia has been both dynamic and subversive of existing régimes is the intelligentsia. Its nearest counterpart in the Arab world were the *ulama*, men trained

in religion and jurisprudence. But because of their religious background the *ulama* were almost necessarily bound to be loyal to any
society based on Islam. Moreover, for many centuries Muslim political theory had stressed the principle of obedience to any government that both had military power and promised to respect the *shar-
ia,* or religious law of Islam. In the absence of an intellectual ferment and of a group that could utilize it to further its own ends,
the various disturbances that occurred in the Arab world—army
insurrections, conquest by one ruler or pasha of another's territory,
bedouin raids, local revolts, etc.—could not lead to any important
modification in the social structure, but only to a change in the composition of the ruling group.

Of course Arab society was not completely static. Economic and
social changes occurred in Syria and Iraq in the eighteenth century.
The Egyptian scholar, Shayyal, already quoted, states that: "Toward
the close of the eighteenth century we detect the first signs of a cultural revival. It was an internal movement which emerged from
within Egypt away from any outside influence whether from the
East or from the West." The Wahhabi movement was a challenge
that might have revitalized Islam. A Soviet scholar has discerned
the beginnings of "capitalist production" in the larger textile and
other establishments in Egypt at the end of the eighteenth century.
It is just conceivable, though highly improbable, that left to itself
Arab society might have evolved into a healthier state. But in fact
it was violently thrown into the mainstream of world history.

The chief responsibility for this may well lie, as Toynbee, Gibb,
and other Western writers claim, with those monarchs and statesmen—Muḥammad 'Alī in Egypt, Mahmud II and Reshid Pasha in
Turkey, Khaireddin in Tunisia—who realized that, without some
thoroughgoing modernization their countries could not survive
a European onslaught. But an equally important factor was the
quest of the Western countries for raw materials, markets, bases,
and spheres of political, religious, and cultural influence. This led
them to open up the Ottoman Empire to Western traders by such
measures as the Anglo-Turkish Commercial Convention of 1838,
to back with diplomatic and other means those of their citizens who
were hunting for concessions, and eventually to impose their rule
over practically the whole Arab world. And it was certainly the presence of the West in the region that caused the latter's development
to take the peculiar form that it did. To put the matter concisely,

Western influence accelerated the transformation of the Arab world from a subsistence to a market economy, and the dissolution of its communal and organizational ties and their replacement by individual, contractual relationships; at the same time, it inhibited the growth of an Arab bourgeoisie.

I

The process of transformation, and the consequent dislocations, took much the same form as in other parts of the world. In the first place, Western medicine and hygiene eliminated the plagues and many of the endemic diseases prevalent in the region, while improved transport and increased food supplies prevented the occurrence of famines. The result was a sharp reduction in the death rate which, since the birth rate remained at its previous high level, led to a rapid increase in population. For a long time the annual rate of growth averaged about 1 percent, but in recent years it has risen to between 2 and 3 and may soon go over the latter figure, which would mean a doubling of the population every 20-25 years. The vast growth that has already taken place, unaccompanied by either massive industrialization or a comensurate extension of the cultivated area, has led to great pressure on the land and, in recent years, to an exodus to the cities. The social consequences have been the appearance of two new phenomena: the landless peasant, and a large, underemployed, amorphous, urban proletariat.

The emergence of a landless peasantry was also promoted by another important transformation: the change-over from a subsistence to a market-oriented, cash-crop agriculture. The economic consequences of this change were predominantly beneficial—a large increase in agricultural productivity and output, greatly expanded exports, and a substantial growth in the national product. But the social consequences were far less favorable. Thus the dissolution of the village community—without which no progress could have taken place—eliminated the security formerly enjoyed by all peasants. Production for the market meant exposure to price fluctuations, which often led to indebtedness and loss of land. Economic progress produced a rapidly widening gap between the able, cunning, or lucky members of the village on the one hand and the inefficient, simpleminded or unfortunate on the other; and such inequalities tended to be self-perpetuating and cumulative. The adoption of Western law codes and their application to land worked in the same direction. Moreover, much of the land was appropriated by former tax-farmers, tribal chieftains, city notables or others, and since rents soon came to absorb a large and growing portion of the total product, the benefits of agricultural progress accrued primarily to a small number of landlords, often absentees. Again, in some countries, notably Algeria, Libya, Tunisia, Palestine, and Morocco, a large fraction of the cultivated area passed—partly by expropriation or chicanery, partly by purchase—into the hands of foreign settlers, thus reducing still further the area available to Arab farmers. Lastly, it should be noted that agricultural techniques showed little or no improvement. The only exceptions were Egypt and such enclaves as the European farms in North Africa, the Zionist settlements in Palestine, the Gezira scheme in the Sudan, and parts of Lebanon. The cumulative effect of all these factors—coupled with the lack of industrialization—was that the Arab countries did not acquire a prosperous, conservative peasantry. Instead, there was an ever-growing number of landless peasants, or of land-hungry farmers with steadily shrinking plots, envious of the neighboring estates of native landlords or foreign planters. Where, as in Egypt and Algeria, the level of living of the rural populations actually declined, the explosiveness of the situation was greatly increased.

Meanwhile, the towns were passing through an even more acute crisis. The handicrafts, which had occupied the greater part of their population, received mortal blows from the competition of machine-made European goods and, in Egypt, from Muḥammad ‘Alī's state factories and monopolies. The disruptive effects of this shock went deepest in such towns as Aleppo, Damascus, Baghdad, Cairo, and Tunis, which had previously supplied the adjoining regions with manufactured goods.[3] And with the ruin of the handicrafts came the dissolution of the guilds that had bound together their members. In their place emerged a mass of unemployed or underemployed workmen, constantly augmented by influxes from the villages and—again in the absence of industrial development—unable to organize and raise its level of living.

The processes so far described do not differ basically from those that took place in Western Europe in the eighteenth and nineteenth centuries, or in many other parts of the world somewhat later. But the crucial difference lies in the fact that Western Europe industrialized. This greatly strengthened its bourgeoisie, which had already become a significant force thanks to the earlier development of trade and finance. And in the course of the nineteenth century the bourgeoisie became the dominant power in society. But the Arab countries began to industrialize only during the last few years, and their economic and social structure was such that—with the exceptions noted below—no native bourgeoisie developed until very recently. This delay, and the consequent weakness of the bourgeoisie, prevented the latter from playing a significant part until hostile forces had developed to the point where they could overwhelm it. And, since the political and economic values and institutions of the West— liberalism, constitutionalism, and free enterprise—are essentially middle-class ones, the crushing of the Arab middle class has meant the elimination of the one class that could still have defended these values and institutions.

The factors that impeded the industrialization of the Arab countries, and of other underdeveloped areas, have often been described. Some would have existed under any political régime: the narrowness of the market, because of low agricultural productivity; the unfavorable social structure; the scarcity of iron and coal, until very recently almost indispensable to industrialization; the dearness of fuel, until the discovery of petroleum and natural gas in the last few decades; the very poor transport systems; the paucity of investment capital; the absence of industrial credit; and the lack of technicians and skilled workmen and, still more, entrepreneurs. But it is no less true that some of these difficulties were greatly aggravated by the nature of the relationships between the Arab countries and the West. Thus the shortage of capital was accentuated by the heavy service charges on the debts contracted—often at usurious rates—by spendthrift monarchs.[4] Industrial credit facilities could have been expanded by government pressure on the banks, which confined their activities almost solely to trade. The lack of skills could have been partly remedied by an appropriate educational policy. But the absence of Western interest in Arab education may be illustrated by the fact that in 1955, after 125 years of French rule, the literacy rate among Algerian Muslims was about 15 percent and only one-sixth of the children of school age (6-14) were attending school. Similarly in Egypt during the first 20 years of British rule government expenditure on education was under 1 percent of the total.

Moreover, the little that was done in education was misdirected, from the point of view of economic development. Thus, whereas under Muḥammad 'Alī (1813-1848) 327 of the 339 students who were sent abroad on government missions studied industrial technology, engineering, medicine, or agriculture, and under his successors (1849-1882) 270 out of 279, during the British Occupation (1883-1919) the figure was 74 out of 289. But the most important point is that a sympathetic government could have given the encouragement and protection without which no industry could possibly have established itself against foreign competition: tax exemptions, rebates on transport rates, preferential purchases and, above all, tariff protection. Instead, local industries were exposed to the full blast of foreign competition. Thus French goods entering Algeria and, with few exceptions Tunisia, and Italian goods entering Libya were exempt from duty, and all imports into the Ottoman Empire and Egypt paid a flat rate of 8 percent, no distinction being made between raw materials, capital goods, and consumer goods. Indeed hostility to local industrialization went further: when a small cotton textile industry did develop in Egypt it was subjected to an 8 percent excise duty, i.e., the rate levied on imports.

Lack of industrial developments and the weakness of the bourgeoisie are closely interconnected. On the one hand industry has everywhere been one of the main sources of middle-class strength. And, on the other hand, in most countries capital and entrepreneurship have flowed into industry from other sectors of the economy dominated by the bourgeoisie, notably trade and finance. But the fact that Arab handicrafts were under such great pressure meant that few if any could expand and develop into workshops and factories, and industrial recruitment from this source was negligible. And in the Arab world all the main sectors of the economy, with the partial exception of agriculture and petty trade, were largely or wholly controlled by foreigners.

This situation comes out most clearly in Arab Africa. In Algeria and Libya almost every single urban activity—finance, transport, trade, real estate, manufacturing, and the professions—was controlled by Europeans, who even provided most of the skilled labor; in addition they ran most of the "modernized" agriculture. In Tunisia and Morocco, the bulk of urban activity and a significant part of agriculture were similarly controlled by Europeans. And the same applied to Egypt until the 1950s, with the not very important difference that here Europeans shared their control, to a certain extent, with various minority groups. In Arab Asia, except for Palestine under the Mandate, foreign investment and immigration were insignificant until the recent expansion of the oil industry. But in several of these countries the middle class consisted to a large extent of minority groups—Jews in Iraq and Christians in Syria and Jordan.

The effect of this phenomenon was that for about a century the entrepreneurial middle class (as distinct from the salaried middle class) became identified with foreigners or minority groups. Of course a Muslim bourgeoisie did eventually develop but, except in Lebanon and to a lesser degree in Syria, it came too late and was too weak to meet the onslaught of the hostile forces that had emerged. In Egypt, the bourgeoisie developed as a result of the efforts of the Misr group, of the 1930 tariff, of the abolition of the Capitulations in 1936, of various government measures to "Egyptianize" business, of the weakening of the Europeans during and after the Second World War, and of the Arab-Israeli War of 1948. In the Arabian peninsula the small middle class that arose owed its existence to the oil boom of the 1940s and 1950s. The same cause was at work in Iraq, supplemented by the exodus of Jews after the Arab-Israeli War. In Libya the sequence was reversed, the withdrawal of the Italians after the Second World War being followed by an oil boom. In Tunisia and Morocco French withdrawal enabled the local bourgeoisie greatly to increase its strength. And in the Sudan a small middle class is being slowly formed, thanks to the country's relatively undisturbed development.

Given sufficient time, these bourgeoisies might have been able to get control of their societies and reshape them in their image. Unfortunately for them, and for the West, the fabric of their societies was already being torn by the various stresses to which they were being subjected. Among such stresses were the population explosion, the hypertrophic urbanization, the agricultural revolution, and the industrial revolution referred to above. Two other processes deserve more detailed treatment: the cultural changes and the political struggles.

The discovery of the West, and the consequent cultural transformation of Arab society, has had the revitalizing—and intoxicating—effect of a renaissance. Its over-all consequences have of course been incalculably beneficial. But it has had a very unsettling effect on Arab society by bringing into being a new class of intellectuals. And whereas the old "intellectuals," the *ulama*, were deeply loyal to the basic values and institutions of their society the new ones did not owe it any such allegiance and looked right and left, East and West, for new sources of inspiration and loyalty. Thus, for the first time in many centuries, new ideas began to corrode the fabric of Arab society.

Meanwhile political strife was being added to social discontent and stirring up the masses. In the Arab East there were the struggles against the British and the French, the traumatic Arab-Israeli War, and the Suez attack of 1956. In North Africa there was the shattering effect of the Algerian Revolution. All these struggles could be waged only by calling on ever wider sections of the population to participate, by digging into ever deeper social strata. The increased participation of the masses meant that new leaders, of more humble origins, soon took command. And these leaders represented not the hitherto dominant upper- and middle-class values but radical ideologies.

II

In the light of the above analysis, the shift in Arab ideologies becomes quite intelligible. For a long time, until the 1920s or '30s, the dominant ideas were those of moderate nationalism, constitutionalism, and political and economic liberalism.[5] The reasons for this are obvious. First, these were the dominant ideologies of the leading powers—Britain, France, and the United States—and to them was given full credit for the prosperity of these countries and their victory in the First World War. Second, Arab cultural contacts were almost entirely restricted to these three countries. Third, liberalism and constitutionalism suited the Arab upper and middle classes, since they controlled parliaments, parties, and the press. And economic liberalism, in addition to being fashionable, was the only policy open to governments whose hands were tied by the Capitulations, Commercial Conventions, and other bonds. But, given the Arab social structure, these ideas made practically no impact on the masses.

During the 1930s and '40s Arab society passed through an acute crisis, caused by such factors as the drastic fall in agricultural prices during the Depression; the presence of hundreds of thousands of Allied troops during the war and the consequent sharp inflation; the growth of unemployment among both unskilled labor and high-school and college graduates; and the unending struggles against foreign occupation. But at the same time the world climate was changing, with the emergence of the Soviet Union and, subsequently, China as powers and with the rapid growth in the "developing" nations of the belief in socialist planning and one-party dictatorship. The result was the collapse of the fragile Arab parliamentary systems and the replacement of the landowner and bourgeois élite by one of army officers, bureaucrats, and technicians drawn from lower strata.

And now, as in so many other underdeveloped countries, an attempt is being made to reconstruct society on the twin bases of nationalism and socialism.

The nationalism consists of an attempt at self-affirmation, primarily against the Western countries which formerly ruled the area and still dominate its economy. But the question immediately arose as to whether that nationalism was to be based on Islam or Arabism. Islam, the religion of 90 percent of the Arabs, had been for centuries the traditional, and is probably still the strongest, bond holding them together. This fact was clearly seen by the Muslim Brotherhood who, in the 1940s and early '50s, achieved great success by appealing to the sense of Muslim solidarity of the masses and by promising radical changes which would bring down the rich and improve the lot of the poor. But such an approach was open to serious objections. First and foremost, the greater part of the educated classes realizes that the ideology and organization of the Brotherhood cannot cope with the complex modernization required by Arab society. Second, the Brotherhood's approach presupposes an essential identity of interests between the Arabs and their Muslim neighbors—the Turks, Iranians, and Pakistanis; but in fact there has been considerable tension between them because of conflicting territorial claims (Alexandretta, Bahrain, and Khuzistan) and opposed international alignments. Third, in the mid-twentieth century it is no longer fashionable to proclaim religion as the official basis of society. Lastly, it created unnecessary difficulties with the Christian minorities, which had played an important part in the development of Arab nationalism and still have a minor contribution to make to Arab society.

Instead, the army groups that crushed the Muslim Brotherhood worked out an alternative, Arab Socialism. Like the socialist nationalism which is sweeping so many underdeveloped countries, it is an amalgam of intense nationalism (with a strong Muslim component), militarism, state ownership, and egalitarianism. In other words, the essential ingredients were the same as those of the Brotherhood but the doses different. The nationalist aims of this movement are the achievement of full independence, which implies the elimination of all foreign military, political and economic positions in the area; cultural independence, which is deemed to require close regulation of the entry of outside influences and the suppression or strict control of foreign schools and other institutions; and Arab unity. Its socialist aims consist essentially of the desire for greater equality and rapid industrialization, since industry is regarded as the main hope for economic development and military and political power. In view of the failure of the native bourgeoisie to carry out sufficiently rapid industrialization, this is to be brought about by state ownership of the principal means of production and by socialist planning. This, it is rightly believed, should reduce private consumption and increase the amount available for investment, though little thought has been given to the concomitant rise in public consumption and the sharp reduction in the efficiency of capital investment under bureaucratic socialism and increasing militarization. Nationalization and planning are also favored because they are expected to eliminate the influence of all private individual or group interests, foreign or local, and give the new rulers full control over their societies.

For it goes without saying that the socialism in question is an authoritarian or perhaps even a totalitarian one, resting on army rule or one-party dictatorship. It is one that gets much more inspiration from Russia, China, or Jugoslavia than from Western Socialism. As for Western political and economic liberalism, its influence and appeal have practically disappeared. It may be added that the new socialist ideas have been spread by, and the new leadership has been recruited from, not the working classes but the lower middle class. In the words of Hisham Sharabi: "It is significant that just as parliamentary democracy has been established without a middle class, revolutionary socialism under army control is now instituted without the firm base of a working class or proletariat."

Of course, the ideological shift described above has not taken place everywhere. Lebanon is still committed to parliamentary democracy and economic liberalism. Morocco, Syria, and Tunisia are struggling hard to find their way. In all four countries a native bourgeoisie had the time to develop, and it is not inclined to give up its power without a struggle. Several Arab countries have not yet reached the stage where either liberal or socialist ideologies are meaningful. But all this is less important than the fact that both Egypt and Algeria are engaged in revolutions to implement their slightly differing versions of Arab Socialism; with the nationalization laws of July 1964, Iraq also seems to have chosen the Arab Socialist way. For well over a hundred years Egypt and Algeria have been the seed beds of change in the eastern and western halves of the Arab world. Because of the reforms started by Muḥammad 'Alī in Egypt and the activity created by the inflow of French capital and settlers in Algeria, economic and social developments in these two countries have, in the past, had deep repercussions on their neighbors. It is hard to believe that this will not also hold in the immediate future.

NOTES

1. G. al-Shayyal in *Historians of the Middle East,* edited by Bérnard Lewis and P. M. Holt (London: Oxford University Press, 1962), p. 410. By way of contrast, by the end of the eighteenth century, a group of Japanese scholars had achieved—through a small chink provided by the Dutch settlement in Deshima—a much clearer picture of contemporary Western civilization. They had accepted the Copernican cosmology and understood the system of the circulation of the blood. (See Donald Keene, "The Japanese Discovery of Europe," London: Routledge and Kegan Paul, 1952).

2. A friend told me that as a young man in Damascus, in the 1860s, wanting to buy some cloth, he was told by the shopkeeper: "I have sold quite a bit today—try my neighbor, who has done very little business."

3. This is an oversimplified account of a long-drawn and complicated process. Some handicrafts gained a new lease on life by using cheaper imported materials, e.g., cotton yarn. Others managed to survive by drastically reducing the earnings of the craftsmen. A handful improved their processes, thus raising their productivity.

4. At the beginning of this century, interest and service charges on the public debt absorbed nearly a third of the Ottoman budget, in Egypt nearly a half, and in Tunisia a quarter. The £5,000,000 thus paid out annually by Egypt represented perhaps 4 percent of its gross national product.

5. Even as late as the mid-1940s, the two heroes of my students at the American University in Beirut were Mazzini and Friedrich List.

15

Economic and Social Foundations of Democracy in the Middle East

It has become commonplace that the parliamentary-democratic[1] form of government has not functioned satisfactorily in the Middle East. During the last few years, a series of *coups d'état* have proclaimed, in no uncertain terms, the dissatisfaction of several countries with their parliamentary governments and in more than one country the army has taken over power.

The failure of democracy in the Middle East has been attributed to widely divergent, though not necessarily incompatible, causes. One explanation, which is current in the West, is that democracy is a plant of slow growth, which gradually developed, over several centuries, in the congenial climate of Europe and North America and which could not possibly be expected to survive when suddenly transplanted to an alien Eastern soil which, since the dawn of recorded history, had bred nothing but the thorns and thistles of despotism. The absence of democratic traditions, and of the historical customs, habits, and attitudes required to make democracy work, was one of the first aspects of the East to strike nineteenth century Europeans and no one has expressed this better than Lord Cromer, who wrote: "Do not let us for one moment imagine that the fatally simple idea of despotic rule will readily give way to the far more complex conception of ordered liberty."[2]

In the Middle East itself, a more popular explanation is that external political factors have been mainly responsible for the inability of democracy to thrive and prosper. The title of Morgan Shuster's book, *The Strangling of Persia*,[3] is indicative of this attitude. It has been cogently argued that no real democracy could develop in Egypt, Iraq, Jordan, Lebanon, and Syria as long as British or French armies of occupation were the determining factor in all political matters and as long as the population continued to be preoccupied, not to say obsessed, with the problem of its relations with

Reprinted with permission from *International Affairs*, vol. 32, 1956.

a foreign Power. Nor was the situation of unoccupied countries, such as Iran and Turkey, very much better, for both have lived under the shadow of two powerful neighbors, one or other of whom periodically made attempts, often successful, to dominate them.

A third explanation, prevalent in both the West and the Middle East, is that, with the exception of the Turks, Middle Easterners are incapacitated, by their extreme individualism, from achieving the degree of cooperation required for the successful functioning of democracy. It is recognized that Middle Easterners develop intense loyalty to small units, such as the family, the clan, the tribe, or the religious sect, but they do not seem to be able to transcend those groups and feel toward any larger body, for example the city or the nation, enough devotion and responsibility to subordinate their individual selfish propensities to some common goal. In other words, the notion of the general will aiming at the general good seems to be absent, and with it any hope of making democracy function. Perhaps the best expression of this view is that of Ibn Khaldun, the most penetrating social scientist who has ever studied the region: ". . . every Arab regards himself as worthy to rule, and it is rare to find one of them submitting willingly to another, be it his father or his brother or the head of his clan, but only grudgingly and for fear of public opinion."[4]

Each of the three views mentioned undoubtedly contains a large measure of truth. Taken together, they may well constitute a sufficient explanation of the shortcomings of Middle Eastern democracy. Nevertheless, it seems relevant to draw attention to another group of factors which have also had a deep effect, the sociological factors. Briefly put, it is the contention of the writer that democracy does not thrive in the present-day Middle East[5] because the economic and social basis which it requires is as yet non-existent. That basis presents the following aspects: size of territory and population, level of economic development, distribution of wealth, industrialization, homogeneity of language and religion, degree of education, and habit of co-operative association. In this paper the common economic and social characteristics of those countries which at present successfully practice democracy[6] will be adopted as yardsticks against which the development of the Middle Eastern countries can be measured.

It is necessary to make explicit one basic assumption which underlies the following argument. For democratic institutions to develop, and for the democratic spirit to flourish, two conditions seem necessary: the community must be bound by a strong social solidarity; and at the same time it must contain enough diversity to produce tension between its constituent parts. In the absence of solidarity, the community is constantly threatened with disintegration, democratic government is too weak to hold it together, and there is a powerful tendency to resort to a strong, absolutist government. On the other hand, unless there is diversity and tension, resulting in the clash of ideas and interests represented by different groups, no effective check on the power of the government is likely to be established.

In Western Europe during the last three or four hundred years, and in the overseas societies which sprang from it, the cementing force has been nationalism which, although only recently articulate and still more recently virulent, has been present since the close of the Middle Ages. The tensions were provided first by the religious differences following the Reformation, and then by economic and social conflicts as first commercial and then industrial development brought into being new classes which could challenge the old landed aristocracy.

Size of population and territory. Whatever errors of application he may have committed, Aristotle was essentially right when he stated that "States, like all other things, have a definite measure of size. Any object will lose its power of performing its function if it is either excessively small or of an excessive size" and further that "experience shows that it is difficult, if not indeed impossible, for a very populous State to secure a general habit of obedience to law."[7] With the exception of the United States, Canada, and Australia, which will be discussed later, none of the democratic countries is very extensive: of the rest, France, the largest, has an area of 200,000 square miles and most of the others are distinctly smaller. Again, with the exception of the United States and the United Kingdom, none of these countries has a population of over 50 million, and the majority fall below the 10 million mark.

It is germane to enquire how the Middle Eastern States compare with the democracies in respect of population and territory. Only Pakistan, with its 75 million inhabitants, ranks among the world's giants. The other countries do not go beyond the 25 million mark, and several of them have less than 5 million inhabitants. It cannot therefore be maintained that the size of the population of Middle

Eastern countries is, in principle, such as to place great obstacles in the path of the democratic progress. Indeed, from the economic point of view, several of them are too small to constitute a market in which division of labor can be carried far enough to secure a high national income and standard of living, a fact which, as will be shown later, has a bearing on their political life. It is worth while noting, however, that in the more populous democracies, for instance, the United Kingdom and France, constitutional government developed at a time when the population was only a fraction of its present size, and that even when the democratic form of government was well established the number of inhabitants was much smaller than at present. Regarded from the point of view of size, the Middle East is not so favorably situated. Iraq is almost as large as present-day France, Afghanistan and Turkey are distinctly larger, and Pakistan, Iran, and Saudi Arabia are twice,[8] three-and-a-half times, and nearly four times as large, respectively.

Experience seems to support the assumption that great size is a handicap in the quest for democracy. In the first place it tends to promote regionalism; French and German political divisions have run on regional lines to a greater extent than have British, while in the United States regional divergences produced a great and disastrous Civil War and have continued to confuse national politics. In a country as large and varied as Iran, regional divergences would have constituted an important political factor even if the population had been perfectly homogeneous, which of course it is not, and the same is true of Pakistan, Turkey, Afghanistan, and Iraq.

The second effect is more fundamental. At any given stage of technical knowledge, there are definite limits beyond which the control exercised by a government ceases to be effective. As Ibn Khaldun put it:

Each State has its apportioned share of territories which it cannot exceed . . . the State is stronger at the center than at the periphery, weakening at the borders and becoming inoperative outside them, like rays and beams radiating from a center, or like circles spreading out on the surface of the water from the point at which it has been impinged upon.[9]

For responsible democratic government an additional condition is necessary, formulated by Aristotle as follows: "The citizens of a State must know one another's characters."[10] It is safe to state that, given the very inadequate means of communication, several of the Middle Eastern States are far too large for effective, let alone democratic, government. The following table shows two criteria, the density of railways, defined as length of line per unit of area and population, and the number of radios per head; other means of communication, such as roads, telegraphs, and telephones, are no better developed.

It may be objected that the United States, Canada, and Australia have succeeded in running a very satisfactory form of democratic government over areas far wider than those of the largest Middle Eastern countries. This is true, but easily accounted for by their very different historical background. For in all three, constitutional government was introduced at a very early stage, in colonies which were small in size and had a tiny population, and responsible government was first practiced on the state or provincial level, by such entities as Massachusetts, Lower Canada, or New South Wales. It was only after democratic government had become firmly established that those states or provinces ventured to federate in a bigger union.

MEANS OF COMMUNICATION IN PRINCIPAL MIDDLE EASTERN COUNTRIES AND
SELECTED WESTERN DEMOCRACIES

| | Railway route kilometers | | Registered Radio |
	Per 100 Square kilometers of total area	Per 10,000 inhabitants	sets per 1,000 inhabitants
Afghanistan	0	0	1
Egypt	0.61	3.2	11
Iran	0.19	1.9	11
Iraq	0.34	3.2	6
Jordan	0.37	8.3	2
Lebanon	4.50	3.5	33
Pakistan	1.23	1.5	1
Syria	0.67	2.5	11
Turkey	1.00	4.0	15
Australia	0.59	55.6	258
Canada	0.75	65.2	189
Belgium	29.03	10.6	164
France	7.55	10.4	172
Sweden	3.38	21.7	307
United Kingdom	23.33	12.0	245
United States	5.13	26.7	600
Uruguay	1.61	13.1	125

And it is very doubtful whether that union would have held together (as in the United States at the time of the Civil War) or even come about (as in Canada and Australia) but for the rapid development of railways and telegraphs.

In the Middle East, however, democracy was introduced at the national level into large areas inadequately provided with means of communication. A glance at the not so distant past, forty years ago, when the bulk of the non-colonial parts of the Middle East belonged to two large States, the Ottoman Empire and Iran, and when the railway and road systems embraced only a few thousands of miles, shows why, until recently, effective government, let alone democratic government, was impossible.

Economic structure. The influence of economic structure on politics may be studied from three angles: level of national income, distribution of wealth and income, and occupational structure. It has been stated that democracy is the child of prosperity, and it is certain, first, that the development of democracy has been intimately connected with the expansion of capitalism and secondly, that a very close correlation can be established between high *per capita* income and the successful working of democracy. A perusal of *per capita* incomes computed by the United Nations[11] shows that the fifteen countries with the highest incomes are, in order: the United States, Canada, New Zealand, Switzerland, Sweden, the United Kingdom, Denmark, Australia, Norway, Belgium, Luxembourg, the Netherlands, France, Iceland, and Ireland—in other words, fifteen of the seventeen democracies listed on page 261. The *per capita* annual income of the poorest of them, Ireland, was computed as $420 and twelve of the fifteen had incomes of over $500 per annum.[12] At the same date, none of the Middle Eastern countries except Lebanon and Turkey had a *per capita* income of over $100. Even making all the reservations which are necessary in any international comparison, it is evident that there is a vast difference in the levels of real income in the Middle East and in the Western democracies.[13]

It is hardly necessary to repeat what has so often been said, namely, that it is only when their basic needs have been satisfied that citizens can find the leisure and energy for active and intelligent participation in politics. Unless real incomes in the Middle East are doubled or trebled, the masses, obsessed by their daily needs, will continue to be the prey of every demagogue who promises relief.

The absolute level of the national income is not, however, the only criterion; no less important is its distribution. Wealth is power and the concentration of wealth in a few hands means that a small group wields excessive political power while the mass of the population, having no economic independence, is in no position to exercise its political rights. This has been clearly realized since the time of Plato, who, in the *Laws*, laid it down that in the ideal commonwealth the richest should not be more than four times as wealthy as the poorest. It has often been remarked that, since the emergence of parliaments in the Middle Ages, and even in ancient Greece, democratic government has rested mainly on the shoulders of the middle class, and it is no coincidence that the most perfect democracies, Switzerland, New Zealand, and the Scandinavian countries, have the most equal distribution of wealth.

Little data are available on the distribution of wealth and incomes in the Middle Eastern countries, but the main outlines stand out only too starkly. A study of pre-war Egypt concluded that "the gap between the two extremes is . . . enormously greater than anything met with in Europe,"[14] and since that time war-time inflation has, if anything, accentuated inequality even further. In Lebanon, Pakistan, and Turkey the situation is distinctly better, but in the other Middle Eastern countries the same pattern of inequality prevails. Hence the often repeated statement that these countries do not have a middle class, a judgment which in this extreme form is certainly untrue but which does bring out one of the basic weaknesses of the region. Hence too, until recently, the complete domination of political life by the large landowners.[15]

The third economic factor to be considered here is the occupational structure. Democracy seems to flourish only when an appreciable proportion of the population is engaged in industry and trade; it appears to be unable to strike roots in an overwhelmingly agricultural country.[16] This generalization seems to be as true of ancient city States, such as Athens, and medieval republics, such as Florence, as of modern nation States such as England or Denmark. Perhaps the best index of industrial and commercial development available for international comparison is the percentage of the working population engaged in agriculture. A table compiled by the Food and Agriculture Organization[17] gives the following percentages for the period 1939-49: United Kingdom 4 percent, United States 13 percent, Australia 15 percent, New Zealand 20 percent, Switzerland 20 percent, Sweden 21 percent, Canada 24 percent, Denmark 27 percent, France 36 percent, and Finland 50 percent. Pre-war figures are also available for another group of countries, for which more recent data are lacking; in the period 1926-39, when the level of employment in agriculture was everywhere distinctly higher than in 1939-49, the percentage of the occupied population working in agriculture was Belgium 17 percent, Netherlands 20 percent, Norway 26 percent, and Ireland 49 percent.

The only comparable Middle Eastern figures refer to the two most industrialized countries, Egypt and Turkey, where the percentage of working population engaged in agriculture in the period 1926-39 was 70 percent and 82 percent respectively. Since that time, industry has developed considerably in both countries, but in neither has it succeeded in drawing away any of the surplus rural population. As for the other Middle Eastern countries it is only in the Lebanon that the proportion is lower than in Egypt, owing to the leading part played in the economy by trade, tourism, and other services; in all the others, a still higher percentage of the working population is engaged in agriculture.

Industrialization and the development of commerce and other services affect political life in several ways. First, they contribute greatly to the raising of the national income. In almost all countries for which figures are obtainable, *per capita* incomes in industry are higher than in agriculture, while in commerce and other services they are higher than in industry.[18] Available data for Egypt, Lebanon, and Turkey show that *per capita* incomes in industry are twice as high as in agriculture,[19] and that the gap between agriculture and services is, if anything, greater than in more advanced countries.[20] It is only in such sparsely populated countries as Australia, Argentina, New Zealand, and Canada that a predominantly agricultural economy succeeded in providing a high standard of living and even there, as has been seen, the bulk of the population is no longer engaged in agriculture.

Industrialization and commercialization also promote democracy in a more direct way. By drawing the peasant away from the land, they at once weaken the power of the landowners and bring into being two new classes, the middle class and the industrial working class. A society consisting predominantly of two classes, landlords and peasants, cannot possibly hope to develop democratic institutions. The emergence of other groups, however, gives it a certain articulation; new interests come into being and with them new points of view. The struggle of the middle class for participation in government is the historical origin of most modern—and even ancient and medieval—democracies. And since the middle class is usually unable to achieve its ends without the help of the urban working class, the latter acquires some share of the benefits.[21] Finally it often happens that both the landed interest and the bourgeoisie compete for the support of the peasantry, which is then drawn into political life.

A special aspect of this process is urbanization. By concentrating large numbers in towns, and thus multiplying their social contacts, industrialization stimulates the intelligence and sharpens political awareness. It is not by chance that democracy has always flourished in an urban environment, in Athens, Florence, Geneva, London, Paris, and Boston. At the same time, it should be noted that in the past European cities were in closer touch with their rural surroundings than were Middle Eastern cities and that democratic ideas were thus more easily diffused.

National, linguistic, and religious homogeneity. It is generally agreed that the absence of national and linguistic[22] homogeneity constitutes a serious obstacle to the working of democratic government. The Scottish and Welsh national movements represent only minor and picturesque anachronisms, and the same may be said of Breton and Provençal nationalism. In Belgium, however, the struggle between Flemings and Walloons has often perilously rocked the ship of State, and in Czechoslovakia even the statesmanship of Masaryk and Beneš could not prevent the quarrel between Czechs, Slovaks, Germans, and Ruthenians from splitting it wide open. Canada's politics are dominated by the tug-of-war between the French and British elements, and United States politics have often been distorted by the centrifugal pull of ethnic groups. The shining success of the Swiss Confederation in fusing its three national ingredients is the more conspicuous because it is the only State of its kind.

In this respect, conditions vary widely in the Middle East.[23] Egypt, Jordan, the Arabian Peninsula, Lebanon, and Syria are entirely homogeneous or contain only insignificant national minorities; the only sizeable non-Arab groups in these countries are the Kurds (some 120,000) in Syria and the Armenians (some 150,000) in Syria and Lebanon, and neither of these presents any real problems. In Iraq, however, the Kurds constitute nearly one-fifth of the total population, and there are also small groups of Persians, Turcomans, and Assyrians. Turkey has been largely "homogenized" by the elimination of its Armenian and Greek minorities, but it still contains a fairly large Kurdish population, estimated at from 1.5[24] million to 2 million.[25] Iran contains many linguistic minorities including the Turks of Azerbaijan (about 1.5 million), Turcomans, Kurds (some 800,000), Arabs (300,000) and Armenians.[26] In Afghanistan there are important differences between Pushtu-speaking Afghans, Persian-speaking Tajiks, and Turkish-speaking Uzbeks, and the task of national integration is complicated by this factor. The situation in Pakistan is difficult to assess, but strains have begun to make themselves felt between the Urdu-speaking West and the Bengali-speaking East, which are separated by over a thousand miles of Indian territory.[27]

It is unnecessary to dwell at length on the effects of the existence of these minority groups, since all students of Middle Eastern affairs agree that they constitute a great handicap to the development of sound government. It may, of course, be said that the minorities are a problem only because the governments have not evolved suitable policies for integrating them into a multi-national whole. This is partly true, but it does not dispose of the fact that their presence adds one more to the many obstacles to democratic government confronting the Middle East. In Iraq, the Kurdish problem has created friction which has occasionally flared up in armed revolt. In Turkey, the friction has been still greater, repression has been more severe, and for a long period the eastern, i.e., predominantly Kurdish, provinces have been under military rule. Afghanistan is in the very earliest stages of nation building.[28] As for Iran, it is periodically threatened with disintegration, as was vividly illustrated by the Azerbaijani and Kurdish separatist movements of 1945 as well as by the Arab separatist movement in Khuzistan after the First World War. What has preserved the country's unity has generally been the Shī'īsm of the great majority of its inhabitants, which has both drawn the Iranians together and marked them off sharply from their Sunnī neighbors.

Middle Eastern minority problems are intensified by the fact that several national minorities still have a predominantly tribal structure. This is true of the Kurds in Iran, Iraq, and Turkey, and of the Turcomans and Turkish-speaking Qashqais in Iran, of the Pathans in Pakistan, and of all the main groups in Afghanistan. The existence of large bodies of tribesmen presents a truly formidable obstacle to any central government attempting to establish a framework of order covering the whole country and to enact uniform legislation for all its parts. This question, too, is not dwelt upon at length here because it has been fully recognized and often discussed by Middle Eastern experts.

While practically all students recognize that the coexistence of more than one national group imposes a great strain on a State, they are not so categorical about religious groups. Indeed it is often maintained that modern liberty and democracy owe their existence to religious diversity. To quote only one of many thinkers who have given this matter their attention, "Political liberty, as a fact in the modern world, is the result of the struggle of religious organisms to live."[29] But while it may be true that without the Reformation and the ensuing religious strife the medieval, all embracing, Catholic church would not have given way to the modern, secular, limited State, it is equally true that, once that State has been firmly established, the presence within its borders of large religious minorities does nothing to promote, and may often retard, political democracy. The conflict between Catholics and Protestants nearly wrecked the Swiss Confederation and has put a great strain on Germany and the Netherlands, while the struggle between Catholics and anticlericals has bedevilled the politics of half of Europe. One of the major reasons for the smooth working of the democratic system in the Scandinavian countries is their religious, as well as their national, homogeneity. Now, except for the Arabian peninsula and present-day Turkey, the Middle East is a veritable mosaic of religions. The fact that the Kurds, Arabs, and Turcomans are Sunnī Muslims further differentiates them from the Shī'ī Muslim Persians. Pakistan contains a 15 percent Hindu and Sikh minority and it is also divided into Shī'īs and Sunnīs. In Iraq, the Shī'īs are almost as numerous as the Sunnīs; in the other Arab countries there are substantial Christian minorities, constituting 7 percent of the population in Egypt, about 8 percent in Jordan, and 12 percent in Syria; in the last mentioned country, heterodox Muslim sects constitute a further 15 percent of the total population. As for Lebanon, it may be said to consist of nothing but minorities: of the seven leading sects, the largest, the Maronite, constitutes 30 percent of the total population, and the smallest, the Armenian Orthodox, under 6 percent.

But it is not merely a question of statistics; much more important is the difference in attitude toward religion prevailing in the West and in the Middle East. In the West, the centrifugal effects of religious divergences have been effectively checked by the centripetal force of nationalism. As Hilaire Belloc somewhat unkindly put it, the predominant philosophy has been: "Worship the nation and you may hold what lesser opinions you please."[30]

In the Middle East, on the other hand, religion is still the strongest social force and the one which arouses the fiercest passions. In the past, after the convulsions of the first few centuries, Sunnī Islam was the cement which held together the greater part of the Middle East; in Iran, after the sixteenth century, Shī'ī Islam performed the same function. Christian and other minorities had a definite, if subordinate, place in society and did not give any trouble.

With the decay of the Ottoman Empire, however, religion, sometimes in alliance with nationalism and sometimes working against it, has proved to be a most disruptive force, and one which has greatly slowed down the formation of stable States. The part played by religious minorities in the different Middle Eastern countries has been fully described in a vast body of literature and need not be discussed here.[31] No unbiased student can deny that their presence, and particularly the pretext they offered for foreign intervention, has greatly complicated the task of government in the region.

Education. This question, too, needs little elaboration, for the main facts are well known. In the West, democracy came into being largely because of the combination of a highly educated ruling class and a literate electorate. The eighteenth and nineteenth century British aristocracy, the Virginia dynasty, and the French middle class during the Restoration and the July Monarchy provide examples of highly educated ruling classes which prepared their countries for democracy. In all European countries, the expansion of education more or less kept step with the broadening of the electorate. This was dramatically signalled in England by the passing of the Education Act in 1870, following the Reform Bill of 1867 which enfranchised the urban artisan class.

In the Middle East, both conditions have been absent. The Middle Eastern States adopted parliamentary-democratic institutions without having either an educated ruling class or a literate mass, although in both respects the situation is improving greatly, thanks to the admirable efforts made after the achievement of independence. Thus, to take only two examples, in Turkey the number of pupils in all schools rose from 360,000 in 1923 to nearly 1,800,000 in 1950 and in Syria, between 1943 and 1950, the school population rose from 147,000 to 301,000. In Egypt, Turkey, and Lebanon competent specialists have begun to appear in the natural and social sciences. But the limited progress achieved serves only to mark the distance from the goal ahead. In only one Middle Eastern country, Lebanon, is more than half the population literate; in Syria the proportion is about one-third, in Turkey one-quarter, in Egypt one-fifth, and in the other countries considerably less. Similarly, while Lebanon provides education for nearly four-fifths of her children of school age, Turkey, Syria, and Egypt can accommodate about half, and the other countries one-quarter or less. Another indication is the newspaper circulation per thousand inhabitants, which stands at 81 in Lebanon, 28 in Jordan, 21 in Syria, 18 in Egypt, 15 in Turkey, 6 in Iraq, 5 in Iran, 2 in Pakistan, and one in Afghanistan. Corresponding figures for some Western democracies are 599 for the United Kingdom, 455 for Australia, 441 for Luxembourg, 415 for the three Scandinavian countries, 357 for the United States, 281 for the Netherlands, and 187 for Uruguay.

It is true that the level of political consciousness of the Middle Eastern masses is much higher than these figures would seem to indicate. Owing to the habit of listening, in groups, to the radio or to a newspaper reader, Middle Easterners have an acquaintance with international and local politics which always astonishes foreigners. But such alternative methods, welcome as they may be, are not a substitute for literacy, and the level of public opinion remains, of course, very much lower than in the developed countries of Europe and America.

Co-operative associations. One of the aspects of the Middle East which impresses, and depresses, Western observers most is the inability of its peoples to associate for co-operative action or to act on the level of local government. Whenever a social need is felt, be it for a village road, an electric station, a school, a football field, or a marketing co-operative, the first impulse is to turn to the central government for help. Recent Middle Eastern history teems with instances of government-sponsored schemes. The great majority of schools and hospitals are government-owned and run and so are the railways and most of the airlines. In Turkey a great part, and in Iran a substantial portion, of industry and mining belongs to the State. In the few countries where it has made headway, i.e., Egypt, Turkey, and Arab Palestine, the agricultural co-operative movement has been sponsored and directed by the government. And it should be noted that in all these cases it is the central government, rather than the provincial or municipal authorities, which is in charge.

It would be foolish in the extreme to condemn such government action outright in the name of abstract principles of individualism and free enterprise. If individual initiative is not forthcoming to build a railway or school, it is surely better that the State should do so rather than that it should be left undone. But at the same time it should be clearly realized that a society that lacks numerous and strong associations, and in which local governments play a negligible part, is not one in which democracy can flourish.

It would be equally rash to conclude that Middle Easterners are congenitally incapable of co-operative association, still less that they lack initiative. There is some evidence that, in its heyday, Islamic civilization was the scene of intense activity conducted by partnerships and joint enterprises. International commercial ventures were on a scale well beyond the financial capacities of any individual, and were carried out by partnerships involving large numbers. Similarly the network of banking, which made it possible to cash in Morocco, Ceylon, or Zanzibar a check drawn on Basra, indicates widespread contacts and habits of trust and co-operation. The collapse of Islamic civilization, following the Crusades and Mongol invasions, seems, however, to have eliminated both individual initiative and co-operation, both of which became equally impossible under the arbitrary and extortionate governments which oppressed the poverty-stricken region.

In the last fifty or hundred years, conditions having become more propitious, there has been a rebirth of individual initiative which is best exemplified by the activities of Persians in India, South Arabians in Indonesia and, above all, the exploits of the Lebanese in West Africa, the United States, and South America. Actions by associations responded much more slowly to the improvement in the environment, being often hampered by the very qualities which account for the increase in individual enterprise, but during the last thirty years there have been such welcome steps as the Banque Misr enterprises and the Committee for Translation and Publication in Egypt, and the foundation of hundreds of societies for educational or philanthropic purposes, such as the Red Crescent, in all the more advanced Middle Eastern countries. Trade unions have also begun to assume some importance. But such associations still play only a minor part in national life. As for local governments, with very few exceptions such as the municipality of Alexandria—which owes its importance and activity to the large number of foreigners who still serve on it—their functions continue to be negligible and there are few signs of an increase in their scope and power. It is significant that Cairo, the largest city in the region, was not allowed to have a municipality until after the Second World War.[32]

The case of Lebanon.   The validity of the observations made in this paper may be tested by applying them to the Middle Eastern country which is furthest advanced on the road to full and genuine democracy, Lebanon. However great the imperfections of her governments, it remains true that Lebanon has enjoyed a freedom of thought, expression, and association far greater than that prevailing in the Middle East—and in many more advanced countries as well. And the bloodless overthrow of the seemingly all powerful President, in September 1952, was an encouraging sign of the power of public opinion and its ability to translate itself into action.[33]

An examination of the criteria enumerated shows Lebanon to be much more favorably situated than any other Middle Eastern country studied here. The very small size of Lebanon's territory and population, which is distinctly hindering her economic growth, has favored her political development. Her means of communication are adequate, an excellent system of roads compensating for the deficiency in railways. Her per capita income, recently estimated at over $250, is well above that of any other Middle Eastern country. Owing to the prevalence of small-scale landholdings in many parts of the country, and to the relatively large number engaged in services, the distribution of wealth and income is less unequal than in other parts of the region. Her population is highly urbanized; only half the population is rural, and of this a substantial fraction earns its livelihood in non-agricultural occupations; the income from industry and building combined is greater than the agricultural income; and commerce plays a most important part in the economy. Education is much more developed than elsewhere; over two-thirds of the population are literate, and nearly four-fifths of children of school age attend school. Newspaper circulation is comparable to that of the less advanced European countries, and the number of radios is relatively high. Nationally and linguistically, Lebanon is homogeneous, the very small Armenian minority presenting no problem whatsoever. The one great handicap of Lebanon is the multiplicity of religious sects, and all observers agree that this, more than anything, has stood in the way of efficient government.

It may therefore be taken that the case of Lebanon confirms the choice of the criteria adopted. A further confirmation is provided by Turkey. The remarkable economic and social advance of the last decade (reflected by such indices as per capita income, literacy, school attendance, and book publishing) following the basic social reforms of Atatürk, paved the way for the emergence of political democracy in that country. These considerations lend support to the hope that economic and social development will bring about, in the other countries, conditions more propitious for the growth of political democracy.

Conclusion. One negative conclusion stands out sharply from the preceding analysis: in the Middle East the economic and social soil is still not deep enough to enable political democracy to strike root and flourish. What is needed is not merely constitutional or administrative reforms, not just a change in government machinery or personnel. It is not even the adjustment of an obsolete political structure to bring it in line with a new balance of forces reflecting changing relations between various social classes, as was achieved by the Reform Bills in nineteenth-century England. What is required is a great economic and social transformation which will strengthen society and make it capable of bearing the weight of the modern State. Such a development is a necessary, if not a sufficient, condition for the establishment of genuine democracy in the region. For, in politics as in religion, a Reformation must be preceded by a Renaissance.

What should be done in the meantime? Clearly, while it is futile to lament the absence of democracy in a region still unprepared for it, it is absolutely necessary to set in motion the forces which will transform Middle Eastern society in the desired manner. Great efforts must be made to improve means of communication, multiply schools, and, so far as possible, bring about a cultural and spiritual unity which will bridge the chasms separating the linguistic groups and religious sects. Great efforts must also be made to develop the economy of the different countries in order to raise the general level and to create opportunities which will allow the individual to emancipate himself from the grip of the family, tribe, and village.

So much would be admitted by all, but the question still remains: who is to carry out all these changes? Most Middle Easterners look to the government for the necessary guidance and initiative and many of them seek a short cut by way of a military dictatorship. Both these tendencies deserve more understanding and consideration than they usually receive from Anglo-Saxon observers. In underdeveloped countries attempting to transform themselves within a twentieth-century economic, social, and political context, the government must inevitably play a large, perhaps a leading, part. This is especially true where it happens to own the main sources of funds which can be used for development, as is the case in the oil producing countries in the Middle East. Nor need the desire for a military dictatorship spring from ignoble, ultra-nationalistic, or reactionary motives. In Asian countries the officer corps tends to be recruited from the middle class and is therefore—unlike the upper class European officer corps—more often a spearhead of change than a bulwark of conservatism. Finally, the need for a strong government is an essential prerequisite of progress, and perhaps even of eventual democracy. Most existing democracies have passed through a prolonged stage of despotic or dictatorial government in which the country was forcibly welded into a coherent whole. One has only to recall the Tudors, the Stuarts, and Cromwell in England and Richelieu, Louis xiv, and Napoleon in France. What Atatürk and Riza Shah attempted to do, with a greater or less measure of success, was to transform a congeries of villages, tribes, and sects into a nation State. The methods were often ill chosen, but it is impossible to deny that without a greater degree of national unity than prevailed when they took power, orderly and efficient government, let alone democratic government, would have been utterly impossible.

All this is true, but it does not represent the final answer to the problem. Ultimately, Middle Eastern society must save itself through the individual and co-operative efforts of thousands of men and women in all walks of life, who will educate and regenerate the people and develop and exploit the human and natural resources of the region. Most Middle Easterners will answer that such efforts are useless under existing conditions, because a malevolent government can thwart the best intentioned and most devoted individuals. This is true, but only up to a point. Sooner or later these efforts will bear fruit, however great the opposing forces may be. And then, the present vicious circle, in which bad governments prevent society from bettering itself and them may be replaced by a "virtuous circle" in which private and public bodies co-operate for the common good. Another objection may also be briefly discussed. Individual, and still more co-operative, action tends to work through, and therefore to reinforce and perpetuate, the existing social framework. This applies particularly to sectarianism. Thus the remarkable expansion of education in Lebanon, which was mainly carried out by church groups, has greatly helped the general development of the country but has undoubtedly strengthened its chronic sectarianism. In recent years, however, there has been an encouraging tendency to transcend sectarian, ethnic, and other group barriers by non-denominational associations working for common political, economic, or social ends. A conspicuous example is that of the *Ruwwad* in Egypt, a group of social workers founded some twenty years ago, several of whose members have served in recent cabinets. Another example is that of the Village Welfare Service in the American University of Beirut.[34] Finally, political parties are tending more and more to cut across sectarian and ethnic lines.

One final remark may be made. The task outlined above is one for the Middle Easterners themselves. Foreign aid can be of great use, but it must be indirect and limited, taking the form of deeper and more sympathetic understanding as well as the provision of technical and financial assistance. The bulk of the work, and all the major policy decisions, must be left to the nationals of the country concerned. The most disastrous mistake would be the belief that because the Middle Eastern countries are unprepared for democracy they are unfit for independence. For one thing, the vast majority of independent States, throughout history and in all parts of the world, have not been democracies. For another, nothing is better calculated to distract Middle Easterners from their real problem than foreign interference. A long and arduous road lies ahead of the Middle East and it is essential that it be not pushed or stampeded into blind alleys but on the contrary encouraged and aided to find the right path.

NOTES

1. In this paper "democracy" denotes exclusively a system of parliamentary government, based on free, popular elections, contested by two or more parties. The term usually covers a much wider range of meaning and in this broader sense several aspects of Middle Eastern life may be said to be "democratic"; in particular, there is a genuine and widespread social democracy in most Middle Eastern countries. It is moreover true that political democracy can express itself in other forms than parliamentary government, and does so in several Middle Eastern countries. However, a study of these broader aspects of democracy would carry the discussion too far afield and the present essay is therefore exclusively concerned with the narrow meaning given above.

2. See "The Government of Subject Races," *Edinburgh Review* (January 1908).

3. (New York, The Century Co., 1912.)

4. *An Arab Philosophy of History: Selections from the Prolegomena of Ibn Khaldun of Tunis 1332-1406,* translated by Charles Issawi (London, John Murray, 1950), p. 57.

5. The Middle East is here defined as the territory bounded by and including Libya in the west, the Sudan in the south, Turkey in the north, and Pakistan in the east, a territory with an aggregate population of not much below 200 million. With the qualifications noted below, much the same economic and social pattern prevails in the whole region, except in Israel, which is consequently not included in this essay.

6. The countries covered by the term "democratic" are: the United States, Canada, the United Kingdom, France, Iceland, Ireland, Switzerland, Luxembourg, Belgium, the Netherlands, Denmark, Norway, Sweden, Finland, Australia, New Zealand, and Uruguay. · Germany and Italy have joined the democratic ranks only recently, while Czechoslovakia has been snatched away from them; the inclusion of these three countries would not, however, in any way affect the conclusions drawn.

7. *The Politics of Aristotle,* translated with notes by Ernest Barker (Oxford, Clarendon Press, 1948), p. 341.

8. Egypt has not been included in this list. Her area is nearly twice as large as that of France, but the population is concentrated· in only 5 percent of the whole territory, making it, in spite of its elongated shape (Napoleon once said that Italy was too long: and Egypt is longer), one of the most compact countries in the world.

9. *An Arab Philosophy of History,* p. 127.

10. *The Politics of Aristotle,* p. 341.

11. Statistical Office of the United Nations, *National and Per Capita Incomes, Seventy Countries, 1949* (New York, October, 1950).

12. The figure for the United States was $1,453; the second highest, Canada, stood at $870. The figures for the two other democracies listed above were Finland $348, Uruguay $331.

13. Other criteria of economic and social development, such as consumption of energy and steel, foreign trade, literacy, newspaper circulation, etc., tend to fall in line with per capita incomes. See Charles Issawi, "The Conditions of Economic Progress in the Middle East," *Economic Development and Cultural Change* (Chicago), December, 1952.

14. Charles Issawi, *Egypt: An Economic and Social Analysis* (London, Oxford University Press for R.I.I.A., 1947), p. 54.

15. See *ibid.,* pp. 173-4, for a discussion of the part played by landlords in Egyptian politics.

16. The United States in the eighteenth century, and perhaps Canada, Australia, and New Zealand in the nineteenth, may be quoted as contrary examples of agrarian democracy. Moreover it may be recalled that, according to Jefferson, democracy can flourish only in an agrarian environment. These facts, however, only apparently contradict the statement made

above. For in all the above-mentioned countries, an immigrant population, from a country with highly developed free political institutions, settled in an empty continent. This meant that, in their new homes, the colonists were not burdened with feudal institutions hampering their economic, social, and political progress; it also meant that agriculture could yield them an exceptionally high income. Neither of these factors could possibly exist in an old, settled society until an economic, social, and political revolution, generated by the expansion of commerce or industry, had broken down their feudal or quasi feudal system.

17. *Yearbook of Food and Agricultural Statistics*, vol. 4, pt. 1, 1950, table 5A.

18. See among others, Colin Clark, *The Conditions of Economic Progress*, new ed. (London, Macmillan, 1951).

19. United Nations, *Review of Economic Conditions in the Middle East, 1951-2*, pp. 37-42.

20. *Egypt: An Economic and Social Analysis*, p. 163.

21. It cannot, however, be denied that at present there is a danger that the working class of underdeveloped countries may choose the path of Communism rather than democracy. It may be found possible to counteract this tendency by raising the economic, social, and cultural level of the working class.

22. In this essay, linguistic and national divisions are assumed to be identical. This may not have been true in the past, but since the national awakenings of the nineteenth century it may be taken that every large group speaking a language differing from those of its neighbors will, sooner or later, experience a feeling of cultural distinctness which will generally translate itself into national consciousness.

23. The best study on this subject is A. H. Hourani's *Minorities in the Arab World* (London, Oxford University Press for R.I.I.A., 1947).

24. A. M. Burton, "The Kurds," *Royal Central Asian Journal*, London, January, 1944.

25. Lewis V. Thomas and Richard N. Frye, *The United States and Turkey and Iran* (London, Cambridge University Press, 1951), p. 78. A figure of 4 million is given by the Kurdish leader, Emir Kamuran Bedir Khan, "Kurdistan," *Cahiers de L'Est*, Beirut, No. I, 1945.

26. *The United States and Turkey and Iran*, pp. 188-90. Somewhat different estimates are given by Haas, Groseclose, and Wilbur in their books on Iran.

27. Europeans minorities which, when protected by the Capitulations, presented a major obstacle in many countries, now no longer constitute a serious problem.

28. Vladimir Cervin, "The Problems in the Integration of the Afghan Nation," *Middle East Journal*, Autumn 1952.

29. J. N. Figgis, *Studies of Political Thought from Gerson to Grotius*, 2nd ed. (London, Cambridge University Press, 1916), pp. 6-7.

30. Hilaire Belloc, *Survivals and New Arrivals* (London, Sheed and Ward, 1939), p. 42.

31. Two points, however, deserve to be made. First, that intermarriage between members of different religious communities was, until very recently, unthinkable and even today is numerically negligible. Secondly, that each religious or national group has generally tended to specialize in one or two occupations, practicing what Professor C. S. Coon has called "an ethnic division of labor." It may also be mentioned that, until recently, each group had its own distinct form of dress.

32. It may be noted that Islamic civilization never witnessed the kind of corporate municipal activity which flourished in ancient Greece and Rome or medieval and renaissance Europe. Only in Spain, where Islam impinged on a European society, did such cities as Toledo, Cordoba, and Seville play an independent part.

33. For an interesting and sympathetic account see: "Peaceful Change in the Lebanon," *The World Today* (R.I.I.A., April 1953), p. 162.

34. In this connection it may be noted that Anglo-Saxon schools in the Middle East have done much to break down sectarian barriers and that a great degree of inter-denominational harmony has been achieved by their students and graduates.

16

European Loan-Words in Contemporary Arabic Writing:

A CASE STUDY IN MODERNIZATION

No one familiar with contemporary Arabic can fail to be struck by the paucity of its foreign loan-words. Indeed, in a very interesting conference held in Paris a few years ago, an eminent French scholar went as far as to describe its resistance to such borrowing as "frénétique."[1]

Various explanations may be given for this imperviousness to foreign linguistic influences. The fact that, for Muslims, the Arabic of the Quran is literally the language of God has naturally made them anxious to keep it "pure and undefiled." With this goes a phenomenon which is almost as widespread among Christian as Muslim Arabs, and which can be described only as "verbolatry": the Arabs have poured almost all their genius into their language—to the great neglect of other arts—and have developed a passionate attachment to it. Lastly, the intense Arab nationalism has, quite rightly, fastened on the Arabic language as the main bond—together with Islam—holding the otherwise rather diverse Arab peoples and the one differentiating them from their non-Arab Muslim neighbors and has further strengthened their attachment to and jealousy for their language; hence any borrowing that might increase the diversity of the Arabic used in various parts is looked upon with deep suspicion as a disruptive factor.[2] It may be added that, as was recognized at the above-mentioned conference, the phenomenon of liguistic nationalism is very widespread in the contemporary world, manifesting itself in France, for instance, in the form of the vigorous attack on "Franglais" pursued by Professor Etiemble.[3]

This article is an attempt to investigate one aspect of the use of foreign words in Arabic through a study of the modern European words in an outstanding contemporary Egyptian novel. These are then compared with the ones in another Egyptian novel and in two articles, as well as with those to be found in two word-lists compiled

Reprinted with permission from *Middle Eastern Studies*, vol. 3, 1967, pp. 110-133.

a few years ago. Lastly, samples have been taken from contemporary Persian and Turkish novels, short stories, and other writings to compare the frequency of modern European words in those languages and some data on Uzbek have also been given. Novels and short stories have been emphasized because, more than any other form of writing, they draw their vocabulary from the mainstream of language and not from the tributaries formed by technical and specialized terms. The choice of Egypt was dictated by the preeminent position, both literary and political, which it occupies among Arab countries and which makes Egyptian by far the most widely read of all modern Arabic writings.

It will be noticed that this study covers only the written language, not the spoken colloquial. No similar work has, to my knowledge, been done on the latter. However, it would be generally agreed upon that the proportion of foreign words in colloquial is considerably larger than in written Arabic. The extent of the difference may be judged by reading a play written in colloquial, for example *al-Farafir* by Yusif Idris (Cairo, 1964).

It should also be pointed out that this study is confined to modern European words. Thus, it excludes borrowings from Persian or Turkish and also the Greek and Latin words taken over in the early Middle Ages and which have become completely acclimatized, e.g., athir (ether), musiqa (music), jins (genus), jughrafia (geography), etc.[4] Hence, except for the names of a few coins which entered Arabic earlier, e.g., qirsh (groschen), the foreign borrowings reflect the impact which Europe began to have—either directly or through the intermediary of Turkish—on the Arab world in general, and Egypt in particular, from the beginning of the nineteenth century.

Most educated Arabs, if asked to name the best novel written so far in Arabic, would probably choose the trilogy by Nagib Mahfuz: *Bain al-Qasrain* (Cairo, 1956), *Qasr al-Shawq* (Cairo, 1957), and *al-Sukkariyya* (Cairo, 1957). This 1,437 page novel tells the story of three generations of a Muslim Egyptian middle-class family, living in one of the old quarters of Cairo, in the years 1918-1919, 1926-1927, and 1935-1944. Although the book is far too long, and wastes much space on tedious descriptions of love-affairs involving enormously fat females, its merits are considerable. In the first place the major characters are real living beings, whose thoughts and emotions are vividly and convincingly expressed. Secondly, the book conveys an excellent idea of that charming and fascinating phenomenon,

Egyptian humor. Lastly, and most interesting for the present study, it shows the gradual exposure to modern and Western influences of a family brought up in what was an essentially traditionalist, Islamic environment. Their attitudes to the dominant political issue in each of the successive periods are typical of those of the petty bourgeoisie, which has been the main formative force in Egypt since the First World War. In 1918-1919 its main preoccupation was the struggle against the British; in 1926-1927 it was the conflict between the Wafd, led by Zaghlul, and the King and his supporters; in 1935-1936 there was again the anti-British agitation culminating in the 1936 Anglo-Egyptian Treaty; and after that, and more particularly during the last years of the Second World War, there was increasing social tension and polarization toward the extremes of the left and right. This is reflected in the fact that of the three grandsons, one becomes a Muslim Brother and another a Communist, while the third has no clear-cut political convictions but occupies a fairly high post in the civil service.

Table I gives a listing, by volume, of the modern European words used by Mahfuz. As mentioned before, it excludes Greek and Latin words which entered the Arabic language in the Middle Ages as well as Persian and Turkish words which came in then or later. It also excludes geographical names, but includes the names of the months of the calendar (January, etc.) which have become universal in Egypt though not in the other Arabic countries where the traditional Semitic names (Tammuz, Ab, etc.) are still used.

The first striking fact in the table is the small number of European words—144 in all, with a total frequency of 788. If one hazards the guess that the vocabulary used in this novel is not less than 10,000 words, European words would constitute at most 1.5 percent of the total. As their frequency is much lower than the average, their total frequency is only some 0.23 percent of the number of words in the book (about 350,000).

These very low figures become even more significant when it is noted that Mahfuz does not go out of his way to avoid foreign words, as do some other writers. Thus, four of the five words he uses most frequently, *salah* (living room), *kanabah* (sofa), *tram* (tramway), *radiu* (radio), and *bulis* (police), have Arabic equivalents which another writer might well have used—indeed, Mahfuz often does use the old Arabic word *shurtah* (derived from Latin) for police. His use of *kanabah* instead of sofa (a word of Arabic origin!) may be

TABLE I

MAHFUZ TRILOGY

Objects of daily use	Volume			Total
	I	II	III	
Food and Drink				
batatah (It. patata ?, potatoe)	1	—	—	1
birah (It. birra, beer)	—	9	—	9
sandwitsh (Eng. sandwich)	—	6	—	6
sigarah (cigarette)	2	4	11	17
shambania (It. sciampania, champagne)	—	5	—	5
shikolatah; shikolatah; shokolatah (It. ciocco-				
lata, chocolate)	10	5	—	15
salsah (It. salsa, sauce)	1	—	—	1
soda (Eng. ? soda [water])	—	3	1	4
tamatim (tomato)	1	—	1	2
faraula (It. fravola, strawberry)	—	—	1	1
koniak (Fr. cognac)	2	6	—	8
murtadilla (It. mortadella, ham sausage)	—	1	—	1
makarunah (It. maccherone, macaroni)	—	—	1	1
wiski, wiski (Eng. whiskey)	1	13	5	19
	14	18	52	20	90
Clothing and Cosmetics				
babiyon (Fr. papillon, bow tie)	1	2	—	3
bantalun (It. pantaloni, pants)	2	5	—	7
budrah (Fr. poudre ?, powder)	4	—	—	4
jakitta (It. giachetta, coat)	3	5	3	11
ridingut (Fr. rédingote, frock coat)	—	1	—	1
rub (Fr. robe [de chambre], dressing gown)	—	—	2	2
ruj (Fr. rouge, rouge)	—	—	1	1
fanillah (It. flanella, flannel, undershirt)	1	2	—	3
kulunia (eau de cologne)	4	1	—	5
manikur (Fr. manicure)	—	—	1	1
	10	15	16	7	38
Household				
bitrul (Eng. petrol ?, benzine)	1	—	—	1
battariyah (It. batteria, flash lamp)	3	—	—	3
bufih (Fr. buffet)	—	—	3	3
tirmus (thermos, flask)	—	3	—	3
tirmumitr (Fr. thermomètre)	—	1	—	1
dushsh (Fr. douche, shower)	1	2	2	5
shizlung (Fr. chaise longue, deck chair)	3	—	—	3
salah (It. sala, living room)	28	9	23	60
viranda (It. veranda)	—	4	8	12
fanar (It. fanale ?, candlestick)	2	—	—	2
villa (villa)	—	—	4	4
kanabah (Fr. canapé ?, sofa)	41	47	19	107
klub (globe ? kerosene lamp)	1	—	—	1
kunsul, kunsul, kansul (console)	3	2	—	5
	14	83	68	59	210

TABLE I continued

MAHFUZ TRILOGY

Objects of daily use	Volume			Total
	I	II	III	
Transport and Communications				
abunih (Fr. abonné, season ticket)	—	—	1	1
asfalt (asphalt)	—	1	1	2
taksi (taxicab)	—	3	—	3
tram (tramway)	2	4	19	25
tilifun, also used as verb talfana (telephone)	3	3	4	10
tilighraf (telegraph)	—	—	1	1
hantur, hantur (Hungarian hinto, horse cab)	8	6	2	16
radiu (radio)	—	—	22	22
tuar (Fr. trottoire ?, sidewalk)	1	1	—	2
farmalah (brake)	3	1	4	8
karru (It. carro, cart)	8	2	2	12
kumsari (It. commissario ?, ticket collector)	5	—	2	7
luri (Eng. lorry)	11	1	—	12
	13	41	22	58 121
Music and Entertainment				
ubira (It. opera)	—	1	—	1
urkistra (orchestra, band)	1	13	—	14
bar (Eng. bar)	—	1	3	4
badrunah (It. padrona, 'madame' in a brothel)	—	—	2	2
biyanu (It. pianoforte)	—	5	3	8
tavirna (It. taverna, tavern)	—	—	1	1
duminu (domino)	—	5	1	6
sirk (Fr. cirque, circus)	—	1	—	1
sinima, sinimai (cinema, cinematographic)	1	5	2	8
taulah (It. tavola, backgammon)	—	—	1	1
fa (musical note fa)	—	1	—	1
klub (Eng. club)	2	1	—	3
luj (F. loge, box)	—	—	1	1
nutah (It. nota, musical note)	—	—	1	1
funughraf (phonograph)	2	1	2	5
	15	6	34	17 57
Diseases and Drugs				
influinza (influenza)	1	—	—	1
tifud, tifuid (typhoid)	1	2	1	4
rumatizm (rheumatism)	—	1	1	2
kallu (It. callo, callous)	—	1	—	1
kukayin (cocaine)	1	2	4	7
kulira (cholera)	—	—	1	1
malaria (malaria)	1	—	—	1
	7	4	6	7 17
Calendar Months				
	8	3	13	— 16

TABLE I continued

MAHFUZ TRILOGY

Objects of daily use	Volume			Total
	I	II	III	
Other				
alagarsun (Fr. à la garçonne, hairstyle)	—	1	1	2
bravu, brafu (It. bravo !)	—	2	3	5
burunzi (bronze coloured)	1	—	—	1
brufa (It. prova, page proofs)	1	—	1	2
blatin (platinium)	—	1	—	1
bumb (bomb)	—	1	—	1
bulitika (It. politica, finesse)	1	1	—	2
granit, graniti (granite)	—	2	—	2
jintilman (Eng. gentleman)	—	2	—	2
dinamit (dynamite)	—	1	—	1
rijim (Fr. régime, diet)	—	—	1	1
ruba bikia (It. roba vecchia, discarded old things)	—	—	1	1
futughrafi (photographic)	—	—	1	1
qirsh (Ger. groschen, a coin)	1	—	—	1
kabtin (Eng. captain of team, leader)	—	—	1	1
surah karikaturiah (Fr. caricature, cartoon)	1	3	—	4
karnafal (carnival)	—	1	—	1
makinah (It. macchina, machine)	1	—	—	1
munawarah (It. manovra ?, manoeuvre)	—	1	—	1
madam (Fr. madame, Mrs.)	—	1	—	1
millim (Fr. millième, a coin)	1	1	2	4
nimrah (It. numero, number in a lottery)	1	—	—	1
wabur (Fr. vapeur, boiler)	—	—	1	1
	23	8	18	12	38
Sub-total	104	178	229	180	587

Abstract and technical terms	I	II	III	Total
Social Sciences				
aristuqratiyy, aristuqratiyya (aristocrat, aristocracy)	—	12	3	15
barlaman (Fr. parlement, parliament)	—	1	1	2
burjuaziyy, burjuaziyyah (Fr. bourgeois, bourgeoisie)	—	—	10	10
bursa, bursah (It. borsa, stock exchange)	—	1	1	2
bulis (Fr. police)	9	2	6	17
dusiah (Fr. dossier, file folder)	—	—	1	1
jurnalji (journalist)	—	—	4	4
diblumasiy, diblumasiyya (diplomatic, diplomacy)	—	3	1	4
diktatur, diktaturiya (dictator, dictatorship)	—	1	3	4
dimuqratiyya (democracy)	—	3	9	12
rutin (Fr. routine)	1	—	—	1
sikritir, sikritariyya (secretary, secretariat)	1	—	10	11

TABLE I continued

MAHFUZ TRILOGY

Abstract and Technical Terms	Volume			Total
	I	II	III	
fashistiyya (fascism)	—	—	8	8
kadr (Fr. cadre)	—	1	3	4
kunstabl (Eng. constable)	—	—	4	4
marksiyya (marxism)	—	—	1	1
milyun, milyunair (million, millionaire)	—	2	1	3
naziyya (nazism)	—	—	6	6
	18	11	26	72	109
Natural Sciences				
mikrub (microbe)	—	2	1	3
biulujiya (biology)	—	1	1	2
duktur (doctor, physician)	—	1	8	9
sikulujiya (psychology)	—	1	1	2
ghaziyy (gaseous)	1	—	1	2
maghnisium (magnesium)	—	1	—	1
mitr (Fr. mètre)	4	1	—	5
	7	5	7	12	24
Education				
bakaluriya (Fr. baccalauréat, school certificate)	—	7	5	12
diblum (Fr. diplome, higher degree)	—	4	—	4
lisans (Fr. licence, B.A.)	—	6	7	13
magistir (M.A.)	—	—	1	1
	4	—	17	13	30
Other				
bragmatizm (pragmatism)	—	—	1	1
drama (drama)	—	—	1	1
rumantikiyya (romanticism)	—	—	2	2
riwayah bulisiyya (Fr. roman policier, detective novel)	1	1	—	2
klasikiyy (classical)	—	—	1	1
mitafiziqa (metaphysic)	—	—	5	5
narfazah, mutanarfiz (nervousness, nervous)	1	1	4	6
mudah (It. moda, fashion)	1	5	6	12
mikaniki, mikanism (mechnical, mechanism)	1	2	2	5
harmuni (harmonic)	1	1	—	2
hirughlifi (hieroglyphic)	—	1	—	1
	11	5	11	22	38
Sub-total	40	21	61	119	201
Grand total	144	199	290	299	788
Approximate number of Arabic words	—	135,000		95,000	
			110,000		350,000

due to his intention to emphasize the fact that he is describing a European-type sofa with a back and side-arms. And sometimes he seems deliberately to go out of his way to use a European word instead of a common Arabic equivalent, e.g., *tirmumitr* instead of *mizan al-harara*.

The second striking fact is brought out by the rather arbitrary division into "objects of daily use" and "abstract and technical terms."[5] Both the number and the frequency of the first group are more than 2.5 times as large as those of the latter. In other words, the author's main need was for the names of *things* rather than for more abstract terms conveying ideas or states of mind. For the latter he judged the resources of Arabic to be adequate.

The third main fact that comes out from the table is the marked increase in the number of foreign words, and in their frequency, as the story advances in time. This is particularly marked in the second group, that of "abstract and technical terms," where the frequency in Volume II is nearly three times as high as in Volume I, and in Volume III twice as high as in Volume II. This increase reflects the growing Westernization of the younger generations. Hence, on the one hand the need for words like beer, sandwich, thermos, radio, and other articles of daily use—including even ham sausages!—and, on the other, the introduction of more abstract terms such as pragmatism, classical, bourgeois, to reflect the objects of their thoughts. Whether this increased use of foreign words is deliberate or subconscious is a question that can only be raised, not answered.

Lastly, a few words may be said regarding the national origins of the loan-words. The predominance of Italian words, followed by French, in "articles of daily use" is very marked. English ranks a very poor third and no other language has made any significant contribution. It is much more difficult to trace the origin of "abstract and technical terms," but the form they take suggests that most of them entered through French, and a few through English. The absence of German words (except for Groschen and Nazism!) is striking.[6]

Closer inspection of the sub-groups brings out further interesting facts. The 14 words in the "food and drink" category apply to articles introduced during the last hundred and fifty years, or in two or three cases somewhat earlier. The 10 words under "clothing and cosmetics" show the Europeanization of middle-class dress, which is worn by the sons and grandsons though not the father, and the 14 words under "household" show a similar invasion of furniture and fittings. The 15 words under "music and entertainment" refer either to Western musical instruments and forms, such as piano, phonograph (however, an Arabic word is always used for discs, *istuwana*), opera, and orchestra, or to various entertainment activities, e.g., bar, cinema, club, tavern, domino, etc.

The number of words dealing with "transport and communications" is relatively high (13) and reflects the fact that not only mechanical transport but even wheeled carriages were introduced into Egypt at only the very end of the eighteenth century.[7] Hence, the names of even the simplest forms of wheeled transport were taken from foreign sources— *karru* (Italian carro, cart) and *hantur* (Hungarian hinto, horse cab);[8] in Syria and Lebanon even the word for paved road, *karrusah*, is derived from Italian. But it should be noted that a vigorous attempt has been made to replace such words by others of Arabic origin; this has met with great success in writing and a lesser, but none the less considerable, one in speech. Thus, *sayyarah* has replaced *utumubil*, *darrajah* has taken the place of *bisiklit* (bicycle), *qitar* is used instead of *trin* (train), *bakhira* instead of *wabur* (vapeur, i.e., steamboat), *barid* (itself of Latin origin) instead of *bustah* (post), *barqia* instead of *tilighraf* (telegraph, telegram), and so on. *Tilifun* (telephone) and the derived verb *talfana* have, however, proved more stubborn and refused to give way to the suggested substitute, *hatif*,[9] while attempts to find an Arabic word for television have so far failed signally[10] and *radiu* (radio) has held its own against *midhia'*, though the word *la-silki* (wireless) is also commonly used.

The most striking fact about the second group, "abstract and technical terms," is their very small number—40 items with a total frequency of 201. The sub-group on "education" shows the influence of French methods and curricula, and the names of the various certificates have remained French. The sub-group "natural sciences" consists of only 7 items, which is not surprising in a novel dealing with people who have no scientific training or interests. As will be pointed out below, however, natural science is the field where Arabic can least dispense with foreign loan-words.

The nature, and relatively small number, of the words shown under "social sciences" point out the success of Arabic in coining words in the vast field designated by this heading. It should be noted that they include some items which could have been omitted, e.g.,

Fascism, Nazism, and Marxism, which are proper nouns, and Aristocracy and Democracy, which were known to the medieval Arabs but were later forgotten and had to be re-introduced, directly or through Turkish, in the nineteenth century.[11] Similarly *Barlaman* (Parliament) is a proper noun like Congress, with Arabic terms for its constituent Chamber of Deputies (*majlis al-nuwwab*) and Senate (*majlis al-shuyukh*). Bourgeoisie has acquired a connotation which makes it untranslatable into Arabic, as into other languages. *Shurta* is frequently used by Mahfuz instead of *bulis*, and *kunstabl* was probably deliberately chosen to emphasize the fact that the constables in question were British. Similarly *jurnalji* is used instead of *sahafiyy* to show the contempt felt by the speaker for journalists; it is an invented compound word consisting of a European stem and the Turkish ending *ji* used for such menial crafts as *'arbaji* (horse-cab driver), *buyaji* (shoeshine, etc.).

The most striking aspect of this sub-group is, however, the words which are *not* there. Thanks to the efforts of Turkish and Arabic translators and thinkers of the nineteenth century, Arabic equivalents were coined for some of the basic terms of European political, economic, and sociological thought.[12] This process has continued without interruption and excellent Arabic words are available for such concepts as capitalism, socialism, communism, anarchism, individualism; conservative, liberal, progressive, reactionary; session, committee, sub-committee, bill, law, decree; executive, legislative; and hundreds of other terms. Even in economics, native resources have met a large part of needs (see p. 279, below). One can predict with a fair degree of confidence that in this vast field Arabic will continue to make very sparing use of foreign loan-words.

The other set of words which are conspicuous by their absence is what may be termed "psychological"—the words used to indicate emotions, states of mind, motivations, etc. In this field the Arabic language offers large resources, and a writer like Mahfuz can easily meet his needs by drawing on old words or twisting them to give a new shade of meaning, as well as by coining a few new ones from old. And of all fields of language, this is perhaps the one that is most important to novelists.

The action of the Mahfuz novel takes place in a large city. As a check, therefore, another novel, with a rural setting, was studied: *al-Haram*, by the gifted playwright Yusuf Idris. The book, which is written in a distinctively more colloquial style than that of Mahfuz, relates the discovery, in a village in the Delta, of a strangled new-born baby, and the search for its mother. The number of European loan-words in it is 41 and their total frequency is 137 or some 0.45 percent of the total number of words (about 30,000). This means that the relative number of European words and their incidence are somewhat higher than in the Mahfuz novel, which is partly due to the greater use of the colloquial. But the most striking fact is that every one of these words deals with concrete objects: machine, auto-mobile, omnibus, garage, cigarette, potato, articles of clothing, names of coins, etc. The author does not seem to have felt the need for a single abstract European term to describe the thoughts, words, or actions of his characters or to use otherwise in his narrative.

As a second check, the foreign words listed in Jacob Landau's *A Word Count of Modern Arabic Prose* (New York, 1959) were studied (see Table II). Dr. Landau's list was based on 136,089 words taken from 20 pages chosen from each of 60 Egyptian books. These books covered a wide range of subjects: literature, biography, history, philosophy, religion, travel, science, economics, politics, sociology, drama, cinematography, etc., and may therefore be regarded as a representative cross section of modern Egyptian prose. Dr. Landau's list consists of 11,284 specific words with a total frequency of 136,089.

In computing the number of foreign words, geographical names and all titles such as Mister, Herr, Baron, Prince, General, etc., were again omitted, but names of calender months were included. Using the same, rather arbitrary, classification as for the trilogy of Mahfuz, gave 56 individual words of "daily use," with a total frequency of 211, and 59 "abstract and technical terms," with a total frequency of 229, or totals of 115 and 440, i.e., 1.04 and 0.33 percent, respectively, of Dr. Landau's total list. It may be noted that a little over half of the second group consisted of terms used in the natural sciences, particularly in chemistry. In other words, the proportion of total foreign words is probably about the same as in the novel by Mahfuz—though their frequency is slightly higher—but the proportion and frequency of abstract terms is much higher, because of the presence of a large number of terms drawn from the natural sciences.

Dr. Landau has also given, alongside his own word-list, the one compiled by Moshe Brill, which was also based on 136,089 words (consisting of 5,981 separate items) but drawn from two newspa-pers, an Egyptian one, *Al-Ahram,* and a Palestinian, *Filastin.* There are 51 foreign words in Dr. Brill's list, or 0.85 percent of the total. This would seem to confirm the impression that journalists— perhaps because they are in more of a hurry and therefore somewhat less careful of their style, or perhaps because they are closer to the colloquial—tend to use European words more frequently than writers of books. But it should be noted that the actual number of foreign words occurring in Dr. Brill's list, as distinct from their frequency, is relatively smaller than in Landau's. And it may be noted that some two-thirds of those words are "objects of daily use," the others consisting mainly of administrative, commercial, and political

TABLE II

LANDAU WORD LIST

Objects of Daily Use	Frequency
asbirin (aspirin)	1
afukatu (It. avvocato, lawyer)	5
ubira (It. opera)	3
utumubil (automobile)	12
urkistra (orchestra)	2
babur (Fr. vapeur, steamship)	2
brafu (It. bravo !)	1
brufa (It. prova, sample)	1
battariyya (It. batteria, battery)	2
bansyun (Fr. pension)	1
bantalun (It. pantalon, pants)	1
bijama (pyjama)	1
biyanu (It. pianoforte)	1
tibgh (tobacco)	1
tram (tramway)	5
tilifizyun (television)	1
tilifun (telephone)	4
tunbak (tobacco)	1
tuwalit (Fr. toilette)	1
jarsuniyira (Fr. garçonnière, bachelor's apartment)	4
jaranit (granite)	9
jurnal (journal, newspaper)	13
junayh (Eng. guinea, pound)	19
dinamit (dynamite)	1
radiyu (radio)	4
riyal (Sp. réal, dollar)	4
sijara (cigarette)	2
sinima (cinema)	31
sinimatughrafiyy (cinematographic)	12
salun (Fr. salon)	1
salah (It. sala, livingroom)	2
frak (Fr. fraque, frock coat)	1
frank (Fr. franc)	2
film (film)	3

TABLE II continued

LANDAU WORD LIST

Objects of Daily Use		Frequency
kazuza (It. gasosa, soft drink)		1
kaskit (Fr. casquette, cap)		1
kamira (camera)		4
kilumitr (Fr. kilomètre)		13
kinin (quinine)		1
mitru (Fr. metro, underground)		2
mitr (Fr. mètre)		8
marsh (Fr. marche, march)		1
makina (It. macchina, machine)		1
millim (Fr. millième, a coin)		2
murfin (morphine)		1
munukl (monocle)		1
hibudrum (hippodrome)		4
wiski (Eng. whiskey)		1
Calendar months	(8)	16
Sub-total	56	211

ABSTRACT AND TECHNICAL TERMS

Natural Sciences

argun (argon)	1
ankilustuma (ankylostoma)	1
uksijin (oxygen)	4
uksid (oxide)	3
batalujiya (pathology)	1
bsikulujiyy (psychological)	1
bilharsiya (bilharzia)	1
tiknik (technique)	1
tiliskub (telescope)	1
tanjistin (tungsten)	2
jiyulujiyy (geological)	4
duktur (doctor)	38
radiyum (radium)	1
fult (volt)	1
karbulik (carbolic)	1
kubra (cobra)	1
karbuniyy (carbonic)	1
kalsiyum (calcium)	1
klurufurm (chloroform)	1
kuk (coke)	1
mikrub (microbe)	2
milyar (milliard)	6
milyun (million)	34
munsun (monsoon)	1
mikruskub (microscope)	3
mikruskubiyy (microscopic)	2
miyusini (miocene)	4

TABLE II continued

LANDAU WORD LIST

Abstract and Technical Terms		Frequency
nitrujin (nitrogen)		4
niyun (neon)		2
hidrat (hydrate)		1
hidrujin (hydrogen)		1
hilyum (helium)		1
Sub-total	32	127
Other		
ithnulujiya (ethnology)		1
arkhabil (archipelago)		1
arkhiyulujiy (archeological)		1
aristuqratiyya (aristocracy)		2
ariy (Aryan)		17
akadimiya (academy)		1
barlaman (Fr. parlement)		12
brutistant (Protestant)		4
bakaluriya (Fr. baccalauréat)		1
balshafiyya (Bolshevism)		1
bank (bank)		25
bursah (It. borsa, stock exchange)		2
bulis (police)		3
dimuqratiyya (democracy)		11
sikritariyya (secretariat)		1
sinfuniya (symphony)		1
filharmuniyy (philharmonic)		1
futughrafiyy (photographic)		1
kalij (college)		1
kumidi (comedy)		2
litiratur (literature)		2
lisans (Fr. licence, B.A.)		1
mikrufun (microphone)		1
makyaj (Fr. maquillage, make-up)		2
mithulujiyy (mythological)		3
miludram (melodrama)		3
haratiqa (heretics)		1
Sub-total	27	102
Grand total	115	440
Approximate number of Arabic words	11,000	135,000

terms. One may therefore tentatively draw the general conclusion that foreign words constitute about one percent of the vocabulary used in current Arabic writing, and their cumulative frequency about 0.5 percent, or less, of the total.

As a third check, I studied the proceedings of the first session of the Congress on Contemporary Literature held in Rome on October 16-20, 1961.[13] The Congress was attended by European, as well as Arab, writers and the discussions were held in Arabic, English, and French. The proceedings of that session run to slightly over 10,000 words. Omitting the title, "Doctor," the only European words used were: *idiyulujiyya* (ideology, 12), *klasikiyy* (classical, 7), *sinima* (cinema, 4), *dinamiyya* (dynamic, 2), *tiknik* (technique, 1), *tiqniyya* (technical, 1), *rumansiyya* (romanticism, 1), *burjuaziyya* (bourgeoisie, 1), and *sikulujiyya* (psychological, 1), a total of eight words with an aggregate frequency of 30, or slightly under 0.3 percent of the total number of words used. In other words, the proportion and frequency of foreign words are much the same as in the Mahfuz novel and Landau word list.

As a last check, I studied a highly technical article in economics, discussing, in a purely theoretical manner, the application of Keynes's Multiplier Theory to Underdeveloped Countries.[14] In this 6,000 word article only three European words were used: *istatikiyy* (static), *dinamikiyy* (dynamic), and *mikanikiyya* (mechanics), with a total frequency of 6, or 0.1 percent of the total. However, 11 other abstruse terms, for which Arabic equivalents were given, also had the English printed alongside, e.g., *al-fasil al-zamaniyy al-tanzimiyy* (Institutional Time Lag) and *Kharitah al-siwa li almujtama'* (Community Consumption Indifference Map). But the bulk of the technical terms used were Arabic, e.g., *mukarrir al-istithmar* (investment multiplier), *al-mayl al-haddiyy li al-istihlak* (marginal propensity to consume), *murunah* (elasticity), *munhana al-'ard* (supply curve), *bitala muqanna'ah* (disguised unemployment), etc.

Naturally most of these terms would be unintelligible to those who have not had a thorough grounding in economics and are not familiar with the English (or more rarely French) terms on which they were patterned. But that would also apply to a similar article written in English or French, and, to a greater or smaller degree, holds true of technical terms in all languages.

The above analysis brings out quite clearly the current Arabic approach toward foreign works. As far as possible the Arabs have tried to find Arabic equivalents for foreign terms, either by giving old words new meanings or by putting together two or more words to form a new composite, e.g., *al-sikkah al-hadidiah* (chemin de fer), *wujhat nazar* (point of view). This procedure has given fairly satisfactory results in the vocabulary of everyday life. It has also made it possible to find Arabic equivalents for most of the terms used in the social sciences, and almost all of those employed in "literature." But although intense—and in this writer's opinion generally misguided—efforts have been made to replace European scientific and technical terms by Arabic equivalents, it is clear that neither Arabic nor any other language can avoid a massive influx of such terms. The international scientific and technical civilization which is sweeping over, and unifying, the world carries with it, perforce, its own terminology.

It remains, in conclusion, to evaluate the Arabic response to the challenge of the foreign vocabulary by comparing it with that of three other Middle Eastern languages—Persian, Turkish, and Uzbek.

A Persian novel by Muhammad Mas'ud, *Dar talash ma'ash* (Teheran 1311, 1932/33) and a volume of short stories by 'Ali Dashti, *Fitneh* (Teheran 1323 1943/44) were studied.[15] Of the approximately 40,000 words of the novel, 2,500 were examined (on pages 14-16, 22-24, 66-67, and 128-129). Of these 18 were European, or 0.72 percent of the total. As for the short-stories, whose aggregate length is about 60,000 words, selections were made from four, with a total of 4,000 words (pages 70-74, 140-144, 207-211, 290-294). Of these, 25 words were European, or 0.63 percent of the total. In other words, the frequency of European words is almost three times as high as in the Mahfuz novel and about twice as high as in Landau's word list.[16]

Only two remarks need to be made regarding these words. First, practically all have been taken from French, and retain their French form. Secondly, although many have their counterpart in Arabic—automobile, salon, docteur, machine, etc.—several others represent terms for which an Arabic equivalent is used, e.g., pacquet, famille, copie, conscient, inconscient, etc.

As a check a study was made of Persian newspapers. For this purpose pages 49-65 of *Ettela'at dar yekrub' qarn* (Teheran, 1329, 1950/51) were chosen, since the newspaper in question is the leading one in Iran. Of the 5,000 words, 70 were European, or 1.4 percent of the total. Here again several European words were found for which the Arabs have coined equivalents, e.g., défilé, moderne, boycott, musée, rapport, clinique, boulevard, compagnie, etc.

Lastly, passages from a book on Public Finance were studied— *Qawanin malieh* by Shams al-din Jazairi (Teheran 1335, 1956/57). Of the total of 3,000 words selected (pages 33-34, 53-54, 232-33, 384-85) 57 were of European origin, or 1.9 percent. These included several terms for which Arabic equivalents have been coined, e.g., régime, budget, contrôle, commission, chaussée, théorie, gendarmerie, etc.

It may, therefore, be stated that Persian has been distinctly more receptive to European words than Arabic.

Turkish has been very much more so. Already before the nineteenth century many Greek, Italian, Hungarian, and Slavic words had made their way into Turkish, and many more—mainly French— came in during that century.[17] But in the last forty years the influx has been enormous and a study of a Turkish newspaper puts the proportion of European words at 5-10 percent of the total.[18] In order to study the incidence of European loan-words in contemporary literary Turkish, two collections of short stories in urban settings were sampled: Oktay Akbal, *Aşksiz Insanlar* (Istanbul, 1949) and Necati Cumali, *Yalniz Kadin* (Istanbul, 1955).[19] In the first, 3,330 words out of a total of about 21,000 were examined. (The second and third pages of each of the nine stories.) Of these, 129 words, or 3.91 percent of the total, were of European origin. In the second set of stories 3,700 words out of a total of 23,000 were studied (the second and third pages of the last eight stories); here 72 words, or 1.95 percent of the total, were European. In other words, the incidence of European words is three times as high as in Persian and about ten times as high as in Arabic. And here, again, one is struck by the multitude of French words for which Arabic equivalents have been coined: appartement, affiche, pacquet, gazette, manchette, roman, groupe, danse, barreau, étiquette, faculté, etc.

As a check, three newspaper articles, written in 1947 by Fuat Köprülü, the eminent Turkish historian and former Foreign Minister, were studied (pp. 231-37 of *Demokrasi Yolunda*, edited by T. Halasi-Kun, The Hague, 1964). Of the 2,500 words, no less than 157 were European, or 6.28 percent, but this high figure is partly explained by the frequent recurrence of the words parti and democratie. Once more one is struck by words for which the Arabs use equivalents, e.g., principe, système, plan, programme, combinaison, syndicat, socialiste, etc.

In other words, the Turks have deliberately taken over European words (practically all French) as part of the attempt to Westernize their country, which was initiated by Atatürk, and which extended to other fields such as dress, law, etc.

If Turkish represents an example of deliberate Europeanization, Uzbek is one of imposed Russification and Europeanization. Already before the Revolution, a very large number of Russian words, or West European words in their Russian form, had entered Uzbek writings—in addition to some that had come in through Turkey. But the proportion rose rapidly under Soviet rule, owing to the closer integration of the Uzbeks in Soviet life and to the massive influx of Russians, Ukrainians, and Bielo-Russians who, by 1959, accounted for 15 percent of the population of Uzbekistan and over half of that of Tashkent. "The Russian word content in modern journalistic Uzbek has risen from 9 percent in 1924 to 18 percent in 1950." The author points out that: "It is doubtful that Russian words have entered into most Uzbek literature in the numbers that would be found in journalistic writings or political oratory." But, on the other hand: "Today, in certain cases, the count of words taken into Uzbek literature from and through Russian is unusually high, the percentage of such terms running well above the 18 percent of 1950."[20] Those words naturally cover a very wide range, including both "objects of daily use" and "abstract and technical terms." Many have replaced Arabic and Persian terms formerly in use.[21]

The conclusion of this study may be briefly stated. Modern Arabic has shown a very marked reluctance to take in European (or other) loan-words, Persian has been somewhat more receptive, Turkish has been very hospitable, and Uzbek has been flooded with such words. The explanation of these phenomena is, in this writer's opinion, to be sought in several fields.

The first is the literary field, using the term in its broadest sense. Here at least three factors may be distinguished. First there is the fact that the Semitic triliteral root of the vast majority of Arabic words imposes on the language a certain pattern which makes long foreign words look very awkward in an Arabic sentence, whereas they fit more easily into Turkish, and perhaps Persian, morphology. This may well have limited, in the past, the adoption of Greek words by the medieval Arabs and, possibly, even have discouraged the translation of Greek epic and dramatic literature.[22] And it may well be that the same factor is at work today. Secondly, there is the fact that Arabic is the "classical" language of the Middle East, just as Chinese is the "classical" language of the Far East. In recent decades, Chinese has adopted far fewer European loan-words than has Japanese, and it may well be that this parallelism illustrates a more general tendency: the greater conservatism of the main "classical" language of a culture area in adopting neologisms and foreign words—here again one cannot help mentioning French. Thirdly, there is the point which all Arabs would give as the main explanation of the phenomenon under study: Arabic is a "richer" language than Persian or Turkish, not to mention Uzbek. This contention is surely true, but a further set of observations may be made on this subject. For, as regards vocabulary—which is the only aspect of language touched upon in this study—Persian and Turkish could be regarded as potentially "richer" languages than Arabic. This is because both languages consist of a native core plus a large accretion of Arabic and Persian, or Arabic and Turkish. Both Persian and Turkish have for centuries used Arabic as their Latin and Greek, the language from which they drew their abstract terms. And to this day most abstract terms in Persian and Turkish are of Arabic origin. Hence, in principle, there was nothing to prevent the Iranians and Turks from drawing on all the resources of Arabic—in addition to "pure" Persian and Turkish—had they so wished, claiming it to be as much a part of their heritage as Latin is of English or French. And that is precisely what both peoples, particularly the Turks, did in the nineteenth century, when they began to feel the need for new terms to express concepts borrowed from Western thought or practice. That they stopped doing so after the First World War is due to a complex set of political and social factors which can be designated by the shorthand term "cultural nationalism." Now, given the reluctance of the Turks and Iranians to continue coining new terms from Arabic roots, it may well be that the relatively restricted range of the "pure" Turkish and Persian vocabularies made it more imperative to borrow Western terms wholesale.

Another possible explanation may be sought in divergent attitudes toward social change. It may well be that, in general, Arabs are more conservative and more reluctant to change their ways than are Turks or Iranians. An important manifestation of this may be their greater attachment to Islam, with which they feel a particularly close identification, for obvious historical reasons; and the close link between Islam and "pure" Arabic has already been noted. But this argument, too, must be treated with great caution, for the degree of social change in Egypt in the last fifty years has not been much less than in Turkey, and has probably been greater than in Iran, and the same is true of several other Arab countries.

A third factor may be the different degree of political evolution of the three countries. It would seem that, before attaining independence, several nations have shown a concern about the "purity" of their language which they lost rather swiftly once they came to feel sure that their nationhood and national independence had been established beyond any shadow of doubt. Thus in Poland before the First World War there was, apparently, much talk about preserving the purity of the language and guarding it against infiltration, but such discussion diminished greatly in the 1920s. And the fact that the Arabs achieved independence only recently may partly explain their linguistic restrictiveness.

Lastly, there is a factor to which this writer attaches much importance as an explanation of the divergent approach of the Arabs and the Turks in the matter of foreign loan-words; it may also partly explain the difference between the Arabs and Iranians in this respect. This centers on the distinction between Westernization and Modernization. Under Atatürk, the Turks set out not only to modernize their society—i.e., to reform it and adapt it to the twentieth century—but also to Westernize it. Rightly or wrongly, they have regarded themselves as part of Europe and have sought to change their society so as to make it European. To a much smaller extent, the same may have been true of Iran under Reza Shah, who took Atatürk as his model; thus, the imposition of male European dress in 1928, the compulsory unveiling of women, and the widespread acceptance of the Aryan racial mythology in Iran are, in this writer's opinion, signs of a desire to Westernize rather than just modernize. This, however, even the most "progressive" Arabs have refused to do. They have accepted modernization, i.e., the adoption of modern technology, science, and—to a lesser degree—political and social ideologies. But, ever since the beginning of the nineteenth century, when they were first exposed to Western influences, they have almost consistently rejected Westernization, seeking in all these changes to preserve their religion, language, and, as far as possible, their culture and way of life. Their very sparing use of foreign loan-words may well be one more example of their attempt to preserve their cultural identity.[23]

NOTES

1. Institut d'études islamiques et Centre d'études de l'Orient contemporain de l'Université de Paris, *'L'Adaptation des Langues "classiques" aux besoins modernes dans le Proche-Orient (Arabe, turc, persan, hébreu et grec modernes)* (25-27 April, 1961), mimeographed, p. 108.

2. The use of a literary language as a link among peoples divided by religion, geography, differing vernaculars and membership in various political units was clearly recognized by several nineteenth century nationalists and language reformers in the Balkans. Among them one may mention Adamantios Korais (1748-1833) in Greece, Dositej Obradovich (1742-1811) in Serbia, Francē Levstik (1831-1887) in Slovenia, and Naim Frasheri (1846-1900) in Albania. These men usually rejected the foreign words that had entered the spoken and written languages of their country. See Stavro Skendi, "The Emergence of Modern Balkan Literary Languages," *Die Kultur Südeuropas, ihre Geschichte und ihre Ausdruckformen* (Wiesbaden, 1964).

3. Institut d'études, *op. cit.*, pp. 2-4. M. Etiemble's defense of the purity of French would have been more effective if it had not been accompanied by a systematic denigration of all aspects of American culture—including the statement that the average mental age of American adults was fourteen. This started a controversy in *Le Figaro* and led the present writer to send a letter in which he pointed out that, but for the sacrifices in blood and resources of the United States during and after the two world wars, the French would have been speaking today not Franglais, but Freutsch or Fruskii.

4. For a study of Turkish words in colloquial Egyptian, see Enno Littmann, "Türkisches Sprachgut im Aegyptisch-Arabischen," *Westöstliche Abhandlungen, Rudolf Tschudi* (Wiesbaden, 1954), pp. 107-127. Several of the words listed by Littmann are to be found in Mahfuz.

5. The inclusion of the names of common diseases in the first group may be justified by their widespread use. Their transference to the second group would in no way affect the conclusions drawn from the table.

6. Groschen entered Turkish during or before the fifteenth century in the form of *qurush* and was later transmitted to Arabic—see H. A. R. Gibb and H. Bowen, *Islamic Society and the West* (London, 1957), Vol. II, p. 50.

7. The first carriage used in Egypt in modern times belonged to Ibrahim Bey, the Mamluk, and the second to Napoleon. Carts were introduced under Muhammad Ali—see Ahmad Ahmad al-Hitta, *Tarikh misr al-iqtisadi* (Cairo, 1957, pp. 221-22) and *Encyclopedia of Islam* (New Edition), articles 'adjala and 'araba.

8. For the derivation of the latter, see E. I. 'adjala and Littmann, *op. cit.* I have included the word *farmalah* (brake) among those of foreign origin. Its form makes an Arabic origin unlikely, and I have not found it in Persian

or Turkish dictionaries. Although the Italian word for brake is "freno," I would venture a guess that *farmalah* is connected with "fermare," to stop. [Mr. Richard Hill, of Durham University, has since informed me that "fermola" is used for brake in Italian railways.]

9. There is an interesting parallelism in Israel, where *mivraq* is used for telegraph and telegram, while *telefon* and the verb *talfen* or *talpen* have survived—see Institut d'études, *op. cit.*, p. 45. For a more general study of the problems of modernization of Hebrew, which presents many analogies with those of Arabic, see Haim Blanc, "Hebrew in Israel: Problems and Prospects," *Middle East Journal* (Washington, D.C.), Autumn, 1957.

10. See Fuad Sarruf, "siyar alfaz 'arabiyya mustahdathah," *Al-Abhath* (Beirut, September, 1963), for an interesting account of the successful attempt to find Arabic equivalents for jet plane *(naffathah)* and spectroscope *(minzar al-taif)* and the failure of the ones proposed for television and streamlined. It would seem, however, that the Arabic word chosen for spectroscope rests on a confusion between two meanings of spectrum, viz., phantom and color-band.

11. For example, both *al-aristuqratiyya* and *al-dimuqratiyya* are used in the old Arabic translations of Aristotle's Rhetoric—see *Aristutalis: al-Khitaba*, ed. by 'Abd al-Rahman Badawi (Cairo, 1959), p. 37. I owe this reference to Dr. Muhsin Mahdi. The word bourgeoisie also enjoyed a brief currency in the Levant during the Crusades. It appears, under the form *birjasiyya*, in *Kitab al i'tibar*, by Usama ibn Munqidh.

12. See Bernard Lewis, *The Emergence of Modern Turkey* (London, 1961), pp. 83-87. Albert Hourani, *Arabic Thought in the Liberal Age* (London, 1962), Chapter IV, and Niyazi Berkes, *The Development of Secularism in Turkey* (Montreal, 1964), pp. 106, 118-20, 278-80.

13. *Al-adab al-'arabi al-mu'asir,* an Adwa publication.

14. Fuad Hashim 'Awad, "Nazariat Keynes . . ," *L'Égypte Contemporaine* (Cairo), October, 1963.

15. These two books were suggested by Dr. Sakina Berenjian, to whom I explained the purpose of this study.

16. Since I am considerably less familiar with Persian or Turkish than with Arabic, it is much more likely that some European words may have escaped my attention in these two languages. The figures given on Persian and Turkish must therefore be regarded as *minimum* ones.

17. Uriel Heyd, *Language Reform in Modern Turkey* (Jerusalem, 1954), p. 76.

18. *Ibid.*, p. 100.

19. These books were suggested by Dr. Kemal Karpat, to whom I explained the purpose of this study.

20. Edward Allworth, *Uzbek Literary Politics* (The Hague, 1964), pp. 182-3.

21. For details, see *ibid.,* pp. 183-87

22. One has only to read Sulayman al-Bustani's translation of the *Iliad,* published in 1904, to realize how incongruous are Greek names in an Arabic context and to appreciate the heroic efforts he made to get around this difficulty.

23. After this article had been sent in for publication, my attention was drawn to an unpublished Ph. D. thesis, presented at Columbia University in 1963: Albert J. Boutros, "English Loanwords in the Colloquial Arabic of Palestine (1917-1948) and Jordan (1948-1962)." The author gave a list of 1,230 words, consisting of "all determinable English loanwords, together with the commonest trademarks of cars, appliances, medicines," etc. Many of these had displaced Italian or French words, and indeed many may have been of French rather than English origin.

The largest category was "locomotion," with 12 percent of the total; followed by "physics, chemistry, and mathematics," 10 percent; "sports and games," 8 percent; "school or bookish words," 7 percent; "food, drink, and smoking," 7 percent; "medical and pharmaceutical," 6 percent; "clothing, fashion, cosmetics, and hair styles," 6 percent; and "building, furniture, and household articles," 5 percent. Thus, except for words relating to the natural sciences, the loanwords fall into the category designated as "objects of daily use."

Boutros also refers to a study by Giuseppe Maria Barbera, *Elementi Italo-Siculo-Veneziano-Genovesi nei Linguaggi Arabo e Turco* (Beirut, 1940), which cites about 1,460 Italian words found in both Arabic (classical and in all dialects of colloquial) and Turkish.

17

Economic Change and Urbanization in the Middle East

Towns are among the most expensive of human artifacts, and among the most durable. It is therefore not suprising that, in a region with as old a history as the Middle East, some urban patterns have shown great persistence. Of these two may be noted here: over the last two thousand years, most of the Middle East has been highly urbanized; and the urban center of gravity has tended to swing to interior regions except when a powerful Western influence (Greco-Roman, from 300 B.C. to A.D. 600; European, from 1800 to the 1920s) has pulled it to coastal areas.

The Middle East entered the Modern Age, at the beginning of the nineteenth century, with two marked characteristics in its urban pattern: a large proportion of town dwellers and a concentration of population in inland towns. The scattered population estimates available for the period of around 1800, although tentative, point to a high degree of urbanization. In Egypt almost 10 percent of the population lived in towns of over 10,000.[1] In geographical or greater Syria, Aleppo had a population variously estimated at 150,000 to 250,000, and Damascus, at about 100,000, while Hama, Homs, Jerusalem, and Tripoli had 10,000 inhabitants or more.[2] Since the total population of Syria was probably below 1,500,000,[3] this implies an extremely high proportion of population living in towns, 20 percent or more. Figures for Iraq are even less reliable, partly because plagues, famines, and floods took heavy tolls and urban population fluctuated sharply, thus greatly affecting the estimates made by European observers. The figures given by Olivier, Rousseau, and Buckingham indicate a population of 50,000 to 100,000 for Baghdad, and of 50,000, or a little less, for each of Mosul, Hilla, and Basra. The total population of Iraq may be estimated to have been under 1,500,000, which again would imply a high degree of urbanization— perhaps as much as 15 percent. As for present-day Turkey—whose population in 1800 may have been around 10,000,000[4]—it contained such cities as Istanbul, with a population of 400,000 to 500,000

Reprinted with permission from *Middle Eastern Cities,* Berkeley and Los Angeles, 1969, ed. Ira Lapidus, pp. 102-119.

in the sixteenth century, 600,000 to 700,000 in the seventeenth, and somewhat more by the beginning of the nineteenth century; Izmir, with over 100,000; Bursa, with probably 50,000 or more; and smaller towns like Erzerum, Konia, and Ankara.[5]

For Iran there are only a few rough estimates. There are many signs, however, that the population of several towns had been greatly reduced from their mid-seventeenth century level. Isfahan, whose population had been put by Chardin at 600,000 (he adds that it was *"aussi peuplée que Londres,"* which at that time had 400,000 to 500,000 inhabitants) had probably half that number by 1800; Tabriz, which had been almost wholly destroyed by the earthquake of 1721, had 30,000 to 50,000 inhabitants in the years 1810-1812; the population of Qazvin, Mashad, and Shiraz had definitely declined; Teheran, which had just become the capital of Iran, had some 15,000; and the population of Yazd was put at the rather high figure of 100,000 in 1810.[6] One gets the impression that the country was somewhat less urbanized than Egypt, Syria, or Iraq, although in the absence of any reliable figures for total population[7] no firm judgement can be made.

The import of these figures may be brought out by comparing them with cities in Europe. In 1800, the percentage of total population living in towns of 100,000 or over has been put at 7 percent in England and Wales, 7 percent in the Netherlands, 2.7 percent in France, 1.6 percent in Russia, and 1 percent in Germany.[8] The proportion living in towns of over 5,000 has been estimated at about 25 percent in England and Wales, under 10 percent in France, and distinctly less in the other countries, with the exception of the Netherlands. As for the United States, the 1790 census showed that only 3.3 percent of the population lived in towns of 8,000 or more, a figure that rose to 8.5 percent by 1840 and 16.1 percent by 1860. It was only with the advent of industrialization and steam transportation that most of Europe and America overtook the Middle East in the degree of urbanization.[9] It may be remarked, parenthetically, that earlier in its history the Middle East had contained still greater cities. It is not clear, however, if this implied a higher degree of urbanization since the total population was also much larger.[10]

Many factors help explain the high degree of urbanization during the late Arab and Ottoman periods despite a marked economic and cultural decline. They include the absence of a strong rural-based feudal system, prevailing rural insecurity, more favorable treatment by the government of townsmen than of peasants, and pilgrim and transit traffic.

The history of the Muslim Middle East shows few examples of strong, independent feudal lords living in country castles. The Mamlūk military leaders and landlords dwelt in Cairo, Damascus, and other cities. This meant that the sums raised by them in rents and taxes, as well as those accruing to the monarch, flowed to the capital or other large cities. This greatly increased the purchasing power of the large urban markets—and correspondingly diminished that of the rural—inducing a concentration of craftsmen, merchants, and others in the cities.

The insecurity of the countryside, which increased in the seventeenth and eighteenth centuries when bedouins extended their raids to the Egyptian Delta and the coasts of Syria and Palestine and order broke down in Anatolia and Iran, caused many farmers to flee to the cities and led to the wholesale depopulation of villages. Volney reports that whereas over 3,200 taxable villages in the Pashalik of Aleppo were recorded in the old Ottoman registers, "at present the collector can scarcely find four hundred."[11] At the same time an appreciable proportion of the inhabitants of most cities consisted of farmers who cultivated adjacent lands, but who lived within the city walls for protection—a practice that has continued to this day in some places, for instance, in Damascus. Other peasants fled to the cities in times of famine believing, rightly, that the government would not let townsmen starve and would somehow or other secure provisions from the countryside, even if it meant rural famine. Again Volney provides interesting examples.[12] The same process seems to have occurred in Iran during the Second World War.

In the absence of commercial or industrial development—or an increase in agricultural production, and a rise in the surplus available for urban use—the towns could not have continued indefinitely to absorb this rural influx if high urban death rates, caused by poor sanitary conditions and raised sharply every few years by an outburst of plague, cholera, or other epidemics, had not reduced city population.[13]

As for pilgrim and transit traffic, it is sufficient to recall the names of such holy places as Jerusalem, Mecca, Medina, Karbala, and Mashad, and to draw attention to the persistence of some trade through the Middle East even after the diversion of most trade between the Far East and Europe to the all-sea route around the Cape.

The second characteristic of Middle Eastern urbanization, inland location, may be dealt with much more briefly. The vast majority of cities in Greco-Roman times were seaports: Athens, Corinth,

Carthage, Syracuse, Ephesus, Alexandria, Antioch, Rhodes, Rome (which was accessible to quite large ships), Constantinople, and so on. So were most large Western cities in early modern times: Genoa, Venice, Naples, Lisbon, Antwerp, Amsterdam, London, Philadelphia, New York, St. Petersburg, and Copenhagen. But in the Islamic Middle East most of the great cities were inland: Damascus, Aleppo, Baghdad, Mosul, Cairo, Rayy, Nishapur, Isfahan, Tabriz, Teheran, Konia. In this, perhaps, the Muslims reverted to the older traditions of the Babylonians, Egyptians, Aramaeans, and Persians. Most of the larger ports inherited from the Romans shrank to insignificance (for examples, Antioch and Alexandria). The major exception was of course Constantinople, whose superb location and great defensibility were fully appreciated by the Ottoman sultans, and Tunis, which grew in North Africa, on the site formerly occupied by Carthage.

Part of the explanation of this phenomenon is no doubt to be sought in the origins of Islamic towns. Many of those founded by the Arabs were camps on the edge of the deserts in which the Arabs maneuvered so effectively—Basra, Kufa, Fusṭāṭ, Kairouan.[14] Others had already served for many centuries as "desert ports," handling caravan traffic, as did Damascus, Aleppo, Kerman, and Yazd. Others were royal cities—Samarra, Baghdad, Cairo, Meknes—and few Muslim rulers felt anything but aversion for the sea. But trade has its exigencies, and one cannot help surmising that great Mediterranean seaports would have developed, or revived, had it not been for the seapower first of the Byzantines and then of the Italians.[15]

In the Middle Ages, the loss of control over the Mediterranean to the Franks led to a shift in the center of gravity to the interior. Thus, in the fourteenth century Aleppo bypassed Antioch, which was falling in ruins,[16] and Cairo conducted much of its international business directly and not through Alexandria, which was vulnerable to raids from Cyprus, Rhodes, and other Christian strongholds.[17] The passage of the centuries merely accentuated the decline of Alexandria, Saida, Beirut, Antioch, and the other seaports, except for Salonica and Smyrna, which began to revive in the sixteenth century, thanks to their large Greek and Jewish populations.

Other striking characteristics of Muslim towns will not be discussed here, since they fall outside the scope of this paper: the complete absence of city-states; the almost complete lack of municipal self-government and institutions; the coexistence of various religious communities, each in its own ghetto; the shutting off of each quarter from the other parts by inner walls and gates;[18] and the concentric layout, with the "nobler" crafts and trades located immediately around the mosque and the "baser" ones on the outskirts.

Evolution: 1800-1920s

In the course of the nineteenth century various parts of the Middle East were drawn, to a greater or lesser extent, into the international network of trade and finance. This entailed the immigration of European businessmen and technicians, the investment of foreign capital, the development of mechanical transport, and the shift from a subsistence to a cash crop agriculture. The introduction of modern hygiene led to a sharp population growth, and foreign competition resulted in the ruin of the handicrafts.

All these trends had marked effects on the location, size, and structure of Middle Eastern towns. Perhaps the simplest way to put it is that the economy began to be oriented outward, toward the export of its primary products, that transport was developed accordingly, with railway lines or steamboat services (in Egypt, Iraq, and Iran) pointing to the coasts, and that the alignment of towns shifted in consequence. Certainly the outstanding feature of the urban history of this period is the growth of "heterogenetic" seaports[19]: Alexandria (population in 1927—573,000), Port Said (104,000), Suez (41,000); Beirut (population in 1932—161,000), Tripoli (51,000); Jaffa (population in 1931—55,000), Haifa (50,000), Tel Aviv (47,000); Basra (population in 1935—60,000); Aden (population in 1921—57,000), Jidda and Bahrain; Abadan (population in 1937—60,000), Khurramshahr (30,000); Izmir (population in 1910 —250,000). In North Africa this development was even more striking: one has only to think of Casablanca, Rabat, Tangier, Kenitra (Port Lyautey), Safi, al-Jadida (Mazagan), Tetuan, and Agadir in Morocco; Algiers, Oran, Annaba (Bone), Bejaya (Bougie), and Skikda (Philippeville) in Algeria; Tunis, Sfax, and Bizerta in Tunisia; and Tripoli and Benghazi in Libya.

The growth of these "heterogenetic" North African seaports was due to the immigration of hundreds of thousands of Frenchmen, Spaniards, and Italians who came to constitute either a majority or a very large minority of their inhabitants. In the Middle East, immigration played a smaller role, except in Palestine, where the Jewish influx began to assume significant proportions in the 1900s, and in the Arabian seaports, which absorbed large numbers of Indians, Indonesians, Somalis, and others.[20] It is worth noting that, at their peak in 1907, foreign citizens constituted 25 percent of the population of Alexandria and 28 percent of that of Port Said, although only 2 percent of the total Egyptian population.

However, the rapid growth in seaports did not entail a corresponding rise in the overall rate of urbanization. A careful study by Gabriel Baer shows the combined population of the twenty-three towns of Egypt to have risen from about 400,000 in 1821 to 1,015,000 in 1882; 1,454,000 in 1897; and 1,596,000 in 1907; their share of total population increased from 9.5 percent to 12.8 percent, 15.0 percent and 14.3 percent, respectively.[21] In Syria, the figures given by Ruppin put the number living in towns of over 10,000, at the outbreak of the First World War, at 1,600,000, or 25 percent of the total population.[22] However, his estimates of the population of some towns seem to be inflated, and it is doubtful whether the proportion of urban dwellers did in fact increase in the course of the nineteenth century. For Iraq, the calculations made by M. S. Hasan show an unchanged urban proportion: 24 percent in 1867, 25 percent in 1890, 24 percent in 1905, and 25 percent in 1930.[23] Evidence for Turkey and Iran is too fragmentary for any firm conclusions to be drawn. *The Encyclopedia Britannica* puts the number of Iranian towns of 10,000 or over in 1910 at forty-five, with a combined population of 1,700,000; only Teheran (280,000), Tabriz (200,000), and Isfahan (100,000) had 100,000 inhabitants or over.[24] The urban population may therefore have been over 15 percent of the total (perhaps 10,000,000), and there is no reason to believe that this ratio was appreciably higher than it had been at the beginning of the nineteenth century.[25] As for Turkey, the 1927 census, which put the total population at 13,648,000, showed that there were five towns with over 50,000 each and with a combined population of 1,055,000: Istanbul, 691,000; Izmir, 154,000; Ankara, 75,000; Adana, 73,000; and Bursa, 62,000. There were another sixty towns with more than 10,000 inhabitants and with an aggregate population of 1,400,000.[26]

The very slow growth of urbanization in the Middle East at a time when the more advanced regions were rapidly increasing their town populations (see footnote 8) may be explained by two factors. In the first place, the growth of some seaports was partly achieved at the expense of other towns. Thus, Cairo's trade was partly diverted to

Alexandria and Port Said, as was that of Rosetta and Damietta.[27] Similarly Beirut took over much business transacted in Damascus and Aleppo, as well as in such small ports as Saida. In North Africa there was also a decline in the relative importance of Fez, Meknes, Constantine, and Kairouan. Second, the decline of the handicrafts— a phenomenon also observable in North Africa—certainly slowed down the growth of such towns as Aleppo, Damascus, Baghdad, Cairo, Tabriz, Isfahan, Bursa, Amasia, and Diyarbakir.[28] Sometimes it may even have caused an absolute decline: thus the Russian consul in Beirut, K. M. Bazili, states that the population of Aleppo dropped from 150,000 in 1820 to 80,000 in the 1840s, and that of Damascus from 120,000 to 80,000. However, although this decline has been attributed to the outflow of craftsmen from these cities,[29] it is not clear how much confidence can be placed in such estimates and whether the decrease was due to economic or other causes. These adverse effects were only partly offset by the favorable impact on urban growth of increasing centralization and bureaucratization, the rise in national incomes, and the spread of Western-style living. And while the combined effect of all these factors was to slow down the rise in the numerator (the size of the urban population), that of the denominator (the size of the total population) was rising steadily. The expansion of agriculture, due to the establishment of law and order, the improvement of transport, the extension of the cultivated area, and the introduction of more valuable crops meant that employment opportunities in the countryside were growing sufficiently fast to absorb the increment in rural population. Migration to the towns was therefore rather small until the First World War.

One last point must be made. As Professors Abu-Lughod and Safran have observed, the composition of the population of the towns changed markedly during this period. To the extent that town-dwelling gave way to persons engaged in more truly "urban" occupations, there was an increase in the degree of urbanization which is not revealed by the statistics.

It remains to add that these developments had a drastic impact on the traditional structure of Middle Eastern cities. New quarters in the Western style were erected alongside the old, throughfares were built through the old quarters,[30] the various communities began to emerge from their ghettos and mingle, and tentative steps were taken toward municipal self-government.[31]

Evolution Since the 1920s

The main trends that have affected economic development and urbanization in the Middle East during the last forty years are: the population growth, the discovery and exploitation of oil, the impact of the Second World War, the exodus of foreigners and minority groups from certain countries, the decline in the foreign trade of some countries relative to their gross national products, foreign aid, and, following independence, the use of state power to promote industrialization and other forms of economic development. The results have been a marked acceleration in urbanization and a reversal of the shift of population concentrations from inland cities to the coast. The ratio of urban (variously defined) to total population has risen at an accelerating rate. In Egypt it was 21 percent in 1917, 24 percent in 1937, 30 percent in 1947, 37 percent in 1960, and 40 percent in 1966. In Turkey it rose from 24 percent in 1927 to 25 percent in 1945, 32 percent in 1960, and 34 percent in 1965, according to official statistics; if the term urban is restricted to places

TABLE I

Urbanization in Middle Eastern and North African Countries in the 1950s[a]

Country	Year	Urban	in cities of	
			20,000+	100,000+
Morocco	1952	—[b]	27[c]	19.2
Algeria	1954	22.9	—	9.9
Tunisia	1956	35.6	18.2	10.8
Libya	1957	—	—	15.0
Jordan	1952	37.7	—	8.1
Saudi Arabia	1954	—	—	8.4
Syria	1955	—	—	28.9
Sudan	1956	8.3	—	2.4
UAR	1957	35.8	36.9	22.4[d]
Iraq	1957	37.3	—	14.5
Kuwait	1957	—	—	50.6
Lebanon	1958	—	—	33.2
Israel	1954	56.4	52.0	36.4
Turkey	1955	25.0	—	10.0
Iran	1956	33.0	—	16.5

Source: Hubert Morsink, "al-Numūw al-ḥaḍarī . . .," *Al-Abḥāth,* (Beirut), June, 1965; [figures on Iran, Israel, and Turkey added]. a) Each entry covers the following ones in the row; thus in Tunisia 35.6 percent of the population was urban; of these, 18.2 percent lived in cities of 20,000 or more (including those of over 100,000) and 10.8 percent in cities of 100,000 or more. b) 29.3 in 1960. c) 14.1 in 1948. d) 1958. The notation — means figure unavailable.

of 10,000 inhabitants or more, the figures are 16 percent in 1927, 18 percent in 1945, and 25 percent in 1960. Comparable figures are not available for other countries, but the same phenomenon has undoubtedly occurred in Iran, where the population of Teheran rose from an estimated 300,000 before the First World War to 500,000 at the outbreak of the Second World War, 1,000,000 in 1950, 1,512,-000 in the 1956 census, and about 2,700,000 in the 1966 census. Table I shows the degree of urbanization in the Middle Eastern countries in the 1950s. The reasons for this rapid growth in town population, which is almost certain to continue, are discussed below.

The relative decline in the importance of seaports compared to inland towns is due to many factors. In some, foreigners and minority groups formed a majority—or a very large minority—of the population and their exodus was bound to leave a very large gap, for instance in Izmir, Istanbul, Alexandria, and Port Said. In some countries, such as Egypt and Turkey, the failure of foreign trade to grow as fast as gross national product has helped to reduce the relative importance of seaports.[32] So has the phenomenal growth of capital cities, discussed below. The development of newly discovered mineral deposits and the growth of towns near them, e.g., Abadan, Kirkuk, and Aswan, and some deliberate attempts to decentralize industry have also contributed to move the urban center of gravity inland.

Characteristics of Middle Eastern Urbanization

Three characteristic features of present-day Middle Eastern urbanization are "overurbanization," the great size of the primate cities, and the emergence of megalopolitan centers.

There is no doubt that the Middle East is distinctly more urbanized than most other underdeveloped regions. The figures in Table I may be compared with the following table:[33]

TABLE II

Percentage City Population, 1950

in cities larger than

	20,000	100,000
World	21	13
South America	26	18
Middle America	21	12
Asia (excl. USSR)	13	8
Africa	9	5

Perhaps more striking is the fact that in 1950 the Middle East, with a little over 3 percent of the world's population, contained four of the world's 49 million-plus cities; if Europe, Anglo-America, and the USSR are excluded, the number of such cities is reduced to twenty-nine. In other words, the Middle East contained 14 percent of the large cities of the underdeveloped world.

The question has been approached from another angle—in some sense, urbanization in the Middle East has far outstripped industrialization.[34] The reasons for the very slow growth of industrialization until the last few years will not be considered here. Those for the acceleration of urbanization can be studied together with a closely connected phenomenon: the abnormally low share of the agricultural sector in gross national product, compared to other countries at the same level of per capita income, and—except in the oil producing countries—the abnormally high share of the service sector.[35] First there is the rapid population growth—accelerating from 1 percent per annum in the 1920s to 2 percent in the 1940s and now approaching 3 percent. In several Middle Eastern countries—notably Egypt, Israel, Jordan, Lebanon, and Saudi Arabia, but also, to a lesser degree, Syria and Turkey—it is no longer possible to extend the cultivated area except by means of costly irrigation works. Hence the growth in the supply of agricultural labor has greatly exceeded the rise in demand for it, and millions have been pushed from the countrysides to the towns. In some countries with no land shortage, such as Iran and Iraq, the land tenure system, by depriving the vast majority of peasants of land, induced the same exodus.

Second, the exploitation of the region's vast oil resources has given its governments huge revenues which at present exceed two billion dollars a year. A very large proportion of this revenue is spent in the cities, especially in the capital, thus making it possible to sustain a much larger urban population than would otherwise be feasible.

The traditional transit, tourist, and pilgrimage services performed by the Middle East, thanks to its location and history, have greatly increased in the age of pipelines and airplanes. Here, too, the benefits accrue to the urban centers: ports, airport cities, places of tourism or pilgrimage. And where such services yield substantial revenue to the government, as does the Suez Canal, for example, the process noted in the previous paragraph occurs.

Foreign aid—which the Middle East has taken in greater abundance per capita and from a wider variety of sources than any region in the world—has operated in the same direction.[36] The initial recipient of such aid is the central government, the bureaucracy in the capital city, and whether the aid is ultimately used for defense expenditure or economic and social development, the ultimate beneficiaries are mainly the urban population. Where the aid is extended in the form of food the connection is even more obvious, since foreign food makes it possible to support a larger number of city people without a corresponding increase in agricultural production.

The last factor is the course and nature of industrialization in the Middle East. In Europe and the United States during the "eotechnic" phase of technology—the era of wood, wind, and water—industry grew up in the countryside, in search of water power; thus in Manchester, which had grown into an important textile manufacturing center, "as late as 1786 only one chimney rose above the town's roofs."[37] During the "paleotechnic" period—the era of steam and coal—industries had to concentrate in seaports, river ports, or towns lying in lowlands, since coal and ores could reach them only by water or railroad. The "neotechnic" phase of electricity, internal combustion, and chemistry, has once more made it possible to set up industries in rural areas, a trend that has been evident in the last few decades. In the Middle East, however, political, economic, and social factors have led to the concentration of industries in cities.

In Europe and the United States it has been observed that the ratio of the size of cities follows a definite rule, the so-called rank-size rule. Thus in the United States the rank of a city (e.g., Chicago, 2; Los Angeles, 3; Philadelphia, 4) multiplied by its population gives a sum very close to that of the largest city, New York.[38] More generally,

the formula is $S_R = \dfrac{A}{R^n}$, where A is the size of the largest city,

R is the rank of a given city, and SR is the size of the city of that rank. No satisfactory explanation has been given for this phenomenon. Since, however, it did not exist in the sixteenth to eighteenth centuries in Europe (where the population of London—Cobbett's "Great Wen"—Paris, Vienna, and other giants was many times as large as that of the next biggest city), it may be surmised that it is connected with the diffusion of transport, industry, wealth, and education over the whole area of an advanced country.[39] Thus in the industrialized countries, including the Soviet Union, indices of industrial concentration show a marked decline with the growth of total industrial production over time.[40]   Similarly the spread of "provincial" universities indicates the diffusion of educational facilities in these countries. Such a diffusion may underlie the hexagonal and circular schemas of central cities described by Walter Christaller, which in turn may help to explain the existence of "a series of city tributary areas arrayed according to the rank-size rule."[41]

In the Middle East, however, the present-day pattern is much closer to that of the pre-industrial West. In most countries a giant capital city towers over the rest: Teheran, with a 1956 population of 1,512,000 compared to Tabriz, with 390,000, and Isfahan, with 255,000; Baghdad, with about 700,000 compared to Mosul, with under 200,000; Beirut, with about 400,000 compared to Tripoli, with a little over 100,000; and the Three Towns of Khartoum, Umdurman and Khartoum North with 240,000,[42] which are the only urban center of any significance in the Sudan.

In other countries two cities dominate the scene: Cairo, with 3,346,000, and Alexandria, with 1,513,000 compared to Ismailiya, with 276,000; and Damascus and Aleppo, with over 400,000 each compared to Hama, with about 170,000. It may be added that North Africa shows the same pattern, with Casablanca, Algiers, Tunis, and Tripoli outclassing all the other towns in their respective countries. In only one country does the rank-size rule seem to hold at all—Turkey, where in 1965 the figures were: Istanbul, 1,751,000; Ankara, 902,000; Izmir, 417,000; Adana, 291,000; Bursa, 213,000; and Eskisehir, 174,000. Interestingly enough, the 1959 census shows that in Soviet Central Asia the rank-size rule holds quite well: Tashkent, 911,000; Alma Ata, 455,000; Dushanbe, 224,000; Frunze, 217,000; Samarkand, 195,000; Ashkabad, 170,000; Chimkent, 153,000; Andijan, 129,000; Namangan, 122,000; Jambil, 113,000; and Khokand, 105,000. It also holds, somewhat more loosely, in Kazakhstan.[43]

The same concentration may also be observed in all economic and social fields. Thus in 1958, 40 percent of the industrial establishments of the UAR were in "Greater Cairo" and 28 percent were in Alexandria; in Iran in 1963, 27 percent of industrial establishments, with 29 percent of employees, were in Teheran, and in 1965, 40 percent of electricity and 50 percent of oil products were consumed in that town and 50 percent of telephones were installed in it;[44] and in Iraq about 70 percent of factory employment was in Baghdad. Similarly, in 1957 Cairo had 48 percent of the UAR's installed electric power and Alexandria 15 percent, and for telephones the figures were 52 percent and 21 percent.[45] In 1953, Baghdad accounted for 65 percent of Iraq's physicians; in 1950, 25 percent of Turkish physicians were in Istanbul; in 1964, 33 percent of Iran's physicians were in Teheran; and in 1955, over 60 percent of the Sudan's technical personnel (physicians, engineers, etc.) were in the Three Towns. And it is only in the last few years that a beginning has been made in setting up institutions of higher education in cities other than the capital or the two main cities: Asyut; Izmir and Erzurum; Tabriz and Shiraz.

Here, too, the main explanation seems to be the administrative centralization and bureaucratization—and more recently the growth of economic planning—which has concentrated so much personnel and income in the capital city. In some countries the presence of foreign communities with high incomes has augmented the purchasing power of the one or two largest cities and enhanced their attractiveness. Industry has been drawn to these cities because of their purchasing power; their good communications; the relative abundance and reliability of their water supplies, electric power, repair shops, and other external economies; and their access to government offices, in which so many decisions affecting economic activity are taken. It is only rarely that Middle Eastern governments have deliberately sought to decentralize industry, as was done by Ataturk in the 1930s, for political, social, and strategic reasons, and as is being done in Iran today, in Isfahan, Shiraz, Tabriz, and other cities.

As for education, in the Middle East the capital has always been the main cultural center (Baghdad, Cairo, Istanbul, Tunis, Fez). There are no examples of provincial Bolognas, Oxfords, Salamancas, Coimbras, Louvains, Leydens, Uppsalas, and Princetons, and few signs that this tradition is about to be broken.

It goes without saying that this centralization of talent and activity in the metropolis has unfortunate economic and social consequences. As regards economics, it seems likely that the benefits accruing from the "external economies" mentioned above are more than offset by the ever rising social marginal costs of the "social overheads" required by the expanding population of the primate cities—water, streets, sewers, schools, and so on; electricity is almost the only such service which operates under decreasing costs over a wide range of output. Socially, two aspects may be noted. First, the flight of talent to the metropolis is self-reinforcing, making it very difficult to persuade technicians, physicians, teachers, and other *Kulturtraeger* to live in the provincial towns, much less the villages. Secondly, the "demonstration effect" of a given amount of modern culture concentrated in the metropolis is presumably much smaller than that of an equal amount divided among, say, half a dozen provincial towns, which could make an impact on a much wider surrounding rural population. Such considerations seem to have influenced Ataturk when he decided to set up many of his new factories—"Ataturk's minarets," as they came to be called—in the provincial towns rather than in Istanbul or Ankara.

Two further observations may be made. First, it may well be that the rank-size rule would apply on the regional scale, even if it does not apply on the national; the difficulty here is to identify the appropriate region (perhaps the Arab Middle East in which one can see an emerging pattern with the following order: Cairo, Alexandria, Baghdad, Beirut? Damascus? Aleppo? etc.). Second, one of the reasons for the concentration of city population in the primate cities may be Middle Eastern geography. The prevalence and pervasiveness of deserts has prevented the emergence of a broad continuum of cultivated, settled areas. Instead, a vegetation or population map of the Middle East shows archipelagoes of settlement surrounded by seas of desert. In these circumstances the hexagonal and other patterns noted in Europe are not likely to emerge, except perhaps after much greater development of transport.

The subject of the emergence of megalopolitan areas can only be touched upon. In the UAR the area between Alexandria and Cairo seems to be developing into one large megalopolis.[46] Another potential one is the coastal strip stretching from Gaza through Jaffa-Tel Aviv, Beirut, Tripoli, and Latakia to Iskenderun or Mersin; at present, however, this coastal band is broken by four frontiers, all unfriendly and two closed. Last, the growth of Istanbul may extend over a large part of the Sea of Marmara, perhaps eventually joining Bursa. In this, as in other fields, the Middle East is erecting, on deep historical foundations, a building with many features of contemporary world civilization.

NOTES

1. Cairo had a population of about 250,000 (see estimates by Volney, Jomard and others discussed by M. El-Darwish in *L'Egypte Contemporaine*,

March, 1929); other towns with 10,000 inhabitants or over were Asyut, Mahalla, Damietta, Rosetta, Alexandria, and Tanta. The total population of Egypt is usually put at 2,500,000 to 3,000,000, but was probably nearer 3,500,000.

Throughout this paper available figures have been reproduced with little or no criticism of their sources, and have been used for calculations of various ratios. This implies a confidence in the accuracy of these figures which is certainly not held by the writer, but the orders of magnitude involved and the general conclusions drawn are probably correct. It is also useful to have the scattered estimates in one place.

2. J. Sauvaget, *Alep*, (Paris 1941), p. 238, and H. A. R. Gibb and H. Bowen, *Islamic Society and the West*, vol. I, part I, (London, 1950), 281. In the seventeenth century Aleppo had about 14,000 hearths (*Encyclopedia of Islam* [new ed.], s.v. Halab).

3. Charles Issawi, *The Economic History of the Middle East*, (Chicago, 1966), pp. 209, 220.

4. The 1831 "census" put the number of adult males (*erkek*) in Anatolia at 2,384,000, implying a total population of about 10,000,000 to which should be added that of Istanbul—see Enver Ziya Karal, *Osmanlı imparatorlugunda ilk nufus sayimi*, (Ankara, 1943), p. 215.

5. O. L. Barkan, "Essai sur les données statistiques des registres Ottomans," *Journal of the Economic and Social History of the Orient*, I (1958); Robert Mantran, *Istanbul dans la second moitié du XVIIe siècle* (Paris, 1962), pp. 44-47, and Bernard Lewis, *Istanbul and the Civilization of the Ottoman Empire* (Norman, Oklahoma, 1963), p. 102. Figures of 600,000 to 900,000 are quoted for "Greater Istanbul" in the period 1815-1844. (Niyazi Berkes, *The Development of Secularism in Turkey* [Montreal, 1964], p. 141). Izmir had a population of about 90,000 in 1650, about 30,000 in 1700, some 100,000 in 1715 and 130,000 in the 1830s (Berkes, p. 141) and Paul Masson, *Histoire du commerce français dans le Levant au XVIIe siècle* (Paris, 1896), p. 416.

6. See Note 25 below and *Encyclopedia Britannica*, eleventh edition, s.v. Isfahan, Tabriz, Teheran, and Yezd. For the general decline in Iran from the end of the seventeenth century see L. Lockhart, *The Fall of the Safavid Dynasty* (Cambridge, 1958), and N. V. Pigulevskaya *et al., Istoria Irana* (Leningrad, 1958), chapters 8 and 9.

7. Estimates for the 1850s to the 1880s range from 5,000,000 to 10,000,-000. The least unsatisfactory estimates are by a Russian scholar, Zolotarev, cited in L. A. Subotsinskii, *Persiya: statistiko-ekonomicheskii ocherk* (St. Petersburg, 1913), who gives a figure of 6,000,000 for 1888, and by Sir A. Houtum-Schindler who cites 7,654,000 in 1881, of whom 26 percent were urban. See *Encyclopedia Britannica* (eleventh edition), s.v. Persia; George N. Curzon, *Persia and the Persian Question*, vol. II (London, 1892), 492-3; and Eteocle Lorini, *La Persia Economica* (Rome, 1900), p. 378.

8. A. Bonné, *State and Economics in the Middle East* (London, 1948), p. 224. By 1900 these figures had risen to 38, 22, 14, 9, and 16 percent, respectively.

9. As for the whole world, it has been estimated that in 1800 less than 2.0 percent of its population lived in cities of 100,000 or more inhabitants; in 1850, 2.3 percent and in 1900, 5.5 percent. (Eric Lampard, "The History of Cities in the Economically Advanced Areas," *Economic Development and Cultural Change* [January 1955]).

10. The population of such Hellenistic cities as Alexandria, Antioch and Seleucia on the Tigris, at their peak, has been estimated at around 500,000 by Beloch, Heichelheim and other authors, and that of Constantinople has been put at not under 500,000 by Andréadès—in Norman Baynes and H. Moss (eds.), *Byzantium* (Oxford, 1948), p.53. But more recent estimates, based on fuller archeological data, have tended to reduce these figures to about 200,000 for Alexandria and Constantinople, and 100,000 for Antioch. (Josiah C. Russell, "Late Ancient and Medieval Population," *Transactions of the American Philosophical Society*, XLVIII [1958], 68-92). Of course the size of urban populations fluctuated sharply, because of wars, epidemics, earthquakes and other disasters.

As for the Islamic period, A. al-Dūrī (*Encyclopedia of Islam, new edition*, s.v. Baghdad) gives a figure of 1,500,000 for tenth century Baghdad, but archeological evidence makes one wonder whether in fact the population could have been much over 500,000. (Robert Adams, *Land Behind Baghdad* [Chicago, 1965]).

Cairo was almost certainly smaller. In this connection, two estimates made at the beginning of the fourteenth century may be quoted: Simone Segoli's of "more than 300,000" and Simon Simeonis' statement: "Cairo is twice as large as Paris, and has four times the population," quoted in Gaston Wiet, *Cairo* (Norman, Oklahoma, 1964), pp. 72-74; Paris had a population of 84,000 in 1292, which "perhaps reached 90,000 before 1348." (Russell, *Late Ancient and Medieval Population*, p. 107). See also other descriptions of Cairo quoted by Raphail Wahba in Morroe Berger (ed.), *The New Metropolis in the Arab World* (New Dehli, 1963), pp. 25-30. In the same period Aleppo and Damascus may have had 100,000 inhabitants each and Tripoli 20,000. (Nicola Ziadeh, *Urban Life in Syria* [Beirut, 1953], p. 97). Marco Polo gave a figure of 80,000 for Aden, probably an overestimate.

11. See Issawi, *The Economic History of the Middle East*, p. 260.

12. Issawi, p. 216.

13. Four examples, out of many, may be given. In May-August, 1669, an estimated 150,000 died of plague in Aleppo (A. C. Wood, *A History of the Levant Company* [London, 1935], p. 246). In Baghdad, in April, 1831, the death toll was 40,000 to 50,000 (S. H. Longrigg, *Four Centuries of Modern Iraq* [Oxford, 1925], p. 266). In Cairo, in 1834-35, "not less than 80,000" died of plague (E. W. Lane, *The Manners and Customs of the Modern Egyptians* [London, 1944], p. 3). In Salonica, according to Rabbi Samuel de Medina, "In 1548 a great pestilence ravaged the city causing the death of about 7,000 Jews. Other plagues followed in the years 1552, 1554, 1561, 1564, and 1568." (Morris Goodblatt, *Jewish Life in Turkey in the XVIth Century* [New York, 1952], pp. 22-23). Earlier outbreaks had been even more

devastating, for example the Black Death in the fourteenth century. For comparable developments in Japan see Irene B. Taeuber, "Urbanization and Population Change in the Development of Modern Japan," *Economic Development and Cultural Change* (October, 1960).

14. Xavier de Planhol, *The World of Islam* (Ithaca, 1959), pp. 3-4.

15. See Archibald Lewis, *Naval Power and Trade in the Mediterranean* (Princeton, 1951).

16. Sauvaget, *Alep*, p. 165. "Her husband's to Aleppo gone, master of the Tiger," *Macbeth*.

17. Subhi Y. Labib, *Handelsgeschichte Ägyptens im Spatmittelalter* (Wiesbaden, 1965), chapter 9.

18. For the striking parallelisms in China, see Wolfram Eberhard, "Data on the Structure of the Chinese City in the Pre-Industrial Period," *Economic Development and Cultural Change*, (April, 1956).

19. See Robert Redfield and Milton B. Singer, "The Cultural Roles of the Cities," *Economic Development and Cultural Change* (October, 1954). The authors give examples of "heterogenetic colonial" cities, including Jakarta, Manila, Bangkok, Singapore, Saigon, and Calcutta.

20. Aleppo also took in perhaps 50,000 Armenians after 1914.

21. Gabriel Baer, "Urbanization in Egypt, 1820-1907." (Paper presented at Conference on the Beginnings of Modernization in the Middle East, Center for Middle Eastern Studies, University of Chicago, 1966).

22. A. Ruppin, *Syrien als Wirtschaftsgebiet* (Berlin, 1916), pp. 187-188.

23. M. S. Hasan, "Growth and Structure of Iraq's Population, 1867-1947," *Bulletin of the Oxford Institute of Statistics* (1958).

24. *The Encyclopedia Britannica*, s.v. Persia.

25. The estimates quoted by Lord Curzon (*Persia*) would indicate a rise in the population of Tabriz from 30,000-50,000 in 1810-1812 to 170,000-200,000 in 1889 (Vol. I, 521) and that of Teheran from 120,000 in 1869 to 200,000 in 1889 (Vol. I, 333), and a fall in that of Isfahan from 200,000-400,000 in 1784-1811 to 70,000 to 80,000 in 1889 (Vol. II, 43), and that of Yazd from 100,000 at the beginning of the nineteenth century and 40,000 in 1860-1870 to 70,000 in 1889 (Vol. II, 240); that of Mashad is given at 45,000 for both 1830 and 1889 (Vol. I, 163). In 1796 Olivier had estimated the population of Teheran at less than 15,000. The population of Hamadan was put at 40,000 by Ker Porter in 1820 and at 20,000 by Curzon in 1889 (*Encyclopedia of Islam* [new edition] s.v. Hamadhan). Kinneir stated that in 1813 Kermanshah contained 12,000 houses (Laurence Lockhart, *Famous Cities of Iran* [Brentford, 1939], p. 55), and Morier put the population of Shiraz in 1811 at 19,000 (Arthur Arberry, *Shiraz* [Norman, Oklahoma], p. 60).

26. In North Africa, however, where European immigration was large and flowed mainly to the cities, urban growth was far more rapid than that of the total population and the percentage of town dwellers rose sharply.

27. Baer, "Urbanization in Egypt, 1820-1907."

28. Issawi, *Economic History of the Middle East,* pp. 41-59.

29. I. M. Smilianskaya, "Razlozhenie feodalnikh otnoshenii v Sirii i Livane v seredine XIX v," *Peredneaziatskii Etnograficheskii Sbornik* (Moscow, 1958).

30. Janet Abu-Lughod, "Tale of Two Cities: The Origins of Modern Cairo," *Comparative Studies in Society and History* (The Hague, July, 1965), and M. Clerget, *Le Caire* (Cairo, 1934).

31. *Encyclopedia of Islam,* s.v. Baladiyya.

32. This is a widespread phenomenon in the underdeveloped countries and is well analyzed by Karl Deutsch and associates in "Population, Sovereignty and the Share of Foreign Trade," *Economic Development and Cultural Change* (July, 1962).

33. Kingsley Davis and Hilda Hertz, "The World Distribution of Urbanization," *Bulletin of the International Statistical Institute,* No. 3 (1954).

34. For a review of the literature and the suggested criteria see N. V. Sovani, "The Analysis of Overurbanization," *Economic Development and Cultural Change* (January, 1964). For Egypt, see Janet Abu-Lughod, "Urbanization in Egypt," *Economic Development and Cultural Change* (April, 1965). The controversy seems to have been started by Kingsley Davis and Hilda Hertz, "Urbanization and the Development of Pre-Industrial Areas," *Economic Development and Cultural Change* (October, 1954).

35. For a table and an interesting discussion see Frederic Shorter, "The Application of Development Hypotheses in Middle Eastern Studies," *Economic Development and Cultural Change,* (April, 1966).

36. For comparative figures see H. B. Chenery and A. M. Strout, "Foreign Assistance and Economic Development," *American Economic Review,* September, 1966).

37. E. Lampard, "History of Cities in Economically Advanced Areas," *Economic Development and Cultural Change* (January, 1955).

38. See Rutledge Vining, "A Description of Certain Spatial Aspects of an Economic System," *Economic Development and Cultural Change* (January 1955), and literature cited therein. To what extent this pattern applies to France, where Paris continues to dominate the scene, is a question worthy of consideration.

39. For still earlier periods, however, the rank-size rule seems to hold somewhat better (Russell, *Late Ancient and Medieval Populations,* pp. 68-70).

40. It is evident that the enormous growth in industrial production, education, and so forth, in the advanced countries had to be accompanied by diffusion since it would have been physically impossible to locate all the factories, colleges and other institutions in a few centers.

41. Edgar M. Hoover, "The Concept of a System of Cities," *Economic Development and Cultural Change* (January, 1955).

42. See Peter McLoughlin, "The Sudan's Three Towns," *Economic Develop-*

ment and Cultural Change (October, 1963; January 1964; April 1964).

43. Edward Allworth (ed.), *Central Asia* (New York, 1967), pp. 98, 107.

44. Bank Markazi Iran, *Annual Report* (1966), and other sources.

45. Said El-Naggar in Berger, *The New Metropolis in the Arab World,* pp. 147-50.

46. Abu-Lughod, "Urbanization in Egypt," *Economic Development and Cultural Change* (April, 1965).

18

Asymmetrical Development and Transport in Egypt, 1800-1914

The history of Egypt during the period 1800-1914 shows a marked asymmetry between economic and social development. The purpose of this paper is to discuss some aspects of this asymmetry, to attempt a general explanation in the light of experience in other regions of the world and in two other Middle Eastern countries, and to explore in more detail one of its particular aspects, the development of transport. It goes without saying that a study of this kind can offer nothing more rigorous than tentative suggestions.

Economic Development and Social Backwardness

According to several economic criteria Egypt, with a population of about 12 million in 1913, was a country with a relatively high level of production.[1] Its per capita income was almost certainly not below— and may have been slightly above—£E 10 ($50), a figure higher than that of Japan, more than twice that of India, about one-half that of Italy, almost one-quarter that of France, one-fifth that of Britain, and one-eighth that of the United States.* No less striking are the figures on foreign trade given in Table 1 which show that, in per capita terms, Egypt was surpassed by only a small number of countries, almost all of them highly advanced. These two sets of figures indicate the high degree of monetization of the Egyptian economy, a conclusion that is confirmed by other facts, e.g., the large share of total agricultural output sold on the market. In addition, it may be pointed out that for a country of its size and population Egypt had received an enormous amount of foreign capital. Total foreign investment in Egypt on the eve of the First World War was over $1,000 million,[2] a figure that may be compared with about $1,000 million for Japan, about $1,750 million for India, about $750 million for China, about $2,750 million for Russia, about $1,100 million for the Ottoman Empire, below $100 million for Iran, a little over $750 million for Brazil, and a little over $500 million for Mexico.[3]

Reprinted from *Beginnings of Modernization in the Middle East* (1968) by William Polk and Richard Chambers by permission of the University of Chicago Press.

TABLE 1

Foreign Trade in 1913

	Imports (Million $)	Exports (Million $)	Total	Population (Million)	Per Capita ($)
Egypt	135	156	291	12	24.3
Turkey	179	94	273	18	15.2
Iran	55	38	93	9	10.3
India	597	786	1,383	320	4.3
Japan	357	311	670	53	12.6
Philippines	53	48	101	9	11.2
Mexico	96	150	246	16	15.4
Brazil	326	317	643	25	25.7
Greece	34	23	57	5	11.4
Bulgaria	35	17	52	5	10.4
Russia	707	782	1,489	161	9.2
Spain	235	191	426	20	21.3
Italy	693	477	1,170	36	32.5
United States	1,775	2,448	4,223	97	43.5
United Kingdom	3,208	2,556	5,764	46	125.3

Source: League of Nations, *International Statistical Year Book, 1928* (Geneva, 1929).

Even twenty-five years later, when Egypt's relative position had greatly deteriorated, it still compared favorably in mass consumption with some countries which were in most respects far more advanced, as is indicated by Table 2.

TABLE 2

Per Capita Consumption of Industrial Goods and National Income
(Pre-war figures, mostly 1937)

Consumption of various Industrial Goods	Western Europe	Czecho-slovakia	Poland	Egypt	Turkey	Pales-tine
Cotton goods (kg)	8	4.2	2.3	2	—	3.3
Paper (kg)	30	13.9	5.1	5.3	2	14.5
Soap (kg)	6	2.5	1.5	2.7	—	7.6
Sugar (kg)	32	21	12.5	9.6	5.3	18.3
Wireless sets (number of licences per 1,000 persons)	120	69	25	4.3	2	21.6
National Income per capita (I-U)	80-120	30	18	12	19	26

Differences of purchasing power have not been allowed for.

Source: Alfred Bonné, *State and Economics in the Middle East* (London, 1948), p. 307.

In sharp contrast to this relatively high economic level was Egypt's social backwardness. Perhaps the best single measure is provided by the illiteracy rates given in Table 3. These show that in mass education Egypt, with an illiteracy rate of 93 percent in 1907 and 85 percent in 1927, lagged behind many countries whose per capita income was probably distinctly lower, such as Burma, Ceylon, the Philippines, Honduras, Mexico, Brazil, Bulgaria, Greece, etc. The contrast with Japan is still more striking.[4] No comparable indices exist for health, but death rates and infant mortality rates were very high and the research undertaken by the Rockefeller Foundation shows that hygienic conditions in Egyptian villages were among the worst in the world.[5]

TABLE 3

*Illiteracy Rates; Percentage of Population Aged 10
or Over at Dates Indicated*

Egypt (1907, 1927)	93	85
India (1911, 1931)	93	91
Burma (1911, 1931)	71	60
Ceylon (1911, 1921)	69	60
Philippines (1918, 1939)	51	51
Turkey (1927)	—	92
Brazil (1900, 1940)	65	56
Mexico (1910, 1930)	78	62
Honduras (1930)	—	67
Colombia (1918, 1928)	58	48
Cuba (1907, 1931)	44	28
Bulgaria (1905, 1926)	66	40
Greece (1907, 1928)	61	42
Hungary (1910, 1930)	32	10
Spain (1910, 1920)	52	44
Portugal (1911, 1930)	69	60
Italy (1911, 1931)	48	22
France (1906, 1926)	14	6

Source: UNESCO, *Progress of Literacy in Various Countries* (Paris, 1953).

The anomalous, or lopsided, nature of Egyptian development may also be illustrated by contrasting it with that of Lebanon, and more particularly with Mount Lebanon, which formed the core of the country. An estimate quoted by a competent observer for "the total incomes of the inhabitants of the mutasarriflik of Lebanon" was 220 million piastres;[6] for a population of 400,000, this works out at only $25 per head, or half of the Egyptian figure. Similarly, although exact data on foreign trade are not available, it is almost certain that the per capita figure was distinctly below that of Egypt.[7] On the other hand, the illiteracy rate for Mount Lebanon was almost certainly not higher than 50 percent and may well have been lower.[8]

General Explanation

At the risk of oversimplification, the explanation of this marked asymmetry in Egypt's evolution may be stated as follows: Egypt felt the impact of the Industrial Revolution before being influenced by the cultural, social, and economic movements that characterized the Renaissance and the Enlightenment, whereas in Latin America, Eastern Europe, Russia, and even Japan the sequence was reversed. In this respect Egypt was typical of the vast majority of countries of non-European culture; what is remarkable however is, on the one hand, the degree of its cultural isolation before about·1820 and, on the other, the swiftness of its economic advance and the slowness of its social progress after that date.

In Latin America, trade, migration, administration, the Catholic Church in the sixteenth and seventeenth centuries, and the intellectuals in the eighteenth, formed a channel between the region and if not the mainstream of Europe at least its Iberian backwater. One has only to recall the establishment of the Universities of Mexico and Lima in 1551 and of Havana in 1728 and to mention the names of the European philosophers and scientists whose books were read in the colonies, as well as the social, intellectual, and political ferment that resulted in the wars of liberation from Spain at the beginning of the nineteenth century. In Eastern Europe the roots go much deeper; to take only Poland, the University of Cracow was founded in 1364 and the names of Copernicus and Nicolas Rej were well known in Europe in the sixteenth century. In the Balkans the multiplication of cultural and commercial links with Western Europe in the seventeenth and eighteenth centuries led to far-reaching intellectual and social changes including the revival of the vernaculars, the emergence of an intellectual elite, the growth of a commercial bourgeoisie, the expansion of the merchant marine, and the replacement of subsistence crops by cash crops. Here again the ferment led to a struggle of national liberation, this time against the Ottoman Empire.[9]

Russia established its first links with Western Europe in the fifteenth century, and by the middle of the seventeenth a relatively large group of foreign merchants, technicians, and officers was playing an important part in Moscow. Other intellectual influences came from Poland through the Ukraine. Under Peter the doors were thrown wide open; by the middle of the eighteenth century universities had been established in St. Petersburg and Moscow, and Euler, Diderot, and other *savants* were gracing the court of Catherine. Concurrently there was a vigorous development of mining and manufacturing, often employing the techniques practiced in the West—indeed for a few decades Russia was the world's leading producer of pig iron, as well as an important producer of textiles and other goods.[10]

But the most striking illustration is Japan, which is mistakenly thought to have lived in complete isolation and stagnation until Commodore Perry pushed it into the modern world in 1853. In fact, Japan had been making important advances in several fields for nearly two centuries. On the one hand, through the intermediary of the Dutch colony in Deshima, there had been much study of European science and technology, and both the Copernican cosmology and the theory of the circulation of blood had been accepted.[11] On the other hand, there were some still more important internal and economic and social changes, apparently unrelated to developments in the West. In agriculture, mention may be made of the spread of commercial crops such as cotton, tobacco, and mulberries for silk, as well as increased use of purchased fertilizers, such as oil cake and dried sardines, which seem to have resulted in an appreciable increase in yields. In industry, there was the establishment of manufactories, both private and public, in such industries as iron, earthenware, and sugar and—in the other branches—the commercialization and organization of household production through a putting-out system. In commerce there was the widespread use of double-entry bookkeeping, some of it at a very high level, and the establishment of what was probably the world's first department store in Tokyo in 1683 by the Mitsui family. In finance there were "exceptionally highly developed" credit institutions and instruments including paper money, checks, and even "futures transactions on rice" in Osaka in 1730. In all these fields the lead was taken by the growing commercial and financial bourgeoisie, the wholesale traders and money lenders.[12] To all of which must be added the extension of education which had raised Japan's male literacy rate to about forty or fifty percent by the 1850s, a figure still unattained in most Middle Eastern countries. Even earlier, by 1700, "books were often published in editions of more than 10,000 copies to satisfy the audiences created by the spread of literacy and the cultural efflorescence of the cities. There were even commercial lending libraries to distribute books to larger audiences."[13]

The fact that in all these countries economic development began early and was accompanied by social development put them in a much better position to meet the challenge of the Industrial Revolution with its urgent demand for the exploitation of their natural resources. In particular it meant that their human resources were relatively developed and that they had a native bourgeoisie, or a government, or both, which could assume some responsibility in guiding the country's economic future. Thus, in Russia, from the early eighteenth century, "the monarch's initiative became the primary factor in economic innovation," and by the end of that century "a new force was evident—the entrepreneural initiative of Russian tradesmen and manufacturers,"[14] and the same combination was also present in Japan. In Eastern Europe the leading role was long played by the German and Jewish urban minorities; but even though distinct from the national majorities of the countries in which they lived, such minorities were not too far removed in culture, and there was much intermarriage and other forms of cultural assimulation.

A few words may be added regarding India. The Portugese seem to have had very little influence on Indian culture, perhaps because their own was so strongly colored by a religion the Indians could not accept. But from the middle of the eighteenth century the British impact, more secular in nature, and striking at many more points and with greater force, had a far greater effect.

The first modern schools were founded in 1781, and by 1857 India had three modern universities. In the 1780s English and other presses, both government and private, were set up in Calcutta and Madras, and books and newspapers were being published. Early in the nineteenth century Bengali and Persian newspapers began to appear. The career of Rammohan Roy (1772-1833), although admittedly exceptional, shows the intellectual awakening that was beginning to take place. Administrative reorganization and reforms had started even earlier. Thus India may be said to have begun its social modernization somewhat before Egypt. But its economic development fell far short of that achieved by Egypt, perhaps because the sheer size of India, and the rigidity of its social structure, necessarily limited the effects of such external impacts as increased trade, capital investment, railways, and irrigation works. And insofar as comparison is possible, it may be said that in India, unlike Egypt, economic growth did not outrun social development. Using the terms adopted in this paper, India may be said to present a case of "symmetrical underdevelopment."[15]

Egypt, by contrast, was almost completely unaffected, until the advent of Muhammad 'Ali, by the momentous changes taking place in the world. The frontier between Christendom and Islam in the Mediterranean seems to have acted as a practically impenetrable barrier; the historian al-Shayyal was to all intents and purposes justified in his statement: "We do not hear of a single Egyptian who had visited Europe in the 16th, 17th, and 18th centuries."[16] The few dozens of European merchants, whose business and numbers shrank in the course of the eighteenth century, were not very interested in propagating culture. The Moravian missionary efforts failed completely and the few Franciscan friars confined their activities to the Catholic Copts (a minority within a minority) and to the small Syro-Lebanese community. The two largest minorities, the Copts and the Jews, seem to have been about as isolated from Europe as the Muslims.[17] One has only to read the writings of such an intelligent and learned man as al-Jabarti to realize that Europe had made no intellectual or social impact on Egypt.[18]

But not only had Egypt not learned from Europe, it had forgotten much of what it had known in the past. In number and wealth the traditional Muslim institutions of learning were far fewer than in Istanbul,[19] and the quality of education had declined even more than the quantity. Thus a perusal of the curriculum prescribed at al-Azhar reveals that the philosophical and scientific works of such men as Ibn Sina, Ibn Rushd, al-Farabi, al-Razi, Ibn al-Haytham, Ibn Khaldun, and even al-Ghazzali were not studied. History and belles lettres were largely neglected, not to mention the natural sciences. The library of al-Azhar was only a fraction of what it had been in the Middle Ages. And hardly any *shaykh* knew another Middle Eastern language, such as Persian or Turkish.[20] As for elementry education it consisted of learning "the orthography of the Arabic language mainly through memorizing the Kor'ān, the whole task taking two or three years," while the rudiments of arithmetic were taught by the *qabbani*, the public weigher in the market place.[21]

Hence, when the Industrial Revolution hit Egypt in the second and third quarters of the nineteenth century in the form of mechanical transport, greatly expanded foreign trade, and capital influx, the country's economic and social institutions were in no position to make an adequate response, and its trained manpower was almost nil. More specifically, there was neither a native bourgeoisie nor a half-way efficient and enlightened government that could take the country's economic development in hand and guide its course. For a few decades this fact was masked by the genius and energy of Muhammad 'Ali, who hit Egypt like a meteorite from another world. But with the collapse of his schemes and the reduction, under external pressure, of the armed forces which had occupied the center of his interest, it became clear that if the country was to be developed at all, it had to be done by foreign enterprise and capital. And as has been seen, foreigners did develop Egypt's resources remarkably swiftly in the period 1860-1913. But this development, whose course and speed were of course prescribed by foreigners to suit their own interests, had four fatal flaws. First, the greater part of the benefit accrued to foreigners or was taken up by higher consumption.[22] Second, development followed the path of least resistance—the extension of the irrigated area and the export of cotton in which Egypt had a comparative advantage. No attempt was made to diversify the economy by creating new forces of production in other fields.[23] Hence, when, after the First World War, the supply of readily available land was exhausted and the relative price of cotton began to decline, Egypt's rapid development came to a sudden end and had to be resumed, after thirty years, on a new basis. Third, in contrast to what had taken place under Muhammad 'Ali, educational and technological development lagged far behind economic development. Fourth, and perhaps most unfortunate, the importation of a foreign bourgeoisie to fill the existing vacuum inhibited the growth of a native entrepreneurial bourgeoisie.

Here again the course of events in Lebanon was very different. Contacts with Europe were reinforced during the reign of Fakhr-al-Din (1585-1635), and the Maronite Church—and to a much smaller extent other Christian churches—formed an important link. This meant that intellectual and social changes accompanied the

economic transformation that began in the seventeenth century—
the development of cash crops and the growth of trade with Europe.
Hence, although Lebanon, unlike Russia and Japan, did not have a
government aware of its economic needs and capable of pursuing
policies designed to meet them, the enterprise of its merchant class
made up for this deficiency.[24]

Another contrast is provided by Turkey, where social development began much earlier but economic progress was distinctly slower
preceding the First World War. In the first place the Turks had the
priceless asset of a ruling group accustomed to govern a vast empire,
lead large armies, and engage in Great Power diplomacy. By contrast the Egyptians had very little chance to acquire the skills needed
for political and military leadership, except during three decades
under Muhammad 'Ali. And although, thanks largely to British
rule, the administrative apparatus in Egypt became more efficient
than that of Turkey, Egyptians seldom rose to high positions, which
were reserved for British or other foreigners; and there seems little
doubt that by the time of the First World War the rulers of Egypt
had received much less training in leadership than those of Turkey.

Second, Turkey's cultural contacts with Europe—or at least those
of Istanbul, Salonica, and Izmir—began almost a hundred years
before those of Egypt. The presence in the three cities of large minority groups, of many Europeans, and of converts to Islam, as well
as the need to modernize the army and navy, helped to stir some
ripples in the hitherto undisturbed pool of the Ottoman government
as early as the reign of Ahmet III (1703-30). A few landmarks may
be noted: the sending of a Muslim Ottoman envoy to Paris in 1720,
followed by a few others; the installation of the first Turkish press,
by Ibrahim Müteferrika, in 1727; the translation of several scientific
and military books into Turkish around the middle of the eighteenth century; the foundation in 1734 of a military engineering
school, which was reorganized in 1769; and the establishment of embassies in the main capitals in 1793. Selim III's more thoroughgoing military and civilian reforms in the 1790s were thwarted by the
reaction of 1807-26, but his work was resumed by Mahmud II and
his successors.[25]

A very tentative comparison of the two countries on the eve of the
First World War seems to indicate that Egypt was far ahead in economic development, as measured by agricultural output, foreign
trade, transport facilities, and, to a lesser degree, employment in

industry. Egypt also had a slightly higher literacy rate. But Turkey seems to have had a broader-based and much more experienced political, military, administrative, and perhaps intellectual elite. The latter fact, together with full political independence, may help to explain Turkey's better performance in the 1920s-50s. By the end of the 1930s Turkey's per capita income had probably caught up with or surpassed that of Egypt,[26] as had its literacy rate. In the 1940s and 1950s Turkey, in spite of the far greater disruption to its economy caused by the war, advanced much faster than Egypt. Thus the index of agricultural production rose from 100 in 1934-38 to 171 in Turkey in 1953-55 but to only 123 in Egypt; in the following decade the two indices moved at roughly similar rates.[27] During the war, manufacturing, being stimulated by Allied Army orders and technical help from the Middle East Supply Center, rose slightly more rapidly in Egypt than in Turkey; but in the late 1940s and 1950s the Turkish rate of growth was distinctly higher.[28]

A comparison of twelve per capita indices of economic and social development for the years 1948-50 shows Turkey to have been ahead in seven (national income, energy consumption, merchandise carried on railways, food consumption, textile consumption, literacy, and registered radio sets) and Egypt ahead in three (foreign trade, cement production, and newspaper circulation). By 1958-59 Turkey was ahead in nine indices (national income, energy consumption, steel consumption, merchandise carried on railways, food consumption, textile consumption, literacy, newspaper circulation, and radio sets) and Egypt in two (foreign trade and cement production).[29]

Transport and Development

In no field was the early and rapid development of Egypt as conspicuous as in transport. Table 4 shows that, relative to its inhabited area, Egypt in 1913 was as well provided with railways as any country in the world and that, relative to its population, it was better off than most.

It may be added that railway building in Egypt—strongly promoted by the British government as an alternative to the projected Suez Canal—started in 1853, well ahead not only of the underdeveloped countries but even of Sweden and Japan.[30] Indeed it was not until the 1870s that the *total* railway mileage of Argentina and Brazil surpassed that of Egypt, whereas Japan did not catch up until the 1890s and China until after 1900.[31] Similarly, Egypt was one of the first countries to be served by regular steamship lines, starting

TABLE 4

Railway Network, 1913

	Length of Railways (kms)	Area (Thousands of sq. kms)	(Million)	Kms of Railway Per thous. sq. kms	Per million inhabitants
Egypt	4,314	40 ᵃ	12	108	·356
India	55,774	4,668	320	12	175
China	9,475	11,080	442	1	2
Japan	10,610	388	53	27	199
Turkey ᵇ	3,513	1,740	18	2	199
Mexico	25,434	1,969	16	13	1,632
Brazil	24,737	24,618	25	1	989
Colombia	1,061	1,196	6	1	193
Greece	1,594	119	5	13	333
Bulgaria	2,109	112	5	19	438
Russia	68,006	21,492	161	3	422
Spain	14,396	505	20	29	718
Italy	16,876	287	36	59	474
France	40,625	536	40	76	1,021
United Kingdom ᶜ	32,582	313	42	104	786

a. Inhabited territory only.
b. Turkey in Asia.
c. Excluding Southern Ireland.
Source: League of Nations, *International Statistical Year Book, 1928.*

in 1836. By the mid-1840s, British, French, Austrian, and Russian lines called at Alexandria; and by 1870 the total had risen to three Egyptian, three British, five French, four Austrian, two Italian, one Russian, and one Turkish regular services.[32] To this should be added the enormous volume of traffic that was beginning to flow through the Suez Canal.

This swift growth stands in marked contrast to both the slow evolution of transport in the more advanced regions and the total lack of previous development of transport in Egypt. The economic development of the West had been heavily dependent on the steady improvement of the sailing ship, which reached its highest technical level only in the second half of the nineteenth century, carried the greater part of international traffic until the 1870s, and continued to compete against steamers until the eve of the First World War.[33] Inland transport was heavily dependent on river navigation, but from the seventeenth century onward this was supplemented by a growing network of canals and highways. Both canal construction and road building increased steadily in Western Europe and the United States until the 1830s, after which railways began to play an increasingly important part. By then, the economic, social, and cultural movements originating in the cities had been widely diffused all over the Western world; as Adam Smith put it: "Good roads, canals, and navigable rivers, by diminishing the expense of carriages, put the remote parts of the country nearly on a level with those in the neighborhood of a town; they are, on that account, the greatest of all improvements." In other words, the transport system developed slowly and spontaneously, in response to local economic and social needs.

In Egypt, on the other hand, as in other parts of the Middle East, with the partial exception of Lebanon, improved transport was introduced by foreigners in the nineteenth century to meet international, not domestic needs. Before that time, owing to the complete absence of roads, wheeled traffic was unknown—a strange state of affairs when one recalls the chariots of the ancient Egyptians, Hittites, and the Assyrians, not to mention the Romans. "The first carriage seen in Egypt was the one received by Ibrahim Bey, one of the Mamluk princes, from France. The second was that used by Napoleon Bonaparte during the French expedition, and the third was Muhammad 'Ali's."[34] And although Egypt, unlike the other Middle Eastern countries, had an internal waterway, the Nile, river navigation was severely restricted by natural obstacles, such as sandbars, piracy, tolls, and other manmade impediments. In Iraq, the only other country with important internal waterways, conditions on the Tigris and Euphrates were even worse.[35]

The advent of steam and British needs for a quick route to India soon changed all that. Steam navigation was eminently suited to narrow seas like the Mediterranean and Red Sea where fueling was easy, and by the 1830s Egypt was linked to both Europe and India.[36] Steamers were also active on the Nile and the Mahmudiyya Canal (opened in 1819), which were regularly dredged and cleared. By the 1850s Egypt was spanned by railways linking Alexandria, Cairo, and Suez, and by 1869 the Suez Canal was open to navigation.

Once the Suez Canal had proved its worth, interest in other railway schemes—e.g., the Mesopotamian-Mediterranean project—slackened. Except for the Berlin-Baghdad line, which was cut short by the First World War, no important schemes were undertaken and the only railways in operation in the Ottoman Empire were a few lines leading inland from such ports as Izmir, Beirut, and Jaffa.[37] Later the use of petroleum pipelines to convey the region's main export item greatly diminished the need for further railways in Arab Asia, as did the development of air traffic for passengers and very valuable goods. And by the 1920s or 1930s, the automobile age had come to the Middle East, as to other parts of the world. In Egypt the course of events was somewhat different. Railway construction continued until the First World War and played an important role in the economic development of the country. Railways made it possible to move Egypt's main export crops, such as cotton, rice, and onions, and to carry its bulky imports, such as coal, timber, building materials, to the remoter parts of the country. In the absence of protection, they also exposed Egypt's handicrafts to the full blast of competition and eliminated most of them—and with them an important potential breeding ground for a native bourgeoisie. But since almost all the materials and fuel needed for railway construction and operation, as well as the skills, continued to be imported from abroad, the railways had practically no "multiplier" effect on the local economy. In other words, they did not provide a market for the products of local industries, did not encourage technical progress in such industries, and did not lead to any important entrepreneurial or financial innovations. In this their effect was very different from what it was in Russia, Japan, or even—though to a far lesser extent—India, not to mention Western Europe and the United States.[38]

Thus the swift development of mechanical transport greatly facilitated the transformation of Egypt into an export-oriented, lopsided economy, heavily specialized in cotton production. To that extent it prepared the way for the difficulties the country was to encounter after the First World War.[39]

But in terms of the problems posed in this paper, the very extension of the transport system raises a further question. By the turn of the century modern transport had reached the greater part of the countryside. In the 1870s the main provincial towns were connected by railways. Light agricultural railways were built by private enterprise, mainly in the Delta and Fayyum, starting in 1895; by 1902 there were over 1,000 kilometers of such lines and by 1914 nearly 1,400. The use made of the railways is shown by the fact that the number of third-class tickets issued by the State Railways rose to 12.5 million in 1900 and over 26 million by 1907. In addition it should be remembered that many irrigation canals were navigable by steam tugs, that Nile and canal tolls were abolished in 1901, and that starting in 1890 agricultural roads—of very poor quality—began to be built, over 2,000 kilometers being in use by 1900.[40] Given these excellent means of transport, and a good postal and telegraph system as well, why was there not a greater response in social development, such as that in Lebanon following the building of village roads during and after the 1850s?

Part—but only part—of the answer is no doubt to be found in the fact that the government sadly neglected education, at both the mass and higher levels.[41] This it could do without arresting economic growth because Egypt was importing not only the capital required to build up a modern economy but also the personnel needed to run it. Europeans supplied the technical skills and managed the larger enterprises. Greeks, Jews, Armenians, Lebanese, and Syrians owned most of the petty business, and even the civil service drew heavily on such groups to fill the more qualified posts. Thus it was perfectly possible to develop Egypt's natural resources without correspondingly developing its native human resources. In such circumstances the best of transport systems could hardly, by itself, elicit much response. To change the metaphor, the transport system provided channels to the remotest villages, but the water that might have flowed through such channels was simply not there.[42] Egypt's social upsurge had to await a new age: the age of national governments working through a native middle class, universities, schools, radios, village roads, and motor cars. This social upsurge may, in turn, be expected to lead to a marked increase in the rate of economic growth.

APPENDIX

The per capita figure of £E 10 agrees with the rough estimate of £E 120 million for national income in 1913 given by the Commission on Commerce and Industry. A. El Sherbini and A. Sherif, "Marketing Problems in an Underdeveloped Country—Egypt," *Egypte Contemporaine* (Cairo, 1956), give an estimate of £E 12.4 for 1913, and an identical figure is given by H. Meunier, in *Revue d'Egypte économique et financière*, December 1, 1951 (Cairo).

Count Cressaty estimated the wholesale value of the principal Egyptian crops in 1908-9 at £E 60 million, i.e., £E 5.370 per head (*L'Egypte d'aujourdhui* [Paris, 1912], pp. 177-80). Since agricultural output rose appreciably between 1908-9 and 1913 (the cotton crop increased by more than ten percent), and since agriculture is unlikely to have accounted for more than sixty percent of the total gross national product, a per capita figure of £E 10 seems reasonable.

The United States figure for 1913 was about $400—GNP was $40 billion and population 97 million (Department of Commerce, *United States Income and Output* [Washington, D.C., 1958], p. 138). The British figure for 1913 was a little over $250—national income was £2,339 miilion and population 43 million (Colin Clark, *National Income and Outlay* [London, 1938], p. 232). The Japanese figure for 1913 was 85 yen, or a little over $40—GNP was 4,245 million yen and population was 51 million (Kazushi Ohkawa, *Growth Rate of the Japanese Economy* [Tokyo, 1957], p. 247). The Indian per capita income in 1900-14 was estimated at 36 rupees (V. K. Rao, *An Essay on India's National Income* [London, 1939], p. 37), and a figure of 40 rupees ($13) has been assumed for 1913. (See also slightly lower estimates given in Vera Anstey, *The Economic Development of India* [London, 1957], p. 439). Needless to say, most of these estimates are very rough, but this does not invalidate the general conclusion.

It may be added that comparison of recent gross domestic product figures shows a marked deterioration in Egypt's relative position since 1913. Thus the Egyptian per capita figure of $156 in 1962 was one-sixteenth that for the United States ($2,691), one-ninth that for the United Kingdom ($1,372) or France ($1,437), one-sixth that for Italy ($917), one-fourth that for Japan ($551), less than one-half that for Greece ($374), one-half that for Lebanon (about $350), and twice that for India ($73). See United Nations, *Yearbook of National Account Statistics, 1963* (New York, 1964), pp. 327-29.

This deterioration, which is due to Egypt's economic stagnation at a time of rapid advance in most of the world, is confirmed by other data, e.g., the value of foreign trade per capita; but needless to say the figures in question are very tentative and should not be pressed too far. Thus, as has been pointed out by several economists, such per capita figures greatly understate the real purchasing power of incomes in the poor countries; for instance, it has been suggested that those for Egypt, Jordan, and Turkey should be raised by fifty percent, and those for India and Pakistan doubled, if they are to be compared to those of advanced countries. But it should be pointed out that this also applies to the somewhat less poor countries—thus, the figures for Greece and Spain should be raised by sixty percent (see P. N. Rosenstein-Rodan, "International Aid for Underdeveloped Countries," *The Review of Economics and Statistics*, 1961).

Although no research has been done on this subject, the present writer is inclined to believe that the gap between the ratios of nominal to real incomes of the underdeveloped countries, compared to the advanced ones, has *widened* in the course of the past fifty or sixty years.[43] If this is so, it would offset part of the relative decline of Egypt compared to the United States, the United Kingdom, France, and Italy.

Another offsetting factor should also be taken into account, the distinction between total population and consumer units. This is based on the fact that children consume less than adults and that therefore a population with a large proportion of children constitutes fewer consumer units than does an equal population with a smaller proportion of children. To this should be added the fact that, because of certain economies of scale, a large household is a more efficient consuming unit than a small one. These two factors may raise the income *per consumer* in underdeveloped countries, with large households and a high proportion of children, by some twenty to thirty percent relative to those in advanced countries with small households and a low proportion of children (E. Kleiman, "Age Composition, Size of Households, and Interpretation of Per Capita Income," *Economic Development and Cultural Change,* October, 1966). Since the proportion of children and the size of households shrank more between 1913 and 1962 in the advanced than in the underdeveloped countries, the gap between their *per capita* incomes must have widened more than that between their *per consumer* incomes.

NOTES

1. The words "high level of production" rather than "developed" have been deliberately chosen to point out the fact that although some of Egypt's productive powers had been raised to a high level, the country's economic and social institutions and skills had not been correspondingly developed.

   * See Appendix to this essay.

2. See A. E. Crouchley, *The Investment of Foreign Capital in Egyptian Companies and Public Debt* (Cairo, 1936); and L. A. Fridman, *Kapitalisticheskoe razvitie Yegipta* (Moscow, 1963), p. 13.

3. Japan's outstanding foreign debt in 1913 was 1,969 million yen (S. Y. Furuya, *Japan's Foreign Exchange and her Balance of International Payments* [New York, 1928], p. 47), but by then Japan's foreign investments amounted to 780 million yen, bringing down net indebtedness to about $650 million (William W. Lockwood, *The Economic Development of Japan* [Princeton, N. J., 1954], pp. 258-59). Russia's foreign debt was put at 5,600 million rubles, and the Chinese *government* debt at $650 million (Herbert Feis, *Europe,*

the World's Banker [New York, 1930], p. 210 and p. 453). The other figures have been calculated from various partial estimates given by Feis and Jean Malpas, *Les Mouvements Internationaux des Capitaux* (Paris, 1934). For figures on the Ottoman Empire see Charles Issawi, *The Economic History of the Middle East* (Chicago, 1966), pp. 94, 106.

4. By the end of the Tokugawa period (around 1850), Japan had a male literacy rate of forty to fifty percent. By the end of the Meiji period (1912) "virtually the entire population had attained functional literacy, and compulsory school attendence was as close to 100 percent as it could be" (Herbert Passin, *Society and Education in Japan* [New York, 1965], pp. 4, 11).

5. See J. M. Weir, "An Evaluation of Health and Sanitation in Egyptian Villages," *Journal of the Egyptian Public Health Asso* (Cairo, 1952).

6. A. Ruppin, *Syrien als Wirtschaftsgebiet* (Berlin, 1916), pp. 192-94.

7. The total trade (exports plus imports) of "geographic" or "greater" Syria on the eve of the First World War was about $50 million (Ruppin, *Syrien als Wirtschaftsgebiet*, pp. 364-71 and Paul Huvelin, "Que vaut la Syrie," *L'Asie française* [Paris, 1921]). Beirut accounted for half the total, but it drew its exports from far inland and distributed its imports much more widely. The population of Syria was about 3.5 million (see Charles Issawi, *Economic History*, part 4), giving a per capita figure of $14, or a little over half the Egyptian figure.

8. The only available figures are for 1932 and refer to the *whole* population and not only to those ten years old and over; they therefore overstate, by a considerable margin, Lebanon's illiteracy rate. For Mount Lebanon, the percentage of illiteracy is given as 40, for North Lebanon as 51, and for the whole of Lebanon as 47. See Sa'īd Himādeh, *Economic Organization of Syria and Lebanon* (Beirut, 1936), p. 11, quoting the 1932 census.

9. See Traian Stoianovich, "Land Tenure and Related Sectors of the Balkan Economy, 1600-1800," *Journal of Economic History*, Fall 1953; *idem,* "The Conquering Balkan Orthodox Merchant," *Journal of Economic History*, June 1960; and L. S. Stavrianos, *The Balkans Since 1453* (New York, 1958).

10. Herbert J. Ellison, "Economic Modernization of Russia," *Journal of Economic History*, December, 1965; Michael T. Florinsky, *Russia* (New York, 1955), pp. 561-64; and Peter Lyashchenko, *History of the National Economy of Russia* (New York, 1949), pp. 287-97.

11. See Donald Keene, *The Japanese Discovery of Europe* (London, 1952).

12. M. Miyamoto, Y. Sakudo, and Y. Tasuba, "Economic Development in Pre-Industrial Japan, 1859-1894," *Journal of Economic History*, December 1965; James I. Nakamura, *Agricultural Production and the Economic Development of Japan* (Princeton, 1966), pp. 75-79; and, more generally, Thomas C. Smith, *Agrarian Origins of Modern Japan* (Stanford, 1959).

13. Passin, *Society and Education*, p. 12.

14. Ellison, "Economic Modernization."

15. See Jawaharlal Nehru, *The Discovery of India* (London, 1946), pp. 262-71; Sir Percival Griffiths, *The British Impact on India* (London, 1957); Nurul

Islam, *Foreign Capital and Economic Development: Japan, India, and Canada* (Rutland, Vt., 1960); and especially Morris D. Morris, "Towards a Reinterpretation of Nineteenth-Century Indian Economic History," *Journal of Economic History*, December 1963.

16. J. al-Shayyāl in *Historians of the Middle East*, ed. Bernard Lewis and P. M. Holt (London, 1962), p. 410. In fact Sonnini mentions a few Coptic Catholic priests who had been to Rome (see J. Heyworth-Dunne, *An Introduction to the History of Education in Modern Egypt* [London, n.d.], p. 89). Professor P. M. Holt has also drawn my attention to a Copt who visited Europe at the end of the sixteenth century and lived for some time at Oxford. He is mentioned in J. G. Graf, *Geschichte der christlichen-arabischen Literatur* (Rome, 1944-53), 4:131-132. An interpreter, Ibn Taghri Birdi, was sent to Venice on a diplomatic mission in 1506 (see Ṣubḥī Y. Labīb, *Handelsgeschichte Aegyptens* [Wiesbaden, 1965], p. 468).

17. Heyworth-Dunne, *An Introduction to the History of Education*, pp. 85-91.

18. It is true that Chateaubriand claims that in 1806 he met in Alexandria "un riche Turc, nommé Ali-Bey el Abassy" who "prétendit connaître mes ouvrages" (*Itinéraire de Paris à Jerusalem* [Paris, 1812], 2:219). But one would like to know who that Turk was and where he came from—indeed one cannot help wondering whether he was not a product of Chateaubriand's fertile imagination.

19. Heyworth-Dunne, *An Introduction to the History of Education*, p. 16.

20. *Ibid.*, pp. 41-83; see also Bayard Dodge, *Al-Azhar* (Washington, D.C., 1961), pp. 52, 92-94; J. al-Shayyāl, *Ta'rikh al-tarjama* (Cairo, 1951).

21. Heyworth-Dunne, *An Introduction to the History of Education*, pp. 2-3.

22. From 1902-14 annual interest payments on Egyptian government and private securities held abroad are estimated to have averaged about £E 8 million (see A. E. Crouchley, *The Economic Development of Modern Egypt* [London, 1938], p. 273). This figure, which represents over 7 percent of Egypt's gross national product for that period, should be further raised by a considerable amount to take into account: first, the tribute to Istanbul, £E 500,000 per annum; second, further payments overseas in the form of remittances of profits made in unincorporated enterprises owned by foreigners residing in Egypt, and remittances of salaries and other incomes earned by other foreigners; and third and most important, income accruing to foreigners residing in Egypt and not remitted abroad but consumed or reinvested in Egypt. These three categories, collectively, probably raised foreigners' share in the Egyptian gross national product to well over 10 percent.

At their greatest concentration, just before the First World War, foreign citizens (221,000 in 1907) constituted 2 percent of Egypt's population. The addition of such minority groups as Jews, Lebanese, Syrians, and Armenians, who being Ottoman subjects were not regarded as foreigners, would raise the total to slightly over 3 percent. At a very rough guess, these foreigners and minority groups may have owned 15-20 percent of Egypt's capital—perhaps closer to the higher figure. This guess is based on the breakdowns given in Charles Issawi, *Egypt: An Economic and Social Analysis* (London, 1947), p. 58.

The ratio between foreigners' estimated shares of capital and income is not out of line with what is known about the distribution of the national product between capital and labor and about the exponents of the Cobb-Douglas function in underdeveloped countries.

For the very marked rise in mass consumption in the period 1880-1913, see Charles Issawi, "Egypt since 1800: a Study in Lop-sided Development," *Journal of Economic History*, March 1961.

23. What aggravated matters and made it practically impossible to change the country's course to a more desirable direction was the fact that the government was severely constrained by the Capitulations and commercial conventions and that after 1882 the captain and officers of the ship of state were British, not Egyptian.

24. For a fuller discussion see Charles Issawi, "Economic Development and Liberalism in Lebanon," *Middle East Journal*, Summer 1964. A striking illustration of the relatively close contacts between Lebanon and Europe is an incident during the peasant uprising of 1840. In proclamations issued on June 8, 1840, slogans embodying French revolutionary ideas were used and the rebels pointed to the example given by Greece. See I. M. Smilyanskaya, *Krestyanskoe dvizhenie v Livane* (Moscow, 1965), p. 209.

25. See Niyazi Berkes, *The Development of Secularism in Turkey* (Montreal, 1961); Bernard Lewis, *The Emergence of Modern Turkey* (London, 1961); and Robert E. Ward and Dankwart A. Rustow, *Political Modernization in Japan and Turkey* (Princeton, 1964).

26. A careful calculation by Alfred Bonné (*The Economic Development of the Middle East* [London, 1945], pp. 44-45), put the net value of Turkish agricultural production in 1934-35 at 366.4 million International Units and the Egyptian at 308.6 million. Output of manufacturing was roughly equal in the two countries (see United Nations, *The Development of Manufacturing Industry in Egypt, Israel, and Turkey* [New York, 1958], pp. 95-96). Turkey's mining production, output of electricity, railway network, and merchant marine were distinctly larger than those of Egypt (see United Nations, *Review of Economic Conditions in the Middle East, 1949-50* [New York, 1951], pp. 54, 60, 64). The size of the populations of the two countries was almost identical.

27. Food and Agricultural Organization of the United Nations, *Production Yearbook, 1955* and *1964*.

28. United Nations, *Development of Manufacturing*, pp. 17-18, 98.

29. Charles Issawi, *Egypt at Mid-Century* (London, 1954), p. 78; *idem, Egypt in Revolution* (London, 1963), p. 110.

30. See *Cambridge Economic History of Europe*, 6:228-49. An attempt by Muhammad 'Ali to build a railway as early as 1834 was unsuccessful, owing to shortage of funds.

31. For Japan, see G. D. Allen, *A Short Economic History of Modern Japan* (London, 1946), p. 178; and Bank of Japan, *Historical Statistics of Japanese*

Economy (Tokyo, 1962), p. 29. For Egypt, Aḥmad al-Ḥitta, *Ta'rīkh Miṣr al-iqtiṣādī* (Cairo, 1957), pp. 230-36; for China, Holland Hunter, "Transport in Soviet and Chinese Development," *Economic Development and Cultural Change*, October, 1965.

32. For the mid-forties, see John MacGregor, *Commercial Statistics* (London, 1847), 2:294; and for 1870, A. E. Crouchley, *The Economic Development of Modern Egypt*, p. 142.

33. G. S. Graham, "The Ascendancy of the Sailing Ships," *Economic History Review* (1956), and Max E. Fletcher, "The Suez Canal and World Shipping," *Journal of Economic History*, December, 1958. As late as 1910, 44 percent of the French merchant marine consisted of sailing ships (J. H. Clapham, *The Economic Development of France and Germany* [Cambridge, 1921], p. 243).

34. al-Ḥitta, *Ta'rīkh Miṣr*, p. 221. See also the excellent articles " 'Adjala" and " 'Araba" in *Encyclopedia of Islam* (New Edition). On a few mamluk attempts to use rollers and wheels for transport of cannon and columns, see Gaston Wiet, *Cairo* (Norman, Oklahoma, 1964), p. 84.

35. See the accounts in *Description de l'Egypte* (Paris, 1809-22), and F. R. Chesney, *The Expedition for the Survey of the Rivers Euphrates and Tigris* (London, 1850).

36. Halford L. Hoskins, *British Routes to India* (London, 1928), and Fletcher, "The Suez Canal."

37. See Issawi, *Economic History*, pp. 91-93, 137-45, 248-57.

38. See Leland H. Jenks, "Railroads as an Economic Force in American Development," *Journal of Economic History*, January, 1944.

39. See Issawi, "Egypt Since 1800."

40. See *L'Egypte: aperçu historique et géographique* (Cairo, 1926), pp. 312-15; L. Wiener, *L'Egypte et ses chemins de fer* (Brussels, 1932), pp. 71-88; *Annuaire Statistique* (Cairo); several articles in *L'Egypte Contemporaine* (Cairo), January, 1933; E. R. J. Owen, "Cotton Production and the Development of the Economy in 19th Century Egypt," (Ph.D. thesis, Oxford, 1965). I am greatly indebted to Dr. Owen for comments he made on an earlier draft of this paper.

41. British reluctance to develop Egyptian education, which is shown both by the slow increase in the school population and by the tiny budget appropriations for education, had two motivations: the desire to keep government expenditure to a minimum and fear that education would breed a class of discontented nationalists who would agitate for independence. The latter sentiment was often expressed by Cromer, who cited the Indian experience.

42. This of course leaves unanswered the question of why, in the absence of government leadership in education, there was so little private initiative in that field. The latter question may be linked with a more general one: Egypt's failure to produce a native entrepreneurial middle class. This failure may be connected with the strength of Egypt's bureaucracy

and the relatively great amount of government control prevailing throughout its history which, in turn, may be explained by the centralization required to run the irrigation system. In Lebanon and Syria, by contrast, rain-fed agriculture led to a more decentralized system which, together with a greater volume of international trade, may have facilitated the growth of a native bourgeoisie.

Another relevant factor is the ethnic difference between the Turkish-Circassian élite of Egypt and its Arabic-speaking population. The importance of this becomes evident when one recalls the role of the Church and aristocracy in the Balkans or Latin America and that of the aristocracy in Japan in leading the country's cultural revival. The point has been suggested to me by Eugene Rothman, a graduate student at Columbia University.

43. This is mainly because services, as distinct from goods, account for a much larger part of the gross national product of the advanced countries than they did fifty or sixty years ago. And it is the fact that the price of services differs so much between advanced and underdeveloped countries (e.g., a haircut in a good barber's shop cost about 20 cents in Cairo in 1961, but $1.25 in New York) that mainly accounts for the discrepancy between the ratio of the purchasing power and the ratio of the exchange rates.

19
The Entrepreneurial Class

The title of this essay is untranslatable. As an economist pointed out, "enterpriser" sounds too dashing and "undertaker" somewhat sinister. It is also vague, and thus allows for some leeway. It has been chosen in order to focus attention on the main topic, the industrial class, shifting whenever necessary to such fields as finance, commerce, or even, in one or two cases, the professions. First, the growth of the entrepreneur class in the principal Middle Eastern countries will be rapidly traced and then the main features will be sketched.

A long historical glance brings out a very significant fact: at its height Islamic civilization was highly commercial. Islam has been described as the one major religion to have been founded by a successful businessman. The Meccan aristocracy, which first opposed, then rallied to and finally took over from Mohammad and his followers, was a trading aristocracy. Unlike agriculture, which was looked down upon by all self-respecting Arabs, and unlike the crafts, which were left to the subject populations, trade was both highly esteemed and widely practiced by the very "best people." The impression of intense commercial activity gained from reading *The Arabian Nights*, is confirmed by more sober accounts. Thus the Iranian traveler Nasir-i-Khusraw in his *Safar Nameh* relates that practically all transactions in eleventh-century Basra were settled by checks, not cash. Indeed, one of the most striking differences between Muslim and Western feudalism is the extent to which the former was based on a monetary economy and used monetary reckonings for its normal transactions. Another important difference for some centuries was the high development of the crafts in the Middle East.

In the twelfth to the fourteenth centuries Islam passed through a terrible crisis, being assailed first by the Crusaders and then by the still more devastating Mongols and Tatars. Islamic society sur-

vived under the Mamluks, but at the crippling cost of militarization
and the debasement of its economic and cultural life. The diversion
of the trade routes completed the ruin of the Middle East.

At this stage, however, a new factor of economic development
began to make itself felt with increasing force. It is significant that,
in its heyday, Islamic commercial activity was directed eastward
and southward—to India, Indonesia, Africa, and for a short while
even China—not westward to Europe. This may perhaps be explained by the poverty of Europe and the wars and piracy which
rendered the Mediterranean insecure. At any rate, when trade
relations did begin, it was the Europeans who initiated them: first
the Amalfians, Genoese, and Venetians, then the Portuguese, French,
and British. By the beginning of the eighteenth century the Middle
East had been drawn into the network of European trade, supplying
such products as silk, cotton, and coffee and receiving in return
manufactured goods. A certain amount of transit trade also continued, Egypt re-exporting the products of Africa and Constantinople those of the Caucasus.

The important thing to notice about this trade is that it was carried
on by European companies and merchants established in Istanbul,
Aleppo, Isfahan, and Cairo. As far as is known, there were no important Middle Eastern merchants. They lacked the liquid capital,
the enterprise, or the security afforded by the Capitulations. But
in the course of the eighteenth century, perhaps because of increasing anarchy in the Ottoman empire, European merchants began
pulling out of Egypt and Syria. Trade, however, did not cease; at
first their place was taken by Aleppo Jews, who became the consular
representatives of some European states, established branches in
Italy, and handled a large proportion of the foreign trade of Egypt
and Syria. In turn, these Jews began to be replaced by Syrian Christians. When Bonaparte established a Council in Cairo, the Christian
Syrian community was deemed sufficiently important—as well as
pro-French—to have five representatives on it.

A parallel development occurred in Greece. In the course of the
eighteenth century Greek shipping and commerce expanded considerably, and when, during the Revolutionary and Napoleonic
wars, British and French ships and merchants withdrew from the
eastern Mediterranean, their place was generally taken by Greeks.
Prosperous merchant colonies were established in Odessa, Venice,
and other Adriatic seaports. Incidentally, these colonies played

an important part in organizing and financing the Greek Revolution.

Greece and Lebanon and Syria are interesting because they furnish the earliest Middle Eastern examples of the spontaneous emergence of an industrial class.

In Greece the development of shipping and trade, especially after 1830, led to the emergence, on the islands and in those parts of Asia Minor lying on the Black Sea—Mediterranean route, of handicrafts related to shipping. The introduction of steam led to the need for fuelling stations and ancillary industries. At the same time the development of agriculture stimulated the making of simple tools and crude chemical fertilizers.

But the real stimulus to Greek industry was the influx of refugees from Asia Minor, following the First World War. A few of the refugees had a little money, which they used to establish small-scale industries. (Incidentally, the same phenomenon is observable today in Jordan.) Most of them were destitute, but they included skilled weavers, carpet makers, and other craftsmen. The vast majority settled in the cities. The International Loan granted to Greece was used to build houses, instead of to resettle the refugees on the land, as had been its original purpose. The result was the development of textile, food-processing, and other industries. When the depression struck in the 1930s, the government helped industry by means of import quotas, tariffs, and foreign exchange control, leading to considerable further development. Some of these industries have now become sufficiently efficient to be competitive, but most still depend heavily on protection. In recent years shippers have not shown much interest in industry, preferring to reinvest their profits in their own line of business.

It may, therefore, be said that Greek industry evolved spontaneously from the handicraft to the manufacturing stage.

Lebanon's economic evolution has run roughly parallel to that of Greece, except that the mainspring of activity has been not shipping but entrepôt and emigration. Early in the nineteenth century Beirut began to establish itself as the foreign trade channel of Lebanon, Syria, Palestine, northern Arabia and Iraq, and southern Anatolia. A prosperous class of Lebanese merchants grew, with close contacts with Europe. At the same time French capital began to interest itself in the country, developing its silk resources and building ports, railways, and public utilities.

The breakup of the Ottoman empire was a heavy blow to the Beirut merchants. They lost their Anatolian market and much of the Iraqi market as well, while Haifa replaced Beirut as the port of Palestine and Transjordan. This was, however, offset partly by the growth of the Syrian and Lebanese markets, partly by the rapid development of tourism, and partly by the development of a money market.[1] At present Beirut is by far the most important financial center in the Middle East, and the Lebanese merchants have been making good use of their wits in foreign exchange transactions. A good example is the gold trade. Gold is bought in Mexico with United States dollars, sent by plane to the Persian Gulf, shipped on little sailing boats which navigate the Indian Ocean, smuggled into India (and until recently into China), and sold for rupees. The rupees are then transferred to Saudi Arabia, where they are exchanged for sovereigns, which are then used to buy dollars, and so the cycle is complete. Other modern *Arabian Nights* stories are told, for instance, about the Lebanese merchant who financed a copper deal between Spain and the Soviet Union, and of another who, learning of a purchase by an American merchant of Iraqi wool, interposed himself between the two offering the American a slightly lower price in dollars and the Iraqi a slightly higher price in dinars, thus concluding the transaction to the satisfaction of everyone except the Iraqi Exchange Control.

These various activities provided one source of liquid capital for the development of industry. Another came from the emigrants who, ever since the 1860s, have been leaving Lebanon for Egypt, the New World, Australia, and, as readers of Graham Greene's novels know, West Africa. Today there are probably as many people of Lebanese descent living outside the country as within it, and the story goes that a Lebanese upon being asked what was the population of his village replied: "Thirty thousand abroad, and ten thousand at home, for purposes of reproduction." Many of these emigrants have done exceedingly well for themselves, the outstanding example being those in Brazil, where Syrians and Lebanese own no less than five hundred large industrial enterprises, including some of the largest textile plants in the world. Thus emigration provided another source of capital in the form of both remittances and transfer of funds.

In the late 1920s some of this capital began to be invested in local industry. The Mandatory authorities directed most French investments into monopolies, such as ports, electricity, water, tobacco, and the like and used their influence to block Lebanese investments in those fields. Some foreign capital also went into the cement industry. But for the rest, most of the businesses were founded by Lebanese capital contributed either by emigrants who had made money, such as Arida, or by merchants, generally importers like Assaili and Tamer. During the 1930s there was further development, but many enterprises were in a precarious state when the war provided them with a shot in the arm. There comes to mind only two firms of any consequence which were not established by either traders or emigrants but grew from the handicraft to the factory stage, a biscuit factory and a jam factory.

Syria's development has differed from that of Lebanon in two important respects. In the first place, it started much later, and so far has made less headway. Secondly, whereas in Lebanon the Christian merchants have kept the lead they won in the nineteenth century, in Syria Muslims have tended to catch up with and overtake them. The example of my maternal family aptly illustrates the evolution of many Damascene Christians. Toward the beginning of the nineteenth century my great-great-grandfather owned a textile workshop. His profits enabled his son to engage, in the middle of the nineteenth century, in large-scale trade with Egypt and other countries. That, however, was the end of any business ability in the family: my grandfather and his brothers, equipped like so many Christians with a French education which gave them a start over their Muslim contemporaries, went into the professions and the civil service, while their sons have tended to concentrate on the professions. Of course, many Christians are still prominent in business, but the Muslims have shown considerable ability and are taking over an ever larger share. And when it comes to modern industry, the Muslims are playing a predominant part.

Except for some French and Belgian capital in railways and public utilities—most of which have now been nationalized—there has been practically no foreign capital investment in Syria. Industrialization has been achieved entirely with local funds, a small start in the prewar period being followed by greater development after the war. Three main groups may be distinguished. First, the so-called Khumasieh group of Damascus, which has established spinning, dyeing, vegetable oil, and soap factories and taken over the Damascus cement plant. It consists entirely of Muslim merchants, most of whom worked in the import trade. Secondly, there is the

Sahnawi group, also of Damascus, which has set up glass, sugar, alcohol, vegetable oil, glucose, starch, and dyeing factories. Its president, and some of its members, are Christians, but the majority are Muslims; almost all of the group consists of traders, practically all being importers or representatives of foreign firms. Lastly, there are various Aleppo industrialists: Mudarris, owner of a large textile plant and notable as the only example of a Syrian landowner who has taken a real interest in industry; Hariri, also a textile manufacturer; and Shabarek who has just set up a cement factory. Both of the latter are traders.

Whereas Greece, Lebanon, and Syria provide examples of the spontaneous and slow growth of a business class, in Israel there has been a completely different phenomenon—the transplantation of a highly developed group of entrepreneurs from Europe. Because of the very diverse origins, both social and national, of the Jewish immigrants into Palestine and Israel, it is difficult to give a clear-cut picture of the background of the industrialists. Broadly speaking, it may be said that the entrepreneurs in Israel established firms either in the industry in which they had previously been employed (as owners, managers, technicians, artisans, or workers) or else in an industry in which their country of origin excelled. As example of the latter tendency, there are the German Jews who founded the chemical industry, the British Jews who set up metalworks, and the American Jews who established the precision instruments industry.

Examples of the former tendency are numerous and diverse. Thus the textile industry was founded by Polish owners of textile factories in Lodz; the chemical and pharmaceutical industry by German chemists, doctors, or merchants dealing in chemical products; the engineering industry by engineers, sometimes in partnership with former importers; and the diamond industry by Belgian diamond cutters who took advantage of the opportunity created by the cessation of Belgian and Dutch exports and the availablity of African diamonds to establish in Palestine a new industry based on a different division of labor. An interesting development is that of printing, carried out by east European Jews who combined a high educational level and a knowledge of several of the many languages current in Israel with experience as printers in Europe.

As in other Middle Eastern countries, but to a lesser extent, there has been a tendency for importers of an article to start producing it; examples are paper, leather, and some textile products. Another trend, which has its counterpart in Lebanon, though the differences are more important than the similarity, is the creation of big enterprises by businessmen who gained their experience abroad, for example the potash, cement, and electricity works, all founded by Russian Jews—Novomeysky, a mining engineer; Lifshitz, the owner of oil wells; and Rutenberg, a politician. A tendency which has gone much farther than in other Middle Eastern countries is the establishment of branches of foreign firms to manufacture such things as Kaiser-Frazer cars, Philco refrigerators, Philips bulbs, Firestone tires. This has been facilitated by the existence of a large supply of skilled technicians and workmen, the opportunity for export provided by Israel's large import surplus and dollar gifts and loans, and the close contacts between Israeli and foreign businessmen. Finally, there is a phenomenon unique to Israel, namely, that of corporations formed by Jews living abroad which raise funds abroad for investment in Israel, e.g., the South Africa Palestine Company, the Palestine Economic Corporation, which is American, and the Palestine Corporation, which is British.

So far the private sector of industry, which accounts for over four-fifths of the whole, has been considered. The rest is owned by the *Histadruth*, whose managers are either former engineers or administrators who have made their way up the ladder of the trade unions or *Kibbutzim*. A high percentage of these men came from Poland or Russia, while the technicians are mainly from Germany and western Europe.

Egypt's economic history differs profoundly from that of the other Middle Eastern countries because of the fact that it was developed much earlier and that that development was achieved by the investment of vast foreign capital and the influx of a large foreign community. Hence, Egypt's entrepreneur class, when it came into being, had to wrest its place from foreign rivals. Apart from a largely foreign-owned public debt of £E 94 million, much of which had been spent on productive works, foreign investments in 1914 amounted to £E 92 million. At that date the foreign community numbered 250,000, out of a total population of 12,000,000, and that figure does not include Europeans or Levantines of Egyptian nationality. Up to World War I these foreigners completely dominated Egypt's financial and commercial life, as well as whatever little industrial activity there was, and even controlled petty trade. As Lord Cromer put it in his *Report* for 1905: "Bootmending, as well as bootmaking, is almost entirely in the hands of Greeks and Armenians. The drapery trade is contolled by Jews, Syrians and Europeans, the tailoring trade by Jews."

Such an unnatural state of affairs could not last indefinitely, and as early as 1879, when the Egyptian press began to enjoy some freedom of expression, a first attempt was made to remedy it by laying the foundations for a native bourgeoisie. Under the leadership of two Lebanese journalists, Adib Ishaq and Amin Shimayyel, a group of prominent Egyptians, including Sultan Pasha and Omar Lutfi Pasha, drew up a prospectus for the creation of a national bank which should buy up and redeem the public debt. In this prospectus they pointed out that the only way open before underdeveloped Oriental countries desirous of getting rich was trade and industry, which required large amounts of capital that only banks, drawing on the savings of the public, could provide. The sponsors disposed of objections based on the Qu'ranic prohibition of usury by different arguments and quotations from an impressive number of authorities.

The moment chosen was, however, most unpropitious, and nothing more was heard of a national bank until 1911, in which year the Egyptian congress recommended the institution of such a bank while a young employee named Talat Harb—later to achieve fame as founder and president of Banque Misr—brought out a book entitled *Egypt's Economic Remedy; or, The Project of a Bank for Egyptians*. This was Harb's fourth book; the other three are worth mentioning as shedding some light on his personality. In 1899 he had opposed Qasim Amin's call for the emancipation of women, a somewhat amusing matter in the light of the fact that his own factories were, in later years, to employ thousands of women workers. In 1905 he had written a history of Arab and Muslim states, in which he showed himself, as always, an orthodox and devout Muslim. In 1910 he had forcefully and cogently argued against the renewal of the charter of the Suez Canal Company, unless accompanied by much more favorable terms including the employment of Egyptian directors and personnel.

In his book on banking he stressed the need for a "really Egyptian bank, alongside the existing foreign banks," which would help and encourage Egyptians to enter various fields of economic activity and give "Egypt a voice in its own money market and defend its interests just as other banks defend those of their countries." At the same time he assured foreigners that an Egyptian bank would not reduce their business, since there was plenty of room for all. He expressed his confidence in the business ability of Egyptians and the availability of Egyptian funds for his scheme.

No immediate results came from this book, but in 1916 Harb was charged by the government Committee on Industry, which formed a landmark in Egypt's economic history, with studying means to develop the country's industry. Basing his arguments on Germany's experience, he urged the creation of a bank which would finance industrial development. By 1920 many prominent Egyptians had come to believe that political independence needed to be consolidated by economic independence, and 126 shareholders subscribed £E 80,000 for the creation of Harb's Banque Misr. By 1927 the capital had been raised to £E 1,000,000. In the meantime the bank began to found affiliated companies in the following fields: 1922, printing; 1924, cotton ginning; 1925, transport and navigation; 1925, cinema; 1926, sugar-cane growing; 1927, silk-weaving, cotton spinning and weaving, fisheries and linen; 1930, cotton exporting; 1932, airways and sale of Egyptian products; 1934, insurance, maritime shipping, tourism, and tanning and leather work; 1938, spinning and weaving of fine cotton goods, mines and quarries, and vegetable oils. The combined capital of these companies amounted to about £E 3,500,000 and their reserves to £E 1,500,000. An affiliated bank was also opened in Beirut and a branch in Hejaz.

There is no doubt that Talat Harb succeeded in his primary aim— that of setting up purely Egyptian businesses, keeping their books in Arabic, and training a body of men in the various economic and financial branches. There is equally no doubt that his enterprises suffered from overextension, neglect of the rules of sound banking (such as not borrowing on short term and lending on long term), favoritism, mismanagement, and in a few cases downright dishonesty. The outbreak of war in 1939 caused a run on Banque Misr which was staved off only with government help. A thorough reorganization was then carried out and, thanks to the war boom, the situation of the Misr group is now basically sound. After the war they added to their long list a large rayon plant.

In addition to the Banque Misr, the 1930 tariff played a large part in stimulating Egyptian industry. Under its shadow, many enterprises sprang up, some owned by Egyptians, others by foreign residents. The Second World War brought more industries into being, mostly Egyptian. As in other Arab countries, most of the Egyptian industrialists have sprung from the trading class.

Perhaps the best index of the progress achieved is the percentage of the total capital of corporations registered in Egypt which is owned by the Egyptians. Whereas in 1933 the percentage of share and bond capital originally subscribed by Egyptians was only 9 percent of the total, it had risen by 1948 to 39 percent. A breakdown by subperiods shows that in 1934-39 Egyptians contributed 47 percent of new capital subscriptions or increase of capital of existing companies; in 1940-45 the proportion was 66 percent; and in 1946-48 it was 84 percent. It should be remembered, moreover, that a substantial amount of share and bond capital originally subscribed by foreigners changed hands and is now held by Egyptians.

Another way of measuring the progress made in Egyptianizing business is to study the *Annuaire des Sociétés Anonymes* (1951), which, of course, covers finance and commerce, where Egyptians are less well represented, as well as industry. Out of a total of 1,406 names which can be identified with any degree of certainty, 31 percent are Egyptian Muslims, 4 percent Copts, 17 percent Jews, 12 percent Syrians or Lebanese, 9 percent Greeks or Armenians, and 31 percent Europeans. The proportion of Muslims and Copts is still very low, but some thirty years before it was almost nil.

If Egypt provides an example of a native business class which gradually pushed its way mainly by its own efforts, Turkey furnishes an example of a business class which was brought into being mainly by state action. This took two forms: elimination of foreign elements and encouragement of natives.

Until the end of the nineteenth century practically all business was in the hands of Europeans or Greeks, Armenians, and Jews. The railways, banks, public utilities, and mines were foreign owned and staffed by foreigners or members of the minority groups. Foreign trade was also in the hands of Armenians, Greeks or Jews, and these groups supplied practically all of Turkey's professional class. Thus almost all pharmacists were Armenians, and there was much rejoicing and considerable publicity accompanying the graduation of the first genuinely Turkish pharmacist. The only nonagricultural economic activity of any consequence which was in Turkish hands was internal trade.

Gradually at first and then much more quickly, things began to change with the disappearance of the Armenian and Greek minorities. Many foreigners, and all the members of the minority groups, thought that the country's economy would never survive such an amputation, but, as usual, foreigners both overestimated the technical difficulties of running anything and underestimated the resilience and resourcefulness of a people determined to make things work.[2] At first Mustafa Kemal expected private Turkish businessmen to step into the breach, but their response was disappointing for the simple reason that there were so few of them.

In these circumstances the government decided it had to do things itself and launched its policy of the state-owned and state-run enterprises. Following the Central Bank and the İş Bank, a purely Turkish commercial bank, came the Sümer and Eti banks, which founded and managed a large variety of industrial and mining enterprises. At the same time foreign-owned railways and practically all mines were nationalized, and coastal shipping, heretofore largely in Greek hands, was reserved for Turks. It was hoped that eventually some of the state-owned enterprises could be sold to private ownership, but this has been a slow and exceedingly difficult step to arrange.

In order to attract capable young men into the government-owned banks and enterprises, much higher salary scales than those prevailing in the civil service were offered. This had the desired result, and with training and education abroad a group of competent managers was formed. Under İnönü a move was made to bring these salaries in line with those of the civil service; as a result many of the most capable employees left for private business. A reversal to the old policy is now taking place.

In the meantime private business was growing, as a result of the country's general development. A good illustration is provided by the career of Vehbi Koç, one of Turkey's leading magnates. As a very young man he came with his father, on a donkey, to Ankara in quest of work. In view of a building boom at the time, he was advised to cart tiles, which he did so successfully that he is now one of the country's richest merchants. Recently, in partnership with foreign capital he founded a large factory for making electric bulbs. Some other merchants have established other industries, such as textiles and cement, while in the south a few landlords set up ginning machines and flour mills to process local produce. Nevertheless, the state still plays a leading part, owning about 30 percent of all industry and having a monopoly of heavy industry and most branches of mining.

It is in commerce, finance, and, above all, the professions that the Turks have taken over from the minority groups. A rapid glance at the shops in Ankara failed to detect a single non-Turkish name.

In Istanbul, which handles two-thirds of the country's foreign trade, although there are many shops which are owned by Greeks, Armenians, Jews, or Levantines, the Turks are taking over an ever-increasing share. Once more they have been helped by a government measure, the *Varlik Vergisi* or Capital Levy of 1942, which fell heavily on minority groups, many of whose members were ruined. The *Varlik Vergisi* undoubtedly played an important part in the Turkification of economic life by enabling Turks to buy up, at very low prices, the businesses and property of other groups.

Lastly, a few words about Iran, about which there is even less information than about the other countries. British capital has developed the oil industry and banking. As in Turkey, members of minority groups have played an important part, the Jews in foreign trade and the Armenians in foreign trade and some handicrafts such as silverwork and furniture making. Neither of these groups, however, has figured at all prominently in industry. Also as in Turkey but to a lesser extent, much of the country's industry has been founded and is operated by the state, which secured the necessary funds by a monopoly of foreign trade and heavy taxes on consumption. The rest has been created mainly by Iranian merchants, mostly exporters or importers, many of whom were enriched by the inflation caused by heavy government investment. Quite a number of Iranians have made their fortunes in trade in India and the Far East. Of these, however, very few have invested in Iran, and even where there has been investment, as in the case of the shipowner Namazi who has been a great benefactor to his native city of Shiraz, it has been on a small scale. It is difficult to think of a single factory which has been founded by an Iranian landlord.

Following this historical account of the development of the industrial classes in different countries, some general statements regarding their origin, character, desires, and influence may not be out of place. In order to create modern industries in the set of circumstances prevailing in the Middle East, four conditions were necessary: capital; business ability and initiative; technical competence; and political prestige and power. Broadly speaking, the first two have been supplied by the merchant class; the third by foreign technicians and foremen; the last by a few politicians who took an interest in industry, such as Sidqi and Hafez Afifi in Egypt and Khaled al-Azm and Faris al-Khuri in Syria. An alternative form has been the creation of industries by the state.

The bulk of Middle Eastern manufacturers has come from the merchant class; indeed, many have continued to practice trade while engaging in industry. A few examples can be shown of landlords setting up industries, and a still smaller number of craftsmen have expanded their business to the size of a modern factory. The vast majority of industrial enterprises have been founded by traders or financiers, generally merchants engaged in foreign trade, for it was the latter class, alone, which had the liquid capital necessary for such an undertaking. This, of course, refers to the pioneers, who first created new enterprises. Once established, industrial firms have attracted an ever-widening circle of investors, who have been encouraged to buy shares by dividends which are high compared to the low rates of interest paid by banks and the almost equally low returns on land bought at inflated values. Thus, in Egypt, successful doctors, lawyers, engineers, politicians, and civil servants have been drawn into industry as shareholders, directors, or administrators, and landlords have taken a rapidly increasing interest in investing in, and even founding, industrial enterprises.[3]

The merchants supplied not only capital but business ability, though not precisely the kind required by industry. To be more precise, they have plenty of entrepreneurial ability but little knowledge of plant management. It takes years to make a Middle Eastern merchant realize that a factory is neither a car, which runs perfectly well if the right buttons are pushed, nor a shop, which an able man can manage with the help of a couple of clerks. They expect immediate and substantial profits and are disappointed when they find that this is not forthcoming. They pinch pennies and stint the technicians on the funds required for experimentation. They grudge these technicians their high salaries, which they cannot help comparing with those paid to their clerks. The following remark by a Syrian industrialist, though perhaps not typical, is worth considering: "I have a clerk who knows perfect English and French, keeps books and makes excellent coffee; I pay him £S 300 a month. Why do you ask for 700 for a technician?" They fail to understand how much has to be done before local raw materials become suitable for processing, local workmen are broken in, and the machines have the "bugs" taken out of them. They try to manage everything themselves and do not appreciate the need for delegation. Above all, they are reluctant to reinvest, preferring to distribute profits.

Technical obstacles have been overcome with the help of foreign engineers and foremen. In general, Middle Eastern workmen have shown intelligence and a remarkable capacity for learning, but good foremen are still scarce and local technicians are not always able to apply in a practical concrete way the lessons that they learned at school. It is still a subject for complaint that the educated Middle Easterner, be he Arab, Iranian, or Turk, is reluctant to dirty his hands, but encouraging progress is being made in this direction. The shortage of managers is more serious, and a long time will have to elapse before it can be overcome.

It would be most unfair to stress all of the shortcomings of the Middle Eastern entrepreneurs without indicating the adverse economic, social and political factors with which they have to contend. Thus, while the inflation of the last fifteen years has undoubtedly stimulated business, the constant depreciation of currencies since the First World War has also strengthened the already ingrained habit of taking the short view and requiring immediate returns. Again, whereas foreign entrepreneurs were completely protected by the Capitulations, local businessmen have to take the rough with the smooth in their relations with the government—and there is plenty of rough. Thus, the International Bank for Reconstruction and Development in its report, *The Economy of Turkey*, states that "private producers in general have grown increasingly apprehensive of expanding state operations and the possibility of expropriation," and urges "prompt elimination of government practices which give public enterprises advantages over their private competitors." Similar conditions prevail in Iran. In the other countries there is no competition from state-owned factories, and the danger of expropriation of native, as distinct from foreign, concerns has been negligible, but there is plenty of administrative red tape, heavy handedness, and the excessive preoccupation with fiscal considerations, which have not created an ideal climate for private enterprise.

So much for the origin and character of the industrialists. Now a few words regarding their desires and influence. Naturally, they all clamor for protection, and in the main their wishes have been met; less has been done, however, to help them in other, more fruitful, directions. Thus, suprisingly enough in view of the abundance of oil, fuel costs are often very considerable because of transport costs, the high price charged by the oil companies, or high excise duties. Inadequate transport facilities hamper industry almost everywhere. Industrial credit, in most countries, is unorganized, and industrialists are forced to borrow on short term, at high rates, from ordinary commercial banks. A Lebanese industrialist has related that he had to pay nine percent on such loans; moreover, the fact that he could not pay in cash compelled him to offer higher prices to his suppliers. He estimated the combined charges at 15 percent of his capital, a figure which cut deeply into his profit margin. This deficiency has been remedied in Israel, and is being remedied in Egypt and Turkey by the recently founded industrial banks, but not in the other countries. Repair facilities are very inadequate and constitute a heavy burden on industrialists, who often have to fly in a spare part from Europe or the United States; they also have to fly in a technician to repair the machine, a fact which has resulted in some Czechs, sent by Skoda, refusing to return and choosing freedom in Syria. And technical education is almost non-existent, except in the more advanced countries, i.e., Israel, Turkey, Egypt, or where it is undertaken by the oil companies.

One more point remains to be noticed in this context—the desire of many industrialists for some form of economic union among the Arab states. Most Egyptian, Syrian, and Lebanese manufacturers realize that such a union would broaden their market and enable them to produce on a larger scale and more efficiently. Naturally, some vested interests oppose such a measure, which would expose them to competition, and, unless steps for union are taken soon, with the passage of years such centrifugal forces may gain in importance.

Lastly, a few words regarding the relations between industrialists and other classes. Needless to say, there have been many clashes with labor concerning wages and conditions of work. As elsewhere, employers have tried to keep wages as low as possible and, except in Israel whose *Histadruth* is the most powerful body of its kind in the world, the unions have not been in a position to offer much resistance. In Turkey, however, state enterprises have offered excellent conditions to their workers, as have several Egyptian firms, notably the Misr textile mills.

Opposition between industrialists and farmers has begun to be manifest. Perhaps the best place to study this is Egypt, where the process has gone the farthest. First, there is taxation, over which, since the 1930s, a closely fought contest has been taking place. The landed interests scored several points in quick succession, such as the imposition of prohibitive duties on imports of wheat, the levying of an income tax on commercial and industrial profits but not on land rents, and, during the war, the raising of the rate of that tax and the imposition of an excess profits tax.

After the war, however, the industrialists had their innings and managed to repeal the excess profits tax, to remodel the tariff to suit their interests, to raise the rate of the land tax, to subject income from land to the general income tax, and, above all, to pass an agrarian reform law. They were also instrumental in the fixing of a minimum agricultural wage and the enactment of compulsory secondary education. These achievements are the more remarkable in view of their slight representation in parliament compared to that of the landlords. So far, however, they have not been able to repeal the measure compelling them to use expensive high-grade Egyptian cotton in their textile factories—an economic absurdity, equivalent to using mahogany for kitchen tables—nor have they succeeded in their primary objective, the raising of the level of the Egyptian peasant.

In Syria, where industry is still embryonic, the beginnings of a conflict can be discerned. The vegetable oil refineries would like to export cottonseed cake, but the landlords prevent this in order to feed their livestock; conversely, the landlords prefer to export maize, which the starch factories require. Industrialists also complain of the labor law, which is very generous to workmen and which was passed by a parliament in which they were practically unrepresented; needless to say, it does not cover agricultural labor.

In Lebanon agriculture plays a very subordinate part in the economy as its contribution to the national income is far less than those of industry and construction combined. Here the clash is between manufacturers on the one hand and merchants and financiers on the other. Thus, importers favor a low tariff while financiers are opposed to the setting up, with foreign help, of an industrial bank on the Turkish model.[4]

But a final word of warning is necessary regarding these conflicts. It must not be forgotten that, unlike European society, and perhaps even more than American, Middle Eastern society is fluid. There is not yet any counterpart to the great industrial and commercial families of the West. Moreover, many industrialists and merchants mark their advent to affluence by the purchase of land. This is usually done for noneconomic reasons, such as prestige, or as a long-term investment, but it nevertheless does help to create a certain community of interests between them and the landowners. Still more important is their common fear of a social revolution, the prospect of which restrains the industrialists from pressing the landowners too hard. The same dilemma faced the German bourgeoisie in 1848 and the Russian bourgeoisie before the Revolution; E. H. Carr's comment on these situations seems to be applicable to the Middle East:

That they were weak was undeniable. But a more significant cause of their hesitancy was that they were already conscious of the growing menace to themselves of an eventual proletarian revolution. One reason why history so rarely repeats itself is that the dramatis personae at the second performance have prior knowledge of the *denouement*.[5]

But precisely because of the greater knowledge and awareness today, it may well be that the Middle Eastern bourgeoisie, with help from abroad, will be able to steer clear of the reefs which wrecked the ships of so many of its predecessors.

NOTES

1. More recently, the development of the Persian Gulf oil fields has had very favorable repercussions on the Lebanese economy.

2. A strikingly similar phenomenon was the exodus of Jewish business-men from Iraq in 1950 and 1951; here, too, foreigners expected a disruption of the Iraqi economy, which did not occur.

3. It may be stated, parenthetically, that developments in nineteenth-century Russia and other parts of eastern Europe were basically similar. When they were not established by the state, by foreign capital, or by resident Germans or Jews, industries were created by local merchants. At a later stage, landowners and other classes began to take an interest in industrial development.

4. In 1954 the Industrial, Agricultural, and Real Estate Bank was founded; its capital is to be provided by both the government and private enterprise.

5. *The Boleshevik Revolution* (London, 1950), I, 42.

20
Schools of Economic History and the Middle East

What can the scholar working on the economic history of the Middle East learn from the leading schools?[1] Very much, if he regards their methods and leading concepts not as cookie-cutters which can be applied to the shapeless Middle Eastern dough to yield ready-to-bake cakes but as faint candles that can help him discern the forms embodied in his material.

I. First the Cliometric school, which is the *dernier cri* in the United States. Its hallmarks are the attempt to fit historical data into econometric models and the application of rigorous economic thought to historical phenomena. One can have one's reservations about the econometrics. Wendell Willkie once said that if what was regarded as a luxury elsewhere were not considered a necessity in the United States, the American economy would stop functioning. The same is true of econometric models for all but the most recent decades. They hold in the United States and certain developed countries—and even there, uncharitable souls often feel that what we have is bad econometrics applied to worse statistics. But for other countries, particularly the Middle East, they are an unaffordable luxury, except perhaps for certain aspects of the Egyptian economy, as shown by Bent Hansen's recently published articles. As Jean Aubin reminds us, for Iran "des suites chiffrées satisfaisantes" are unavailable before the second half of the nineteenth century, and the situation is not much better elsewhere. In such circumstances, there is very little on which the econometrician can exercise his skills. But it goes without saying that we should apply the most rigorous methods available to those statistics that we do manage to compile.

So much for the econometricians. For economists, however, nothing human is alien. Indeed some of them, notably the Chicago school, not content with studying the economics of education, discrimination, and crime, have poked their noses into other people's beds and discussed the economics of marriage and procreation. And, it should be added, they have made valuable contributions to knowledge, along with rather bizarre statements. For, stripped of its jargon and verbiage, economics consists of the systematic application of concepts such as the following, all capable of being expressed in simple mathematical terms, which are indeed relevant to a very wide range of human activities.

a. Opportunity Cost: every use of a good or factor of production (labor, land, capital) entails a cost, which can be measured by the most productive alternative use to which the good or factor could have been put.

b. Diminishing Returns: the increased application of any one factor of production, the other factors being held constant, results in steadily diminishing increments of production.

c. Diminishing Utility: increased use of any good results in steadily diminishing additional utility to the consumer. This principle is regarded as superfluous by most economists, but it is useful for the layman and the historian trying to understand economic phenomena.

d. Maximization: both consumers and producers act rationally, that is, they seek to obtain the desired output with the smallest possible input of means or, alternatively, to get the greatest possible output from the factors of production and materials at their disposal.

e. Equilibrium: the market provides an equilibrating mechanism which brings it about, for example, that a shortage of a good, by raising its price, sets in motion forces that increase its supply and thus, eventually, push down its price again. Of course, this can be partly or totally offset by other, more powerful forces (e.g., a sustained rise in demand for that good or a general price inflation).

f. Remuneration According to Marginal Productivity: the earnings of each factor of production are determined by its relative contribution to total output, or, more strictly, by its marginal productivity, which varies (see [b] above) according to the Factor Mix, i.e., the relative scarcity of labor, land, and capital.

g. Lastly, for monetary phenomena, some version (more or less elaborate or refined) of the Quantity Theory at least to the extent that a large increase in money supply will, unless offset by other factors, tend to raise prices and a decrease to lower them. A minor, though especially for earlier periods, useful, principle is Gresham's Law—that bad money tends to drive out good.

Now, there is no doubt that the first three principles are of universal application; they hold for any past, present, or conceivable future society. But with the others, we enter the realm of controversy. Do men in fact seek to maximize, and, if so, what—income? capital? satisfaction? prestige? leisure? security (i.e., minimize risk)? etc. Anthropologists who have studied village and tribal economies in the Middle East, Africa, and elsewhere have come up with very different answers to these questions. Some maintain that the responses are economically very rational, though the underlying constraints may be different (see Clifford Geertz's work on Moroccan bazaars), whereas others say that the economist's usual maximizing model may apply to stockbrokers in Europe or North America but not to Middle Eastern or Latin American or Asian or African peasants.

Or take the question of the market. A most distinguished economist, John Hicks, made the Rise of the Market the central theme of his very stimulating incursion into history, *A Theory of Economic History*, tracing its origins to remote antiquity. But some highly learned and intelligent historians, like Karl Polanyi and M. I. Finley, have assured us that the concept of market, and its associated mechanisms and phenomena, is very misleading when applied to ancient times, including Rome.[2]

As for remuneration according to marginal productivity, the mere concept strikes many people as highly comical. It is not, really, but a good deal of explanation would be required to convince the average reader that the relative incomes of lord and serf in Europe, or Mamluk and *fallah* in Egypt, reflected their marginal contributions to *economic* production. Surely, at this stage, it is advisable to introduce some non-economic considerations.

II. This is done by the next school to be considered, the *Marxist*. This school is fully aware of the political and sociological elements that make up any given historical situation, often without a corresponding awareness of strictly economic factors. The central concept of "mode of production" directs the economic historian's attention to the core of the social structure. It urges him to understand first the material forces of production—the human and natural resources at the disposal of the society at any given moment and the technical knowledge and methods available. It then asks him to relate the individuals and groups constituting that society to the process of production, in other words, to determine the economic bases of the various classes and their interrelations. The mode of production and class structure between them determine the superstructure; i.e., the political, cultural, and other institutions and ideas.

The notion of class struggle, arising out of the various groups' attempt to appropriate a larger part of the social product, explains the dynamics of social change and transformation and accounts for the successive stages of antiquity, feudalism, capitalism, and socialism. This makes it possible to add to the economist's analytical kit many new, powerful, and versatile tools. One is that of coercion and exploitation, which surely tells us more about the distribution of land and income over long historical periods than does marginal productivity. Another is class interest and class ideology, which are better explanatory concepts than the traditional economist's "tastes," and bring out much more clearly the constraints within which thought, innovations, action, and policy can operate at any given time. The list could be prolonged, but this is not the place to do so.

In the past few decades, Marxist historians, working on Western and Eastern Europe, have done fine work, but there is nothing comparable on the Middle East and the rest of Asia. This is not suprising: Marx and his followers were Europeans, thoroughly familiar with European history, society and politics, but like everyone else, ignorant of those of other regions. And it is by no means self-evident that the basic categories of Western economics hold for these regions. Take feudalism—was there such a system outside Europe, except perhaps in Japan and parts of Lebanon? Claude Cahen has examined the question in some penetrating articles, and is very much aware of the difference between *iqta'* and fief. Or was there an Asiatic mode of production? The pronouncements of Maxime Rodinson and others on the subject are far from clear. Did the Islamic guilds play a role similar to those of Europe—and indeed were there any guilds at all before the Ottoman period? The excellent works of Bernard Lewis, S. M. Stern, Claude Cahen, and Gabriel Baer reveal our ignorance. Can one speak of a feudal aristocracy, or even a hereditary nobility, in the six centuries dominated by the Mamluks and the Janissaries, or their successors the *multazims*? Do the *Çiftliks* in the Balkans and elsewhere mark the beginnings of a capitalist agriculture? There are some interesting observations on this last subject in an unpublished manuscript by Bruce McGowan. In what sense can one speak of a Middle Eastern bourgeoisie before the nineteenth or twentieth centuries? Why did it remain so weak, comparatively? Why was property so precarious and the accumulation and retention of family fortunes—the power base of the bourgeoisie

—so rare? Why did the middle class not consolidate its power in city states, but remain so subservient to the central government— the contrast between the fate of the Hansa and Karimi merchants is suggestive. And why was authority so overwhemingly concentrated in the hands of bureaucrats and military? And how does the latter square with the Marxist assertion that the state must represent the interests of an *economic* class drawing its power from the process of production?

One last point needs to be made. In the Middle East today everyone, like Molière's M. Jourdain, speaks prose Marxist—or, more precisely, Leninist. But, except in the Balkans, where, thanks to the Ottoman archives in Sofia, Sarajevo, and elsewhere, very useful if often tendentious work is being done on the Ottoman period, hardly anyone is putting Marxism to its optimum use. True, Arabs, Iranians, and Turks are busy reexamining their late medieval and modern history, but their Marxism goes no further than denouncing Feudalism (used mainly as a term of abuse) and Imperialism—the latter term covering every aspect of economic, religious, and cultural relations with the West. Some excellent economic history is also being written—mostly in Turkey, but also in Egypt and elsewhere— but mainly by scholars influenced by either the Annales school or by the classical British economic historians.

III. The Annales school compensates for many of the deficiencies of the Marxist and Cliometric. This is not the place to examine this school, but some of its strengths may be pointed out. First, its stress on physical and human geography, including climate, which have been so largely ignored, or taken as constants, by the other two schools. It may be parenthetically pointed out that in a region lying at the edge of the main rainfall systems (monsoon, Atlantic) like the Middle East, fluctuations in the precipitation are frequent and have a decisive influence on agricultural production and other economic activities; hence any rainfall cycles that may be discerned[3] could go a long way toward explaining the course of economic and social change.

Secondly, its great interest in a whole set of disciplines closely related to economic history, such as sociology, anthropology, psychology, archaeology, and art history. These are more important in the Middle East than elsewhere since the region has, in the course of the last seven or eight centuries, undergone less economic and social transformation than, say, Europe, which means that its old "structures," to use an Annalist term, have survived in a better state and are of greater relevance today. Micro-studies at the level of the village, urban quarter, or tribe carried out by geographers, sociologists, and anthropologists with a historical vision can be of incalculable help to the economic historian. More specifically, the Annalists have done superb work in demography, another discipline neglected by Marxists but which provides the clue to one of the main determining forces of history—e.g., it is probable that the depopulation caused by the Black Death was the most important single event in Middle Eastern history in the period A.D. 1000-1800 (see Michael Dols, *The Black Death in the Middle East*). The absence of parish registers in the Middle East means that the work done on medieval and early modern Europe cannot be duplicated here, but the Ottoman archives offer an alternative source which is just beginning to be tapped. Another interest of the Annales school, by no means peculiar to or pioneered by it, is "serial history," in particular that of prices. This, too, has no counterpart in the Middle East but, particularly for the Ottoman period, much can be done in this field.

It should be added that for a person trained in economics, the analysis done by this school falls far short of its descriptive power—a reproach that has often been made by Cliometricians. The construction of models and their testing is almost completely absent, and the laboriously compiled statistics used are not subjected to the revealing torture to which Cliometricians put them. The Annalists retort that there is not much point in building elaborate theoretical structures on the very shaky data provided by all but the most recent history and argue that history is more akin to Biology than to Mechanics or Hydrostatics; therefore, they are more interested in structure, growth, and evolution than in equilibrium. In this they could claim the support of the high priest of modern economic analysis, Alfred Marshall.[4] We are dealing with a fundamental *Methodenstreit,* and the debate continues.

The contribution of this school to Middle Eastern historiography can be gauged from the monumental volumes of André Raymond (his *Artisans et Çommercants au Caire au XVIIIe siècle* is perhaps the most important piece of research on Egypt since Napoleon's *Description de l'Egypte*), Dominique Chevallier, and Ömer Barkan. May their good work continue and spread! It should be added that excellent studies are also available on North Africa by such scholars as Miège, Nouschi, Noin, Poncet, Despois, and Valensi, but this area falls outside the scope of the present paper.

IV. The Dependencia is a school whose doctrines have emanated mainly from Latin America and have been expressed most forcefully by André Gunder Frank, A. Emmanuel, and Samir Amin. Its interest is focussed on one burning question: why is the economic center of the world (Western Europe, the United States, and, presumably, Japan, but how did Japan get to the center, surely a very significant and revealing question?) so rich and the Periphery (Latin America, Asia, and Africa) so poor? The answer is that the former enjoyed Development whereas the latter experienced the Development of Underdevelopment, the two being as inextricably bound up as Siamese twins. The prosperity of the Center was derived by sucking up the resources of the Periphery: "all of these regions [in Latin America], like Bengal in India, once provided the lifeblood of mercantile and industrial development in the metropolis."[5] Conversely, the influence of the Center on the Periphery was in every way baleful, which is not suprising since, except under "socialism," *all* exchange is exploitive; thus, in Latin America, provincial metropoles "by being centers of intercourse are also centers of exploitation."[6] More specifically, the countries of the Periphery are said to have suffered the following:

a. Their mineral wealth was pillaged, their lands exhausted by monoculture, their populations enslaved, and, in some countries, decimated.

b. Under the hypocritical slogans of Free Trade and the Open Door, British, and, subsequently, other, including American, manufactured goods invaded their markets and destroyed their handicrafts. Where some factory industry showed signs of developing, as in parts of Latin America, it too was stifled by foreign competition.

c. The import surplus shown by Britain and other European countries in their trade with tropical countries from about 1870 on represents a massive transfer of resources from the latter.[7]

d. Even a perfectly balanced trade would mean very little, since all trade between the Center and the Periphery is one of Unequal Exchange, in which the latter is forced to give far more than it takes. The only evidence adduced (apart presumably from the fact that since the Center is rich and the Periphery poor the former must be exploiting the latter) is the alleged constant deterioration in the terms of trade for primary products. But this assertion violates historical reality. Between 1800 (or 1820) and the 1860s-1870s, the net barter terms of British trade—the only ones about which we have adequate information for the first half of the nineteenth century—showed a sharp decline, due to the drastic cheapening of manufactured goods, followed by a small advance (due partly to the steep fall in freight rates, which reduced c.i.f. import prices) to 1900-1913, and mild fluctuations thereafter.[8] A study of France's terms of trade with Latin America in 1827-1856 also shows a sharp movement in favor of the latter, a conclusion which, as the author points out, is in line with other research but directly contrary to those of Frank and Celso Furtado.[9] The period since the Second World War has seen sharp swings but no definite trend in the relative prices of primary goods and manufactures. And, anyway, it is worth noting that "as late as 1883, the first year for which we have a calculation, total imports into the United States and Western Europe from Asia, Africa, and tropical Latin America, came only to about a dollar per head of the population of the exporting countries,"[10] which could not have given rise to either much riches or much impoverishment.

What the Dependencistas refuse to admit is that the wealth of the Center was due partly to certain favorable natural factors, such as good climate and a high land-man ratio after the Black Death had reduced the population of Europe, but mainly to steady technical and economic progress since the eleventh century, which raised crop yields per acre and per man and equipped the craftsman with increasing amounts of both physical capital (watermills, windmills, ships, wharves, etc.) and human capital (education, health), raising his productivity. And it is hardly exploitation when a more productive factor earns a higher income than a less productive one. Of course, the loot of Empire and superior bargaining power played their part, but it was a smaller one. As for the economic backwardness of the Periphery, the most important single factor is one that is hardly ever mentioned in the Dependencia writings: "Thus in effect the tropics were held back by their need for a technological revolution in agriculture such as had been occurring in Western Europe for two centuries [actually much longer]. This view, however, is not the popular one."[11]

e. Capital investment has converted the receiving countries into satellites of the Center. And since the amount transmitted back to the Center over the years exceeds its cumulative investment in the Periphery which it must if interest and profits are to be paid (unless massive losses have occurred) investment becomes another channel for transferring resources from the poor to the rich.

f. The social structure of the Periphery is transformed, in a highly vicious way, by foreign economic and political influence. The ruling oligarchies expropriate and exploit their peasants and, in turn, enter into a subservient relation with foreign capital—"The so-called national and progressive bourgeoisie in Latin America is neither nationalist nor progressive; it is dependent comprador bourgeoisie"—and the working class is no better.[12]

g. The present state of the Periphery is dismal and shows no signs of improvement: "Thus, higher GNPs in certain Latin American countries (e.g., Mexico and Peru) certainly do not constitute development in this sense." Industrialization is a sham: "Far from having become more developed since then [i.e., Second World War], industrial sectors of Brazil and most conspicuously of Argentina have become structurally more and more underdeveloped and less and less able to generate continued industrialization and/or sustain development of the economy. This process, from which India also suffers . . ." One should add that, for nearly three decades, these economists have been yearly announcing the demise of Brazilian and other Latin American industrialization. There is, however, one hope: "The Soviet industrialization model in which the state, rather than consumer demand, determined the goods—capital goods—to be produced first. But for that they would have had to have a Soviet state, that is, a socialist class structure."[13] Their reward would, presumably, be to become another Uzbekistan or Albania.

Where does the Middle East fit into this model? Before attempting to answer this question, it is necessary to point out that, unlike Latin America or sub-Saharan Africa, the Middle East has been in close touch with Europe for some 2,000 years, during most of which it was the stronger partner, militarily and economically, and fully used its powers. In the last 200 years it has, of course, been on the receiving end. As for specifics:

a. It did not have any mineral wealth to plunder and its soil was not devastated, though Egypt did suffer some water-logging and loss of silt deposits, both caused by the shift from basin to perennial irrigation. Its population was neither enslaved nor ravaged by disease; on the contrary, it has grown prodigiously: Egypt's from some 3.5 million in 1800 to 11.3 in 1907, and over 40 million today, and other countries in a slightly smaller proportion; of course this is not a sign of prosperity! Its oil wealth yielded fabulous riches to the foreign capital that discovered and developed it. From the 1920s to the early 1950s the share of the local governments in the net income generated by the industry was only some 20 percent, but this soon rose to 50 and over and, since 1973, has been above 90 or even 95 percent.[14]

b. Already in the eighteenth century, foreign handicraft goods were penetrating Middle Eastern markets, and with the Industrial and Transport Revolutions, and the opening of the Middle East by the 1838 Anglo-Turkish Treaty, manufactures poured in. This ruined some Middle Eastern handicrafts, causing economic losses and social distress. European competition, and political influence, also undoubtedly inhibited the growth of a factory industry until the First World War, but there were also numerous local factors impeding industrialization.[15]

c. All available figures show that, in the nineteenth century, Turkey, Egypt, Iran, and other Middle Eastern countries had import surpluses. Presumably, these were covered partly by import of capital and partly by dishoarding of gold and silver accumulated over the ages; but the statistics are too shaky for firm conclusions.

d. The scanty information available suggests that the price of Egyptian cotton and other Middle Eastern exports followed world trends. As regards their terms of trade, those of Egyptian cotton improved greatly in 1820 to 1913 and those of other goods presumably followed world trends. The terms of trade of oil have risen greatly.

e. The Middle East received huge amounts of foreign capital: in 1913 the Ottoman Empire's public and private debt was some $1,000 million and so was Egypt's, while Iran owed a little over $100 million. The public debt was almost entirely wasted, because of the monarchs' extravagance and the increasingly unfavorable terms of the loans, but the private (about half the total) made a contribution to development. Debt servicing constituted a heavy burden and drained resources. Of course, today the Middle East is the main capital-exporting region of the world, a development that opens interesting perspectives.

f. Long before the European impact, the social and political structure of the Middle East was thoroughly unfavorable to economic and social development. Power lay in the hands of bureaucrats and soldiers for whom economic and social development was the last of their worries. European capitalists, administrators, and adventurers may not have been more concerned about the welfare of the people, but in their effort to exploit the resources of the region, they started many processes that eventually led to economic and social progress. The level of living of the masses seems to have risen slightly, but the bulk of the increase in income was absorbed by population growth, foreign capitalists, minority groups,[16] local landlords, and the very small native bourgeoisie.

g. As regards the present state of the Middle East, there is room for divergence of opinion, but no one who has lived through and remembers the last fifty or sixty years can doubt that great progress has been made. Egyptians, Iranians, Turks, Iraqis, Syrians, and others have recovered much control over their economies. They are investing large sums in development. Their infrastructure has greatly expanded and so has their industry. Their populations are healthier, far more educated, and so on. They are still, in many ways, dependent on the West (or the Soviet Union), but that is a fact of life that is unlikely to change for many years to come. Whether they will eventually choose Soviet-type socialism, a Western-type pattern, or develop their own economic and social design, will be determined by themselves.

Where, in conclusion, does that leave us? I am afraid in the category of spineless eclecticism so despised by the Schools. For good economic history we need method, tools, and materials. We also need some theory. As Werner Sombart put it: "No theory, no history." But, in as rudimentary a field as ours, fairly simple but sturdy tools will do, and the method and theory do not have to be elaborate, though they must be sound and consistent. As indicated, the Middle East historian can learn something useful from all the above-mentioned schools (even the Dependencia!), but he must not let himself be enslaved by any of them. He can also learn at least as much from the classical scholars who laid the groundwork of European economic history: Thorold Rogers, Clapham and Tawney in England, Usher and Nef in the United States, Henri See and Paul Mantoux in France, and countless Germans, Italians, Swedes, and others. For they, after all, grappled with the problems when the discipline was at its beginnings, which is where we, in the Middle East, stand today, except that they started from a much more favorable position.

This is now being done by a handful of scholars whose work is radically transforming our knowledge of the economic history of the region. S. D. Goitein has exploited the unsuspected and seemingly inexhaustible riches of the Geniza documents, and is being ably followed by A. L. Udovitch. E. Ashtor has put European archives as well as Arabic sources to excellent use and cast floods of light on the medieval Arab economy. The books and articles by Hassanein Rabie, Subhi Labib, Abd al-Rahim Abd al-Rahim and Ali Barakat show that a very promising new school is developing in Egypt.

For the Ottoman Empire, the material is much more abundant and the scholarship more advanced. To the well-known names of O. L. Barkan, Halil Inalcik, Halil Sahilioglou, Robert Mantran, Stanford Shaw, and Kemal Karpat, and those of Mehmet Genç and Gündüz Ökçün, should be added a young English scholar, M. A. Cook, for his excellent work on the population of sixteenth century Anatolia and three American scholars—Bruce McGowan,[17] who has shown with what effect statistical techniques can be applied to the Ottoman *defters*; Donald Quataert, who has explored the Ottoman archives and produced valuable series;[18] and Ronald Jennings, who has done fine work on the seventeenth century *defters*.[19] Mention should also be made of at least one Soviet scholar working in this field.[20] And recently a French historian has shown to what good use foreign sources can still be put.[21]

Modern Egypt has also attracted many good scholars who have produced valuable works: Ali al-Gritli on industry, Helen Rivlin, Gabriel Baer, Ahmad al-Hitta, E. R. J. Owen, P. O'Brien, and Bent Hansen on agriculture, Justin McCarthy on population, A. E. Crouchley and another Soviet scholar, L. A. Fridman, on capital investment. For Iran, A. K. S. Lambton still stands in solitary eminence. Other parts of the region await their turn, but one can be confident that the coming decades will see some very good work done on the economic history of the Middle East.[22]

NOTES

1. In this essay I shall confine myself to the period ending with the First World War, for after that the nature of the available sources and data calls for a different methodology.

2. For a recent penetrating discussion, see Douglass North, "Markets and other Allocation Systems in History: The Challenge of Karl Polanyi," *Journal of European Economic History*, VI, 3, pp. 703-16; all of North's writings are extremely valuable for those interested in methodology.

3. See Karl Butzer in *Erdkunde* (XI), 1957.

4. *Principles of Economics,* (8th edition 1920), pp. 50, 315-16, 323, 461, 777.

5. Frank in James Cockcroft *et al., Dependence and Underdevelopment,* (New York, 1972), p. 14.

6. Quoted approvingly in *ibid.,* p. 5.

7. This thesis is most recently expounded in Frank's article in the *Journal of European Economic History,* V, 2, pp. 407-38; see also comments by Paul Bairoch and Sidney Pollard and Frank's reply in *ibid.,* pp. 467-74 and VI, 3, pp. 745-53. Frank's figures are taken from the pioneering work by my late colleague and friend Folke Hilgerdt, who, however, would not have drawn conclusions from comparison of f.o.b. export and c.i.f. import prices of the advanced countries, since the latter include payment for transport, insurance, and other financial services; however this does not bother Frank, since he presumably regards these services as parasitical. Other difficulties have been pointed out: The United States and White Dominions had consistent export surpluses, and so do Japan and Germany today, while China and many other poor countries had an *import* surplus.

See also A. J. Latham in *ibid.,* VII, I, pp. 33-60; and, the exchange between D. Platt and Stanley and Barbara Stein in *Latin American Research Review,* XV, I, 1980.

Frank also seems to contradict the Hobson-Lenin thesis that the main motive force of imperialism is the capitalists' desperate search for markets in which to dump the surplus goods they cannot sell at home. If so, surely they would have seen to it that their governments did not aggravate their difficulties by allowing an import surplus that would drain an appreciable fraction of the scant purchasing power of their own impoverished masses!

8. See table in B. R. Mitchell, *Abstract of British Historical Statistics* (Cambridge, 1971), pp. 331-32.

9. J. Schneider, "Terms of Trade between France and Latin America, 1826-1856," in P. Bairoch and M. Levy Leboyer, *Disparities in Economic Development Since the Industrial Revolution* (New York, 1981), pp. 110-19.

10. W. Arthur Lewis, *The Evolution of the International Economic Order* (Princeton, 1977), p. 5; for further details see *idem, Growth and Fluctuations 1870-1913* (London, 1978).

11. Lewis, *Growth, op. cit.,* p. 202.

12. Cockcroft *et al.,* pp. xviii, xxii.

13. *Ibid.,* pp. xvi, 12, 14.

14. For a detailed study, focussing on 1948-60, see Charles Issawi and Mohammed Yeganeh, *The Economics of Middle Eastern Oil* (New York, 1962), chapter V.

15. On this and other topics in this section, see Charles Issawi, *Economic History of the Middle East* (Chicago, 1966); *idem, Economic History of Iran* (Chicago, 1971), and *idem, Economic History of Turkey* (Chicago, 1980).

16. See *Christians and Jews in the Ottoman Empire* (in press), Benjamin Braude and Bernard Lewis (eds.).

17. "Food Supply and Taxation on the Middle Danube (1568-1579)," *Archivum Ottomanicum* I (1969), pp. 139-96.

18. "Ottoman Reform and Agriculture in Anatolia, 1876-1908," unpublished dissertation, U.C.L.A., 1973.

19. "Loans and Credit in Early Seventeenth Century Ottoman Judicial Records," JESHO 1973.

20. O. G. Indzhikyan, *Burzhuaziya Osmanskoi Imperii* (Erevan, 1977).

21. Jacques Thobie, *Intérêts et impérialisme français dans l'Empire Ottoman (1895-1914)* (Paris, 1977).

22. For further details on the state of scholarship, see Charles Issawi, "Economic History of the Middle East to 1914," *Middle East Studies Association Bulletin*, vol. 2, no. 2 (1968) and *idem*, "Economic History and the Middle East," *ibid.*, vol. 8, no. 1 (1974).

21

The Change in the Western Perception of the Orient

The West has often, and increasingly, been castigated for its contemptuous and hegemonic attitude toward the Orient.[1] The charge contains a large measure of truth but requires two qualifications. First, every civilization worth its salt has been arrogant and xenophobic. The Greeks thanked the Gods that they had been born "Greek and not barbarian, man and not woman, free and not slave." The Chinese did not hide their horror at the "ugly foreign devils" who came to their shores and, for two thousand years or so, do not seem to have taken a serious interest in any aspect of any foreign culture except for Indian Buddhism and Persian carpets and ceramics. In 1793, their attitude to Europe was expressed, wisely and presciently, but not very tactfully, by the Emperor to a British envoy seeking to establish diplomatic and commercial relations:

If you assert that your reverence for our Celestial Dynasty fills you with a desire to acquire our civilization, our ceremonies and code of laws differ so completely from your own that, even if your Envoy was able to acquire the rudiments of our civilization, you could not possibly transplant our manners and customs to your alien soil . . . . Our Dynasty's majestic virtue has penetrated into every country under Heaven, and kings of all nations have offered their costly tribute by land and sea. As your Ambassador can see for himself, we possess all things. I set no value on objects strange or ingenious, and have no use for your country's manufactures.[2]

The Indian attitude was simple: anyone who traveled to foreign lands was polluted. As for the Muslims, in the fourteenth century, the great Ibn Khaldun stated that, because of unfavorable climate, the nature of Negroes was "close to that of dumb animals . . . . The same applies to the Slavs."[3] In spite of the fact that Europeans were regarded as fully human, and even civilized, neither Ibn Khaldun nor his predecessors and successors made the slightest effort to learn their languages or study their cultures. The twelfth century traveller, Ibn Djubayr, when describing Sicily and other Christian

lands, shows no interest in the customs and institutions of their inhabitants but never fails to call down God's curses on the infidels.
Similar examples could be multiplied. When in the middle of the
seventeenth century, the French ambassador announced to the
Grand Vizier, Mehmet Köprülü, "that his master had taken the strong
city of *Arras* from the *Spaniard*"—the reply the Vizier gave was no
other than this (*What matters it to me whether the Dog worries the Hog,
or the Hog the Dog, so my Master's Head be but safe?*)"[4] On another plane,
the historian Naima, a contemporary of Newton, Leibniz, and Euler,
concluded his account of a set of thoroughly mediocre Ottoman
scholars with this remark: "This much is sufficient to awaken the
envy of the Christians:

> If this does not please you—
> Turn away your face: never mind it[5]

The other qualification is that Europeans (and Americans) have
shown an interest in and curiosity regarding other cultures that
is unique in human history and is witnessed by the innumerable
artifacts they excavated, bought, or looted from the four corners
of the earth. In doing so, they deciphered scripts that had remained
unintelligible for thousands of years, edited and translated musty
manuscripts, and restored to many peoples glorious but forgotten
epochs of their own past. Here again the contrast with other civilizations is striking. As far as we can tell, no Greek or Roman bothered
to read inscriptions in hieroglyphics or cuneiform. With one or
two possible exceptions mentioned in Yaqut's *udaba* no Arab Muslim ever learned Greek or showed interest in Roman civilization—
in spite of the awesome monuments stretching from Syria to Spain
and the presence of large Christian populations that could have
taught them Greek or Latin. Nor were the Indians and Chinese any
more receptive.

But, all this having been said, it is a fact that Europe's attitude
toward the Orient—China, India, and Islam—changed markedly
between the eighteenth and nineteenth centuries, becoming much
more arrogant and condescending; the reasons for this deserve
attention and are brought out best by examining the image of China.

Until the end of the eighteenth century Europeans tended to be
awed by China. Its size and numbers impressed them and so did
its prosperity. Hume speaks of "the happiness, riches, and good
policy of the Chinese."[6] Malthus, who had a pessimistic view of
things in general, declared that China was the richest country in

the world; he was surely right if he was referring to total gross national product but even on a per capita basis China ranked high. But admiration went further. The Europe of the Enlightenment was very favorably impressed by a state not governed by priests but by "philosophers." Confucian tolerance was contrasted with Chritian persecution. In a society where nepotism was rampant, the Chinese Civil Service, recruited by examination, was regarded as a model for imitation. The fad for "Chinoiseries" in art was only one symptom of a much more general fascination.[7]

The sudden shift in perception may be illustrated by two quotations. In his preface to "Hellas," written in 1821, Shelley, urging Europe to help Greece in its struggle for independence states: "But for Greece . . . we might still have been savages and idolaters; or, what is worse, might have arrived at such a stagnant and miserable state of social institution as China and Japan possess." Thirty-five years later, De Tocqueville was even more emphatic. Discussing the Enlightenment's infatuation with China, which, at the time, "was still very little known," he says: "This imbecilic and barbarous government, which a handful of Europeans masters at will, seemed to them to be the most perfect model that all the nations of the world could copy. It was for them what, later on, England and then America became for all Frenchmen."[8] Tennyson's "better fifty years of Europe than a cycle of Cathay" is well known. The predominant characteristics of China are now no longer seen as stability, order, tolerance, efficient government, and prosperity but poverty, oppression, ignorance, and, above all, stagnation.

The very unhappy history of China in the nineteenth century lent credence to such a view. The Empire disintegrated politically and declined economically. Famines and floods were frequent and devastating. Opium, forced on China by the British, spread rapidly among the demoralized population. China's impotence against either foreign aggression or internal disruption was repeatedly demonstrated. And a change in European attitudes in two basic fields converted what had been regarded as Chinese virtues into intolerable vices. The revival of Christianity led to a deep horror of Chinese "godlessness." And the development of a historical sense led to the drawing of a contrast between Europe and China's past very unfavorable to the latter; this was perhaps best expressed by Karl Marx, who could accept Western Feudalism as a necessary precursor of Capitalism and Socialism but saw no future in the Asiatic Mode of Production and looked forward with eagerness to its speedy demise at the hands of European capitalism and imperialism.[9]

   For India, a similar, but perhaps less dramatic, shift occurred.

In the imagination of Europe, India had always been the fabulous land of untold wealth and mystical happenings, with more than just a normal share of wise men. . .The association of India with wealth, magic, and wisdom remained current for many centuries. But this attitude began to change in the nineteenth century when Europe entered the modern age, and the lack of enthusiasm for Indian culture in certain circles became almost proportionate to the earlier over-enthusiasm. It was now discovered that India had none of the qualities which the new Europe admired.[10]

This change in attitude is traceable to the tremendous upsurge of Europe in the eighteenth and nineteenth centuries, which manifested itself in the huge expansion of science and scholarship, the Industrial Revolution, and the growth of technical and military power that spread European rule all over the globe.[11] Two other factors were important. As mentioned above, the revival of Christianity led to a revulsion at Indian and other Asian religions. And, secondly, the emphasis on rational thought and the exaggerated importance attached to both progress and political freedom led to a profound contempt for civilizations deficient in any of these respects. To this should be added the status of women. European and American women had always enjoyed more freedom than the Oriental ones, and the nineteenth century saw many calls for further emancipation. Such practices as polygamy, suttee, in India, veiling and seclusion, in the Islamic world, and foot-binding, in China, further confirmed the growing conviction of Western superiority. To resume the quotations: "There was apparently no stress on the values of rational thought and individualism. India's culture was a stagnant culture and was regarded with extreme disdain, an attitude best typified in Macaulay's contempt for things Indian. The political institutions of India, visualized largely as the rule of the Maharajas and Sultans, were dismissed as despotic and totally unrepresentative of public opinion. And this, in an age of democratic revolution, was about the worst of sins."[12]

   The "free, progressive, prosperous, compassionate" West was now held up against the "servile, poor, stagnant, callous" East. This image originated in a profound historical experience, which could not have been argued away. Hume is certain that the Europe of his day was superior to Greece and Rome—and therefore to all mankind—both politically and economically:

In those days there was no medium between a severe, jealous aristocracy, ruling over discontented subjects; and a turbulent, factious, tyrannical democracy. At present there is not one republic in Europe, from one extremity of it to the other, that is not remarkable for justice, lenity and stability, equal to, or even beyond, Marseilles, Rhodes, or the most celebrated in antiquity. Almost all of them are well-tempered aristocracies.

There are many other circumstances, in which ancient nations seem inferior to the modern, both for the happiness and increase of mankind. Trade, manufactures and industry were no where, in former ages, so flourishing as they are at present in Europe.[13]

Some eighty years later, Macaulay was even more emphatic; more than once he states that the England of his day is much freer, more prosperous and intellectually more advanced than it had been in earlier times.

This feeling of Western progress and superiority weakened only when Europe began to decline, following its Civil War of 1914-45, with the intervening Depression and rise of Hitler, and when the Eastern countries—Japan and China and, much more slowly, India— began their military, political, and economic ascent. At the same time, and not coincidentally, Europe began to discover the finer aspects of their art, religions, and philosophies.

The evolution of the West's perception of Islam was very different. Europe did not have to wait until the sixteenth century to discover Islam, which was the only foreign civilization that ever ruled over European soil. From the very birth of Western civilization, in the seventh century, it was painfully aware of Islam's intrusive and threatening presence—as a great ideological, political, and military power—in Spain, France, and Italy. This threat waxed and waned, and its thrust shifted to Eastern and Central Europe, but it did not disappear until the eighteenth century.[14] In the intervening millennium vivid, hostile images were imprinted on the consciousness of both civilizations regarding the other and, strange as it may seem to those on the opposite side of the dividing line, the word Crusade evokes positive responses among Christians, as does *Jihad* among Muslims. When General Allenby captured Jerusalem, he is reported to have made a reference to the Crusades,[15] and, three years later, General Gouraud is reported to have declared, at Saladin's tomb in Damascus, "Saladin, we have returned." Eisenhower called his book "Crusade in Europe." By the same token, the Algerians fighting the French and the Palestinians struggling against the Israelis called themselves *Mujahid*.

But it was not only in warfare that Christianity and Islam were interlocked. Because of their common origin, the closeness yet divergence of their central doctrines, their numerous points of physical contact and the large size of their adherents—which soon indicated that both were there to stay—they had, at an early stage, to come to terms with each other. From the beginning of his prophetic mission Muhammad grappled with the problem; the image he drew of Christianity and the subordinate position he assigned to Christians (and Jews) may offend our sensibilities, but it endured, practically unchanged, down to the present. On the other side, St. John of Damascus (c. 675-c. 749), who knew Arabic, made a serious attempt to understand, as well as refute, Islam. But in Western Europe knowledge of Islam was minimal, and the accounts of the beliefs and practices of Muslims are fantastically wild and inaccurate—for example that they worshipped three idols: Mahound, Tervagant, and Apollo! For a brief moment, in the thirteenth and fourteenth centuries, European scholars made a sustained effort to study Islam and Arabic thought, but this ended with the emergence of a new Muslim threat, that of the Turks. This is not the place to discuss this subject, which has been ably studied by Daniel, Hourani, and Southern, nor do I have the competence to do so.[16] Suffice it to say that, with Islam, Christianity had a relationship very different from that with India, China, and Japan. They were *"frères ennemis"*; each looked at the other, thought he saw his own face in a distorting mirror, and recoiled in horror.

Eventually the religious fervor subsided in Europe and Oriental scholarship—beginning with Hebrew, Syriac, and Arabic—began to develop. Increasing knowledge sometimes led to liking or respect. Thus Busbecq, a sixteenth century Imperial Ambassador to Turkey, described Ottoman institutions with accuracy and admiration.[17] Early in the eighteenth century, Lady Mary Wortley Montague was enchanted with Turkish ways.[18] Back at home, chairs of Arabic and other Middle Eastern languages were established at the leading universities; translations of the Quran, the Arabian Nights, and other Arabic and Persian classics were published. Although to a lesser extent than China, Islam also benefitted from the universalist, secularist attitude of eighteenth century Enlightenment and was favorably spoken of by Leibniz, Voltaire, and Gibbon.[19] Several Romantic poets and writers, notably in Germany, were attracted by Persian and other Islamic poetry and introduced Oriental themes and images into their languages.

But even at the height of the Romantic interest in the Middle East, a shadow interposed itself—that of Greece. As an Indian historian points out, in Europe "it was firmly believed that the greatest human achievement was the civilization of the ancient Greeks—*le miracle grec*. Consequently, every newly discovered culture was measured against ancient Greece and invariably found to be lacking. Or, if there were individual features worth admiring, the instinct was to try to connect others with Greek culture."[20] In this respect, Islam suffered from a special disability: it had overrun the home of the ancient Greeks and supplanted their language and culture. Hegel's refutation of Geographic Determinism is devastating: "where the Greeks once lived, the Turks now live." A modern historian develops this theme: "The conquest of Asia Minor by the Turks and its transformation into the country of Turkey has always appeared to Europeans to constitute without question something incomprehensible, inadmissible, and slightly outrageous."[21] Islam had committed a sin of which India, China, and Japan were innocent. And the attempts by the Turks to suppress the Greek struggle for independence—which, significantly, the future president of Harvard, Edward Everett, called a Crusade—only drove the conviction deeper in.

The Romantic Era was succeeded by the Imperialist and relations between Europe and the Muslim world shifted to a new basis: that of dominator and dominated. The Netherlands in the East Indies, Russia in Azerbaijan and Central Asia; France in North and West Africa; Britain in India, the Middle East, and Africa; Spain in Morocco; and Italy in Eritrea, Somalia, and Libya ruled over large Muslim populations.

Islamic movements were often the main force opposing colonial expansion, as in Algeria, the Caucasus, Sudan, and Cyrenaica, and many sensed that much of the resistance put up by Turkey, Iran, and Afghanistan was due to Islam. The Europeans could hardly be expected to look with sympathy on a religion and culture that gave them so much trouble. The more far-sighted of them, like Lord Cromer, clearly saw that modern European imperialism would prove to be much more ephemeral than Roman precisely because it had to contend with religious and national forces that the Romans very seldom encountered.[22] But few people looked that far into the future, and almost all soon came to regard Islam as the main obstacle to the order, justice, economic development, and enlighten-

ment they believed they were introducing. A well-known scholar, Sir
William Muir, writing shortly after the First World War, summed
up such feelings: "The sword of Muhammad, and the Kor'an, are
the most stubborn enemies of Civilization, Liberty and the Truth
which the world has yet known.[23] Other exasperated colonial administrators—Persian, Macedonian, Roman, Arab, Chinese, and
Ottoman—must have held similar views on the religion and culture
of their "natives," but they were not so articulate and did not go into
print. This attitude colored the views of thinkers like Schlegel, Burck-
hardt and Weber, who had no connection whatsoever with colonialism
and who "tended to put [Islam] somewhere near the bottom of the
scale of human faiths."[24]

One more remark is in order. The world of Islam, or at least its
Middle Eastern and North African component, proved to be a hard
nut to crack and, moreover, one with a rather small kernel. European manpower losses—British in Afghanistan, French in Algeria,
French and Spanish in Morocco, Italian in Libya, and so on—were
high compared to those in other colonial areas like India, Indonesia,
and Central Africa. And, except in the oil bonanza years 1945-73,
when very high profits were made, the economic returns to Europe
from the region were rather low, compared to such areas as India,
Indonesia, Central and South Africa, and, in the colonial period,
Mexico and Peru.[25] This fact, however dimly perceived, cannot
have increased Europe's affection for Islam.

At a more popular level, there was an unprecedently massive
contact between European (and American) soldiers and Muslims
during the two World Wars. Neither side was at its best and neither
was edified by what it saw of the other.

Imperialism was eventually succeeded by Decolonization, which
included the World of Islam along with the rest of Asia and Africa.
All the Arab countries of the Middle East and North Africa gained
their independence, most rather easily, some like Algeria after a
hard struggle, because of the presence of a large body of European
settlers. Two factors, however, have prevented the development
of the easy relations between ex-ruler and ruled that mark, say,
Anglo-Indian or Dutch-Indonesian connections. The establishment of Israel, seen as a mortal threat by Arabs, has profoundly
influenced their attitude to Europe, and, still more, to the United
States. And the fact that the Arabs and Iranians control two-thirds
of the world's oil-reserves has made the Europeans, and later the
Americans, highly apprehensive about the safety of their economic

lifeblood. What had been a Middle Eastern dependence on the West was suddenly converted into an even more complete Western dependence on the Middle East.

The huge surplus generated in the oil industry has also created much bitterness, first on the part of the producing countries, who complained that they were getting only a small fraction of the profits and then on that of the consumers, who were being forced to pay what they regarded as extortionate, rapidly rising prices.[26] And in the last few years, the Arabs and Iranians have acquired a new, and most unattractive picture, that of the money grubbers, money lenders, and ostentatious *nouveaux riches* of the world.

The last few years have also seen a new phenomenon, the Islamic Revival, whose most spectacular achievement so far has been the Iranian Revolution. Some Westerners are attracted by its underlying principles of social justice, group solidarity, puritanism, rejection of Western values (and fundamental hostility to the United States and Europe); but most are repelled by its narrowness, xenophobia, violence, and intolerance.

Once more, the identity "Mahomet ou le fanatisme" seems to have been firmly established in the popular consciousness. The legacy of the long, sad past is still very much with us, and will continue to color images and bedevil relations between the West and the Islamic World for a long time to come.

NOTES

1. See, for example, Edward W. Said, *Orientalism,* New York, 1978.

2. Quoted in Arnold Toynbee, *A Study of History,* London, 1934, vol. I, p. 161.

3. Ibn Khaldun, *The Muqaddimah,* translated by Franz Rosenthal, New York, 1958, vol. I, p. 168.

4. Paul Ricaut; *The History of the Present State of the Ottoman Empire,* London, 1682, p. 167; the treatment of foreign ambassadors, described by Ricaut on pp. 155-66, also hardly indicates respect for the countries they represented. Ricaut's story presents a minor difficulty: Arras was captured in 1640, and Köprölü did not become Grand Vizier until 1656.

5. Naima, *Annals of the Turkish Empire,* translated by Charles Fraser, London, 1832, vol. I, p. 9.

6. David Hume, *Essays,* "Of the Rise and the Progress of the Arts and Sciences."

7. For these and other topics see Raymond Dawson (ed.), *The Legacy of China,* Oxford, 1964, chapter I.

8. A. De Tocqueville, *L'Ancien Régime,* Book III, chapter III.

9. Dawson, *loc. cit.*; see Karl Marx, *Pre-Capitalist Formations*, ed. by Eric Hobsbawm, New York, 1964; and "The British Rule in India."

10. Romila Thapar, *A History of India*, London, 1966, vol. I, pp. 15-16.

11. On this last point see Daniel Headrick, *The Tools of Empire*, Oxford, 1981.

12. Thapar, *op. cit.*, p. 16.

13. Hume, *Essays*, "Of the Populousness of Ancient Nations."

14. Charles Issawi, "The Christian Muslim Frontier in the Mediterranean," *Political Science Quarterly*, December, 1961.

15. However, his biographer states: "It always annoyed Allenby if anyone referred to his campaign as a 'crusade.' He pointed out that a number of his troops, and such valuable assistants as the Egyptian Camel and Labour crops, were Muslims, not Christians," Field Marshall Viscount Wavell, *Allenby*, London, 1946, p. 194.

16. N. Daniel, *Islam and the West: The Making of an Image*, Edinburgh, 1960; Albert Hourani, *Europe and the Middle East*, London, 1980; R. W. Southern, *Western Views of Islam in the Middle Ages*, Cambridge, Mass., 1962.

17. Edward Forster (trans.), *The Turkish Letters of Ogier Ghiselin de Busbecq*, Oxford, 1927.

18. Robert Halsband, ed., *The Complete Letters of Mary Wortley Montague*, Oxford, 1965. The Arabs were not so fortunate. The Emperor Philip the Arab is described by Gibbon as "An Arab by birth and consequently—a robber by profession," *Decline and Fall*, chapter 7.

19. Bernard Lewis, *Islam in History*, London, 1973; J. W. Fück, *Die arabische Studien in Europa*, Leipzig, 1955; Maxime Rodinson, *La fascination de l'Islam*, Paris, 1980: for Gibbon's views on Islam see: Bernard Lewis "Gibbon on Muhammad," *Daedalus*, Summer, 1976, pp. 89-101.

20. Thapar, *op. cit.*, p. 17.

21. Claude Cahen, *Pre-Ottoman Turkey*, London, 1968, p. 64. In the Middle Ages, the hope of acquiring Greek philosophy and science in their Arabic translations attracted Europeans to the study of Muslim sources. But when the Greek originals became available, in the fourteenth century, and a new world view set in, Arabic suffered from the general revulsion against "Gothic barbarism." "Petrarch (1304-1374) vigorously expresses his disgust at the style of Arab poets, whom he surely did not know," Rodinson, *op. cit.*, p. 51.

22. Earl of Cromer, *Ancient and Modern Imperialism*, London, 1910.

23. Sir William Muir, *The Caliphate, Its Rise, Decline, and Fall*, Edinburgh, 1924, cited by Hourani, *op. cit.*, p. 34.

24. Hourani, *op. cit.*, p. 35; see also pp. 62-72.

25. This topic is dicussed in my forthcoming *Economic History of the Middle East and North Africa since 1800*, chapter XI, "The Balance Sheets."

26. For company profits up to 1960, see Charles Issawi and Mohammed Yeganeh, *The Economics of Middle Eastern Oil*, New York, 1962; prices since 1973 speak for themselves.

22

The River and the Fire: A Cautionary Tale

Once upon a time, there were some people called the Ar, who lived in a pleasant village. The Ar were very much like other people, very nice and likeable, but unable to see much beyond their noses. Although warm blooded and given to occasional outbursts of temper and violence, they were, like other people, on the whole peaceful and wished to be left alone to carry on their daily business. Unfortunately, again like other people, they had their troubles.

To the West of the village ran a mighty River, which was at once the source of much of their prosperity and the origin of many of their woes. From that River came much of their drinking water; with it they irrigated their crops and on it they sailed to distant and exciting lands. But that was not the whole story. The River was powerful and capricious and often swelled in wrath and overflowed its banks, devastating fields, levelling houses, and occasionally drowning a few men and women.

Things had not always been so. The village elders had been told by their grandfathers, who had heard it from their grandfathers, that in previous times the village had been independent of the River. The climate had then been very different, rain was more abundant, and the Ar could grow crops without irrigation. It is true that these crops were much poorer than the ones they now raised, but then the number of Ar was much smaller and their life was much simpler. Moreover, at the same time, a great change had come over the River. Formerly it had been much smaller and flowed at a great distance from the village. But, perhaps because the change in climate had resulted in a much greater rainfall upstream, the River had burst the mighty dam, called the Ott, which had held it back, and shifted its course, coming very close to the village of the Ar.

Ever since, the River had dominated the lives and thought of the Ar. Their wisest men spent their time devising means to contain

Written in 1958; published, in Arabic, in *Adab*, Spring, 1962.

it and limit its damage without losing all the benefits it gave. They built powerful dykes and banks and dug channels to divert its waters. The young men stood always ready to take up their pickaxes and spades and fight the flood. The neighboring villages, some of which were friendly and others hostile, often helped them in their struggle. But even when they were not actually fighting the River, they were always thinking of it. Every morning and evening they implored their gods to deliver them from its evil. Each year they sacrificed twelve youths, chosen for their beauty and courage, in the hope of celestial aid. The River was the subject of every conversation, and almost every thought. Mothers frightened their children by telling them "If you don't behave, the River will get you." When a man wished to offend another, he would say, "You are a Riverite," and there was no greater term of abuse. If anyone wanted to oppose any new project, such as the building of a road, all he had to say was: "This will make it easier for the River to reach the village," and the whole idea would be dropped at once.

In recent years, however, things had greatly improved. Owing to another change of climate, rainfall had once more shifted a little. The village now received more rain, and was able to grow more of its crops away from the River. At the same time, the destruction wrought by the River had greatly diminished. In part, this was due to the fact that the River level had fallen considerably, because of less rain upstream. In part, it was because of the dykes and channels built by the villagers, which had been improved over time and could now hold back the floods more effectively than before. It is true that certain outlying portions of the village, notably those in its western and southern extremities, were still subject to flooding, with much damage and loss of life, but by far the greater part was now safe. And the master builders, seeing the level of the River sink lower and lower, and learning new ways of building dykes, were confident that in the near future the whole village would be adequately protected.

But feeling toward the River had not changed. It was still regarded as the Great Enemy. Curses were still heaped on it. All thoughts were still directed toward fighting it and weakening its power.

Just about that time, messages reached the village about a new cataclysm that was sweeping the country, in the shape of a great and consuming Fire from the East. Many distant villages had already been laid waste by it—Pol and Fin, and Hun and Bul, and many others. Refugees streamed out from these villages, a few reaching that of the Ar, and their condition was truly pitiful. The Ar were sorry for them, but they had enough troubles of their own with the River and did not feel that they could do much about other people's misfortunes. In fact, they soon began to get very angry with the refugees, who were spreading foolish and dangerous words. For they would say again and again, "You are so much more fortunate than we were; if we had been as close to the River as you we would have used its waters to fight the Fire, and then we would have been saved." This made the Ar furious: "You don't know what you are talking about because you have never experienced the River. Better a thousand Fires than one flooding. Fight the Fire with River water indeed! As if any good could come out of the River."

The words of the refugees convinced some people in the village of the danger of the Fire, and of the need for preparing to fight it, but they formed only a very small group. The vast majority of the Ar continued to believe that there was one danger and only one, that of the River. They stuck to their old ideas, and regarded the others as either fools or traitors.

In the meantime the Fire drew nearer and nearer. It did not spread very fast, for it did not move to a village until it had completely devastated the one before. However, its progress was unmistakable and more and more Ar began to get worried. But the majority of the village would not change their ideas. Who ever heard of any danger other than that of the River? Soon the neighboring village of Ir was aflame, and then the Ar became scared. They realized, at last, that the danger facing them now was not the River, but the Fire. As the flames caught on to the outskirts of the village, they began to clear the debris lying in their path and to remove all inflammable material that might assist their progress. They even started feverishly to dig channels which could draw River water to the village. But who knows if by then it was not too late?

INDEX